D0080969

# MULTICULTURAL FILMS

## A Reference Guide

JANICE R. WELSCH AND J. Q. ADAMS

GREENWOOD PRESS
Westport, Connecticut • London

**Library of Congress Cataloging-in-Publication Data**

Welsch, Janice R.
Multicultural films : a reference guide / Janice R. Welsch and J. Q. Adams.
p. cm.
Includes bibliographical references and index.
ISBN 0–313–31975–8 (alk. paper)
1. Minorities in motion pictures. 2. Motion pictures—United States—Catalogs. I. Adams, J. Q. II. Title.
PN1995.9.M56W45 2005
016.79143'6556—dc22 2004022529

British Library Cataloguing in Publication Data is available.



Library of Congress Catalog Card Number: 2004022529
ISBN: 0–313–31975–8

First published in 2005

Greenwood Press, 88 Post Road West, Westport, CT 06881
An imprint of Greenwood Publishing Group, Inc.
www.greenwood.com

Printed in the United States of America

The paper used in this book complies with the Permanent Paper Standard issued by the National Information Standards Organization (Z39.48–1984).

10 9 8 7 6 5 4 3 2 1

*In memory of*
*John Ogbu*

# Contents

# Preface

*Multicultural Films: A Reference Guide* could easily be subtitled "What Movies Tell Us about Race/Ethnicity in the United States." It offers educators, librarians, students, and other film viewers brief synopses and critiques of a variety of motion pictures that take up, in one way or another, issues of race/ethnicity. Though this may appear to be an uncomplicated, straightforward statement, it demands clarification because "multicultural," "race," and "ethnicity" can be difficult concepts to define, and in selecting a variety of films, criteria are needed to provide some semblance of coherence within that variety.

Definitions attempt to establish lines, or borders, around ideas, relationships, and entities and to offer a common ground for communication and interaction. While working on this book, however, we have been repeatedly reminded of how difficult defining ideas or establishing parameters around concepts can be. We, like multicultural educators generally, consider gender, class, sexual orientation, ability, and age as well as race/ethnicity when exploring cultural diversity. However, in this book, we have deliberately chosen to work within a narrower scope while recognizing the significance of these other cultural factors and knowing that they cannot and should not be completely separated from issues of race/ethnicity. They will surface in some of our critiques though our principal interest remains race/ethnicity.

We use this compound term, race/ethnicity, to draw attention to the ways in which "race" has been used within the United States and to refute its accuracy as a sound scientific concept, while admitting its continued relevance as a sociological construct. That is, because scientists have no clear criteria for defining race or distinguishing one race from another, because "most of the world's people are of 'mixed stock' " (Allen 94), and because "[m]ost human characteristics ascribed to race are . . . [actually] ethnic, not racial," the term has no genetic or biological viability (Allen quoting Allport 94; See also Allen and Adams 46 and Cavalli-Sforza et al.). Yet, the term continues to be used to ascribe identity to various groups on the basis of physical differences or similarities, such as skin color, eye shape, or hair texture, and to determine access to political, economic, and social resources for these groups (Weber 80–82). As a socially constructed term, its meaning has changed as society has changed, a phenomenon evident, for example, in the different racial identities given to Italians and Greeks in the United States in the early twentieth century and today, and in the different racial categories used in the U.S. Census from decade to decade (Barrett and Roediger 29–34; Omi, Omi and Winant).

People all over the world belong to one race, the human race, but their ancestral origins give them diverse ethnic identities: Ethiopian, Mexican, Irish, Japanese, Lebanese, or Vietnamese, for instance. Within the United States, when referring to a citizen of this country, we regularly make ethnic distinctions among European Americans, identifying them more specifically as German, French, Polish, or Italian American; but we usually refer to people who came from Africa, whatever their actual country of origin, as African American. We tend to do the same when referring to Native Americans from different tribal nations, Hispanics or Latinos/as, Asian Americans, and Arab Americans. To bring some symmetry to these categories, we have adopted the following designations for the first six sections of this book, even though we realize that each is problematic in one way or another: African, Arab and Middle Eastern, Asian, European, Latino/a, and Native American. Unfortunately, by doing so, we gloss over valid and interesting distinctions among peoples from different nations. When possible, we do identify characters' ethnicities more specifically within individual film analyses. This is very rarely possible with African Americans because most first generation African Americans were brought involuntarily to the United States without country-of-origin records and were forced to give up their ethnic identities during their enslavement.

Because it was often to the economic and social advantage of immigrants to shed their ethnic origins if they could, many individuals and families did so as they took root in the United States of America, referring to themselves simply as American, a designation that has become, in the minds of many, synonymous with white Americans living in this country though all the people of the Americas, whatever their skin color, can lay claim to it. The pluralism of the United States encompasses people of color as well as people who have been identified or have identified themselves as white. A multihued pluralism offers a far more accurate picture of the United States than one seen as white, and in the "Intercultural" category we include films featuring people of different ethnicities and colors as well as of multiple ethnicities. We acknowledge that the work, talent, and very presence of indigenous people and immigrants of color have helped enormously in shaping this country and are as much a part of it as the immigrants who identify as white. We also recognize that the people in this country, whatever their color and ethnicity, frequently interact. Watching that interaction play out in films can lead to greater understanding of our cultural diversity and human similarity.

We include films made over the past century, giving greatest weight to the last quarter because of its immediate relevance but aware that contemporary cultures have been shaped significantly by the cultures that preceded them and from which they evolved. Our concentration on the past several decades also reflects the greater awareness of racial/ethnic stereotyping in films that came about through the civil rights movements that began in the 1950s and the greater number of films that now attend to interracial and interethnic interaction.

This slowly growing awareness has resulted in increased efforts to broaden the movie presence of some previously underrepresented groups and to offer more filmmaking opportunities to individuals from these groups. Only in the past quarter century has the industry moved beyond the narrowest of stereotypes. It still frequently falls back into stereotypical portrayals and limits to a notable extent the range of films possible even when it hires producers and directors from traditionally excluded groups. Clear examples of this phenomenon are the blaxploitation films, such as *Shaft* and *Superfly* of the 1970s, and the black ghetto films, like *Boyz N the Hood* and *Menace II Society*, of the 1990s.

Because of their constant pressure on the industry, African Americans have made more progress than have other traditionally underrepresented groups even though they have not enjoyed the range or number of possibilities European American filmmakers have open to them. Particularly neglected have been Arab and Middle Eastern Americans, with the situations of Native Americans, Asian Americans, and Latino/a Americans only marginally better. Viewers of Hollywood features are more likely to see Arabs, invariably portrayed as terrorists, than Arab Americans on screen. Even documentary filmmakers have, to a great extent, ignored Arab and Middle Eastern Americans. Documentarians, however, have made some of the most compelling and insightful films about African, Asian, Latino/a, and Native American cultures; we therefore have included reviews of documentaries as well as fictional features in this collection. Because of their relevance, we have also included a few films, fictional and documentary, that have been made for television or direct video distribution rather than theatrical release.

For several historically underrepresented ethnic groups, independent productions have provided the most promising and satisfactory avenue of access to film audiences and to the kind of stories they are most interested in telling. Independent filmmaking ventures usually mean greater freedom as well as limited budgets and limited audiences. Although limited funding can be frustrating, it is not necessarily detrimental; well-crafted, meaningful films, such as *Smoke Signals*, *To Sleep with Anger*, and *The Wedding Banquet*, can be made for comparatively little money, and the freedom to tell one's stories as one chooses is an invaluable advantage over submitting to strictly commercial interests. Independent film production often means forgoing the technical sophistication associated with Hollywood movies, but authenticity and the ability to take viewers beyond stereotypes take precedence over technical wizardry in these instances. We therefore have included such films here and have provided distributor information for them if they are not available through video stores or large distributors like Facets Video or Netflix. They are among the most interesting and provocative films to explore ethnicity in the United States.

Given its nature and primary interest in profits, the film industry's relative lack of commitment to focused, in-depth, three-dimensional portrayals of any culture, including European American, is not surprising. Hollywood films do depict culture, at times in spite of themselves. Independent films are often more conscious of their cultural context. Both give us stories. Those stories inevitably exist within a context, a culture, since culture is omnipresent. Films in effect put a frame around a particular culture or an aspect of culture and, in doing so, call attention to what is included and what is excluded, thus giving it boundaries and definition. They are mirrors through which we can explore culture, including cultures defined by race/ethnicity. Though they seldom present a fully developed portrait, they often provide insight and, as cultural artifacts, can evoke or provoke valuable discussion.

Regarding films as cultural artifacts and considering the continuous output of the various arms of the film industry, the number of films to choose from for this project was enormous. Couple this with the huge number of events and issues that reflect or reinforce various aspects of the cultures that characterize the United States, and it becomes clear that our film choices are not the only ones possible. The films in this book were chosen because they depict a variety of cultures and culturally significant moments or issues, they can serve as starting points for discussions that revolve around these cultures, moments, and issues, and they are currently available. We were also conscious of including films that would be appropriate for different audiences—young children, adolescents, young adults, and older adults—and for this reason we have included the film rating when possible.

We hope the films we have critiqued and the brief synopses, analyses, and suggestions for use we offer prove useful to a variety of individuals, from casual filmgoers to reference librarians, from community organizers to educators working in K–12 schools as well as colleges and universities, from recreational leaders to Elderhostel and other lifelong learner programmers. This guide bridges the worlds of educators in a range of settings and across disciplines, including multicultural education, film history and criticism, literature, sociology, psychology, history, ethnic studies, political science, philosophy, ethics, religious studies, and economics.

Films have been an integral and accessible part of the cultures of the United States for a long time, so many viewers are used to watching them and responding to them. By situating films, for instance, within a psychological study of identity development, a historical survey of a civil rights movement, a comparative exploration of family structures and relationships, an introduction to the United States' class divisions, a study of representations of race/ethnicity in literature and film, the evolution of musical traditions in the United States, or the spiritual values and priorities of diverse racial/ethnic groups in the United States, educators can move viewers from accessible texts to new ideas, diverse perspectives, and greater understanding of some of the basic concepts that shape their own worlds and those of their neighbors. The films we have chosen for inclusion can help in many of these moves. The thematic guide will help readers choose a single film or a series of films that address specific topics and issues that interest educators and programmers. Librarians will find the guide useful when working with patrons who are looking for assistance in connecting films and themes or in planning programs around specific topics that are related on some level to the nation's ideological, political, social, psychological, or aesthetic underpinnings.

Our film analyses are relatively brief. They contain a summary of the plot or of the major action, followed by points we find especially relevant given our focus on race/ethnicity; at times we also mention how gender, sexuality, or class comes into play in a movie before suggesting how the film can be incorporated into a course or discussion. Our comments are meant to stimulate ideas and discussion. Because they are far from exhaustive, we have concluded many of them with specific suggestions for further study; we have also appended a more general Selected Bibliography to assist readers who are looking for further information and insight into various facets of race/ethnicity, whether they are interested on a theoretical or experiential level. The films themselves, of course, through "flesh-and-blood" characters demonstrate how race/ethnicity is experienced in the United States under many different circumstances. The Works Cited and the Selected Bibliography help readers and viewers explore these individual portraits and representations within wider contexts, such as poverty, civil rights, education, or U.S. history. We envision readers using our comments, perspectives, and suggestions for further research as points of departure for their own analyses and discussions.

We welcome feedback. Have our critiques prompted greater insight or new ways of looking at the films included here? Have they led to fruitful discussions around the issues we identify as significant? Do they seem wrongheaded or off the mark? In what way? Do other films have greater potential as catalysts for understanding race/ethnicity as it exists in the United States of America? Readers who want to share their perspectives can contact us at jq-adams@wiu.edu or jr-welsch@wiu.edu.

Though we are responsible for any errors in this book, many of the insights are the results of dialogue between the authors and their friends, family, and colleagues. We also have received help from distributors and filmmakers who provided review copies of their work. Particularly helpful were Daniel Bickley at the University of California's Center for Media and Independent Learning, Rick Derby at Shiprock Productions, Audrey Felton at Red-Horse Native Productions, Inc., Felicia Gustin at Speak Out Speakers, Sandra Sunrising Osawa at Upstream Productions, Nanci Rossov at Filmanthropic, David Wayne, manager of Family Video in Macomb, Illinois, and employees at the American Indian Film Institute, Bullfrog Films, California Newsreel/Resolution, Chip Taylor Productions, First Americans in the Arts, and Rich Heape Films, Inc.

We must thank Penny Corder, typist extraordinaire, Marc Vawter, and Mary Killip for assisting in the preparation of the manuscript, as well as our editors, Lynn Araujo and Debby Adams, for their ongoing support. Our families and friends have lived with this project for longer than they would have chosen, and we owe them our thanks for their patience and good cheer.

## WORKS CITED

Allen, Bem P. "Personality and Prejudice." In *Cultural Diversity: Curriculum, Class, and Climate Issues*, edited by J. Q. Adams and Janice R. Welsch, 91–101. Macomb: Illinois Staff and Curriculum Developers Association, 1999.

Allen, Bem P., and J. Q. Adams. "Why 'Race' Has No Place in Multicultural Education." In *Multicultural Education: Strategies for Implementation in Colleges and Universities*, edited by J. Q. Adams and Janice R. Welsch, 45–50. Macomb: Illinois Staff and Curriculum Developers Association, 1992.

Allport, Gordon W. *The Nature of Prejudice*. Reading, MA: Addison-Wesley, 1954.

Barrett, James R., and David Roediger. "How White People Become White." In *White Privilege: Essential Readings on the Other Side of Racism*, edited by Paula S. Rothenberg, 29–34. New York: Worth, 2002.

Cavalli-Sforza, L. Luca, Paolo Menozzi, and Alberto Piazza. *The History and Geography of Human Genes* [Abridged]. Princeton, NJ: Princeton University Press, 1996.

Omi, Michael. "Racial Identity and the State: The Dilemmas of Classification." In *Dealing with Diversity*, edited by J. Q. Adams and Pearlie Strother-Adams, 91–101. Dubuque, IA: Kendall/Hunt, 2001.

Omi, Michael, and Howard Winant. *Racial Formation in the United States*. 2nd ed. New York: Routledge, 1994.

Weber, Lynn. *Understanding Race, Class, Gender, and Sexuality: A Conceptual Framework*. New York: McGraw-Hill, 2001.

# African American Films

## OVERVIEW

Historically, mainstream commercial films in the United States have offered viewers very limited portraits of African Americans, keeping them, with few exceptions, in the roles of servants and buffoons for decades, then expanding their roles to include drug dealers, prostitutes, and pimps in 1970s blaxploitation films. Since then variations on these roles have persisted, but in the past quarter century, in large part due to persistent pressure by African American activists, the kinds of roles available to black actors have grown.

Because Hollywood filmmaking remains primarily a commercial enterprise, and because movies are marketed first as entertainment, the number of well-crafted, insightful films featuring three-dimensional characters that are financed and distributed through the industry remains low. However, opportunities for independent productions do exist, and the greater influence of African Americans in Hollywood is apparent in their increased presence both in front of and behind the camera, and in the larger variety of genres and roles in which they appear.

One of the more subtle aspects of this phenomenon is the appearance of African Americans (and other people of color) in a wide range of secondary and minor roles in films whose plots do not specifically call for African Americans but which more realistically depict their growing diversity and mobility within U.S. society. Black character actors are no longer confined to service or comic roles but regularly appear as responsible professionals.

Beyond these secondary roles, African American male actors have achieved star status in unprecedented numbers, at times cast in roles that do not highlight their race/ethnicity. African American women have yet to be recognized at the same level, though Halle Berry's Oscar-winning performance in *Monster's Ball* (2001) may help open the Hollywood door to them as well. We would like to take these developments as harbingers of a more open and diverse movie landscape as the twenty-first century unfolds. Meanwhile, we can point to some movies we judge to be well worth viewing and discussing because of their depictions of important historical events that have made this progress possible, or because they explore aspects of African American culture and experience in some of its complexity and richness.

Historical events and figures are represented primarily in documentaries, including *Africans in America*, *Eyes on the Prize*, *Hoop Dreams*, *When We Were Kings*, and *Miles of Smiles*, *Years of Struggle*. The fictional films we critique range from classic features like *Stormy Weather* and *Raisin in the Sun* to more recent independently made films like Julie Dash's *Daughters of the Dust* and Charles Burnett's *To Sleep with Anger*, from family dramas such as *Sounder*, *Soul Food*, and *Eve's Bayou* to tough-minded political statements like Melvin Van Peebles's *Sweet Sweetback's Baad Asssss Song* and Spike Lee's *Bamboozled*. All of the films we review are appropriate for mature audiences, but some are also suitable, in whole or in part, for elementary and secondary school students. Among the latter are *The Autobiography of Miss Jane Pittman*, *Hoop Dreams*, *Eyes on the Prize*, and *Sounder*.

Collectively the films raise issues related to identity and self-respect, the debilitating legacy of enslavement and Jim Crow laws, empowerment through personal commitment and political action, family tensions and betrayals as well as family loyalties and love, internalized self-hatred and overt violence, redemption and healing, poverty, injustice and marginalization, resistance and perseverance, the value of creativity and education, and the importance of one's ethnic and family heritage.

Though they are not the only choices we could have made given the number of films available that focus on African American culture, they are diverse in the stories they tell and the forms they take and can serve as appropriate starting points for explorations of that culture as it has been portrayed in movies.

## THE FILMS

### *Africans in America: America's Journey Through Slavery* (1998/1999)

Producers: Orlando Bagwell and Susan Bellows

Distributor: PBS Video

Length: 360 min.

Rating: Not Rated

Historical Documentary

*Africans in America: America's Journey Through Slavery* is an excellent historical account of the experiences of Africans in what is now the United States of America. The series is divided into four parts: Part 1: The Terrible Transformation (1450–1750); Part 2: Revolution (1750–1805); Part 3: Brotherly Love (1791–1831); and Part 4: Judgment Day (1831–1865). Each part is a comprehensive examination of the role Africans have played in the development of this country during a particular period. Part 1 chronicles the transition of early African immigrants from indentured servitude to slavery, from servitude for a specified number of years to enslavement for life. It also documents free, landowning African immigrants as they witness the encroachment upon their rights. Part 2 examines the role African Americans played in the American Revolution as they sought the same freedoms as their European counterparts. Part 3 documents the fight to push the fledging nation to live up to the promises so boldly written into its Constitution. The end of the international slave trade, the emergence of new black leaders, and a growing abolitionist movement are among the subjects covered. In the final part, the nation is shown to be increasingly divided as slavery spreads west and as court rulings, including the devastating Dred Scott decision that declared that African Americans could not become U.S. citizens, work against justice and equality.

*Africans in America* will probably prove to be extremely informative for viewers because it covers much material that is often overlooked in history surveys. The series can be used very effectively in the classroom to give students an understanding of how Africans and their progeny have impacted the United States in the past and how that past continues to inform the present. To make the series even more valuable than it already is as a stand-alone program, PBS has developed extensive resource materials to support *Africans in America*, including teachers' guides, bibliographies, documents, and commentaries.

**Work Cited:** WGBH Interactive. "Africans in America." PBS Online. http://www.pbs.org/wgbh/aia/home.html.

## *Amistad* (1997)

Director: Steven Spielberg

Cast: Morgan Freeman (Joadson), Nigel Hawthorne (Martin Van Buren), Anthony Hopkins (John Quincy Adams), Djimon Hounsou (Cinque), Matthew McConaughey (Roger S. Baldwin), Stellan Skarsgård (Tappan)

Length: 152 min.

Rating: R

Early American Slave Drama; Courtroom Drama

In 1839 enslaved Africans aboard the Spanish ship the Amistad forcefully overthrow the crew and gain control of the vessel. Although they kill most of the crew during the revolt, they spare the life of the navigator on the promise that he will steer the ship back to Africa. The navigator, however, deceives the Africans and sails the ship toward North America. Six weeks later, running short of provisions, they come into contact with a U.S. naval ship. The fugitive Africans are placed in chains and imprisoned awaiting a decision about their fate.

Tappan, a northern white abolitionist, becomes interested in the fugitives' case after Joadson, a freed African American, brings their plight to his attention. At the first hearing, several parties, including representatives of the queen of Spain, the naval officers who intercepted the vessel, and the surviving crew members, claim the enslaved Africans as well as the hijacked vessel as their property.

Important national issues concerning slavery begin to swirl around this event. For instance, President Van Buren is running for reelection and is influenced by pro-slavery forces warning him that freeing the Africans could bring the South closer to secession. Abolitionists see the case as an important statement about the humanity of the Africans and of African Americans. The case finally goes to the Supreme Court and former President John Quincy Adams is persuaded to defend the Africans. His defense plea is legendary, a brilliant appeal to the Declaration of Independence and the principles behind it. The Africans are freed, and they return to their homelands.

This is an excellent example of how a film can bring historical events into contemporary times. Before *Amistad* was made, most people in the United States had not heard about this important civil rights case. Even though the case is given the Hollywood treatment in *Amistad*, with dramatic license trumping historical accuracy at times, the film renewed interest and prompted educators to study the case itself and its historical context. Director Steven Spielberg glamorizes the African defendants, especially Cinque, who leads them in their revolt and in their courtroom testimony. Spielberg creates the character Joadson and diminishes Tappan's role; in doing so, he elevates Africans and African Americans and gives them a status they often deserve but rarely receive.

*Amistad* illustrates how African Americans, European Americans, and Africans worked together to fight for freedom during the era of enslavement in the United States. Educators who choose to screen *Amistad* or to introduce their students to the historical events that prompted the movie will find books for all age groups as well as numerous websites available. One website that could prove particularly useful is entitled "Exploring Amistad at Mystic Seaport." Its curriculum ideas and resources can provide much solid background information about the events that inspired the Spielberg film.

**Works Cited:** Mystic Seaport. "Exploring Amistad at Mystic Seaport." http://www.amistad.mysticseaport.org.

## *Antwone Fisher* (2002)

Director: Denzel Washington

Cast: Derek Luke (Antwone Fisher), Denzel Washington (Lt. Cmdr. Jerome Davenport), Joy Bryant (Cheryl), Viola Davis (Eva)

Length: 120 min.

Rating: PG-13

Psychological Drama: Coming to terms with one's past

*Antwone Fisher*, the directorial debut of two-time Academy Award winning actor Denzel Washington, is an emotionally gripping film based on the real life story of Antwone Fisher. An excellent first effort for both Washington and newcomer Derek Luke, the film opens with Fisher dreaming about himself as a little boy sitting at a large dinner table full of food and surrounded by a large, loving extended family. He loves being the center of attention. Suddenly a loud noise wrenches him awake aboard the aircraft carrier on which he is serving. Later that day he fights with a shipmate and, after a judicial hearing, is not only fined, reduced in rank, and confined to base, but is also ordered to undergo a psychological evaluation. The psychiatrist, Lieutenant Commander Davenport, quickly realizes Fisher has emotional problems that often lead to violent outbursts.

Once Davenport wins his trust, Fisher reveals a childhood filled with violence, abandonment, and abuse. Though the revelations do not automatically quell his rage, Davenport is gradually able to help Fisher dredge up his demons and slay them one by one. In the process, Fisher becomes a fictive member of Davenport's family and joins them for Thanksgiving dinner at the Commander's home. He also seeks out his own family with Davenport's encouragement and the support of Cheryl, a sailor with whom he falls in love. Together Fisher and Cheryl seek out his past and, through tenacious effort, locate members of his family.

Reunited with his father's side of the family, Fisher pushes on to a meeting with the mother he has not seen since infancy. In an extraordinary scene, he asks the questions that have governed his whole life while she acknowledges his presence but can offer only silence and tears, testimony to a life of denial and regret.

*Antwone Fisher*, a powerful film about a remarkable young man, explores the painful underbelly of family life for some African Americans. Few people within the black community want to acknowledge this phenomenon of dysfunction, much less to examine it publicly from a psychological perspective. Though blaxploitation films often show black gang activity and dysfunctional black families, they generally focus on violence and action, not on the social or psychological factors behind such activity. *Antwone Fisher* exposes the psychological damage inflicted on an individual through abuse, violence, drugs, crime, and a lack of family integrity. But most of all, *Antwone Fisher* is about resiliency; Antwone is the phoenix rising from the ashes, the triumph over impossible odds. *Antwone Fisher* is a powerful statement of how hope, friendship, and love can transcend almost any earthly obstacle.

This film has excellent teaching potential and could be used effectively with a variety of audiences, especially preadolescent and adolescent viewers. Many of the themes in this film are universal: for example, the need for love, protection, and compassion. Given the problems and challenges faced by African American communities, the message in *Antwone Fisher* is a timely one. Viewers who want to learn more about Antwone Fisher may want to read his autobiography, *Finding Fish.*

**Work Cited:** Fisher, Antoine Quentin, and Mim Eichler Rivas. *Finding Fish*. New York: HarperCollins, 2002.

## *The Autobiography of Miss Jane Pittman* (1974)

Director: John Korty

Cast: Cicely Tyson (Jane Pittman), Odetta (Big Laura), Richard A. Dysart (Master Bryant), Rod Perry (Joe Pittman), Michael Murphy (Quentin)

Length: 120 min.

Rating: G

Family Drama: One hundred years as experienced by an African American woman

This made-for-television movie is based on the incredible life of Jane Pittman, an African American woman whose life spanned over 110 years. Born into slavery, Pittman, who is superbly played by the accomplished Cicely Tyson, recounts the story of her life to a New York magazine writer named Quentin, who seeks her out with the hope of writing a feature story on her life if it is merited. The year is 1962 and the Civil Rights Movement is at its zenith. Pittman, the grand-matriarch of her community, is being lobbied by local civil rights activists to help break the tradition of whites-only facilities like the water fountain outside the town courthouse. This was part of the Jim Crow system "of separate but equal" that discriminated against African Americans following the *Plessy v. Ferguson* Supreme Court decision in 1896.

Pittman agrees to tell her story to the writer and does so through a series of vignettes that chronicle some of the high and low points of her extraordinary life. Her story begins with an explanation of the significance of the two rocks that she has kept for almost a century. They symbolize her will to survive slavery, the reconstruction, Jim Crow laws, and the civil rights struggle. Each story testifies to the courage, intelligence, and resilience of Pittman and other African Americans as well. The film's ending exemplifies the life of this special person and carries a message to all who seek social justice, equity, and equality. Simply stated, social change requires a lifetime commitment.

*The Autobiography of Miss Jane Pittman* is an excellent film for all age groups, but especially for middle and secondary school students, a generation that has no real-life connections to the Civil Rights Movement and only a limited acquaintance with Reverend Martin Luther King, Jr., and other participants in civil rights activities. This film can help fill this historical vacuum. Other excellent films including *Roots, Ida B. Welles*, and the documentary series *Eyes on the Prize* can also educate young people about these important chapters of our nation's history.

**Works Cited:** *Eyes on the Prize*. PBS Video. Produced by Harry Hampton. 1986/1989; *Ida B. Welles: A Passion for Justice*. Produced by William Greaves Productions, 1990; *Roots*. DVD. Produced by Stan Margulies. Performances by Levar Burton, Louis Gossett, Jr., Madge Sinclair, Leslie Uggams, 1977.

## *Baby Boy* (2001)

Director: John Singleton

Cast: Tyrese Gibson (Jody), Tarajh P. Henson (Yvette), Candy Brown Huston (Ms. Herron), Ving Rhames (Melvin), Omar Gooding (Sweet Pea)

Length: 130 min.

Rating: R

Urban Drama: African American adolescent survival in a post-industrial society

*Baby Boy*, the final leg of director John Singleton's trilogy on African American urban life in South Central Los Angeles, examines the hard-core realities of African American males and females in late adolescence. Although the language and behavior of the central characters may shock mainstream middle- and upper-class viewers, it paints a very realistic picture of a segment of the African American urban working and poor classes in contemporary U.S. society.

Through Jody, Singleton portrays choices open to many working class and poor urban African American males. Jody still lives at home with his mother, who looks barely older than her son. Her boyfriend, Melvin, competes with Jody for his mother's affections and a place in the house. Jody's complex South Central community contains a range of African American classes from small business owners who run hair salons and restaurants to street vendors who work in less-than-legal occupations peddling items like incense, food, and CDs, and hustlers who sell drugs. Jody, in need of money to help support the two children he has fathered with two different young women, starts his own business selling clothing to women in the community.

Sweet Pea, Jody's partner, is high-strung and has neither a job nor the marketable skills to get one. When Jody asks him, "What are you good at?" Sweet Pea replies, "Robbing!" Sweet Pea is also burdened with guilt from the actions of his past and desires "redemption" through the act of being "saved" through Christianity.

Yvette, the mother of one of his babies, is Jody's central love interest. She is caught up in Jody's physical and sexual mystique but is frustrated by his lack of devotion and the fact that he still prefers to live with his mother. She works in a telecommunication business and holds their small alternative family together. When her first boyfriend, Rodney, comes unannounced to live with her after he is released from jail, the resulting chain of events leads to Rodney's death and the resolution/redemption of the film's central character.

This film is not for minors; it is full of graphic language and sexuality and violence. It requires a skilled and knowledgeable facilitator who understands the multilayered complexity of the African American experience, but as a powerful statement about African American culture in the urban community, it merits attention and analysis. Though not likely to change middle-class sensibilities about what is legal and what is illegal, *Baby Boy* does expose the huge gray world that lies between these two poles and that is part of the economies of each of this nation's social classes. It powerfully illustrates the difference in how the criminal justice system responds to white-collar and blue-collar crime and in the penalties individuals in these different classes receive, as is vividly shown in the sentences given for the possession of crack cocaine versus powdered cocaine.

*Baby Boy* is a story about surviving in a post-industrial economy in which oppressed people are still victimized not only by their own internalized demons but by the realities of living in a racist and classist society that refuses to acknowledge the ongoing effect of these realities. A number of scholars have addressed this situation, among them Michael Eric Dyson in *Reflecting Black* and William Julius Wilson in *The Truly Disadvantaged* and in *When Work Disappears.*

**Works Cited:** Dyson, Michael Eric. *Reflecting Black: African and American Cultural Criticism.* Minneapolis: University of Minnesota Press, 1993; Wilson, William Julius. *The Truly Disadvantaged: The Inner City, the Underclass, and Public Policy.* Chicago: University of Chicago Press, 1987; Wilson, William Julius. *When Work Disappears: The World of the New Urban Poor.* New York: Vintage Books, 1997.

## *Bamboozled* (2000)

Director: Spike Lee

Cast: Damon Wayans (Pierre Delacroix), Michael Rapaport (Thomas Dunwitty), Jada Pinkett (Sloan Hopkins), Savion Glover (Manray/Mantan), Tommy Davidson (Womack/Sleep'n Eat), Mos Def (Julius/Big Blak Afrika)

Length: 135 min.

Rating: R

Social Satire: Racism and the media

Without a doubt, *Bamboozled* is Spike Lee's most controversial movie. From start to finish, this biting satire attacks the racial sensitivities of both African and European Americans. Lee provides us with a historical lesson wrapped in the contemporary context of a prime-time minstrel show. Pierre Delacroix, in an attempt to get fired from his network job because it refuses to air balanced black programming, creates this outrageous farce. He and Sloan, his assistant, are totally surprised and dismayed when the show is enthusiastically received by both the network and its audience. "Mantan: The New Millennium Minstrel Show" features Manray, a street dancer, and his street partner Womack as Mantan and Sleep'n Eat, respectively. This black face comedic duo portrays the basest elements of black buffoonery in a watermelon patch, while a cast of Alabama porch monkeys supports them.

Thomas Dunwitty, a network producer who pitches the show to the network, is married to a black woman, has two children by her, and identifies himself as being blacker than Delacroix. While the Harvard-educated Delacroix speaks with a French accent, Dunwitty uses Ebonics and the "N" word in almost every other sentence and understands the commercial potential of the show Delacroix has created.

The film reaches its climax when audience members start wearing blackface and identifying themselves as "N"s. This pressure splinters the relationship between Womack and Manray as well as that of Sloan and Delacroix. The Mau Maus, a gangsta rapper group, are so outraged by the program that they kidnap Manray and assassinate him live on network television. In despair Delacroix commits suicide.

This film is not for the squeamish; it is an over-the-top satire. It screams at us from the deepest part of our racial socialization. The intent is clearly to disturb us regardless of our race/ethnicity and to create enough cognitive dissonance to make us examine our racial stereotypes and the products, movies, television programs, and other racist media images that are not only among the artifacts of our society but are still being perpetuated in media today. Further analyses of these images and of *Bamboozled* can be found in a Spike Lee interview and a symposium published in *Cineaste* (Crowdus and Georgakas 2001; Landau et al. 2001).

**Works Cited:** Crowdus, Gary, and Dan Georgakas. "Thinking about the Power of Images: An Interview with Spike Lee." *Cineaste* 26, no. 2 (2001): 4–9; Landau, Saul, Armond White, Michael Rogin, Greg Tate, and Zeinabu irene Davis. "Race, Media and Money: A Critical Symposium on Spike Lee's *Bamboozled*." *Cineaste* 26, no. 2 (2001): 10–17.

## *Bird* (1988)

Director: Clint Eastwood

Cast: Forest Whitaker (Bird), Diane Venora (Chan Parker), Michael Zeinker (Red Rodney), Samuel E. Wright (Dizzy Gillespie), Keith David (Buster Franklin), Michael McGuire (Brewster), James Handy (Esteves), Bill Cobbs (Dr. Caufield)

Length: 160 min.

Rating: R

Fictionalized Biography: Charlie Parker, world-class musician and troubled genius

*Bird* is the poignant and bittersweet story of the legendary jazz musician Charlie Parker. It covers many of his trials and tribulations as he struggles with his creative genius and the oppression of blacks in the United States in the 1940s and 1950s. Diane Venora provides a solid supporting role as Chan, Bird's faithful wife, the mother of his children, and the one person who understands him in all of his complexity. We get glimpses of his interaction with fellow musicians like Dizzy Gillespie and Red Rodney, who are witnesses to the development of his genius and the internal demons that would destroy him.

Director Clint Eastwood effectively shows Parker's struggle with heroin and how it cuts his life tragically short. Parker's life is full of pain. He constantly struggles with the paradoxes he encounters in his life: the love of family and the death of a young daughter, his musical creativity and the never-ending difficulty of holding a paying job. These difficulties carve a hole in his soul that never heals. While everyone recognized his genius, no one really knew how to help him—not his psychiatrist, his physician, or the musicians who knew him. He was an enigma as well as a prophet who signaled a new way of playing music that still contributes to jazz and many other forms of contemporary music.

The soundtrack is taken from original recordings of Charlie Parker that were remastered specifically for this film. This film makes an important contribution to our understanding of jazz culture and one of its central architects. It reveals the challenges that African American musicians faced in the pre-civil rights era as well as the ravages drugs can have on those who abuse them. Watching *Bird* in tandem with Ken Burn's *Jazz* could add to the meaning of both.

**Works Cited:** *Jazz*. Directed by Ken Burns. PBS Video, 2001.

## *The Birth of a Nation* (1915)

Director: D. W. Griffith

Cast: Lillian Gish (Elsie Stoneman), Mae Marsh (Flora Cameron), Henry B. Walthall (Ben Cameron), Miriam Cooper (Margaret Cameron)

Length: 154 min.

Civil War and Post-Civil War Melodrama: The rise of the Ku Klux Klan and acceptance of racism

*The Birth of a Nation* dramatizes the Civil War and Reconstruction, weaving these nineteenth-century national events into the fictional story of the Stoneman family in the North and the Camerons in the South. Permeated with the racist thinking prevalent at the time it was made and greatly distorting actual history, the film is one of the most controversial films ever produced. It paints virulent, demeaning portraits of African Americans as it glorifies the Ku Klux Klan and rationalizes the lynching of black men. The film does this while introducing and consolidating narrative and cinematic techniques that had never before been so effectively marshaled to tell a story.

Griffith's skill in advancing narrative filmmaking as he reflected and reinforced racism raises questions about whether narrative and cinematic form can be divorced from ideology when evaluating a film. Many film historians seem to think the separation is possible and continue to praise the film as a critical step in the development of film art. For example, David A. Cook, in *A History of Narrative Film*, acknowledges that Griffith assaults "our sensibilities beyond the bounds of decency in order to drive home an ideological point" (83), but he devotes more space to Griffith and *The Birth of a Nation* than to any other director and film and concludes that "*The Birth of a Nation* is the cinema's seminal masterpiece" (86).

In *A History of Film*, Jack C. Ellis and Virginia Wright Wexman are somewhat more circumspect. They recognize that "thoroughly embodied in the film . . . is an assumption of innate inferiority of black people . . . with the nastiest aspect of Griffith's representation of black and white relationships . . . his preoccupation with possible sexual intermingling of the races" (30–31). They assert, too, that critics "all agree that in *Birth of a Nation* Griffith's formal control over the medium achieved an unprecedented power," with some "deplor[ing] the content while praising the form" (31). Vincent F. Rocchio, however, directly challenges the idea that content and form can be disconnected (29–30). In *Reel Racism*, he analyzes the film's representation of African Americans in detail (29–54) and, like film scholars Charles Taylor (Rocchio 30), Manthia Diawara (Rocchio 47), and James Snead (37–45), illustrates that racism is inseparable from Griffith's use of images and editing to create meaning in the film.

Despite its blatant racism and the pain involved in watching *The Birth of a Nation*, the film remains relevant as a depiction of early twentieth-century attitudes and assumptions, the residue of which is still present in our society and still perpetuated, though more subtly, in media representations of African Americans as well as in institutional policies and cultures that deny people of color equal opportunity. A trilogy of *California Newsreel* documentaries that trace and analyze images of African Americans in popular culture are Marlon Riggs's *Ethnic Notions*, *Color Adjustment*, and *Black Is . . . Black Ain't.* Combining screenings and discussions of *The Birth of a Nation* with these films could lead to greater understanding of the form and content or aesthetics versus ideology issues that Griffith's film raises as well as of the interplay between cultural representations and social attitudes.

**Works Cited:** *Black Is . . . Black Ain't.* Directed by Marlon Riggs. California Newsreel/Resolution, 1995; *Color Adjustment.* Directed by Marlon Riggs. California Newsreel/Resolution, 1987; Cook, David A. *A History of Narrative Film.* 3rd ed. New York: Norton, 1996; Ellis, Jack C., and Virginia W. Wexman. *A History of Film*, 5th ed. Boston: Allyn and Bacon, 2002; *Ethnic Notions.* Directed by Marlon Riggs. California Newsreel/Resolution, 1987; Rocchio, Vincent F. *Reel Racism: Confronting Hollywood's Construction of Afro-American Culture.* Boulder, CO: Westview, 2000; Snead, James. *White Screens, Black Images.* Edited by Colin MacCabe and Cornell West. New York: Routledge, 1994.

## *The Color Purple* (1985)

Director: Steven Spielberg

Cast: Danny Glover (Albert), Whoopi Goldberg (Celie), Margaret Avery (Shug), Oprah Winfrey (Sofia), Willard Pugh (Harpo), Akosua Busia (Nettie), Deserta Jackson (Young Celie), Adolph Caesar (Old Mister), Rae Dawn Chong (Squeak)

Length: 154 min.

Rating: PG-13

Family Drama: Complexities of African American relationships

*The Color Purple* depicts African American life in the early decades of the twentieth century in the South. This film adaptation of Alice Walker's book is largely about the lives of two sisters, Celie and Nettie, who are forced to deal with various forms of abuse, including incest, beatings, and, perhaps even more painful, separation for many years. Celie is particularly brutalized, not only by losing Nettie and Nettie's two children, but also through the violence of a husband, Albert, who despises her. Celie's relationships are not all painful, however. She finds a welcome ally in Shug, a blues singer and Albert's mistress, who helps her recognize her own value, and she, Nettie, and the children are ultimately reunited.

This is a richly textured tale that is full of human emotions, often sad and cruel, but at times generous and warm. Its characters find ways to survive and in time to triumph over their adversity. The film explores a range of relationships within an extended family and beyond, but primarily in the African American community. It does not ignore the additional pressure imposed on its central characters by the existence of white racism, however. This is most evident when Sofia, the wife of Celie's stepson, is jailed for eight years for defying two white people.

Spielberg provides a coherent rhythm to the lives of each main character; the film flows smoothly and elicits genuine empathy for Celie and Nettie. The settings are realistic; you can almost smell Celie's country breakfast. The soundtrack meshes juke joint boogie sounds with foot-stomping gospel spirituals, along with somber orchestral strings and rhythmic African melodies. Altogether, this music embraces the visual landscapes and heightens the viewer's connection to the story.

*The Color Purple* has been seen by many viewers as an insightful depiction of the complexities of the African American experience in the United States, but others have found it problematic, particularly in its portrayal of African American men. Much has been written about the film, but educators may find Jacqueline Bobo's "*The Color Purple*: Black Women's Responses" and Ed Guerrero's "The Slavery Motif in Recent Popular Cinema" especially useful because they reference many of the early responses to the film.

**Works Cited:** Bobo, Jacqueline. "*The Color Purple*: Black Women's Responses." *Jump Cut* 33 (1988): 43–51; Guerrero, Ed. "The Slavery Motif in Contemporary Film: *The Color Purple* and *The Brother from Another Planet*." *Jump Cut* 33 (1988): 52–59.

## *Daughters of the Dust* (1991)

Director: Julie Dash

Cast: Barbara O. Jones (Yellow Mary), Adisa Anderson (Eli), Cora Lee Day (Nana), Kaycee Moore (Haagar), Trula Hoosier (Trula), Tommy Hicks (Snead), Alva Rogers (Eula), Bahni Turpin (Iona)

Length: 114 min.

Rating: Not Rated

Family Drama: An exploration of tensions between the past, present, and future

*Daughters of the Dust* chronicles the activities of the Peazant family on the day in 1902 that many of them leave Ibo Landing, an island off the coast of South Carolina, and journey north to the U.S. mainland. Their activities encompass a celebration: a meal, stories, group photographs, children's games, disagreements, reconciliations, and farewells. Describing the film this way, however, is at once accurate and very misleading because Julie Dash, the film's writer–director, goes far beyond traditional Eurocentric filmmaking practice in telling her story. For example, she engages two narrators, one an unborn child, the other, Nana, the child's great grandmother; both slide into and out of the past, present, and future without the usual film markers that keep viewers on track. Other characters similarly slip from era to era as Dash weaves history, memories, impressions, and the present into an enigmatic and evocative work based on Gullah culture and heritage.

Though not readily accessible to viewers unfamiliar with Gullah culture or whose film-viewing skills and expectations have been learned by watching only mainstream commercial movies, *Daughters of the Dust* is worth seeing. Visually, it is stunningly beautiful, and even though grasping all of its allusions may be difficult without repeated viewings and considerable study because it is so richly layered, it offers multiple meanings and pleasures to viewers willing to stretch beyond their usual film experience. Dash adopts a revolutionary film style and the perspective of African American women to explore culture and history, memory and roots, change and dreams—concepts that she presents in culturally specific terms but that are important to everyone concerned about identity and wholeness.

In Erich Leon Harris's interview with her, Julie Dash discusses *Daughters in the Dust* and her approach to the film. In her own essay, she talks about "Making *Daughters of the Dust.*" Toni Cade Bambera critiques the film at length in "Reading the Signs, Empowering the Eye: *Daughters of the Dust* and the Black Independent Cinema Movement." Bambera seems to be translating into words the visual style Dash employed in her film. In doing so, she provides considerable insight into the film's structure and its themes.

**Works Cited:** Bambera, Toni Cade. "Reading the Signs, Empowering the Eyes: *Daughters of the Dust* and the Black Independent Cinema Movement." In *Black American Cinema*, edited by Manthia Diawara, 118–144. New York: Routledge, 1993; Dash, Julie. "Making *Daughters of the Dust.*" In *Cinemas of the Black Diaspora: Diversity, Dependence and Oppositionality*, edited by Michael T. Martin. Detroit: Wayne State University Press, 1995; Harris, Erich Leon. *African-American Screenwriters Now: Conversations with Hollywood's Black Pack.* Los Angeles: Silman-James Press, 1996.

## *Eve's Bayou* (1997)

Director: Kasi Lemmons

Cast: Jurnee Smollett (Eve Batiste), Meagan Good (Cisely Batiste), Samuel L. Jackson (Louis Batiste), Lynn Whitfield (Roz Batiste), Debbi Moran (Mozelle Batiste Delacroix), Jake Smollett (Poe Batiste), Edith Ayler (Gran Mere), Diahann Carroll (Elzora)

Length: 109 min.

Rating: R

Family Drama: Understanding complex interpersonal relationships; coming of age

Eve Batiste, a young Creole woman, begins her account of the "summer [she] killed [her] father" by alerting viewers that "Memory is a selection of images, some elusive, others printed indelibly on the brain." How old Eve is when she recounts the events of that summer remains unclear, but she lived them as a ten-year-old and chooses to speak from that perspective. Her story revolves around her family: her handsome, loving father, Dr. Louis Batiste; her beautiful, solicitous mother, Roz; her vulnerable adolescent sister, Cisely; her younger brother, Poe; and her supportive, clairvoyant aunt, Mozelle. Eve begins the account with the night her socially prominent family hosts a big party. Upset because of the attention she sees her father giving Cisely and her mother giving Poe, she takes refuge in the carriage house and falls asleep. She awakens to see her father and Matty, a family friend, in a passionate embrace. Though her father glosses over the situation, Eve's perception of what she has seen, together with subsequent observations of her parents' behavior and interactions, and of Cisely's sudden estrangement, prompt her to take action.

Placing the blame for the family's unhappiness on her father and spurred by her conviction that he has molested Cisely, Eve pays the voudon (i.e., voodoo) fortune-teller Elzora to help her kill him. Almost immediately, Louis is killed by Matty's husband after discovering Louis and Matty together in a bar. Eve witnesses the murder and instantly regrets her actions. Her confusion about the course of events intensifies when she finds a letter Louis had written to his sister Mozelle explaining not only his infidelities but also his actions the night of his alleged incestuous behavior. Confronting Cisely for clarification, Eve realizes that even with her gift of sight, "the truth changes color depending on the light," for the flashbacks that show what happened are shaped by Cisely's, then Louis's, perceptions, and even Eve's clairvoyance conjures up ambiguous images.

When Eve begins her story, she explains that she is the descendant of Lieutenant Jean-Paul Batiste and the African slave woman Eve, whose powerful medicine saved Batiste's life when he was stricken with cholera. In gratitude he freed Eve, gave her land near the bayou, and began a relationship with her. The younger Eve and her family reflect this ancestry and their complex, sometimes contradictory Creole roots in African, French, and U.S. cultures as well as in African and Christian religions, which offer very different blends of faith, mystery, and myth—and suggest areas for further study.

*Eve's Bayou*, through stunning cinematography and multilayered perspectives, evokes a sense of mystery and wonder as it interweaves the preternatural with everyday human behavior. By choosing to focus exclusively on her Creole characters, Lemmon captures multiple levels of that culture while suggesting reconciliation with one's past is critical if one is to live fully in the present. She explores the "tenuous aspect of truth" (Donalson 190) and connections between the personal and cultural with an insight and sensitivity that provide viewers with a catalyst for discussing those concepts.

**Work Cited:** Donalson, Melvin. *Black Directors in Hollywood.* Austin: University of Texas Press, 2003.

## *Eyes on the Prize* (1986/1989)

Producer: Harry Hampton, Blackside, Inc.

Distributor: PBS Video

Length: 14 60-min. segments

Rating: Not Rated

Historical Documentary: The Civil Rights Movement

*Eyes on the Prize* remains the most comprehensive and in-depth documentary history of the United States. Civil Rights Movement that has been produced. Its 14 hour-long episodes begin in the mid-1950s with the lynching of 14-year-old Emmett Till in Mississippi and with the bus boycott in Montgomery, Alabama; the series ends with the 1980 racial disturbance in Miami and the election of Harold Washington as the first black mayor of Chicago. Linking these events are ongoing civil rights actions that involve and challenge the country's religious, social, economic, educational, judicial, legislative, and political institutions. Some of the specific events chronicled are the integration of Central High School in Little Rock, Arkansas; the Freedom Rides; the 1963 march on Washington, D.C.; the Mississippi voting rights campaigns; the Selma-to-Montgomery march; the Howard University sit-ins; the Poor People's Campaign; the emergence—and suppression—of the Black Panther Party; the Attica prison riot; and elections of black mayors in Cleveland and Atlanta.

Leaders of the Civil Rights Movement are seen in action via archival footage and, in many cases, through interviews. These men and women include some as well known as Dr. Martin Luther King, Jr., Malcolm X, and Muhammad Ali, but many others are seen and heard. Mose Wright, Rosa Parks, E. D. Nixon, Fannie Lou Hamer, Coretta Scott King, C. T. Vivian, John Lewis, Andrew Young, James Forman, Stokely Carmichael, and Jesse Jackson are among them. Even this abbreviated list suggests the size of the movement, the diversity of its leaders, and the many facets of life in the United States that needed to be addressed. Again and again these leaders point to the absolutely essential involvement of large numbers of committed ordinary people who were willing to risk their lives for the rights and freedoms they sought.

Still photos, newspaper headlines, live-action news footage, and audio tapes gathered from many different archives are interwoven with contemporary interviews conducted specifically for *Eyes on the Prize* to give viewers a particularly instructive and important chronicle. Both African and European Americans are interviewed and the conflicts and confusion within the movement are included, but the perspective adopted by the makers of *Eyes on the Prize* is never in doubt. In Dr. Martin Luther King, Jr.'s words, "We must come to see that the end we seek is a society at peace with itself, a society that can live with its conscience." *Eyes on the Prize* is an extraordinarily rich resource for anyone wanting to learn about the Civil Rights Movement and to understand the people who were involved in it. Among the printed materials available to provide additional information and insight into the Civil Rights Movement and *Eyes on the Prize* are Juan Williams's *Eyes on the Prize: America's Civil Rights Years*, 1954–1965 and Elizabeth Amelia Hadley's "*Eyes on the Prize*: Reclaiming Black Images, Culture, and History."

**Works Cited:** Hadley, Elizabeth Amelia. "*Eyes on the Prize*: Reclaiming Black Images, Culture, and History." In *Struggles for Representation: African American Documentary Film and Video*, edited by Phyllis R. Klotman and Janet K. Cutler. 99–121. Bloomington: Indiana University Press, 1999; Williams, Juan. *Eyes on the Prize*: *America's Civil Rights Years, 1954–1965*. New York: Penguin, 1987.

## *Hoop Dreams* (1994)

Director: Steve James

Length: 169 min.

Rating: PG-13

Documentary: Urban adolescence, sports

*Hoop Dreams* is an insightful view of two African American basketball phenoms as they begin their first year at basketball powerhouse St. Joseph High School where NBA great Isaiah Thomas starred. This documentary follows the prep careers of Arthur Agee and William Gates as well as their relationship with their families as they struggle to fulfill their ambitions of making it someday in the NBA.

In the beginning, basketball is their all-consuming love, but being at St. Joseph means a three-hour round trip by train each day into a world of white people, a sharp cultural and social contrast to their inner-city lives. Both athletes have promising first year seasons: Arthur is the starting point guard on the freshmen team, while William is a sensation on the varsity leading St. Joseph to the super-sectional championship. Academics on the other hand are a major struggle for both students.

In addition to their academic problems, tuition money is a factor, forcing Arthur to leave school midway through the fall semester. William, however, inherits a sponsor who takes care of his money problems for the remainder of his prep career. Arthur transfers to Marshall High School but loses a full semester of credit. He plays on the sophomore team. William's academics improve significantly, but once again St. Joseph comes up short of making it downstate to compete for the state championship.

Director Steve James allows us to share in the lived experiences of these two young African American teens as they struggle with the complexities of adolescence, low income, family issues, and high athletic expectations. Their roads are similar but also different. Arthur has to overcome the abuse of a father who abandons his family and forces them onto welfare. William fathers a child out of wedlock and suffers a knee injury that threatens his athletic hopes. Even though both survive these obstacles, only Arthur is able to realize the dream of leading his team to the coveted trip downstate.

This is more than a basketball movie. This is a treatise on one of the perceived options out of the inner city. James provides viewers with a detailed look at the odds thousands of would-be NBA stars have to overcome to make their dreams of stardom come true.

## *John Q* (2001)

Director: Nick Cassavetes

Cast: Denzel Washington (John Quincy Archibald), Kimberly Elise (Denise Archibald), Daniel E. Smith (Mike Archibald), Anne Heche (Rebecca Payne), James Woods (Dr. Raymond Turner)

Length: 118 min.

Rated: PG-13

Family Drama: Challenges and dilemmas for working class parents

The film *John Q* is not likely to win any awards for movie excellence, but the story is worth its weight in gold as a portrayal of a working class African American family facing a major crisis. The story revolves around an intact loving family struggling to pay its bills. Both parents have jobs. John Q works in a factory part time due to a downturn in the economy, while his wife works at a grocery store and receives few benefits. They attend church every Sunday and are well liked by their community. Their lives are centered on their son, who loves action heroes and plays Little League baseball. At one of his games he collapses on the playing field and is rushed to a nearby hospital where he is diagnosed as having an enlarged heart. He will die soon unless he has a heart transplant operation. Because of John Q's part-time job status, he does not have comprehensive medical insurance or the $250,000 it would cost for the surgery. After exhausting what little resources they have and the good will of family and friends, John Q and Denise are able to raise only $20,000.

A by-the-book hospital administrator, an indifferent heart specialist, and the worsening condition of his son compel John Q to take desperate action. He kidnaps the heart surgeon and takes over the emergency ward of the hospital.

During the standoff with the police, while John Q and his hostages alternately challenge and engage each other and the police play out their own internal conflicts, *John Q* explores several complex issues: health care for the working and lower classes, the overuse of lethal force by the police, ethical suicide, and, through two of the hostages, spousal abuse. Even though aspects of events are overplayed, the hopelessness experienced by John Q and Denise's situation will strike a chord in the hearts of parents.

In the end, John Q's crisis is handled in typical Hollywood feel-good fashion: The child is saved and John Q becomes a folk hero, despite an anticipated short jail sentence. The question of the working poor and health care is not resolved. This film works similarly to other mainstream commercial films that take on social issues: Individual solutions are found but the roots of the problem remain unaddressed. William Julius Wilson does address those roots in *When Work Disappears: The World of the New Urban Poor*.

**Work Cited:** Wilson, William Julius. *When Work Disappears: The World of the New Urban Poor*. New York: Vintage Books, 1997.

## *Malcolm X* (1992)

Director: Spike Lee

Cast: Denzel Washington (Malcolm X), Angela Bassett (Betty Shabazz), Albert Hall (Baines), Al Freeman, Jr. (Elijah Muhammad), Spike Lee (Shorty), and Delroy Lindo (Indian Archie)

Length: 194 min.

Rated: PG-13

Historical Drama: African American leadership, coming to awareness

This is a film about the life of one of the United States' most controversial national leaders, Malcolm X. Director Spike Lee's interpretation of this historical character is loosely based on Alex Haley's book, *The Autobiography of Malcolm X*. The film has four major sections; the first details the early life of "Red" Malcolm Little, the son of a black minister who is murdered by the Ku Klux Klan for preaching Garveyism, a twentieth-century back-to-Africa movement, and for standing up to them as a black man. His mother has a nervous breakdown brought on by the death of her husband and her inability to support her children. The children are eventually taken by the state and raised in separate households.

Red receives a good K–12 education but also a healthy dose of skepticism. In his early adult life, he is concerned with "dressing to the nines" and being cool. He partners with a hairdresser named Shorty, who shares his passion for the fast life and white women. During this time, Red meets Indian Archie, who teaches him how to run numbers (an illegal lottery) and use drugs. This lifestyle eventually leads to Red's and Shorty's arrests and their sentencing to ten years' hard labor in the state prison.

Red's incarceration is the beginning of the second major section of the film and of his life. In prison he meets Baines, who becomes his spiritual teacher, his guide to Islam, and his connection to the Honorable Elijah Mohammad. Baines rescues Red from a life of growing self-hatred as symbolized by the conking (straightening) of his hair. Once he accepts Islam he changes his name to Malcolm X. When he gets out of prison and has the opportunity to meet the Honorable Elijah Mohammad, he is humbled, overwhelmed, and awed. For the next twelve years, the third major phase of his life, he serves the Nation of Islam faithfully.

The final phase encompasses Malcolm X's liberation from the Nation of Islam and his transformation into a global, independent thinker. This ideological change creates intense animosity between him and the Nation and leads to his assassination. Who actually killed him has never been substantiated.

The significance of this film is that it brings knowledge of this important American to a wider audience. We are able to see through this man's life the impact of racism on him and on society in general. His life also provides an example of how one individual learns to overcome his own prejudice and become a leader in his community. A remarkable film about the life of a remarkable man, Malcolm X can be an effective point of entry into an exploration of the pre–civil rights and civil rights eras through the lived experiences of a man who is both a product as well as an architect of his times. As is usually the case when public figures become the subject of a motion picture, Spike Lee's *Malcolm X* sparked considerable controversy, some of which is recounted by Ed Guerrero in *Framing Blackness.* It, of course, would be reasonable to go beyond the film and dig more deeply into Malcolm X's life and times, reading, for example, his autobiography or speeches. As Guerrero indicates: "Malcolm and his ideas, in large part due to the efforts of Spike Lee and Company, are more alive today and available to a new generation than at any time during his life" (204).

**Works Cited:** Guerrero, Ed. *Framing Blackness: The African American Image in Film.* Philadelphia: Temple University Press, 1993; Malcolm X. *The Autobiography of Malcolm X.* With Alex Haley. New York: Ballantine, 1965, 1992; Malcolm X. *By Any Means Necessary.* Edited by George Breitman. New York: Pathfinder Press, 1970, 1992.

## *Miles of Smiles, Years of Struggle* (1983)

Producers and directors: Paul Wagner and Jack Santino

Distributor: California Newsreel/Resolution

Length: 58 min.

Rating: Not Rated

Documentary: African American labor struggles

*Miles of Smiles, Years of Struggle*, a history of black Pullman porters, their union the Brotherhood of Sleeping Car Porters, and their arduous but successful efforts to negotiate with the Pullman Palace Car Company for better pay and working conditions, is probably the only documentary narrated by a 100-year-old African American woman. Mrs. Rosina Tucker's role as narrator is appropriate given her status as the wife and then widow of a Pullman porter, as a very involved participant in the porters' union activities, and as a person whose life spanned most of the 100-year history of black Pullman porters.

While Rosina Tucker's narrative connects the documentary's historical information, archival photos, and film footage, retired porters actually tell most of the story of their service and struggles. They relive the work they did in Pullman dining, parlor, lounge, and sleeping cars to make their passengers comfortable. An excerpt from the 1933 movie *Emperor Jones*, starring Paul Robeson, illustrates the pride, respect, and commitment associated with their jobs and symbolized by their uniforms. Other film clips, however, present contrasting images of porters as Uncle Toms and figures of ridicule, images the interviewees counter by asserting, "if a person respects himself and others, he can be a man while being a servant."

Besides exploring porters' on-the-job skills and intelligence, *Miles of Smiles* looks at some of the negative aspects of their work, including low wages, poor accommodations, job insecurity, and discriminatory treatment by Pullman passengers. The film also explores what the porters accomplished through the substantial leadership of the indomitable labor and civil rights activist A. Philip Randolph and the Brotherhood of Sleeping Car Porters. It documents their twelve-year struggle with the Pullman Company for recognition and bargaining rights and examines the Brotherhood's little-known but significant contributions to the Civil Rights Movement, beginning with the Montgomery bus boycott.

*Miles of Smiles, Years of Struggle* is an apt title for this documentary, clearly indicating the perspectives from which "the Untold Story of Black Pullman Porters" is presented and contributing an important piece to the larger mosaic of African American history. For a more extensive exploration of the many contributions of A. Philip Randolph to the labor and civil rights movements, see *A. Philip Randolph: For Jobs and Freedom.*

**Work Cited:** *A. Philip Randolph: For Jobs and Freedom.* Directed by Dante James. California Newsreel/Resolution, 1996.

## *A Raisin in the Sun* (1961)

Director: Daniel Petrie

Cast: Sidney Poitier (Walter Lee Younger), Claudia McNeil (Lena Younger), Ruby Dee (Ruth Younger), Diana Sands (Beneatha Younger), Ivan Dixon (Joseph Asagai), John Fielder (Mark Lindner), Louis Gossett, Jr. (George Murchison), Stephen Perry (Travis Younger).

Length: 128 min.

Rating: Not Rated

Family Drama: Clashing dreams and values in a working class family

Set almost entirely in a cramped 1940s ghetto apartment in Chicago, *A Raisin in the Sun* tells the story of the Younger family—Mama, her son Walter and daughter Beneatha, Walter's wife Ruth, and their son Travis. They are waiting for the $10,000 check Mama is to receive from Big Walter's life insurance policy. Each of the adults dreams of the opportunity the money represents for them: Walter wants to buy a liquor store; Beneatha, a college education; and Mama and Ruth, a house with a yard. Their opposing expectations and desires lead to a series of clashes with Walter, who at age 35 is particularly angry when Mama says no to financing the store. Having equated being an entrepreneur with being a man, he chafes at the idea of continuing to work as a chauffeur, but Mama sees a house as a priority and makes a down payment on one. Its location in a segregated European American neighborhood adds one more level of conflict and complexity through which the family must work.

*A Raisin in the Sun* began life as a play written by Lorraine Hansberry, and the film version, with its limited setting and unusually rich dialogue, reflects it origin. Its current relevance suggests not only Hansberry's perceptiveness but also the complexity of the issues she raised. Walter is caught in a narrow, socially imposed definition of masculinity that equates being a man with material success, interpreted by Walter to mean owning his own business and having money. He sees himself as a "giant surrounded by ants," a man of vision stymied by unsupportive women. Beneatha, unlike Walter, is very aware of traditionally defined roles and intentionally rejects them. She wants to reinvent herself and her world, and she continuously investigates what seems innovative. She tries to defy traditional gender roles by becoming a doctor, not a housewife, but at the same time she attempts to recover her African roots and honor African tradition.

Mama Lena and Ruth define themselves in terms of family and as widow or wife and mother whose primary focus is the spiritual, psychological, and physical health of their family. Their desire for a healthy family informs their desire to leave the ghetto and live in a place where people (and plants) can grow. That this means integrating a previously European American neighborhood and fighting the prejudice of neighbors does not deter them.

In the course of their confrontations, numerous issues are exposed: the existence of God; abortion; personal integrity; spiritual and material values; the importance of ethnic and family heritage; the roles of men and women, parents and children; the nature and place of dreams; the function of work, and the definitions of authority and privilege. One powerful scene follows another, each skillfully crafted and seamlessly unfolding as the Younger family crisis deepens. The intensity is most vividly portrayed when Mama, addressing Travis but speaking to Ruth and Walter as well, tells them she has bought a house, and we see in close-up Walter's hand crushing the glass he holds. From his perspective, his dream has been crushed, and he sees no future for himself. Later, after he has lost the $6,500 Mama entrusted to him, and he has decided to sell out, Mama challenges him to tell Travis he will capitulate to the demands of the European American neighborhood association. Only then does he reclaim the values and the dream of the five generations of his people who have lived in the United States.

Because of its artistry, its dramatic intensity, and its incorporation of universal themes with historical realities, *A Raisin in the Sun* can still be appreciated and serve as a medium that leads to greater understanding of African Americans and of the humanity people share, whatever their ethnic/racial identity.

## *Roots* (1977)

Directors: David Greene, John Erman, Marvin J. Chomsky, and Gilbert Moses

Cast: Levar Burton (Kunta Kinte as young man), Ji-Tu Cumbuka (Wrestler), Louis Gossett, Jr. (Fiddler), John Amos (Kunta Kinte in middle age), Richard Roundtree (Samuel Bennett), Madge Sinclair (Bell), Leslie Uggams (Kizzy), Ben Vereen (Chicken George), Georg Stanford Brown (Tom Harvey)

Length: 573 min.

Rating: Not Rated

Historical Drama: Epic journey from Africa through enslavement to freedom

*Roots* is an extraordinary achievement. When first aired on television, this twelve-hour miniseries became a national event, with an estimated 130 million viewers following the saga of Kunta Kinte as he is torn from his family in Gambia, West Africa, enslaved, and subsequently made to suffer all of the indignities and horrors of an enslaved person. Kinte's story takes viewers from the security of his close family and community affiliations, through the tortures of the Middle Passage and the humiliation of a slave auction, to Kinte's life of enslavement and service, of attempted escapes and punishment.

Because he refuses to deny his true identity or to reject his African heritage, Kinte is able to pass on his inner strength, his sense of dignity, and his African traditions to his daughter Kizzy. She lives her life with a fierce determination to hold onto that heritage and to pass it on, in turn, to her son, Chicken George, and to her grandchildren. She does so despite being sold to a new owner, being repeatedly and brutally raped, losing her son for fourteen years, and, with her family, being terrorized by the newly formed Ku Klux Klan. It is after Chicken George has bought his own freedom, fought in the Civil War, and returned to his family that the whole family, through a carefully devised plan, secures its freedom and is able to make its way to a new home in Tennessee. The epic concludes with author Alex Haley picking up the story. By making the links between himself and Chicken George, he brings us back to Kizzy, Kunta Kinte, and their roots in Gambia.

That so many viewers watched this story unfold over eight consecutive evenings in January 1977 suggests its power. Filled with information and commentary on the history and reality of slavery in the United States, it conveys its lessons through compelling events, strong expressive faces and telling gestures, realistic settings, and recognizable human interactions. As history and as drama, it remains a relevant introduction to a defining facet of the U.S. experience and an effective reminder of the importance of our roots as members of a family and of a nation that is unique in its pluralist composition and in its democratic ideals.

*Roots* was followed in 1979 by *Roots: The Next Generation*, an effective continuation of the story of Kunta Kinte's descendants from 1882 to post-World War II. A decade later *Roots: The Gift* aired, but rather than bringing Alex Haley's story forward, this spin-off, starring Lou Gossett, Jr. and Levar Burton, circled back to the nineteenth century and a pre-Emancipation narrative. *Roots* and *Roots: The Next Generation* are the stronger representations of the Kunta Kinte saga.

## *Slam* (1998)

Director: Marc Levin

Cast: Saul Williams (Ray Joshua), Sonja Sohn (Lauren Bell), Bonz Malone (Hopha), Lawrence Wilson (Big Mike), Beau Sia (Jimmy Huang), Andre Taylor (China)

Length: 100 min.

Rating: R

Urban Drama: Street life, rap, and self-realization

*Slam*, a riveting portrait of urban life in Washington, D.C., centers on the African American community in a place called Dodge City. In Dodge City rival gangs rule the streets. A person's street reputation is critical for respect and safety. Ray Joshua, a small-time street hustler, makes his living selling marijuana and rhymes. His street rep has garnered him a small following of aspiring young rappers, 9- to 12-year-olds, whom he mentors. He also has the respect of Big Mike, a gang leader who is Ray's source for drugs and an outlet for his love lyrics, which Mike buys from Ray to impress his girlfriends. During an exchange of drugs and lyrics on the street, members of a rival gang attempt to assassinate Big Mike. Because he is standing next to Big Mike when he is shot, Ray is arrested, and when the police discover he is selling drugs, he is arraigned and sent to jail to await trial.

In lock-up gang boss Hopha informs Ray that a rival gang wants to take him out because they think he set up the hit on Big Mike, whom they all think has been slain. He is pressured to side with one of the gangs for his own safety, but Ray refuses to do so, and when gang members make a move on him, he unleashes one of the most powerful pieces of urban poetry audiences are likely to hear. It resonates with so much verve that it defuses the attack, and Ray escapes. Overhearing this incredible display of talent, Lauren Bell, a writing instructor in the prison's soon-to-be-cancelled educational program, invites Ray to attend her last class. He is as taken with her talent and beauty as she is with his poetry.

Hopha is so impressed with Ray that he arranges to pay his $10,000 bail, and Ray is released. When he discovers Big Mike had been wounded, not killed, they reunite and together try to change the eye-for-an-eye culture of Dodge City. Ray also finds Lauren, who introduces him to a world of poets and poetry that challenges and energizes him. At a time when he is almost paralyzed by not knowing what awaits him in court, he and Lauren face off in an exciting, spirited poetry slam where they steal the show.

Marc Levin assaults viewers' senses through his powerful direction and comes up with a superb urban hip-hop film. Because of its explicit language, brief nudity, and violence, this film is not appropriate for younger audiences; however, its messages are important, and with the proper preparation, mature adolescents could gain a great deal from this work. *Slam* is a musical that replaces catchy tunes with earthy rap and poetry. It examines with insight and passion the best and worst of what is taking place in the urban ghetto. That it takes place in the shadow of the nation's capital adds to the ironies the film explores.

## *A Soldier's Story* (1984)

Director: Norman Jewison

Cast: Howard E. Rollins, Jr. (Captain Davenport), Adolph Caesar (Master Sergeant Waters), Art Evans (Private Wilke), David Harris (Private Smalls), Dennis Lipscomb (Captain Lipscomb), Larry Riley (C. J. Memphis), Trey Wilson (Capt. Nievens), Denzel Washington (Private Peterson)

Length: 98 min.

Rating: PG

Military Drama: Self-hatred and questions of African American identity

This screen adaptation of Charles Fuller's play *A Soldier's Story* is a complex tale of the influence racism can have on the psyches of human beings who try to adapt to survive and evolve within a hostile sociocultural milieu, like that experienced by African Americans in the U.S. Army during World War II. The film unfolds around the murder of Master Sergeant Waters, who is killed returning to a segregated Mississippi military base after a night of drinking in the "colored" section of the local town. Captain Davenport, a black lawyer, is sent from Washington, D.C., to investigate the crime. As Davenport begins his investigation, he encounters resistance from white officers Colonel Nivens and Captain Taylor, who instruct him on the rules of the segregated South and the consequences of not staying in one's place. While interviewing the soldiers, Davenport uncovers their hatred for Waters, a hatred that is the result of his contempt for himself as well as for his men.

Waters loathes C. J. Memphis, a multitalented musician and athlete who he considers to be the type of colored person who brings amusement to white people and shame to the "Negro race." Waters sees himself as the new Negro, an evolved colored person who is ready to take his place as an equal to the white man. He also believes it is his job to weed out the type of colored person C. J. represents. This belief leads to the entrapment, imprisonment, and eventual suicide of C. J. His death acts as a catalyst for the psychological unraveling of Waters and provides viewers with a case study of racial self-hatred. Water's attempt at assimilation results in his being ostracized by his own group and by the group he wants to join.

Ultimately Water's story is about the criteria used to judge a person's worth. Do we adopt an arbitrary system of "race" that limits or supports a person's potential on the basis of skin color, or do we weigh the full range of individual characteristics of each human being? *A Soldier's Story* makes clear that choosing the former can lead to hatred and discrimination within a group as well as between oppressed and privileged groups.

## *Soul Food* (1997)

Director: George Tillman, Jr.

Cast: Vanessa L. Williams (Teri), Viveca A. Fox (Maxine), Nia Long (Bird), Michael Beach (Miles), Mekhi Phifer (Lem), Brandon Hammond (Ahmad), Jeffrey D. Sams (Kenny), Gina Ravera (Faith), Irma P. Hall (Mama Joe/Big Mama)

Length: 114 min.

Rating: R

Family Drama: Matriarchal strengths and challenges; multifaceted relationships

Mama Joe, or "Big Mama," brings her daughters and their husbands and children together every Sunday for a magnificent soul food dinner that her daughters, Teri, Maxine, and Bird, help her prepare. The dinners keep the family together even though they do not always go smoothly because of various tensions among family members, most notably between Teri, an ambitious, successful lawyer, and Maxine, a full-time wife and mother. Tension escalates when Mama Joe is hospitalized with diabetes, suffers a stroke, becomes comatose, and after several days, dies. Crises in the marriages of Teri and Miles and of Bird and Lem erupt while Teri and Maxine square off over the sale of the family home. Ahmad, Maxine and Kenny's young son, is convinced the problems can be resolved if they resume the forty-year-old family tradition of Sunday dinner, so he finagles just such an event. Lots of sparks fly as family members express their anger and their frustrations, but the outcome is very close to the perfect ending Ahmad envisions.

Ahmad, via voice-over narration, provides the perspective adopted to tell this story, but the women, Mama, Teri, Max, and Bird, are the film's center. These women, despite their mistakes and hang-ups, are all competent and accomplished in most areas of their lives. The sisters' husbands are also hard working and capable. The rifts among them arise from interpersonal relations, but a few of their comments link the family to the larger society. Ahmad, for example, picks up on the self-hatred plaguing Lem—characteristic of many traditionally underrepresented group members—after Lem fails to find a job. Ahmad suggests he try loving himself. Lem himself places blame for his difficulty finding a job on a racist society. The film's primary focus, however, is on the interaction within a middle-class African American family, not on discrimination based on race/ethnicity.

*Soul Food* calls attention to race/ethnicity issues to some extent because it contrasts so vividly with films like *Boyz N the Hood* (1991) and *Menace II Society* (1993) that depict inner-city drug culture. Another contrast is the film's use of a young male narrator and central adult female characters. Given that writer–director George Tillman, Jr. based the story on his own family experiences, his choice of narrator can be justified, but his choice positions a preadolescent boy as the voice of wisdom. Because Big Mama has lost her voice, Ahmad assumes the role of her surrogate and, for a time, virtual head of the family, the mediating voice of reason and reconciliation.

Ahmad/Tillman's perspective also favors the traditional woman's role of wife and mother over that of successful career woman by presenting Maxine as the most mature and complete of the three sisters, while Teri has hard, sharp edges that place her in a negative light in relation to her husband and her sisters. The character portrayals in *Soul Food* need to be questioned because of their perpetuation of gender stereotypes. As a depiction of an aspect of African American life neglected by most mainstream feature films, *Soul Food* offers a welcome change in focus. Its clearly stated theme—the importance of family and tradition—resonates across cultures.

## *Sounder* (1972)

Director: Martin Ritt

Cast: Cicely Tyson (Rebecca Morgan), Paul Winfield (Nathan Lee Morgan), Kevin Hooks (David Lee Morgan), Carmen Mathews (Mrs. Boatwright), Janet MacLachlan (Camille Johnson), Taj Mahal (Ike)

Length: 105 min.

Rating: G

Family Drama: Love, sacrifice, purpose

Black sharecropper Nathan Lee Morgan, pressed hard during the 1930s Depression to care for his family adequately, steals meat from a neighbor. He is apprehended, sentenced to a year of hard labor, and transported to a work camp in another Louisiana parish. The local sheriff, pleading "it's the law," refuses to tell his family where he is. His wife, Rebecca, and their three children, David Lee, Earl, and Josie, are devastated but persist in keeping up the farm and trying to locate Nathan. They all work incredibly hard throughout the planting, growing, and harvesting seasons and succeed in bringing in the sugarcane crop. At one point, with information given to them by a sympathetic European American neighbor, Rebecca sends David, with the family's dog, Sounder, to visit his father.

Reaching the work camp where Nathan purportedly is, David is turned away. The journey proves serendipitous, however, when David, lost and discouraged, asks schoolteacher Camille Johnson for help. Their meeting leads Miss Johnson to invite David to attend her school in the fall. Back home, David resumes his share of farm work. He, Rebecca, Earl, and Josie are ecstatic when Nathan returns home early. That his release is due to a leg injury does not diminish the joy of their reunion, but it does lead to David's decision to stay on the farm rather than go to school—until Nathan convinces him of the value of the opportunity he has been given.

*Sounder* is a beautifully realized story of a family sustained by their mutual love, a love that motivates them to work incessantly to remain a family in the best sense of the word. Their close ties are conveyed through their respectful interactions, the glances they exchange, their excitement when Nathan pitches a winning baseball game, the sacrifices they are willing to make, and the chances they are willing to take to help each other. Though the film's cinematography is stunning and conveys the beauty of the area, it also captures the poverty and hardship of the lives of sharecroppers in the Jim Crow South of the 1930s.

*Sounder* contrasts sharply with the blaxploitation films of the early 1970s (Guerrero 103–104). Rather than exploiting filmgoers' interest in stories of drug trafficking, gangs, and violent action, *Sounder* focuses on a far more dominant aspect of African American culture: family love and solidarity. It does so without sentimentality but with honesty, simplicity, and candor.

**Work Cited:** Guerrero, Ed. *Framing Blackness: The African American Image in Film*. Philadelphia: Temple University Press, 1993.

## *Stormy Weather* (1943)

Director: Andrew L. Stone

Cast: Lena Horne (Selina Rogers), Bill Robinson (Bill Williamson), Cab Calloway (Himself), Katherine Dunham (Herself), Fats Waller (Himself), Fayard Nicholas (Himself), Harold Nicholas (Himself), Ada Brown (Herself), Dooley Wilson (Gabe Tucker), Eddie "Rochester" Anderson (Himself), Emmett "Babe" Wallace (Chick Bailey), Mae E. Johnson (Herself)

Length: 77 min.

Rating: G

Musical: Showcase for major 1940s African American entertainers

This film will never be mistaken as having a great storyline or subtle acting, but what it does have is a fine assembly of black entertainers and musical performances. Anchored by the solid performances of the legendary Bill "Bojangles" Robinson as Bill Williamson and the beautiful and multitalented Lena Horne as Selina Rogers, *Stormy Weather* is pure fun. The story loosely follows the life of Williamson through a series of flashbacks as he returns from the Great War and tries to establish himself as a marquee dancer in the black musical reviews of the time. Along the way he falls in love with Selina, prompting a typical romantic pursuit.

The performances throughout the film become more exhilarating as the narrative unfolds. They include the comic relief of Johnny Horace and Ned Stanfield, the musical talents of Fats Waller, Cab Calloway, and Ada Brown as well as the extraordinary dancing talents of the Nicholas Brothers. All build to the film's centerpiece: Lena Horne as Selina singing "Stormy Weather" while the famous Katherine Dunham dances in the background.

*Stormy Weather* is a treasure chest filled with smoothly paced performances by some of the best black entertainers in the United States during the first half of the twentieth century (Berry 63).

**Work Cited:** Berry, S. Torriano. *The 50 Most Influential Black Films*. With Venise T. Berry. New York: Kensington, 2001.

## *Sweet Sweetback's Baad Asssss Song* (1971)

Director: Melvin Van Peebles

Cast: Melvin Van Peebles (Sweetback), Simon Chuckster (Beetle), Hubert Scales (Mu-Mu), John Dullaghan (Commissioner), Rhetta Hughes (Old Girlfriend), John Amos (Johnny Amos), Mario Van Peebles (Kid)

Length: 97 min.

Rating: R

Political Satire: Controversial, hard-hitting Jim Crow era urban drama

Written by, directed by and featuring Melvin Van Peebles, *Sweet Sweetback's Baad Asssss Song* is an acidic assault on the exploitation of the black man by the white oppressor and one of the most provocative films about the black experience in the United States of its era. It follows the maturation of Sweetback, a character who earned his name through his sexual prowess with the prostitutes who rescue him and then provide him with employment. As an adult he stars in a live pornographic show where his technique has become legendary. During one of his exhibitions, the police arrive looking for a patsy to take downtown to make themselves look good. Beetle, the proprietor, gives them Sweetback; on the way to the station, they arrest an agitator named Mu-Mu, who the police physically abuse during an interrogation.

The abuse of Mu-Mu causes Sweetback to snap psychologically; he uses the police officers' handcuffs to beat them unconscious. This action symbolizes the black revolt taking place at this time in the United States and in many other countries around the world. The theme is simple: The black man is not going to take it anymore. In the movie, Sweetback's action triggers a massive manhunt, with the police using all the dirty tactics they know to get information on Sweetback and Mu-Mu's whereabouts. Each time the police close in on the two, they are able to escape largely through the cooperation of the extended black and underground community who view them as celebrated folk heroes.

Sweetback uses his sexual prowess to win the support of a female-headed California bikers' club, which symbolizes various other forms of oppression at this critical time in the 1960s and early 1970s. Van Peebles is sometimes heavy-handed in his use of symbols, perhaps most obviously when he includes a sign that says "Jesus Saves" in scenes that show a corrupt and immoral police force constantly harassing the black community.

This film is a jagged tour of the black inner city seen through the eyes of Sweetback and is filled with a variety of sordid images, from brothels to a jack-legged preacher, would-be revolutionaries, and an assortment of drug addicts and alcoholics. The film is

dark but not without hope. It has strong sexual content complete with nudity and some pornographic sexual acts. Sweetback is hunted, hounded, and wounded, but he survives. He becomes a catalyst that unites a larger community and provides a radical role model for the oppressed, showing them one way to strike back against the tyranny of the "Man" and prevail.

As Gladstone L. Yearwood puts it, *Sweet Sweetback* "presents a character from the streets . . . , who despite the seemingly impossible task of altering his life, strikes a small, but nonetheless important blow for his freedom" (195). This film was and still is a bold statement about oppression and the civil disobedience often necessary to change it. In *Framing Blackness*, Ed Guerrero discusses the conflicting responses it evoked among African American scholars and film critics (86–91) while acknowledging its breakthrough status as a black independent production that appealed to "a critical mass of black people eager to see heroic images of themselves rendered from a black point of view" (146).

**Works Cited:** Guerrero, Ed. *Framing Blackness: The African American Image in Film.* Philadelphia: Temple University Press, 1993; Yearwood, Gladstone L. *Black Film as a Signifying Practice.* Trenton, NJ: Africa World Press, 2000.

## *To Sleep with Anger* (1990)

Director: Charles Burnett

Cast: Danny Glover (Harry), Mary Alice (Suzie), Paul Butler (Gideon), Carl Lumbly (Junior), Richard Brooks (Babe Brother), Vonetta McGee (Pat), Sheryl Lee Ralph (Linda), Devaughan Walter Nixon (Sunny)

Length: 102 min.

Rating: PG

Family Drama: Mystical intergenerational conflict

Harry shows up at the Los Angeles home of old friends Gideon and Suzie and proceeds to accept and abuse their hospitality while exacerbating the frictions and frustrations among the couple, their sons, Junior and Babe, and their sons' wives, Pat and Linda.

Just before Harry appears at Gideon and Suzie's door, things begin to go wrong: Gideon has an unsettling dream and misplaces a charm his grandmother had given him, a teapot breaks, and a trumpeter sounds a sour note—all harbingers of the disruption Harry represents and all symbolically meaningful within African American culture. Charles Burnett skillfully laces the traditional rural cultural beliefs and imagery of the South into the modern urban and materialistic world of Los Angeles in his portrayal of an African American family on the verge of disintegration. Harry becomes the catalyst that pushes the family toward destruction but ultimately to reconciliation and rebirth when he enters the home, feigning gratitude and humility, but slyly and purposefully invading every aspect of his hosts' lives. He is the congenial trickster, the accommodating evil spirit that quickly identifies and plays on the weaknesses and rifts that threaten the stability of Gideon and his family. It is Suzie's faith, strength, and determination to keep the family together that finally defeat him.

Burnett ably intertwines not only the spiritual and material worlds, but also different spiritual realities—that of traditional black culture with its mix of African, Christian, and voodoo elements and that of contemporary black Christianity. He effectively juxtaposes generations, lifestyles, and values as well in this evocative story. Because it so seamlessly reflects multiple aspects of African American culture, *To Sleep with Anger* will probably not be as accessible to viewers unfamiliar with that culture as it will be to those who are; but for those interested in learning about some aspects of the culture, this film provides an entertaining and engaging entry and helps counter the blatantly negative stereotypes of 1970s blaxploitation films (such as *Shaft* and *Superfly*) and the more recent movies revolving around gangs, ghettos, and drugs. Excellent analyses are available to help viewers explore this richly textured film. Among these are Nathan Grant's "Innocence and Ambiguity in the Films of Charles Burnett" (135–155) and reviews by Sheila Benson (1) and by Georgia Brown (59).

**Works Cited:** Benson, Sheila. "Magical, Mystical Tour of South-Central." *Los Angeles Times*, October 24, 1990, sec. 1; Brown, Georgia. "The Trouble with Harry." *Village Voice*, October 16, 1990, 59; Grant, Nathan. "Innocence and Ambiguity in the Films of Charles Burnett." In *Representing Blackness: Issues in Film and Video*, edited by Valerie Smith, 135–155. New Brunswick, NJ: Rutgers University Press, 1997.

## *When We Were Kings* (1996)

Director: Leon Gast

Cast: Muhammad Ali, George Foreman, Don King, James Brown, B. B. King, Mobutu Sese Seko, Spike Lee, Norman Mailer, George Plimpton, Thomas Hauser, Malick Bowens, Lloyd Price, Wilton Felder, Wayne Henderson, Stix Hooper

Length: 89 min.

Rating: PG

Documentary: Inside look at the world of professional boxing

*When We Were Kings* won the Academy Award for best documentary film in 1996. Director Leon Gast captures the rollercoaster story of one of the greatest upsets in the annals of professional boxing. However, it is more than a sports story; it is a tribute to the civil rights era around the world, a testament to the rise of the oppressed as they strive for self-determination, and a defining chapter in the legend of "The Greatest," Muhammad Ali.

The film takes viewers into the camps of both champion George Foreman and the challenger Muhammad Ali as they prepare for the fight in Zaire, Africa. It chronicles the different adjustments both fighters make to this new land as well as the perceptions of the indigenous people of Zaire when the fighters interact with them.

Gast also provides insights into the politics of planning and implementing a major entertainment spectacle in a third world country. The flamboyance and charisma of Don King is tested as he tries to keep all the major parties in Zaire after Foreman is injured during training and the fight is postponed for six weeks. We also see the stark contrast between the affluence of the visitors from the United States and the economically struggling but proud people of Zaire. We hear incredible stories of the cruelty of Zaire's dictator Mobuto Sese Seko.

The story is told by intercutting film footage from Ali's and Foreman's fight careers with historical civil rights events in Africa and the United States. Transitions are made through interviews with people such as Spike Lee, Norman Mailer, George Plimpton, and Thomas Hauser. The powerful music on the soundtrack, present throughout the film, combines actual footage of performers from the United States, like James Brown and B. B. King, with footage of musicians and dancers from Zaire.

The film concludes with the much-anticipated fight. The build-up is extraordinary, as viewers receive a microanalysis of Ali's creative ring genius, a genius enabling him to develop a strategy that defies the odds and brings him an improbable but clear victory.

*When We Were Kings* takes viewers beyond the sports event it chronicles. It showcases some of the best of African and African American culture, and it documents the triumph of the human spirit through its multifaceted portrait of Muhammad Ali, arguably the best-known being on our planet as well as one of the most resilient and respected. To learn more about him and his remarkable life's journey, you may want to read Thomas Hauser's *Muhammad Ali: His Life and Times*.

**Work Cited:** Hauser, Thomas. *Muhammad Ali: His Life and Times*. New York: Simon and Schuster, 1992.

# Arab American and Middle Eastern American Films

## OVERVIEW

When discussing race/ethnicity, we continually run into problems with language. We need categories if we want to establish some kind of order among the innumerable individual entities we encounter in life, but the categories we develop inevitably fall short. This is definitely true when naming the various racial/ethnic groups that comprise the population of the United States. The categories we have adopted, African, Asian, European, Latino/a, and Native American, are each problematic in some way; the categories Arab American and Middle Eastern American are no different.

Twenty-two countries make up the Arab world. They and the countries of the Middle East are sometimes misidentified as being coextensive, but they are not. Some Arab countries are not in the Middle East—Morocco and Mauritania, for instance—and some countries in the Middle East, such as Iran and Israel, are not Arab. Arabs are also at times assumed to be Muslim, even though many are not. Arab American is the category some people in the United States at times use when speaking of Americans who have immigrated not only from Arab countries but from non-Arab Middle Eastern countries as well. The situation presents a conundrum for those who would like to be as accurate as possible without giving up categories altogether. We have not solved the problem, but in acknowledging it we hope to invite more people to consider the issues it encompasses and become more aware of the importance of accuracy in naming groups and the individuals within groups.

In bringing up the issue of naming in relation to immigrants from Arab or other Middle Eastern countries, we are aware of an irony, because very few films, either fiction or documentary, feature immigrants from these areas. Jack G. Shaheen, the author of *Reel Bad Arabs: How Hollywood Vilifies a People*, has looked at over 900 movies made in the past century that feature Arabs, but only a handful of those focus on Arab Americans, and in its special supplement, "The Arab Image in American Film and Television," *Cineaste* includes only three films about Arab Americans in its admittedly limited filmography (21). Arab Film Distribution also focuses primarily on films from Middle Eastern countries though it carries several documentaries on the Arab American experience.

Among Arab American actors who have had significant roles in movies are F. Murray Abraham, Salma Hayek, and Tony Shalhoub, though they are not usually cast as Arab Americans; however, an important exception is Shalhoub's role in *The Siege*, a film that has led to much controversy and that Shaheen and other film critics condemn for its racist and stereotypical depiction of Arabs, Arab Americans, and Arab Muslims as terrorists (430–433). For Shaheen, Shalhoub's nonstereotypical role as an FBI agent and a man of integrity can "never offset all those scenes that show Arab Muslims murdering men, women, and children" (431).

Even films made by Middle Eastern American directors do not always avoid the formulaic equation of Middle Easterner = Muslim = terrorist, as is apparent in Ramin Serry's *Maryam*, a film that creates conflict within the story of an Iranian American family by casting the newly arrived Ali in the role of a hotheaded, political radical bent on killing the deposed Shah of Iran. In contrast, Daisy von Scherler Mayer's *Party Girl* features a Lebanese American leading an "ordinary" life. Omar Townsend plays Mustafa, a former Lebanese teacher who makes a living in New York as a street vendor selling falafel and babaganush. He aspires to improve his English, become a teacher in the United States, and bring his mother and siblings to New York. He falls in love with Mary, a party girl and a hustler who is the epitome of New York cool. Though upbeat and fun, Mary's central role, her colorful, offbeat friends, and their hip parties dominate the film, leaving little space to explore the quietly supportive, responsible Mustafa or his culture.

In the wake of 9/11 more films about Arab and Middle Eastern Americans are being made. For instance, *In My Own Skin* brings together the responses of several young Arab American women who talk about what it has been like for them since the attacks, and in *With Us or Against Us: Afghan Americans Since 9/11*, Afghan Americans in Fremont, California, discuss the impact of 9/11 on their lives. Though the tragedy that prompted these and similar documentaries is unquestionably deplorable, the subsequent attempts to open dialogue and broaden understanding across ethnicity and race are laudable.

With greater public support, Arab and other Middle Eastern Americans can go beyond independent cinema and documentaries to effect a positive change in mainstream commercial features as well. This probably will not happen without lobbying, but a precedent has been set by African, Native, and Latino/a Americans who "have by protest and education effectively altered their images in the media" ("Editorial" 2); they have also secured more opportunities to control their images as directors, writers, and actors. Not all demeaning and misleading representations have been eliminated for people in these groups, but progress has been made. Similar progress is possible in the representation of Arab and Middle Eastern Americans.

**Works Cited:** "Editorial." *Cineaste* 17, no. 1 (1989): 2; Georgakas, Dan, and Miriam Rosen. "The Arab Images in American Film and Television." With the American-Arab Anti-Discrimination Committee. *Cineaste* Supplement 17, no. 1 (1989): 1–24; Shaheen, Jack G. *Reel Bad Arabs: How Hollywood Vilifies a People*. New York: Olive Branch Press, 2001.

## THE FILMS

### *Collecting Stories from Exile: Chicago Palestinians Remember 1948* (1999)

Director: Jennifer Bing-Canar

Distributor: Arab Film Distribution

Length: 28 min.

Rating: Not Rated

Documentary: Arab American oral history

The title of this documentary, *Collecting Stories from Exile: Chicago Palestinians Remember 1948*, is almost self-explanatory because it alludes to the video's dual focus: the Arab American Oral History Project and the memories a number of Palestinian Americans living in Chicago have of the 1948 Palestinian–Israeli conflict. The history project provides a context in which the Palestinian American interviewees discuss not just their memories of the conflict, but the meanings the conflict has had for them and the larger Palestinian and Palestinian American communities.

The video begins and ends with commentary by the late U.S.-based Palestinian author and scholar Edward Said, who suggests that the Palestinians are unique in the way their existence has been challenged; that they have, through their leaders, given up their history by being silent about the events of 1948; and that because Palestinian history since 1948 revolves around those events, they must reclaim this history if they are to have an identity. Other interviewees speak about leaving their villages to escape the fighting, but often, as the project organizers note, the interviewees, in keeping with their cultural values, speak more readily about the experiences of Palestinians in toto than about their individual experiences. They also comment on the difficulty of becoming politically active in the United States given the strong support Israel receives from the U.S. government and the prominence of anti-Arab media representations.

This video is a joint project of the American Friends Service Committee and the Arab American Action Network and presents Palestinian American rather than Palestinian, Israeli, or Jewish American perspectives. The voices are those of exiles, of people who have lost their homeland and who link that loss specifically to their 1948 expulsion from Palestine. Though their voices are not often heard in attempts to resolve the extremely complex, multifaceted Palestinian–Israeli situation, they can help audiences understand that situation more fully.

### *Covered Girls* (2002)

Producers and directors: Janet McIntyre and Amy Wendel

Distributor: Filmakers Library

Length: 22 min.

Rating: Not Rated

Documentary: Adolescents' commitment to Muslim beliefs and practices

*Covered Girls* features a number of Muslim girls, all adolescents from various ethnic groups, who live in New York. They are shown playing basketball, enjoying various rides at an amusement park, bowling, shopping, praying, and discussing various aspects of their lives, including wearing the *hijab*, or veil, and the long, loose-fitting garments favored by many Muslims. They talk about the impact of 9/11 on their lives and the increased hostility evoked by wearing the hijab after the tragedy of that day. They also talk about relationships and marriage and about what their faith means to them.

Viewers unfamiliar with Muslims may be surprised at how similar the interests of these adolescents are to those of mainstream adolescents in the United States. Their energy and spirit are also similar. Their devotion to their religion is not unlike that of devout teenagers of other religions, though some of their beliefs differ, of course. *Covered Girls* could work well as a starting point for a discussion of these beliefs. It could also help initiate a study of dress that is identified with religious commitment. What roles for example, do the habits of Catholic nuns, the collars of priests and ministers, or the yarmulkes of Orthodox Jews, the dark buttonless dresses and suits of the Amish, and the turbans worn by Muslim men play in these people's lives? What is their significance? Does their value go beyond symbolism? Beyond self-identification? Why have the hijab and the burka worn by Muslims generated intense interest and concern? How have various forms of religious dress changed over time? Seeking answers to these questions could lead to a greater understanding of the values of various religious groups.

## *House of Sand and Fog* (2003)

Director: Vadim Perelman

Cast: Ben Kingsley (Colonel Massoud Amir Behrani), Jennifer Connelly (Kathy Nicolo), Ron Eldard (Deputy Lester Burdon), Shohreh Aghdashloo (Nadi Behrani), Jonathan Ahdout (Esmail)

Length: 126 min.

Rating: R

Psychological Drama: Clashing cultural and personal values result in tragedy

When the Shah's regime in Iran topples, Colonel Massoud Amir Behrani, his wife Nadi, and their son Esmail move to the United States, become U.S. citizens, and begin to work toward the realization of the American Dream. The Colonel takes on multiple jobs while looking for opportunities to restore the family's fortune. Because of his hard work and extremely careful planning, he is ready to pay cash for a house that is seized and auctioned by the county after the owner fails to pay the taxes on it. He buys it with the intent of making a few relatively inexpensive improvements and selling it at a substantial profit, though while he owns it, he and his family occupy it.

The home's earlier owner, Kathy Nicolo, a recovering alcoholic who makes a modest living housecleaning, inherited the house from her father and believes she has dealt with the tax question satisfactorily. However, because of personal crises, she has failed to follow up. Devastated by her loss, she secures the help of a lawyer to retrieve the property, but, too impatient to wait for a resolution, she confronts Behrani personally. Her explanations and pleas become threats and only affirm for him the legitimacy of his purchase. As others become involved, the two become more entrenched in their positions, but when Behrani finds Kathy about to commit suicide one night, he immediately takes her into the house and, with Nadi, cares for her.

A second suicide attempt that same night follows and is thwarted, but Lester, a deputy sheriff who has fallen in love with Kathy, misreads the situation, holds Behrani and his family hostage, and demands the return of the property. They agree on a plan for the transfer, but in the process of carrying it out, Esmail is shot. Desperate, Behrani promises Allah everything in exchange for his son's life, but the boy dies, and Behrani collects himself and returns home. Unable to bear the loss and to protect Nadi from its excruciating pain, Behrani gives her tea laced with a deadly amount of drugs and, lying beside her dressed in his Iranian military uniform, he suffocates himself. Kathy discovers their bodies and is left absorbing the situation.

Colonel Behrani is introduced celebrating the marriage of his daughter with family and friends. The event is festive, elegant, and orderly and contrasts with Kathy's introductory scene. Shortly after she is awakened by a phone call from her mother at 6:00 AM, she walks through her house to answer a knock on the door and is served with an eviction notice. Both she and the house are disheveled. We learn fairly quickly that she is prone to obsessive behavior, is a recovering alcoholic, and is separated from her husband, something she has not told her mother. Behrani responds with great joy or anger to various situations, but his fierce determination is usually controlled and moderated by principle, foresight, and a deep love for his family. Kathy is more volatile, far more likely to act spontaneously and without thought of the consequences. To her the house represents her father's life and love, stable elements in her chaotic world. To Behrani it represents a way to provide for his family; it is a means to an end.

The Behranis' Iranian roots and culture along with their immigrant status play a significant role in *House of Sand and Fog*. Their values, their family interactions, and their daily home life reflect their heritage. They are U.S. citizens and both father and son speak English well. Behrani also understands his rights and the process governing real estate transactions. Nadi speaks English haltingly and can be easily intimidated by threats of deportation. Her realm, defined by patriarchal values, is the home, family, and relationships.

The Behranis' Iranian culture and immigrant status are evident in their daily lives, but Lester's behavior, in his misguided zeal to help Kathy, underscores some of the differences between their cultural values and those of the U.S. mainstream. He tries to intimidate and coerce, regularly coming across as the "ugly American" who thinks loud talk and threats of violence will get him what he wants. In using these tactics he not only loses Kathy, but also what many consider the American Dream: his home, family, and career. Initially he appears to be a concerned and empathic deputy, but his ambivalence about his family and his desire for Kathy expose his insecurities and racism. In terms of diversity, he provides the greater contrast with Behrani and, with Behrani, the easiest point of departure for discussion of the cultural values explored in the film. Though Kathy is more central in many ways, she is defined primarily in psychological rather than cultural terms.

*House of Sand and Fog* is one of the very few full-length fictional films made in the United States that feature immigrants from the Middle East. How effectively does it depict Iranian culture and the lives of immigrants who are responding to particular push (political upheaval) and pull (freedom and opportunity) factors that prompt them to leave their homeland and that draw them to the United States? The film provides a platform from which to launch a discussion of these issues. In addition, Behrani's murder–suicide, though the conduct of an individual who is acting against the values of his Iranian culture, suggests the importance of family within that culture and the desperation of a person caught between cultures and countries. The changes in Iran that caused the Behranis to leave make a return impossible or suicidal, but the loss of Esmail destroys any desire or possibility of realizing the American Dream.

*House of Sand and Fog* offers adult viewers enough substance to make discussion rewarding but can also lead to further study of Iranian history and culture. Persis M. Karim and Mohammad Mehdi Khorrami's *World Between: Poems, Short Stories, and Essays by Iranian-Americans* provides a starting point.

**Work Cited:** Karim, Persis M., and Mohammad Mehdi Khorrami, eds. *A World Between: Poems, Short Stories, and Essays by Iranian-Americans*. New York: George Brazilier, 1999.

## *In My Own Skin: The Complexity of Living as an Arab in America* (2001)

Producers and directors: Jennifer Jajeh and Nikki Byrd

Distributor: Arab Film Distribution

Length: 16 min.

Rating: Not Rated

Documentary: Young Arab American women and the impact of 9/11

Filmed after the September 11, 2001, attacks on New York's World Trade Center, *In My Own Skin* offers a brief but rich introduction to five young Arab American women who live in New York and have felt the impact of that attack specifically as Arab Americans living in the United States. Anneh, Giulia, Maka, Renda, and Rabyaah represent multiple ethnic backgrounds—Egyptian, Syrian-Filipino, Palestinian, and Yemeni—and all identify as Arab Americans. Filmmakers Jajeh and Byrd interviewed the women separately in their homes and on the streets of New York, then intercut excerpts from those interviews around several ideas that surfaced repeatedly. Among the themes that evolved are the pain of being stereotyped, the rewards of acknowledging and celebrating one's beliefs, and the caution, unease, and questioning the 9/11 attacks and their aftermath have generated for Arab Americans.

Because several of the women were interviewed as they participated in traditional Arab practices, viewers not only learn from what they say, but also from what they do. For example, while Renda is speaking, she is having an elaborate henna design painted on her hand, and part of Anneh's interview takes place as she prepares coffee. Rabyaah wears a veil while she discusses her family's experience in the United States; she talks about the veil's positive meanings but also demonstrates how, after 9/11, she has chosen to change the way she wears it when she is outside her own home so she doesn't call undue attention to her Arab or Muslim identity.

*In My Own Skin* covers significant themes in just sixteen minutes, making it ideal for class discussions, but educators and students may want to do further research. Resources teachers can easily access for further information about Arab Americans include the American-Arab Anti-Discrimination Committee of the National Association of Arab Americans, the Arab American Institute Foundation, and the Center for the Study of Islam and Democracy.

**Works Cited:** American-Arab Anti-Discrimination Committee. http://www.adc.org/; Arab American Institute Foundation. http://www.aisa.org/aaif.htm.

## *The Siege* (1998)

Director: Edward Zwick

Cast: Denzel Washington (Anthony "Hub" Hubbard), Annette Bening (Elise Kraft), Bruce Willis (General William Devereaux), Tony Shalhoub (Frank Haddad), Sami Bouajila (Samir Nazhde), Ahmed Ben Larby (Sheik Almed Bin Talal)

Length: 115 min.

Rated: R

Terrorist/Military Drama: Exploration of terrorism and civil rights

*The Siege* evokes one of our worst national fears: terrorism. In this action thriller we see a sequence of events that turn our domestic tranquility into a state requiring martial law. The story begins with the kidnapping of Sheik Ahmed Bin Talal, who is turned over to William Devereaux, a rogue U.S. general. This action leads to the operation of an Arab terrorist cell in New York and starts a series of escalating bombings that challenge the resources and abilities of Anthony (Hub) Hubbard, the FBI Bureau Chief in the city, and his Arab American partner, Frank Haddad. After the bombing of the FBI headquarters, when military forces under the command of General Devereaux take over the city and invoke martial law, Haddad is pressured to choose between his loyalty to the FBI and his family.

This film provides a vile picture of Arab culture in the world and in the United States. In one scene the Arabs are at the Mosque praying, and in the next scene they are building bombs and plotting terrorist actions. Director Edward Zwick spins an intriguing and disturbing tale of how fear and power can lead to the dehumanization of an entire ethnic or religious group. Because no specific Arab country or group is ever identified, the audience is left without a place to affix blame; therefore, every Arab is suspect. General Devereaux exemplifies this dehumanization as he and his men squeeze the Arab community—regardless of the nationality of community members and without regard for their constitutional or human rights—and ultimately execute Muezzin, an Arab American who is loosely affiliated with the terrorists. The execution finally brings Devereaux's own reign of terrorism to an end.

Although the potential for this type of tragedy is real, Hollywood has a long history of singling out Arabs as the people most likely to carry out terrorist acts of violence (Shaheen, 1–2). We then must ask these questions: Do the positive roles of Hub and Frank Haddad offset the callous actions of the terrorists and a fanatical army general? Do they affect the negative representations of Arab and African Americans that so frequently appear in the popular media? Do General Devereaux's actions affect the image of the military or of European American males in negative ways? Is the linking of Arabs and Muslims justified? What freedoms and constitutional rights are jeopardized when a group of people are habitually dehumanized or when the actions of a few people are identified with an entire group? The essays by film critic Jack Shaheen and *The Siege* co-author Laurence Wright in *Taking Sides*, suggest that they would respond to these questions differently.

**Works Cited:** Shaheen, Jack G. *Reel Bad Arabs: How Hollywood Vilifies a People.* New York: Olive Branch Press, 2001; Shaheen, Jack G. "We've Seen This Plot Too Many Times." In

*Taking Sides: Clashing Views on Controversial Issues in Race and Ethnicity*, 3rd ed., edited by Richard C. Monk, 210–212. Guilford, CT: Dushkin/McGraw Hill, 2000; Wright, Lawrence. "Open Your Mind to the Movie We Made." In *Taking Sides: Clashing Views on Controversial Issues in Race and Ethnicity*, 3rd ed., edited by Richard C. Monk. Guilford, CT: Dushkin/McGraw Hill, 2000.

## *Tales of Arab Detroit* (1995)

Director: Joan Mandell

Distributor: New Day Films

Length: 45 min.

Rating: Not Rated

Documentary: Intergenerational concerns within Arab community

Made before the September 11, 2001, attacks on the World Trade Center in New York, *Tales of Arab Detroit* focuses on generational differences and evolving traditions in Detroit's large Arab community. Most of the older generations speak Arabic and are very much in tune with their traditions. Because they want to pass on their values and believe one way to do this is through the stories that embody these values, they invite an elderly Egyptian storyteller to recite an important ancient epic poem of migration and romance for the people in their community. The poem, accompanied by a single musical instrument played by the storyteller, takes 100 hours to recite and is done from memory.

The performance or storytelling becomes the occasion for parents and children to talk about their different perspectives on Arab culture. The parents are particularly interested in having their children pick up this culture, including an understanding of the importance of the extended family and the primacy of the community over the individual. The parents try to introduce these values through their own storytelling, through community celebrations of Arabic poetry, music, and dance, and in some cases having their children study Arabic. The children, especially the adolescents, are torn between their Arabic culture and the more pervasive modern culture of the United States. Some prefer rap and other contemporary styles of music and poetry to the less familiar sounds and rhythms of tradition. The parents' reactions to these moves away from their heritage differ. One mother, for example, is comfortable with her son being away from 10:00 PM to 4:00 AM several evenings a week so he can participate in a music group, but another couple sends their son, an aspiring rap artist, back to Yemen as a way of severing his connections to rap.

Though several young men seem to bridge their Arab and American cultures successfully, several express their commitment to protecting their sisters in a way that seems more in line with their Arab heritage than with contemporary life in the United States. Several women, including an artist and a poet, speak of wanting to honor their parents through an acceptance of Arab culture but also wanting to forge their own multicultural identity.

Some of the most vibrant scenes in *Tales of Arab Detroit* are those in which young and old perform traditional dances. Seeing them could help viewers understand the Arab Americans' desire to preserve elements of their culture while also availing themselves of what the United States offers. The American Arab Anti-Discrimination Committee maintains a comprehensive website where viewers can begin to learn more about Arab Americans not only in Detroit but throughout the United States.

**Works Cited:** American-Arab Anti-Discrimination Committee. http://www.adc.org/.

## *With Us or Against Us: Afghan Americans Since 9/11* (2002)

Producers and directors: Mariam Jobrani and Kenneth Krauss

Distributor: Filmakers Library

Length: 27 min.

Rating: Not Rated

Documentary: The lives of Afghan Americans in a California community

When Russia invaded Afghanistan in the early 1980s, many Afghan people fled the country, and some eventually immigrated to the United States of America. Like previous immigrants, rather than scattering throughout the country, many settled in enclaves, where they found maintaining certain cultural beliefs and practices easier and where they could more readily expect to be understood. Little Kabul, an Afghan community of 15,000 people in Fremont, California, population 210,000, is such an enclave. Though the Afghan Americans living there are second and third generation as well as first generation, they are often perceived by others as more Afghan than American. This was particularly apparent in the weeks immediately following the 9/11 tragedy when people in the community suffered hate mail and property damage.

*With Us or Against Us* gives Afghan Americans an opportunity to talk about their experiences in the United States, about their connections to Afghanistan, and about the impact of 9/11 on their own lives as well as on Afghanistan and its people. Most prominent among the interviewees in the film are an artist, an editor, a journalist, a community activist, a marketing professional, and a restaurateur. All still have strong ties with their or their parents' homeland and are interested in helping rebuild a post-Taliban Afghanistan by sending money and supplies or by actually working there themselves. They also have strong ties to the United States and legitimately see themselves as citizens of this country.

For the many people in this country who have not had the opportunity to interact with immigrants from Afghanistan, Pakistan, or the countries of the region, the documentaries emerging after 9/11 and introducing Arab Americans and Muslims to the rest of the country can be very helpful. Though still not available in great numbers, their emergence augurs well for viewers who want to learn more about the many cultural groups that comprise the United States.

While *With Us or Against Us* spends considerable time on issues raised by the 9/11 catastrophe and its subsequent impact on the people and country of Afghanistan as well as on Afghan Americans, it also humanizes people who have too often been seen only as members of a group rather than as human beings who share aspects of history and culture. The film can effectively introduce secondary school and college students as well as adults to a number of articulate Afghan Americans as they express various views on their own situations before and after 9/11 and on post-9/11 events in Afghanistan.

# Asian American Films

## OVERVIEW

A surge of filmmaking activity occurred among African and Latino/a Americans as part of the civil rights movements that took root in the 1960s and 1970s. Around the same time, Asian American activists and artists participated in a similar increase in independent, politically engaged filmmaking, often to counter the limited and stereotypical representation of Asian Americans in Hollywood movies (Feng, *Screening* 4; Hirano 295–298, 301). Peter X. Feng, in *Screening Asian Americans*, points to Eugene Franklin Wong's 1978 study, *On Visual Media Racism*, when suggesting "that the U.S.A. motion picture industry's racism manifests itself in role segregation (wherein white actors can portray non-whites, but non-whites can never portray whites), in role stratification (wherein the larger the role, the greater the likelihood that a white actor will be cast), and in the relatively limited (that is to say, stereotypical) dimensions of Asian characters" (Feng, *Screening* 8).

Feng identifies shortcomings in the representations of Asian Americans in mainstream movies but suggests that representations in all movies, whether mainstream or marginal, be read—and judged—within contexts rather than as simply negative or positive depending on whether or not Asian Americans created them (*Screening* 5). The race/ethnicity of the filmmaker is only one factor in assessing the value and virtue of a work. The contexts in which viewers see films, their own values and perspectives, and their purpose in watching and analyzing a film all come into play. Though relevant whenever exploring a movie, this may be of particular importance for viewers who are not Asian American when they attempt to interpret Asian or Asian American cultures as these are presented on screen.

People of the East tend to approach the world in fundamentally different ways from people of the West. These "approaches include profoundly different social relations, views about the nature of the world, and characteristic thought processes" (Nisbett xx). Even when these differences have been filtered through the experiences and perspectives of Asian Americans who have learned to navigate effectively in a world dominated by the West's linear, logic-driven standpoints, viewers unfamiliar with Asian or Asian

American cultures cannot assume Asian Americans, whether filmmakers or characters, have abandoned completely the holistic, interdependent thinking patterns of the East. We have considered this in viewing and discussing the Asian American films we critique, but switching mind sets is difficult, and we urge all readers, whether or not they are Asian American, to consider this when watching these films or reading our responses to them.

Readers will probably notice that Chinese and Japanese Americans are disproportionately represented among the Asian American films we review. Immigration patterns that brought Chinese and Japanese people to the United States earlier than Cambodians, Koreans, Vietnamese, Indians, or other Asians help explain this, as do the number of immigrants within each group, their historical relationships to the American mainstream in the United States, and their material circumstances in the 1970s and 1980s when Asian Americans began making films in significant numbers.

Simply naming some of the ethnicities and nationalities referred to as Asian American calls attention to the diverse cultures subsumed under that name. Lisa Lowe points this out when she writes, "From the perspective of the majority culture, Asian Americans may very well be constructed as different from . . . Euro-Americans. But from the perspectives of Asian Americans, we are perhaps even more different, more diverse, among ourselves: being men and women at different distances and generations from our 'original' Asian cultures—cultures as different as Chinese, Japanese, Korean, Filipino, Indian, and Vietnamese" (27).

Even while acknowledging this diversity, and the continual pressures that keep these and (all cultures) in flux, Lowe also acknowledges the importance of Asian Americans identifying as such (27–28). Similarly, Peter Feng notes that using "the label 'Asian American Cinema' does not imply that there is such a thing as 'Asian American culture,' given the diversity of Asian cultures and the different patterns of acculturation that have greeted the immigrants from various Asian countries." He suggests "Asian 'American' is a political category: the name of a coalition of Americans who have come to realize that their political situation . . . requires them to act together" ("State" 20–21).

Considering all of this, certain broadly defined themes still seem to emerge in a study of Asian American films: Identity (*Chan Is Missing, A Great Wall, Living on Tokyo Time*), intergenerational respect and expectations (*Chutney Popcorn, Eat a Bowl of Tea, The Joy Luck Club, The Wedding Banquet*), and the immigrant experience (*Combination Platter, The Green Dragon, Sa-I-Gu, Snow Falling on Cedars, Who Killed Vincent Chin?*) are among them. Most of these films have been made by Asian Americans, their variety and quality encouraging but their limited distribution emblematic of the difficulty independent filmmakers, especially filmmakers from traditionally underrepresented groups, have in ensuring that their work is seen. We hope our calling attention to them prompts educators, and curious moviegoers generally, to see them. As windows through which viewers can see some aspects of Asian American cultures, they vary in size, shape, and translucence, but they can offer enough of a view to spark interest and suggest points of contact among cultural groups.

**Works Cited:** Feng, Peter X., ed. *Screening Asian Americans*. New Brunswick, NJ: Rutgers University Press, 2002; Feng, Peter X. "The State of Asian American Cinema: In Search of Community." *Cineaste* 24, no. 4 (1999): 20–24; Hirano, Ron. "Media Guerillas." In *Counterpoint Perspectives on Asian America*, edited by Emma Gee, 295–302. Los Angeles: Asian American Studies Center, University of California, 1976; Lowe, Lisa. "Heterogeneity, Hybridity, Multiplicity:

Marking Asian American Differences." *Diaspora* 1, no. 1 (Spring 1991): 24–44; Nisbett, Richard E. *The Geography of Thought: How Asians and Westerners Think Differently . . . and Why*. New York: Free Press, 2003.

## THE FILMS

### *Catfish in Black Bean Sauce* (2000)

Director: Chi Moui Lo

Cast: Chi Moui Lo (Dwayne Williams/Sap), Sanaa Lathan (Nina), Paul Winfield (Harold Williams), Mary Alice (Dolores Williams), Lauren Tom (Mai), Kieu Chink (Thanh)

Length: 119 min.

Rating: PG-13

Family Comedy/Drama: Exploring identity within an interracial family

While Harold is working in a government-sponsored adoption agency responsible for placing Vietnam refugees, he overhears Mai's pleas not to be separated from her younger brother. Separation is a distinct possibility not only because finding adoptive parents for one child is easier than for two but also because adoptive parents often prefer younger children to preadolescents. Harold and his wife Dolores respond to Mai's pleading, adopt Mai and Dwayne, and rear the children in their African American community.

Dwayne becomes thoroughly assimilated, while Mai chooses to remain closer to her Vietnamese heritage. Dwayne, a bank manager in the African American community, dates Nina, an African American who has completed college and is weighing job possibilities while Dwayne debates asking her to marry him. Mai marries Vinh, like her a Vietnamese refugee; she continues her long search for Thanh, her birth mother, though Dwayne and her adoptive parents are unaware of this until she announces Thanh's imminent arrival.

Thanh's presence heightens the existing unease between Mai and Dolores and creates tension in most of Dwayne's relationships. Thanh insists on moving in with him rather than with Mai and then, in an attempt to recoup her role as his mother, tries to undermine his relationships with Nina and Dolores. The result is much unhappiness for everyone as Dwayne tries, often without success, to scramble through one awkward situation after another.

Chi Moui Lo treats these situations comically, at times incorporating the kind of bungling associated with traditional screwball comedy and interspersing funny fantasy scenes as Dwayne's imagination runs wild. Chi Moui Lo even manages to introduce scenes of sexual misidentification related to dates of Dwayne's roommate, Michael. At times, the director simply goes too far, not only in reaching for zany comic turns some viewers will not find funny, but also in bringing in distracting elements of a subplot that revolves around Michael. The film seems to get away from him in these instances and suggests he may not trust the value of his central story enough, or he may not want to give up any of the ideas that came to mind while writing the screenplay.

Despite its sprawling narrative, *Catfish in Black Bean Sauce* is worth looking into. The refugee, adoption, identity, and intercultural relationship issues it raises are important, and the film does give viewers enough material on these issues to form a basis for discussion and further exploration. One relationship that seems particularly difficult to resolve is that between birth mother and adoptive mother. The devotion, claims, and expectations of each are conveyed effectively, as is their need to step back in ways that are extraordinarily selfless. Mai's struggle to define her relationships with Thanh and Dolores is presented convincingly though more quietly than Dwayne's efforts to rethink his relationship to his dual heritage. Both call attention to the unique challenges of interracial identities and interracial adoptions, subjects that continue to be debated in light of increasing numbers of biracial children in the United States and growing opportunities for parents here to adopt children from other countries. Useful resources on this issue are Michael Omi and Howard Winant's *Racial Formation in the U.S.: From the 1960s to the 1990s* and Maria P. P. Root and Matt Kelley's *Multiracial Child Resource Book: Living Complex Identities*.

**Works Cited:** Omi, Michael, and Howard Winant. *Racial Formation in the U.S.: From the 1960s to the 1990s*. New York: Routledge, 1994; Root, Maria P. P., and Matt Kelley. *Multiracial Child Resource Book: Living Complex Identities*. Seattle: Mavin Foundation, 2003.

## *Chan Is Missing* (1982)

Director: Wayne Wang

Cast: Wood Moy (Jo), Marc Hayashi (Steve), Laureen Chew (Amy), Peter Wang (Henry the Cook), Presco Tabios (Presco), Frankie Alarcon (Frankie), Judi Nihei (Lawyer)

Length: 80 min.

Rating: Not Rated

Investigative Parody: Coming to terms with diverse perspectives

When their friend and associate Chan Hung disappears with the $4,000 they gave him to buy a cab license, Jo and his nephew Steve take on the role of amateur sleuths and try to find the missing Chan and their money. Self-consciously and simultaneously mimicking and critiquing Charlie Chan and his Number One Son, the two begin interviewing people who might give them some information about where Chan is: his ex-wife, his daughter, the manager of the hotel where he lived, and acquaintances. Instead of bringing them closer to a resolution of Chan's mysterious disappearance, they find themselves more and more perplexed, as their interviewees give them widely dissimilar views about Chan's character and activities.

That the primary focus of Jo's investigation is Chan rather than the money becomes evident as he and Steve continue their search even after Chan's daughter returns the $4,000. Elements of traditional film mysteries emerge throughout their odyssey: a saved newspaper with a missing article, allusions to a murder and a political controversy, a gun found in Chan's car, a threatening phone call, multiple false leads, and melodramatic music. Through voice-over commentary, however, Jo points out that the clues do not lead to a satisfactory conclusion—at least not if that means Chan is found and his disappearance explained. Rather, Jo learns that Chan cannot be pinned down; his identity cannot be fixed once and for all; he cannot be located. Each "witness" sees Chan differently: as a naïve immigrant, a software genius, a responsible father, an irresponsible husband, a loser, a political activist, a person who is at once slow-witted, sly, hot-headed, paranoid, honest, patriotic, and eccentric (Feng 200–201).

In presenting Chan through multiple perspectives as a complex, changing, and ultimately elusive figure, Wang, the film's director, undercuts Asian American stereotypes. Playing with recognizable genres, including detective films and films noir, Wang also continually reminds viewers that he can bend genre guidelines to reflect his Asian American perspective and to critique Hollywood-generated expectations. A light comedic touch and an indirect approach help convey his critique of mainstream media stereotyping of Asian Americans without undermining its seriousness.

Questions of identity are important to individuals and to groups and can be addressed from many angles. Wang adds to his own exploration by casting Marc Hayashi, a Japanese American actor, as the Chinese American Steve. He thus calls attention to pan-Asian American identities as opposed to a specific ethnic identity and suggests that "later generations of Asian Americans have more in common with each other than with the specifics of their cultural ancestry" (Feng 207; See also Dittus 19), a hypothesis that is worthy of further investigation.

*Chan Is Missing* is a small, independent black and white film that was made for less than $25,000. It is not a technically polished production, but audiences can enjoy and analyze it to learn more about issues of identity, media representation of Asian Americans, and some aspects of Asian American culture. Unfortunately, early in the film, Steve and Jo's niece Amy, invite Jo and viewers to laugh at the possibility of electing a gay Chinese American to the San Francisco Board of Supervisors. In his in-depth analysis of *Chan Is Missing*, Peter Feng discusses what he refers to as Steve's "insecure masculinity" in terms of Chan's immigrant (FOB/fresh off the boat) versus Steve's ABC (American-born Chinese) status (202–203), but Feng does not link this to Steve's apparent homophobia even though sexual orientation certainly is a significant aspect of identity.

**Works Cited:** Dittus, Erick. "*Chan Is Missing:* An Interview with Wayne Wang." *Cineaste* 12, no. 3 (1983): 16–20; Feng, Peter X. "Being Chinese American, Becoming Asian American: *Chan Is Missing*." In *Screening Asian Americans*. 185–216. New Brunswick, NJ: Rutgers University Press, 2002.

## ***Chutney Popcorn*** **(2000)**

Director: Nisha Ganatra

Cast: Nisha Ganatra (Reena), Jill Hennessy (Lisa), Sakina Jaffrey (Sarita), Maaher Jaffrey (Meenu), Nick Chinlund (Mitch)

Length: 92 min.

Rating: Not Rated

Light Family Drama: Adapting to changing family structures

To Meenu's delight, her older daughter, Sarita, marries and, with her husband Mitch, looks forward to having children. To Meenu's dismay, her younger daughter, Reena, is in a lesbian relationship with Lisa and has no intention of providing her with grandchildren. When Sarita finds out she cannot have children, her and her mother's disappointment is palpable. Reena, to Lisa's consternation, offers to become a surrogate mother, an offer that is initially dismissed but gradually takes hold even though, after Mitch and Reena initiate the process of artificial insemination, Sarita becomes increasingly wary of the arrangement and ultimately pressures Reena to stop. However, Reena does become pregnant, thus alienating Sarita and prompting Lisa to leave—temporarily. By the time the baby arrives, Lisa and Reena's love, Meenu's delight in having a grandchild, and Sarita's strong family ties assure the baby's welcome and reunite all involved.

*Chutney Popcorn* intertwines Indian, mainstream U.S., and lesbian cultures, alternating the family gatherings and traditions Meenu presides over with the get-togethers of Reena, Lisa, and their friends. Reena is initially posed as an outsider during the Indian celebrations, but she brings some elements of Indian culture into her work, as when she makes henna painting an important focus of her photography. And Meenu, having already accepted Sarita's marriage to a European American, learns to adapt the Indian rituals associated with childbirth and family to the reality of Reena and Lisa's relationship. This upbeat resolution fits the light tone that prevails throughout the film despite the upheavals and disappointments the characters experience.

*Chutney Popcorn* celebrates the value of change and a willingness to adapt to new circumstances while also recognizing the value of cultural traditions. It suggests that relationships are more important than the forms used to define—and limit—them, but the forms need not be abandoned altogether, just adjusted to the reality of the relationships. The relationships depicted in *Chutney Popcorn* are sufficiently varied to make the film an appropriate starting point for many discussions, including discussions of both traditional and changing cultural values, family structures and expectations, and individual needs and responsibilities.

## *Combination Platter* (1993)

Director: Tony Chan

Cast: Jeff Lau (Robert), Colleen O'Brien (Claire), Colin Mitchell, (Benny), Kenneth Lu (Andy), Lester Chan (Sam)

Length: 84 min.

Rating: Not Rated

Comedy/Drama: Efforts of a Chinese immigrant to secure legal status

Tony Chan, in his first feature film, *Combination Platter*, directs attention to the issue of undocumented immigrants. His protagonist, Robert, has immigrated to the United States from Hong Kong and has found steady employment as a waiter at the Szechuan Inn. He wants to legitimize his position by getting a green card, but only two ways of doing this seem open to him: marry a U.S. citizen or persuade his employer to initiate an application process. Robert's lack of confidence and poor communication skills undercut his attempt to develop a relationship with Claire that could lead to marriage. Mr. Lee, the restaurant owner, although a decent employer, has his own worries and suggests "now is not a good time" when Robert approaches him about the application. Robert thus remains in the precarious position of an undocumented worker, on the one hand assuring his parents in Hong Kong that everything is going well for him, while on the other experiencing the constant pressure of possible discovery, detention, and deportation.

*Combination Platter* avoids the extreme horrors suffered by many illegal immigrants. Robert has a sympathetic, if beleaguered, boss, relatively pleasant working conditions, a concerned friend, and a fairly comfortable living space. He and his coworkers get along well, with the exception of Sam, an addicted gambler who resorts to stealing tips. Robert, through a combination of luck and quick thinking, avoids discovery when immigration officials pay an unexpected visit to the Szechuan Inn. His attempt at being honest with Claire is not so successful, but the help he gives James, one of his regular customers, when James proposes to his girlfriend Noriko, suggests to Robert that interethnic and interracial relationships can work, hinting, perhaps, that he will try to reunite with Claire or at least consider pursuing a relationship that crosses ethnic lines.

Definitely low-key, *Combination Platter* appears to be honest and realistic in its portrayal of Robert and his situation. Since, like most people, whether immigrant or citizen, he avoids cataclysmic relationships and events, viewers can easily relate to him and to his life as it unfolds, picking up in the process some understanding of the ongoing challenges and cultural adaptations Chinese immigrants face, particularly those who are undocumented.

## *Eat a Bowl of Tea* (1989)

Director: Wayne Wong

Cast: Cora Miao (Mei Oi), Russell Wong (Ben Loy), Victor Wong (Wah Gay), Siu-Ming Lau (Lee Gong)

Length: 102 min.

Rating: PG-13

Family Drama/Comedy: Intergenerational pressure prompted by a desire for progeny

Because early Chinese immigrants were not allowed to bring their wives to the United States or to marry here, their virtual bachelor community was relieved and delighted when these rules were rescinded after World War II. Wah Gay happily sends his G.I. son Ben Loy back to China to marry Mei Oi, a friend's daughter, and return with her to New York. Their prearranged marriage appears to have great promise as they fall in love and begin a new life together. The promise quickly dissolves, however, because of the pressure exerted by Ben's father and his friends as they wait for signs that Mei Oi is pregnant.

Ben's stress is compounded by the demands of a new job, and he becomes impotent. His efforts to reverse the situation prove unsuccessful, and Mei Oi, feeling neglected and unloved, succumbs to the advances of a neighborhood rake eager to become her lover. When she becomes pregnant and Ben and the rest of the community discover the truth, the chaos that follows leads to Ben's and Mei's fathers leaving New York. Ben and Mei's marriage survives.

Given the historical content of *Eat a Bowl of Tea*, the older generation's interest in Ben and Mei seems easy to fathom. Though many of the men are married, most did not see their own children grow up because of the restrictive immigration laws in place until after World War II. Viewers who want to look into this further can explore the content and impact of the Chinese Exclusion Act of 1882 as well as the 1946 War Brides Act; they might also follow the development of other immigration laws such as the McCarran Act of 1952 and the Immigration Act of 1965, which affected major reform in U.S. policy.

*Eat a Bowl of Tea*, like *Chutney Popcorn* and *The Wedding Banquet*, focuses on the parents' desire to see their children married and have children. In each of these films, this desire borders on obsession and plays out in interesting and unorthodox ways. In

*Chutney Popcorn*, the lesbian sister of a new bride offers to submit to artificial insemination and become the surrogate mother of her sister's baby; in *The Wedding Banquet*, a gay man enters into a marriage of convenience to satisfy his parents and in his only sexual contact with his wife, impregnates her. In *Eat a Bowl of Tea* the much awaited pregnancy occurs because of Mei Oi's relationship with a lover, not her husband. Each of the films ends happily, or relatively so in the case of *Eat a Bowl of Tea*, with parents and children looking forward to the birth. Because having descendants is so important to the older generation, they are willing to overlook the means used to that end. In doing so, ironically, a very traditional and conventional value—progeny—fuses with contemporary relationships that challenge tradition.

Parent–child relationships, the meaning of family, intergenerational expectations, and the impact of historical events on personal relationships are some of the issues *Eat a Bowl of Tea* raises. Exploring them in relation to *The Wedding Banquet* and *Chutney Popcorn*, or to the history of the immigration policies of the United States can lead to greater understanding of an important segment of the country's population. Such an exploration can also show how public policies can impact very personal relationships, a point Oliver Wang makes in his review of *Eat a Bowl of Tea*.

**Works Cited:** *Chutney Popcorn*. Directed by Nisha Ganatra. Performances by Nisha Ganatra, Jill Hennessey, Sakina Jaffrey, and Maaher Jaffrey. First Look Pictures, 1999; Wang, Oliver. "Performing Under Pressure." *Pop Matters*, June 9, 2003. http://www.popmatters.com/film/reviews/e/eat-a-bowl-of-tea.shtml (accessed June 22, 2004); *The Wedding Banquet*. Directed by Ang Lee. Performances by Winston Chao, May Chin, Ah Lei Gua, Sihung Lung, and Mitchell Lichtenstein. Samuel Goldwyn, 1993.

## *A Great Wall* (1986)

Director: Peter Wang

Cast: Wang Xiao (Liu Yida), Li Qinqin (Lili Chao), Xui Jian (Yu), Sharon Iwai (Grace Fang), Shen Guanglan (Mrs. Chao), Kelvin Han Yee (Paul Fang), Hu Xiaoguang (Mr. Chao), Peter Wang (Leo Fang)

Length: 97 min.

Rating: PG

Comedy/Drama: Chinese Americans return to China for family visit

Leo Fang left China at age ten and has lived in the United States ever since. He has married Grace, a Chinese American, and has one child, Paul, who is a college student. Having excelled as the supervisor of an important computer project, Leo is angry enough to quit his job abruptly when his boss passes over him and appoints a younger European American director of his division. He uses the unexpected "gift" of time to return to China with Grace and Paul for an extended visit with his sister, her husband, and their daughter Lili, who is preparing for the annual college entrance exams. Almost as soon as they have been reunited, the Chaos invite Leo and his family to stay with them rather than at a hotel, making it possible for the two families to observe each other very closely. Both are often fascinated or bemused by the other's culture.

*A Great Wall* invites viewers to observe and compare the cultural practices of the Fangs and the Chaos and to note similarities as well as differences. In California the

Fangs enjoy Chinese art and food, though Grace admits she can make only one such dish, beef noodles. The décor of their home reflects their Asian roots, but neither Grace nor Paul can speak Chinese, though they have studied it. Both identify completely with mainstream American culture and know little about Chinese history and traditions. The Chaos' knowledge of the culture of the United States is just as limited, though Lili does study English because she cannot pass the college entrance exam without it and is considering a career that will require it.

Differences in clothes, food, music, dance, transportation, exercise, and sports are all made apparent through the characters' connections and interactions. To Mr. Chao, for instance, Paul's Pierre Cardin burlap blazer with leather elbow patches and his drab Calvin Klein slacks are far from chic, and to Lili the dress Grace brings her simply doesn't fit right. The single computer his Chinese counterparts so solemnly and proudly show Leo is clearly a letdown given his technical expertise and experience. But the characters also reveal the similarities between Chinese and mainstream American culture as they interact. Lili's and her schoolmate Liu's shy behavior as they become more and more attached to each other does not differ significantly from that of shy adolescents in the United States. Mr. Chao and Leo both want their children to marry within their Chinese culture, even though Leo has absorbed many aspects of U.S. culture; and Liu's and Paul's competitiveness when they play for the ping pong championship is comparable.

*A Great Wall* revolves around quiet but insightful observations and revelations rather than dramatic confrontation or conflicts (Ebert). The cross-cultural encounter has an observable impact on Leo that is evident in his switch from the more tense and stressful jogging he had been doing to the quiet, graceful moves of tai chi. That he has no intention of giving up his life in the United States, however, is suggested not only by his return, but also by the arrival of his boss, no doubt to offer Leo the promotion he had previously denied him. Paul resumes his relationship with his European American girlfriend Linda and does not appear to have been affected at all by the visit to his Chinese relatives. Nor do Lili and Liu seem changed by the encounter. We see them after Liu has passed his exams; while he is feted by his neighbors, he and Lili demurely establish eye contact, suggesting the resumption of their slowly developing romantic relationship.

How much influence do cross-cultural encounters have on the individuals involved? How much depends on the individuals' circumstances: their age, their immigrant or nonimmigrant status, the likelihood of ongoing communication? *A Great Wall* may prompt these and other questions for viewers, but its primary appeal is its skillful, nonjudgmental depiction of two cultures and how they might intersect as well as differ, making it a valuable educational tool.

**Work Cited:** Ebert, Roger. Review of *A Great Wall. Chicago Sun-Times*, July 18, 1986. http://www.suntimes.com/ebert/ebert_reviews/1986/07/68758.html (accessed July 15, 2003).

## *The Green Dragon* (2001)

Director: Timothy Linh Bui

Cast: Patrick Swayze (Jim Lance), Forest Whitaker (Addie), Don Duong (Tai Tran), Trung Nguyen (Minh Pham), Hiep Thi Le (Thuy Hoa)

Length: 115 min.

Rating: PG-13

Drama: Vietnamese refugees struggle to adjust in a new land

*The Green Dragon* tells the stories of some of the many refugee families who came to the United States of America as the result of the Vietnam conflict. The film intertwines several stories being lived out in the relocation camp at Fort Pendleton, California.

One story is told through the eyes of Minh, a young Vietnamese boy who with his sister has arrived in the camp with their uncle Tai. They wait day after day for their mother, who sacrificed herself in order to enable her children to escape. Because she promised to join them in the United States, they meet each new group of arrivals with the hope she will be among them, but they are repeatedly disappointed.

Addie, the character played by Forest Whitaker, befriends Minh and wins his heart through his sensitivity and his ability to cross the cultural barriers that separate them. Together they paint a mural that creates a solid bond between them and offers hope to Ming. Addie, however, is in the last stages of a terminal illness and has given his last days to working as a volunteer cook for the refugee camp. Minh is as important to Addie as Addie is to Minh.

The story of Loi and his two wives focuses on differences in cultural traditions but also encompasses the universal problems identified with close personal relationships. In this case the jealousy of the first wife causes discomfort and tension with Loi as well as with the younger second wife, who sees Loi as her only chance for some semblance of security.

Tai, while caring for his niece and nephew meets Thuy Hoa, who has assumed responsibility for her father and younger sister. Tai and Thuy Hoa's story is of hope, connection, and new beginnings. They learn to recognize the need to let the past go in order to start anew. Though not easy, they both find the courage to move forward and come together as a couple.

Patrick Swayze plays Jim Lance, the camp coordinator. An administrator whose job is to keep the camp running smoothly, he recognizes Tai's bilingual ability and offers him the job of camp manager. Their interaction throughout the film reveals the difficulty of developing understanding across different cultures and the necessity for humans to use their hearts as well as their brains when attempting to do so.

This film helps fill the historical void surrounding the large post-Vietnam War influx of Southeast Asians who now call this country their home. It gives us insights into the difficulty all immigrants face as they seek to create a new life in a new land, a process made all the more difficult for those who come as involuntary refugees rather than voluntary immigrants.

The spectrum of characters allows Bui to present a variety of situations and responses that can remind viewers of the diversity among refugees. Though at times regarded simply as Vietnamese refugees who share a culture, they also reflect different personal perspectives and priorities. Because of this, *The Green Dragon* can be helpful in introducing and discussing immigration issues. Two useful resources on these issues are Hien Duc Do's *The Vietnam Americans* and Ronald Takaki's *Strangers from a Different Shore.*

**Works Cited:** Do, Hein Duc. *The Vietnam Americans.* Westport, CT: Greenwood Press, 1999; Takaki, Ronald. *Strangers from a Different Shore: A History of Asian Americans.* Boston: Little, Brown, 1989.

## *Heaven & Earth* (1993)

Director: Oliver Stone

Cast: Hiep Thi Le (Le Ly), Tommy Lee Jones (Steve Butler), Joan Chen (Mama), Haing S. Ngor (Papa)

Length: 140 min.

Rating: R

Vietnam War Drama: Surviving in a war-torn country and as a refugee in the United States

*Heaven & Earth*, the third film of Oliver Stone's trilogy about the United States' involvement in the Vietnam War, begins in the rice fields of South Vietnam, where viewers meet Le Ly, the movie's heroine, as a child. Le Ly tells the story of the invasion of her country by the French in the early 1950s, and the subsequent incursion by the Chinese and the U.S. military in the 1960s. She feels pain as her brothers are forced to go off and fight with the Viet Cong. Left behind with her parents and a younger sister, her father warns her of the responsibility she has to both her country and to her ancestors.

Her allegiances are torn between the southern regime allied with the U.S.A. and the North led by the popular Chinese leader Ho Chi Minh. By day the village is prosouthern, but by night it belongs to the Viet Cong. The division splits families and brings constant danger, as Le Ly learns most harshly when government troops brutally torture her one day, and Viet Cong interrogate, torture, and rape her soon afterwards. To escape, her mother takes her to the city, where they are hired as servants by a rich family. When the master of the house, Anh Lien, becomes intimate with her and she becomes pregnant, Madame Lien forces her husband to send Le Ly and her mother away. Le Ly hustles cigarettes and contraband on the streets and accepts help from her sister Kim until her child, Jimmy, is born.

After Jimmy arrives, Le Ly meets Steve, a G.I., who pursues her persistently for three years and, after she gives birth to their son, takes her to the United States. Initially, the opulence of life in this society overwhelms Le Ly, but she gradually becomes more independent and, in time, establishes a successful business. As she prospers, Steve becomes increasingly resentful, depressed, and angry. A mental breakdown leads to his suicide.

Returning to Vietnam after thirteen years in the United States, Le Ly is reunited with the father of her first child, her mother, and her oldest brother. She has come full circle and for the first time understands that her fate is to live between North and South, between Vietnamese and American cultures, between heaven and earth.

*Heaven & Earth* provides a more comprehensive history of the lives of Le Ly and her family than most mainstream movies made in the United States. Le Ly is not just a refugee, not just the wife of an American G.I., not just a survivor of the atrocities of war; she's all of these and more: a three-dimensional human being, a daughter, a sister, a wife, a mother, an entrepreneur, with stories that should be told. By basing *Heaven & Earth* on the autobiography of Le Ly Hayslip and following her experiences, director Oliver Stone goes beyond the worlds of the U.S. military in Vietnam he explored in *Platoon* (1986) and *Born on the Fourth of July* (1989). By giving viewers a more complete picture of an average peasant family in an average Vietnam village caught in the brutality of a civil war that tears families and souls apart, *Heaven & Earth* invites audiences to question the identity of the enemy from the perspective of an "ordinary" person. From which invading government, under which flag, and in which uniform does the enemy come? Additionally, Le Ly's adaptation to life in the United States of America provides some excellent discussion points about immigration and the ongoing assimilation-versus-acculturation debate as well as the practice of religion, specifically Buddhism, in the lives of some of the more recent immigrants to this country.

**Works Cited:** *Born on the Fourth of July*. Directed by Oliver Stone. Performances by Tom Cruise, Kyra Sedgwick, Willem Dafoe, Raymond J. Barry, and Tom Berenger. Universal, 1989; Hayslip, Le Ly. *When Heaven and Earth Changed Places: A Vietnamese Woman's Journey from War to Peace*. New York: Penguin, 1990; *Platoon*. Directed by Oliver Stone. Performances by Charlie Sheen, Tom Berenger, Willem Dafoe, and Forest Whitaker. MGM, 1986.

## *The Joy Luck Club* (1993)

Director: Wayne Wang

Cast: Kieu Chinh (Suyuan), Tsai Chin (Lindo), France Nuyen (Ying Ying), Lisa Lu (An Mei), Ming-Na Wen (June), Tamlyn Tomita (Waverly), Lauren Tom (Lena), Rosalind Chao (Rose)

Length: 139 min.

Rating: R

Mother–Daughter Drama: Differences in experiences and expectations

*The Joy Luck Club* encompasses the stories of four mothers and their daughters. The mothers are Chinese immigrants who came to the United States as young adults; their now-grown daughters are U.S.-born Chinese Americans. Their stories are told primarily through flashbacks triggered by various remarks made during a party for June, who is about to leave for a reunion with her stepsisters in China. Each story revolves around mother–child relationships and, in all but one, mother–daughter relationships. Each of the mothers has faced great traumas brought on by war, poverty, or male privilege, while their daughters have each faced a crisis of identity and confidence they link to their mothers' expectations and hopes for them.

*The Joy Luck Club* begins with a story told in voice-over during the opening credits. It is about a woman who bought a swan, which, she was told, was a duck "that stretched its neck in hopes of becoming a goose." The woman decided it was too beautiful to eat and sailed with it to the United States, where she hoped to have a daughter who would escape pain and sorrow and who would recognize her mother's hopes for her when she gave her the swan, "a creature that became more than what was hoped for." When the swan was taken by immigration officials, the woman was able to hold onto only one feather. She resolved to give the feather to her daughter, telling her "this feather may look worthless, but it comes from afar and carries with it all my good intentions."

This allegory introduces and, to a great extent, explains the action in *The Joy Luck Club*. The mothers in the film have survived unspeakable pain, immigrated to the United States of America, married, and had daughters for whom they have great hopes. For the daughters, their mothers' hopes have been translated into pressures that have caused anxiety and feelings of inadequacy and failure. Only when these reach crisis proportions do the mothers and daughters confront each other and come to a greater understanding of their different perspectives—and the deep love they have for each other.

Amy Tan, the author of the novel *The Joy Luck Club*, is the coauthor of the film's screenplay and one of its producers as well, giving the film a greater chance of reflecting Tan's own intentions and her knowledge and experience of Chinese and Chinese American cultures. However, the film has relevance for everyone. It may have special interest for immigrant parents and their children and for anyone interested in the acculturation process because the film, like the allegory of the swan, mirrors in many ways the experiences of immigrants who come to the United States with the desire for a better life for themselves and their children, but who also want to give their children an appreciation of the culture of their homeland. Under these circumstances, relationships between generations, between parents and children, whether female or male, take on cultural as well as personal significance. *The Joy Luck Club* underscores how the two are intertwined.

Viewers who want to learn more about the experience of Chinese immigrants to the United States will find Ronald Takaki's *Strangers from a Different Shore* a very insightful resource.

**Works Cited:** Takaki, Ronald. *Strangers from a Different Shore: A History of Asian Americans*. Boston: Little, Brown, 1989; Tam, Amy. *The Joy Luck Club*. New York: Vintage Books, 1991.

## *Living on Tokyo Time* (1987)

Director: Steven Okazaki

Cast: Minako Ohashi (Kyoko), Ken Nakagawa (Ken), Kate O'Connell (Lana), Brenda Aoki (Michelle), Mitzie Abe (Mimi), Bill Bonham (Carl)

Length: 85 min.

Rating: R

Drama: The gulf between first and second generation immigrants

The film opens with a soliloquy by Kyoko in which she explains her rationale for coming to the United States of America from Japan. She is preoccupied with justifying her desire to stay in the United States to her family and to her best friend, both who want her to come home. The next scene, in a Japanese restaurant in the United States, shows Kyoko practicing her English so that she can get into a university. Ken, a Japanese American whose girlfriend has just broken up with him, visits the same restaurant and has a conversation with a friend who suggests that he marry Kyoko so she can get her green card and he can have someone to talk to. After dinner and a movie they do get married. She moves in with him and they begin their relationship.

Though her friends think Ken is boring, Kyoko defends her new husband by saying he is very nice and reminding everyone that this is the best way to get a green card. Life carries on with its own unique rhythm, but over time their cultural gulf begins to wear on Kyoko. Ken, a guitar player, clearly does not see himself as Japanese, at least not in the same way Kyoko does. Kyoko still calls him Mr. Ken, and they simply do not connect on an emotional level.

When Ken tries to interact with her, Kyoko doesn't know how to respond. He reaches out to her, but she has reservations about a long-term commitment, having entered into the marriage only because it was expedient. She is threatened by his change in the relationship and begins to distance herself from him; for example, in one scene, she begins speaking in Japanese, knowing he cannot speak the language. Their cultural differences work against their getting to know and understand each other, so it is not surprising when the interview at the immigration office does not go well. The many discrepancies in their responses to the questions they are asked and their lack of knowledge about each other and their families undermine their claim to be a couple.

Kyoko, disheartened by the interview and seeing no viable way to stay in the United States legally, decides to return to Japan. She packs her clothing and leaves. When Ken reads her farewell note, he smashes his guitar in frustration, though he remains painfully and unrealistically optimistic that someday she will return.

This is an intriguing examination of the issues new immigrants face when interacting with second-generation hyphenated Americans. It provides multiple openings for discussing differences in perspective in male–female relationships, homesickness, language and cultural barriers, and the challenges of immigration. Viewers may also want to compare and contrast this film with Peter Weir's *Green Card* (1990), in which a marriage of convenience between a French immigrant (Gérard Depardieu) and a U.S. citizen (Andie MacDowell) turns into a romance with a typical Hollywood happy ending. See a review of the film in this volume.

**Work Cited:** *Green Card.* Directed by Peter Weir. Performances by Gérard Depardieu and Andie MacDowell. Buena Vista, 1990.

## *Maya Lin: A Strong Clear Vision* (1994)

Director: Freida Lee Mock

Distributor: Sanders & Mock Productions/American Film Foundation

Length: 83 min.

Rating: Not Rated

Documentary: Biography of architect who designed the Vietnam Memorial

At age 20, while an architectural student at Yale, Maya Lin entered the competition for the design of a national Vietnam Memorial and won. Her proposal, while the clear choice of the jury, was strongly supported by some veterans' groups but vigorously opposed by others, and Lin was called upon to defend her design. In her words, the design was meant to say that "the cost of war is these individuals and we have to remember them first . . . because it's only when you accept the pain, it's only when you accept the death, can you then come away from it, can you then overcome it."

*Maya Lin: A Strong Clear Vision* devotes considerable time to the Vietnam Memorial, the design and its meaning as Lin understood it and as visitors to the memorial came to understand it. The documentary also covers the initial controversy that threatened its implementation, as well as the tenth anniversary of its installation. That so much time is given to the context that surrounded the conception and realization of the monument is fitting, given how Lin works. Before designing any sculpture or building, she must understand the context—historical as well as physical—in which it exists. Out of that understanding comes the "strong clear vision" her works reflect. This is true not only of the Vietnam Memorial, but also of the Juniata Peace Chapel, the Civil Rights Memorial commissioned by the Southern Poverty Law Center, the Museum for African Art in New York, the fountain honoring Yale's women graduates, and the other public and private structures she has designed.

Appropriately, *Maya Lin*'s portrait of the artist encompasses her work and her ideas about that work. It relies more on interviews with her than about her but includes a sketch of her family and home life in Athens, Ohio, where her parents, both Chinese immigrants and university professors, taught her to value creativity and to measure success more in terms of the significance of what she does than in terms of financial rewards.

That the filmmakers admire Lin and see her accomplishments as very significant is evident in this documentary. The film is a tribute to a Chinese American woman who entered the public sphere with remarkable insight into what the Vietnam War meant to people in the United States. Her subsequent work has shown her to be consistently thoughtful and perceptive and to have the creativity and skills to translate her insights into memorable works of art. She can easily serve as a role model for young people, for women, for Chinese and other Asian Americans, for aspiring artists, and for citizens who want to make a positive difference in society. *Maya Lin: A Strong Clear Vision* is an appropriate introduction to this artist.

## *Picture Bride* (1995)

Director: Kayo Hatta

Cast: Youki Kudoh (Riyo), Tamlyn Tomita (Kana), Akira Tahayama (Matsuji), Cary-Hiroyuki Tagawa (Kanzaki)

Length: 95 min.

Rating: PG-13

Drama: The lives of sugarcane field workers in Hawaii

*Picture Bride* traces one aspect of the history of Hawaii through the story of Riyo's arranged marriage to Matsuji, a field worker in Hawaii. Riyo, a 16-year-old from Yokohama, Japan, is pressured by her aunt to accept marriage to Matsuji after both of her parents die from tuberculosis. Shunned by her neighbors and with no apparent alternatives, Riyo agrees after she and Matsuji exchange photographs and letters. She makes the journey to rural Hawaii only to find Matsuji has sent a photograph depicting himself as a young man rather than the 43-year-old he now is. Matsuji himself, his shabby two-room house, and hard physical work in the sugarcane fields for sixty-five cents a day are all disappointments to Riyo, and she quickly vows to return to Japan as soon as she can pay Matsuji the $300 he spent on her voyage. Matsuji, having anticipated a strong country girl as a bride, is as unhappy with the frail-looking Riyo as she is with him, but with the help of Kana, a neighbor who also immigrated to Hawaii as a picture bride, they begin to appreciate each other and to respond to each other's needs and desires.

*Picture Bride* is dedicated to the more than 20,000 women who made the journey from Japan, Korea, and other Asian countries to Hawaii as picture brides between 1907 and 1924. Each woman, on the basis of an exchange of photographs and letters, and at times the services of a matchmaker, crossed an ocean to enter into marriage with a plantation worker from her own country who, having settled in Hawaii, was willing to pay the cost of the voyage for a woman with whom he could share his life.

According to film critic James Berardinelli, director Kayo Hatta spent five years researching the subject of picture brides and, with her sister Mari Hatta, wrote the screenplay. Rather than make a documentary, they chose to integrate the historical context and facts about these marriages within the fictional story of one of the brides.

This story is complicated not only by Matsuji's deception but also by Riyo's. Riyo would not have consented to the partnership had she known Matsuji was almost three times her age, but Matsuji would not have considered Riyo had her aunt been honest about the cause of her parents' deaths. Eventually the marriage works out because both husband and wife are essentially alone and have few options, but also because they are both decent people who come to respect and love each other. Deception and disappointment as well as accommodation were, no doubt, aspects of many of these arranged marriages. The disappointment, as in Riyo's case, was often linked to personal relationships and to the hard labor and harsh working conditions awaiting the brides when they joined their husbands in the sugarcane fields. *Picture Bride* quietly but clearly illustrates this as well as a plantation hierarchy based on ethnicity—Scottish overseer, Portuguese field supervisor, Japanese and Filipino field hands—that led to discrimination, ill will, and at times tragedy. The film, however, ends on a note of hope: Riyo and Matsuji have come to appreciate each other and their marriage, and the Japanese workers have begun establishing a strike fund and planning to solicit Filipino support in a strike for better wages and working conditions.

Besides its portrayal of an aspect of Asian American history that is not well known, *Picture Bride* depicts a number of Japanese customs and cultural events that bring Riyo and Matsuji closer and show them within the larger community. The film also gives viewers a glimpse of how labor-intensive growing sugarcane was at the time and how the field hands were able to keep up their spirits by singing in their native language, using their lyrics to criticize the field boss or even articulate their desire to strike.

Though it unfolds at a leisurely pace, *Picture Bride* can easily hold the attention of viewers interested in the issues it explores. For further information about the historical situation on which it is based, viewers can check Ronald Takaki's *A Different Mirror*. His chapter on "Pacific Crossings: Seeking the Land of Money Trees" directly addresses the picture bride phenomenon.

**Works Cited:** Berardinelli, James. Review of *Picture Bride*, directed by Kayo Hatta, 1995. http://www.cybernex.net/~berardin (accessed March 15, 2004); Takaki, Ronald. "Pacific Crossings: Seeking the Land of Money Trees." In *A Different Mirror: A History of Multicultural America*, 246–276. Boston: Little, Brown, 1993.

## *Sa-I-Gu: From Korean Women's Perspectives* (1993)

Writer and director: Dai Sil Kim-Gibson

Producers: Christine Choy, Elaine Kim, and Dai Sil Kim-Gibson

Distributor: National Asian American Telecommunications Association

Length: 36 min.

Not Rated

Documentary: An exploration of the 1992 L.A. riots from the viewpoints of Korean shopkeepers

Three months after the April 29, 1992, Los Angeles riots that were set off by the acquittal of the police officers who were tried for the Rodney King beating, Kim-Gibson, Choy, and Kim asked a number of Korean American women to give their perspectives on the riots and the events surrounding them. Among the women interviewed are several shop owners whose stores were looted and destroyed during the riots, including Jung Hui Lee, the mother of the only Korean killed as part of the disturbances. The women express a range of viewpoints as they share their perceptions, insights, experiences, and feelings.

In a prologue, the producers explain their purpose in making the video, and in an epilogue, they comment on its content, underscoring their desire to give Korean American women a chance to give their perspectives on what happened and why it happened. The documentary begins and ends with Jung Hui Lee talking about her son's death and her effort to understand it not only as a personal tragedy but also as a social phenomenon that represents a much more far-reaching problem. She and several of the other interviewees are able to assess the L.A. riots and their own losses within the larger context of race/ethnicity and class issues in the United States and to offer a perceptive critique based on their observations and experiences.

Though Korean American women are rarely heard in mainstream media, *Sa-I-Gu* suggests they should be. Their intelligent and passionate voices can bring a valuable dimension to discussions of multicultural issues.

## *Snow Falling on Cedars* (1999)

Director: Scott Hicks

Cast: Ethan Hawke (Ishmael), Youki Kudoh (Hatsue), Rick Yune (Kazuo), Max von Sydow (lawyer), James Rebhorn (lawyer), Eric Thal (Carl Heine, Jr.), Daniel von Bargen (Carl Heine, Sr.), Celia Weston (Etta Heine)

Length: 130 min.

Rating: PG-13

Courtroom Drama: Interracial romance, anti-Japanese prejudice

*Snow Falling on Cedars* is a multilayered story, told through a series of flashbacks, that examines a small island community in the Pacific Northwest prior to and after World War II. This film gives us a quasi-historical account of the fragile alliances between European and Japanese Americans. The story centers on the mysterious death of Carl Heine, Jr., whose body is found in the fishing nets of his boat. Suspicion falls on Kazuo, and he is arrested. Post-World War II prejudice, pain, and hatred come to a boil in both communities during his ensuing murder trial.

The two lawyers do an excellent job in representing the heated emotions in this case. As the trial unfolds, the past relationship between Hatsue, who is now married to Kazuo, and Ishmael, the newspaper reporter covering the trial, resurfaces. One question that emerges as the trial proceeds is whether Ishmael can overcome his own personal pain from the past, the loss of his arm in the war, and the loss of the one woman he loves, to bring balance, justice, and truth back to this small island community.

Ishmael and Hatsue's childhood friendship buds but never blossoms into love because of the tensions that arise in their community after the Japanese attack on Pearl Harbor. The potential for their love is drowned out by the noise created by nationalism, paranoia, suspicion, and tradition. Director Scott Hicks gives us a glimpse of what it must have been like for the Japanese Americans as they packed their belongings and were loaded on the trucks that would carry them to the Manzanar relocation center. He also reveals reactions of the European Americans who were their neighbors and friends.

After the war, this island community seeks to restore harmony between its Japanese and European residents. Kazuo returns from fighting on the European front to find that the land his father made a deal for with Carl Heine, Sr., has been sold by his wife, Etta. Kazuo seeks to reclaim what he feels has been stolen from his family by confronting Carl Heine, Jr. After a meeting at sea on their fishing boats, they establish a gentleman's agreement, but as with the first agreement, tragedy strikes before the deal can be legally consummated.

The photography and sound of this film come alive, adding detail that helps carry and underscore the plot; the shrouded foggy ocean scenes, the snow, and the trees are particularly evocative. The music score, blending European American and Japanese traditional orchestration, drives the tempo of the film and helps to tie together the very separate but sometimes fused cultures we witness.

This film can help audiences begin to understand the delicate conditions that existed between Asian and European American communities in the 1940s and to see how the human heart and our capacity to love can transcend the fetters of culture and tradition. *Snow Falling on Cedars* presents aspects of the litmus test each generation in this country needs to pass as it becomes more and more diverse.

To learn more about the treatment of Japanese Americans during World War II, viewers can explore Roger Daniels's *Prisoner Without Trial* and Gary Y. Okihiro's *Whispered Silences*. Educators are also likely to find the "Children of the Camps" and "Rabbit in the Moon" web sites very rich resources.

**Works Cited:** "Children of the Camps." PBS Online. http://www.PBS.org/childrenofcamp/; Daniels, Roger. *Prisoners Without Trial: Japanese Americans in World War II*. New York: Hill and Wang, 1993; Okihiro, Gary Y. *Whispered Silences: Japanese Americans and World War II*. Seattle: University of Washington Press, 1996; "Rabbit in the Moon." PBS Online. http://www.PBS.org/pov/pov1999/rabbitinthemoon/index.html.

## *Two Lies* (1990)

Director: Pam Tom

Cast: Dian Kabayashi (Doris), Sala Iwamatsu (Mei), Marie Nakano (Esther)

Length: 25 min.

Rating: Not Rated

Short Family Drama: Identity crises and mother-daughter relationships

A day after having plastic surgery to make her eyes look more "European," Doris drives her two daughters, Mei and Esther, from Los Angeles to Cabot's Old Indian Pueblo Museum. The trip is sparked by Esther's interest. She, along with the rest of her class, is studying the homes of different cultural groups. This month they are learning about pueblos and building papier-mâché models of them, so the trip is to be a special treat for Esther. Mei, however, is upset about her mother's surgery and the particular way she is attempting to "get a new grip on life." Doris's effort to create a new image seems to go hand in hand with her apparent need for male attention: she flirts with almost every man with whom she interacts, much to the adolescent Mei's chagrin.

When the Cabot's tour guide explains that Cabot came from Boston and built the thirty-five-room pueblo, Mei challenges its authenticity, but Doris responds under her breath with, "Don't ruin this trip for your sister. Who the hell cares who built it? It looks like one, doesn't it?" to which Mei retorts, "But it's not one." As the three prepare to eat a picnic lunch, Mei tells her mother that her operation is called "two eyes, two lies," but Doris suggests it is no different than piercing one's ears, dying one's hair, or dieting. The two argue, and Mei runs off. Doris tries to follow but becomes disoriented and returns to their picnic spot still angry. She quickly moves from anger to tears, prompting Mei to understanding and empathy.

Though some of the acting in *Two Lies* is amateurish, the film's overall impact and the issues it raises make it worth seeing and discussing. One of those issues, appearance or image, has been the subject of a number of films such as *Killing Us Softly 3: Advertising's Image of Women; Slim Hopes; Mirror, Mirror*; and *The Body Beautiful*; little attention, however, seems to have been given to the effect of current Western standards of beauty on Asian and Asian American women. *Two Lies* helps counter this omission. In *Two Lies*, appearance is juxtaposed with authenticity, as these relate not only to Doris but also to Native American artifacts. Mei criticizes her mother because of her "two eyes, two lies" and because of her lack of concern about Cabot's ersatz pueblo, thus giving the film's title a double meaning. Given this focus, the director's use of Japanese American actors for her Chinese American characters seems unfortunate even while it is understandable and provides an opportunity to consider the compromises filmmakers must make if they are to complete a project.

For educators, *Two Lies* has the advantage of being a short film that can be shown and discussed in a single class period. Its representation of Doris and her daughters centers attention on their interaction, but viewers will do well to pay attention to the background images as well, because many of these raise questions about how traditionally underrepresented groups are viewed by the mainstream.

**Works Cited:** *Body Beautiful, The*. Directed by Ngozi Onwurah. Women Make Movies, 1991; *Mirror, Mirror*. Directed by Jan Krawitz. Women Make Movies, 1990; *Killing Us Softly 3: Advertising's Image of Women*. Directed by Jean Kilbourne. Media Education Foundation, 2000; *Slim Hopes*. Directed by Jean Kilbourne. Media Education Foundation, 1995.

## *The Wedding Banquet* (1993)

Director: Ang Lee

Cast: Winston Chao (Wai-Tung), Mitchell Lichtenstein (Simon), May Chin (Wei-Wei), Sihung Lung (Mr. Gao), Ah-Lah Gua (Mrs. Gao)

Length: 108 min.

Rating: R

Romantic Comedy: Parental pressure and filial obligations intertwined with gay and immigrant relationships

At the suggestion of his partner, Simon, Wai-Tung agrees to marry Wei-Wei. They think the marriage will satisfy Wai-Tung's parents while concealing their homosexual relationship; it will also allow Wei-Wei to obtain a green card and stay in the United States. Complications arise when Wai-Tung's parents, the Gaos, fly from Taiwan to New York for the wedding, turn a simple civil ceremony into a huge traditional community celebration, and extend their stay in New York. The deception cannot be sustained, but all the parties involved manage to get what they want: Wai-Tung and Simon continue their relationship; Wei-Wei is able to remain in the United States and to become part of Wai-Tung's life, and Wai-Tung's parents not only see them married, but also get the grandchild they want so much.

Though a twist on traditional romantic comedies, *The Wedding Banquet*, like many films in the genre, spills over into screwball comedy at times, particularly during the incredibly elaborate and farcical wedding banquet at the film's center. For some viewers, the celebration may seem overdone, especially when it continues in Wai-Tung and Wei-Wei's honeymoon suite, but the guests' intrusiveness actually leads to the consummation of the marriage and Wei-Wei's pregnancy. Wai-Tung's parents' desire for a grandchild is, it seems, at the heart of their interest in Wai-Tung's getting married, though he does not weigh this possibility when responding to his parents' continual pressure. Neither does he consider the possibility that his parents would accept his homosexuality were he honest about it. Would they have accepted it as readily as they do had Wai-Tung and Wei-Wei not first given them the grandchild that ensured the continuation of the family? That remains an open question given the plot and a resolution that has each of the major characters getting what they want, albeit in a slightly different form than anticipated. Ironically, as James Schamus points out, Mr. Gao's "desires are fulfilled through the subversion of the very traditions that instilled those desires in him in the first place" (xii).

Director Ang Lee is straightforward and comfortable in presenting Wai-Tung and Simon's relationship even though his character, Wai-Tung, is not. Wai-Tung's failure turns his life upside down and causes him and those closest to him much pain and discomfort. When he finally tells the truth, everything—or everyone—falls into place. Lee's resolution confirms the value of being truthful as well as the validity of homosexual relationships and alternatives to traditional family structures. It does so without undercutting the importance of culture or child–parent love and respect.

Mr. and Mrs. Gao embody Chinese culture, though Wai-Tung seems to identify more with gay culture and with his role as a young entrepreneur than with his ethnic background. His relationship with Simon is an issue as a gay, not an interethnic or interracial, partnership, but their choice of Wei-Wei as a suitable marriage partner indicates that ethnicity is a consideration if only as part of their effort to placate Wai-Tung's parents. That Wei-Wei is from mainland China and the Gao family is from Taiwan presents no problem.

The characters' relationships offer viewers multiple pathways into *The Wedding Banquet* and the complications that diverse backgrounds, motivations, and goals can generate. A number of essays explore the film in depth and with different emphases. See, for example, Gina Marchetti's "*The Wedding Banquet*: Global Chinese Cinema and the Asian American Experience" and Mark Chiang's "Coming Out into the Global System: Postmodern Patriarchies and Transnational Sexualities in *The Wedding Banquet*."

**Works Cited:** Chiang, Mark. "Coming Out into the Global System: Postmodern Patriarchies and Transnational Sexualities in *The Wedding Banquet*." In *Screening Asian Americans*, edited by Peter X. Feng. 273–292. New Brunswick, NJ: Rutgers University Press, 2002; Marchetti, Gina. "*The Wedding Banquet*: Global Chinese Cinema and the Asian American Experience." In *Countervisions: Asian American Film Criticism*, edited by Darrell Y. Hamamoto and Sandra Liu. 275–297. Philadelphia: Temple University Press, 2000.

## *Who Killed Vincent Chin?* (1988)

Producers and directors: Renee Tajima and Christine Choy

Distributor: Filmakers Library

Length: 82 min.

Rating: Not Rated

Documentary: In-depth exploration of Vincent Chin's murder and its aftermath

In 1982, Detroit resident Vincent Chin was killed after leaving a topless bar where he and some of his friends had gathered for his bachelor party. While in the bar Chin had argued with Ronald Eben, who was there with his stepson, Michael Nez. Shortly after both parties left the bar, the two clashed again. Eben and Nez chased Chin down, and as Nez held Chin, Eben beat him with a baseball bat, leaving him critically injured. He died four days later. When tried for manslaughter, Eben and Nez were sentenced to three years' probation and a $3,000 fine. The Asian American community, outraged by the light sentence and convinced that Chin's ethnicity was a factor in the killing, were further galvanized by his mother and her desire for justice. Supporters succeeded in having the federal government investigate the case and charge Eben with violating Chin's civil rights. Though this trial resulted in a guilty verdict and a twenty-five-year sentence for Eben, the ruling was reversed on appeal.

*Who Killed Vincent Chin?* presents this information through interviews, television and newspaper coverage of the case, photographs and home movies depicting aspects of Chin's and Eben's lives, and footage showing Detroit's automobile plants, assembly lines, and workers, its topless bars, and its neighborhoods, as well as parades, rallies, and demonstrations. The information makes clear that Eben and Nez were responsible for Chin's death, providing a simple answer to the film's title question. The issues raised through the killing, however—questions of motivation and of the role of race/ethnicity in Chin's death—are more complex. These are related to a slump in auto sales and a 17-percent unemployment rate in Detroit, to inroads Japanese auto manufacturers had made into the American market, and to the possible misidentification of Chin as Japanese rather than Chinese. More specifically, Eben's and Nez's unemployment status, Eben's and Chin's tendencies to be outgoing and argumentative, and the fact that both men had been drinking and had apparently evaluated the abilities of one of the dancers very differently, may also have played into the eruption of violence. Tajima and Choy open these possibilities through their extensive interviews and in-depth investigation. Instead of a "traditional advocacy documentary," they focus on the "gray areas of the story," on "subjective factors of intent," and on the ambiguities that arise when perpetrators, witnesses, jurors, and judges see, remember, or evaluate an event differently (Tajima-Peña 248).

Bill Nichols argues "that *Who Killed Vincent Chin?* is the most important political documentary of the 1980s" (160), underscoring the relationship between the diverse viewers of the film and the filmmakers' willingness to present their material so viewers can provide the interpretation or meaning of that material. Where the viewers are historically and ideologically will determine their interpretations and responses. They are invited to put together the story of Chin's killing from the montage—or collage—provided. Because most directors, whether making documentaries or fiction films, try to guide audiences to particular ways of seeing, clueing viewers in to the more open structure of *Who Killed Vincent Chin?* could be helpful. Alerting them to the film's ambivalence can help them adjust their expectations, work through the information they are offered rather than look for what is not given, and prepare them to discuss their take on the Chin–Eben story and the issues it raises, those identified with specific people in a particular time and place—Detroit 1982—and those with broader ramifications—race/ethnicity, class, and gender (Nichols 166).

**Works Cited:** Nichols, Bill. "Historical Consciousness and the Viewer: *Who Killed Vincent Chin?*" In *Screening Asian Americans*, edited by Peter X. Feng. 159–172. New Brunswick, NJ: Rutgers University Press, 2002; Tajima-Peña, Renee. "No Mo Po Mo and Other Tales of the Road." In *Countervisions: Asian American Film Criticism*, edited by Darrell Y. Hamamoto and Sandra Liu. 245–262. Philadelphia: Temple University Press, 2000.

# European American Films

## OVERVIEW

Until recently studying race/ethnicity in the United States of America usually meant studying African, Asian, Latino/a, and Native Americans. Arab and Middle Eastern Americans as well as European Americans were not considered. Arab Americans are now increasingly included in multicultural education though they rarely appear in fictional or documentary films and, therefore, receive little attention in film studies. Although their absence is due to a lack of representation in films, the absence of European Americans in studies of race/ethnicity in films is for an altogether different reason. They have so thoroughly dominated film that their presence is not marked. They are, like the air we breathe, so widely taken for granted that their absence rather than their presence is noticeable.

Since the late 1980s and through the 1990s, a host of publications on "whites" and "whiteness," have appeared across academic disciplines, including film studies. Though scholars adhere to the terms "whites" and "whiteness," European Americans are the primary racial/ethnic subjects of this work. In films, because of their pervasive presence, their racial/ethnic identity is seldom an issue. European Americans are more likely to be identified in terms of class, gender, age, occupation, family, education, and temperament. Examples abound but include films as different as *Sergeant York*, *Fail Safe*, *Thelma & Louise*, *The Insider*, *Seabiscuit*, and *Songcatcher*. The European American characters in these films, just as European Americans in life, are far more likely to be seen simply as Americans than European Americans, as men and women, waitresses or reporters, scientists or politicians rather than European American men, women, waitresses, or politicians. Being an unqualified American has worked to their advantage.

Yet race/ethnicity is as much a part of the basic identity of European Americans as it is of African, Arab, Middle Eastern, Asian, Latino/a, and Native Americans. If how individuals in these latter groups see themselves and are seen by others matters, how European Americans identify themselves and are identified by others also matters. That their race/ethnicity advantages them (Johnson; McIntosh) is just as significant as the fact that the racial/ethnic identity of African, Arab, Middle Eastern, Asian, Latino/a, and Native Americans disadvantages people in those groups.

From another perspective, of course, retaining one's racial/ethnic identity can enrich one's life while losing it can diminish it. That for many European Americans this is unimportant is reflected in the lack of attention given to the ethnic/racial identities of European American film characters. When it is a dimension of these characters, it often plays a central role in the plot. For example, in *Gangs of New York*, nativists and recent Irish immigrants are pitted against each other; in *A Bronx Tale*, the protagonists' Italian roots dictate much of the action; and in *My Big Fat Greek Wedding*, a family's ethnic heritage is paramount.

Though we are aware our choices of films in this European American category are arbitrary to a great extent, and the category itself is extremely slippery (Guglielmo and Salerno), especially when we include films featuring Jewish Americans, acknowledging the racial/ethnic backgrounds of European Americans is so important we are willing to open this Pandora's box. Leaving out such an enormously comprehensive and powerful racial/ethnic group and letting it remain invisible while so much in the lives of African, Arab, Middle Eastern, Asian, Latino/a, and Native Americans hangs on their racial/ethnic identities vis-à-vis European Americans would be unconscionable. Scholars from many disciplines, including film and multicultural studies, have begun to focus on whites and whiteness, on race/ethnicity as it helps define people who are in fact European American (Benshoff and Griffin; Bernardi; Friedman; Girgus; Rothenberg; Shohat and Stam). They provide multiple possibilities to follow up our brief remarks with further study. The effort can be extremely rewarding.

**Works Cited:** Benshoff, Harry M., and Sean Griffin. *America on Film: Representing Race, Class, Gender, and Sexuality at the Movies*. Malden, MA: Blackwell, 2004; Bernardi, Daniel, ed. *Classic Hollywood, Classic Whiteness*. Minneapolis: University of Minnesota Press, 2001; Friedman, Lester D. *Unspeakable Images: Ethnicity and the American Cinema*. Chicago: University of Illinois Press, 1991; Girgus, Sam B. *America on Film: Modernism, Documentary, and a Changing America*. New York: Cambridge, 2002; Guglielmo, Jennifer, and Salvatore Salerno. *Are Italians White? How Race Is Made in America*. New York: Routledge, 2003; Johnson, Allan G. *Privilege, Power and Difference*. Mountain View, CA: Mayfield, 2001; McIntosh, Peggy. *White Privilege: Unpacking the Invisible Knapsack*. Wellesley, MA: Wellesley College Center for Research on Women, 1998; Rothenberg, Paula S., ed. *White Privilege: Essential Readings on the Other Side of Racism*. New York: Worth, 2002; Shohat, Ella, and Robert Stam. *Unthinking Eurocentrism: Multiculturalism and the Media*. New York: Routledge, 1994.

## THE FILMS

### *Almost Famous* (2000)

Director: Cameron Crowe

Cast: Billy Crudup (Russell Hammond), Frances McDormand (Elaine Miller), Kate Hudson (Penny Lane), Jason Lee (Jeff Bebe), Patrick Fugit (William Miller), Philip Seymour Hoffman (Lester Bangs)

Length: 122 min.

Rating: R

Rock 'n' Roll Drama: Coming of age story of an aspiring journalist and rock 'n' roll fan

*Almost Famous* is a semiautobiographical account of director Cameron Crowe's adolescent experience as a rock journalist for *Rolling Stone* magazine in the 1970s. This charming and lighthearted account of the mysterious world of rock 'n' roll seen through the eyes of an innocent fifteen-year-old is firmly positioned in a particular period. The film follows William Miller in his first solo adventure as a journalist and represents the breaking away that all young people face as they journey into adulthood. Paralleling his odyssey is his mother's efforts to let go. Her struggle is made more difficult as a single parent and the family breadwinner, dual responsibilities that contrast with those of the previous generation when two-parent households were the norm.

Given the rock 'n' roll culture, the protests against restrictions of any kind, and intense dissatisfaction with government, the world William was entering differed even more sharply than his mother's did with her parents. This becomes apparent in the unwritten code of the "circus" that William experiences. In a world of promiscuity, alcohol, and drugs, the participants try to live up to their interpretation of what they think is the appropriate role for a rock musician, roadie, manager, groupie, and "band aid." This results in the bizarre range of behaviors elicited by the "circus" performers in this film.

Another major issue raised by *Almost Famous* can be put in the form of a familiar question: "What is love?" Does it differ from one relationship to another? What is its role in mother–daughter, mother–son, rock star–band aid, rock star–girlfriend, band aid–journalist, and brother–sister relationships? What is its role in friendships such as those between colleagues or between professionals, such as a rock star and a journalist?

A further set of questions is suggested by the title of *Almost Famous*. In a country where the rich and famous are considered royalty, what does it mean to be almost famous? What does it do to one's ego? To one's professional competence? How does it affect one's relationships? William Miller's journey suggests some possible answers.

The film captures the reckless abandon of a culture dominated by the frenzy of electric guitars and a generation trying to make sense of a country divided by the civil rights struggles and protests against our involvement in Vietnam. Does *Almost Famous*, under the guise of a coming-of-age film, reflect the death of rock 'n' roll and the birth of the Disco Age? Does it reflect, more sinisterly, a move away from liberalism and the Civil Rights Movement and a return to a greater emphasis on individualism and more conservative policies in the United States?

## *Avalon* (1990)

Director: Barry Levinson

Cast: Armin Mueller-Stahl (Sam), Aidan Quinn (Jules), Elizabeth Perkins (Ann), Elijah Wood, (Michael), Joan Plowright (Eva)

Length: 126 min.

Rating: PG

Family Drama: The story of two generations of Russian Jewish immigrants living in Baltimore

*Avalon* tells the story of Sam Krichinsky, a Jewish immigrant from Russia who arrives in the United States of America on the fourth of July, 1914, and is awed by the festivities and the fireworks. Over the next fifty years, he works hard and supports his family; he sees his son Jules grow up, marry, move to the suburbs, change his last name to Kaye, and open a discount store.

Sam also witnesses major changes in his extended family. Meetings where family matters were discussed and decisions made collectively are superseded by rifts and separations. Intragenerational and intergenerational tensions surface as strong family values are challenged by an increasing interest in business and the business opportunities offered after World War II. For Sam, attention once given family and relationships seems to be redirected to things, like televisions, appliances, and automobiles.

Levinson effectively captures the evolving mood and styles of an era through his attention to detail—to early television clips, TV dinners, and period dress, for instance. More important to his recreation of an era are family conversations, Sam's observations, and the stories he shares with his grandson Michael. Sam, with his close ties to an extended family, sees no need to change his name or to assimilate, but Jules, faced with more options and eager to succeed in business, chooses to do both. His move to the suburbs facilitates his shift from his father's Old World values to the more materialistic values associated with financial success, though he certainly maintains strong relationships with both his father and with Michael.

*Avalon* raises questions about intergenerational relationships, evolving values, changing technologies, and the impact of national and world events on peoples' lives. Given its PG rating, educators should find it useful when discussing any of these issues.

## *A Beautiful Mind* (2001)

Director: Ron Howard

Cast: Russell Crowe (John Forbes Nash, Jr.), Ed Harris (William Parcher), Jennifer Connelly (Alicia Larde Nash), Paul Bettany (Charles Herman), Christopher Plummer (Dr. Rosen), Judd Hirsch (Professor Helinger)

Running Time: 129 min.

Rating: PG-13

Family Drama: A study of paranoid schizophrenia as experienced by John Forbes Nash

*A Beautiful Mind* ostensibly chronicles the life of Nobel Prize winner John Forbes Nash, Jr., a brilliant mathematician who suffered from paranoid schizophrenia throughout his adult life. Like most biographical films, this one strays from the facts, yet it does give viewers a rare glimpse into what it might be like to have one's world split between reality and delusion. Early in the film, director Ron Howard deceives us into believing that Charles, John's roommate, is a real person, not the beginning of a trio of delusional characters that will plague him throughout his life. This confusion furthers audience dissonance as it struggles to make sense of the fractured reality Nash faces every day of his life.

Nash triumphs through his mathematical genius and his love for Alicia, but his story turns tragic as he slips into a delusional world of espionage and paranoia. Perhaps the most interesting and significant delusional character Nash relates to is Marcee, Charles's niece, a young girl about nine years old. After Nash's hospitalization and the trauma of insulin shock therapy, Nash's condition improves and he is able to return home, but his ongoing delusional episodes exert tremendous pressure on him, Alicia, and their marriage. Just at the point when Alicia decides she can no longer cope with the situation, Nash makes a conscious breakthrough: He realizes that Marcee never ages. This becomes the handle he needs to retain his grip on reality.

*A Beautiful Mind* works as a compassionate and engaging story about the human condition and about one of the great thinkers of the twentieth century. It also works as an exploration of mental illness and a world created by such a condition. Because of film's ability to visualize alternate worlds and to have them intersect convincingly while inviting viewers to identify with the characters in these worlds, it can further understanding of a condition such as Nash's. Nash, after all, has many sane moments and experiences the excitement of falling in love and the satisfaction of doing meaningful work. Though he loses his hold on reality and tries the patience of his wife and colleagues, he does not lose their support.

Film characters with mental and emotional illness have appeared in a number of mainstream movies and in independent films, but they are still relatively rare. Those that do exist usually revolve around European American characters rather than people of color, an interesting but perhaps not surprising situation because traditionally in U.S. society, European Americans are more likely to have the time, energy, interest, and money to consider their psychological well being and more support to do something about it. There is much to learn about individuals with a mental illness, whether one is a member of traditional mainstream society or of a historically underrepresented segment of society. Studying *A Beautiful Mind* and John Nash's (Nasar; Nash) life can prompt more people to deepen their understanding of this alternate world.

**Works Cited:** Nasar, Sylvia. *A Beautiful Mind: The Life of a Mathematical Genuis and Nobel Laureate*. New York: Simon and Schuster, 2001; Nash, John F., Sylvia Nasar, and Harold W. Kuhn. *The Essential John Nash*. Princeton, NJ: Princeton University Press, 2001.

## *The Believer* (2001)

Director: Henry Bean

Cast: Ryan Gosling (Danny Balint), Summer Phoenix (Carla Moebius), Theresa Russell (Lina Moebius), Billy Zane (Curtis Zampf)

Length: 99 min.

Rating: R

Adolescent Drama: Jewish and fascist beliefs and identities clash within one individual

This film is based on the true story of Danny Balint, a Jewish adolescent who appears to be obsessed with hatred of his own people and his religion, but who is deeply ambivalent, equally fascinated and repulsed by his faith and its many traditions. Even as a child he questions the teachings of his rabbis, always offering alternative interpretations to the teachings of the Torah. This eventually leads to his expulsion from school.

As he grows older, he identifies with Nazi and other fascist groups. His actions become more and more brazen, and he begins to speak out in ever larger public circles. He claims that while Jews are obsessed with abstractions, he has a sophisticated rationale for all his beliefs. When a writer for *Rolling Stone* magazine interviews him about his anti-Semitic views and then confronts him with his knowledge that he is a Jew, Danny vehemently denies his heritage. He becomes so agitated that he pulls out his revolver, sticks it in the reporter's mouth, and warns him that he will kill himself if the information is printed. Another powerful scene takes place following a fight at a Jewish delicatessen. He and his racist friends are ordered by the court to attend sensitivity training with a group of Holocaust survivors; the outcome is disastrous and humiliating. Danny challenges the survivors by asking them why they didn't fight back. When one asks him what he would have done, he responds without hesitation, "Kill your enemy."

Though often decisive and firm, Danny's ambivalence comes through, especially when he and his white supremacist associates desecrate a Jewish temple. When some of the members are about to damage the Torah, he intervenes, stops them, and takes the Torah back to where he is living. His girlfriend, the daughter of fascists, discovers the Torah and when she finds out he can read it, asks him to teach her; he does. When a Nazi associate accuses him of showing sympathy for Jews because he saved the Torah and fails to carry out a planned assassination, Danny shoots him. Though he does protect the Torah, Danny subsequently plants a bomb in a synagogue, intending to kill the Jewish congregation. Then, unable to go through with his plan, he in essence kills himself while intervening to save the worshipers. He becomes the victim of his desperate desire to kill a Jew.

*The Believer* is a powerful story about historical and contemporary forces of anti-Semitism that impact the life of an intelligent, very articulate Jewish boy who questions too deeply his faith, religious beliefs, and traditions. Director Henry Bean effectively intersperses flashbacks from Danny Balint's childhood, when he began to question his faith, throughout the film. He also shows flashes of a story Danny heard from the Holocaust survivors that contribute to the film's power.

This very disturbing film contains scenes of violence and anti-Semitic behavior. It could be effective for mature audiences, however, especially if a rabbi or another adult well versed in the underlying tenets of Judaism helped facilitate the discussion. Organizations like the Anti-Defamation League can provide materials and speakers to support a quality program on this controversial film. Another comprehensive site where viewers can find helpful information is the Simon Wiesenthal Museum of Tolerance Web site.

**Works Cited:** Anti-Defamation League. http://www.ade.org; Simon Wiesenthal Museum of Tolerance. Simon Wiesenthal Center. http://www.wiesenthal.com.

## *A Bronx Tale* (1993)

Director: Robert DeNiro

Cast: Robert DeNiro (Lorenzo Anello), Chazz Palminteri (Sonny), Lillo Brancato (Calogero, "C"), Taral Hicks (Jane Williams), Kathrine Narducci (Rosina Anello), Joe Pesci (Carmine)

Length: 121 min.

Rating: R

Urban Crime Drama: A coming-of-age story spans opposing lifestyles and diverse cultures

In *A Bronx Tale*, Calogero, the son of bus driver Lorenzo Anello, relates the story of his own coming-of-age in an Italian American neighborhood in New York City. Though blessed with strict but loving parents, as a youngster Calogero was more attracted to the lifestyle of Sonny and other gangsters in his neighborhood than to the lifestyle of his steady, hard-working father. Because he doesn't identify Sonny in a police lineup after seeing him kill someone, Sonny befriends Calogero, nicknames him "C," and gives him a chance not only to work in the local bar for tips from the mobsters, but also to sharpen his knowledge of the street. Sonny's interest angers Calogero's father so much that he confronts Sonny; they exchange threats and never speak to each other again.

Eight years later C is still hanging around Sonny but now has his own crew. When he meets Jane, an attractive African American girl, they are immediately drawn to each other, but when C's crew assaults a group of African Americans that includes Jane's brother, the bad blood spills over into C and Jane's relationship. Tragedy—including the accidental deaths of C's crew and Sonny's murder—follow, but so does Calogero's reconciliation with both Jane and his father. At Sonny's wake he recounts some of the lessons he has learned about love, friendship, and loyalty and is reminded by his father that "the saddest thing in life is wasted talent."

*A Bronx Tale* captures the racial/ethnic tensions that still exist in many ethnic neighborhoods, especially when new groups move into an established area and housing patterns change, but it also shows, through Jane and Calogero's connection, the potential for interracial relationships based on respect and love. Love scenes such as theirs are rare even in current films. The film also exposes the tensions within a racial/ethnic group as it contrasts Lorenzo's principled but tedious life with Sonny's flashy criminal activity. All in all, *A Bronx Tale* gives viewers a starting point from which to investigate a number of significant issues.

## *Clueless* (1995)

Director: Amy Heckerling

Cast: Alicia Silverstone (Cher Horowitz), Stacey Dash (Dionne Davenport), Brittany Murphy (Tai Fraiser), Paul Rudd (Josh Lucas), Donald Faison (Murray Duvall), Breckin Meyer (Travis Birkenstock), Dan Hedaya (Mel Horowitz)

Length: 97 min.

Rating: PG-13

Teenage Comedy: An update of Jane Austen's *Emma* set in a multicultural high school

High school students and best friends Cher and Dionne enjoy the admiration and envy of their classmates as they negotiate and shop their way through adolescence. Daughters of wealthy parents, they seem to have limitless financial resources as well as some understanding of their privilege and popularity. We do not meet Dionne's parents, but Cher's father Mel, an attorney, takes greater satisfaction in Cher's ability to leverage her way to good grades than he would if she earned them legitimately.

As part of one attempt to improve their grades, Cher and Dionne successfully spark a romance between two of their teachers, thus prompting the new couple to a more generous view of life in general and more lenient grading policies in particular. Cher is so satisfied with their efforts, she makes intervening to make others happy her mission. Dionne is on hand to help. Together they make over Tai, a new student, and try to steer her into a relationship with Elton, one of their most sought-after classmates. The attempt proves unsuccessful.

When coupled with a loss of popularity at school, a misjudgment about another new student, and her failure to pass her driving test, Cher begins reassessing her activities and strategies and decides everything she has been doing is wrong. She bounces back quickly, however, and directs her efforts to a makeover of herself. She takes on the organization of a relief effort, supports Travis, whom she had earlier dismissed as a loser, and generally becomes less judgmental and a bit less self-centered.

*Clueless*'s energetic characters, bright colors, quick pace, and light touch work well to set the film's breezy comic, slightly ironic tone. Though the story parallels Jane

Austen's *Emma*, its 1990s California setting calls for a number of shifts in characterizations and action. Among the most significant of these is the cultural diversity of Cher, Dionne, and their friends. Cher is a very blonde European American while Dionne is African American. Because of their shared socioeconomic status, their values and outlook are very similar; race/ethnicity is not an issue for them or for their classmates, at least not on the level of same-sex friendships.

Students' socioeconomic status and behavioral preferences, not race/ethnicity, determine which group or clique they fall into. Elton effectively voices this focus when, after finding out Cher envisioned him and the middle-class Tai as a couple, he exclaims, "Don't you even know who my father is? . . . Me [*sic*] and Tai, we don't make any sense." Ethnic/racial diversity appear to be taken for granted among the students, the school's staff, and if Mr. Horowitz's law practice is exemplary, in society overall. Because Cher's major interest is drawing individuals into romantic relationships, however, viewers might question the complete absence of interracial couples within Cher and Dionne's circle of friends. Viewers might also note Cher's limited understanding of ethnicity when she identifies Lucy, who works for her and her father as a maid, as Mexican rather than Salvadoran. And they can legitimately point out that Cher controls the point of view and Dionne's importance recedes when Cher starts her personal makeover. Still, *Clueless* proves refreshingly open.

*Clueless* has been a favorite among high school students though it appeals to a more general audience as well. Engaging and upbeat, it easily captures students' attention. They may not immediately zero in on the film's cultural diversity, but directing their attention to it through questions and writing prompts can spark a fruitful exploration of its significance and how that significance continues to evolve.

## *Fail Safe* (1964)

Director: Sidney Lumet

Cast: Dan O'Herlihy (General Black), Walter Matthau (Groteschele), Frank Overton (Edward Binns), Larry Hagman (Buck, Fritz Weaver), Henry Fonda (president of the United States)

Length: 113 min.

Rating: Not Rated

Cold War Drama: Tense international distrust and miscommunication result in disaster

*Fail Safe* is a classic example of the worst fears of the Cold War coming true. Filmed in 1964, director Sidney Lumet creates the austere world of a military base, the conservative world of military think tanks, and the chain of command that keeps both running. Early in the film a bureaucrat questions the dependability of the fail-safe box and the other machines the military utilizes. This foreshadows the tragedy about to unfold.

Lumet shows meetings of the Joint Chiefs as they discuss such topics as limited war and accidental war. General Black encourages slowing down and suggests developing strategies to eliminate war while Professor Groteschele insists they must speed up war. During their briefing, a UFO is sighted and causes an alert system to shift from yellow to green while the country's patrol aircraft respond as if the threat is real. After the UFO is correctly identified, the planes are contacted to return to normal patrol status, but something goes wrong and some of the planes are sent a false signal to attack the Soviet Union. The pilots and crew follow their protocols and begin heading to their targets in Soviet territory.

As their briefing continues, the Joint Chiefs become aware of the impending situation. Buck, a Russian linguist, is summoned by the president as attempts are made to recall the attacking bomber group. When those attempts fail, the men inform the president that the best course of action is to shoot the bombers down, but the fighter jets are unable to do so and the president is forced to contact the Soviet premier. As the two speak and the president tries to convince the Soviet premier that this is a mistake, the Soviet leaders admit they jammed the planes' radio signals, which may have triggered the false signal to attack. The comments heard in both war rooms as these world leaders talk parallel each other and express similar fear, suspicion, and loathing for the enemy.

The president orders General Black to drop a thermonuclear weapon on New York City—and the U.S. armed forces—to aide the Soviets in shooting down the U.S. aircraft. When the Soviets ask for specific help on how to blow up the American air-to-air missiles, two officers, unable to transcend their training and staunch ideological beliefs, are incapable of sharing this critical information. The film ends with the nightmare imagined earlier and with the knowledge that the politics of two world super powers have cost the world millions of innocent lives.

*Fail Safe* can easily be used in classrooms with adolescents and adults. For many viewers it will be just as powerful as it was forty years ago. An effective character study, it allows careful examination of each role and how each character's script is shaped by the times and by his or her particular place in society. The discussion between the technocrats and the intellectuals is amazing; we hear the classic arguments of the hawks and doves. We also hear about the hopes and limits of technology.

Viewers may want to compare *Fail Safe* to the British production *Dr. Strangelove: Or How I Learned to Stop Worrying and Love the Bomb* (1964), directed by Stanley Kubrick. Kubrick's cutting black comedy captures the same era, the same cold war fears, and the same disastrous responses. Though both films present characters who differ in ethnicity and nationality, neither goes beyond traditional roles when representing historically underrepresented groups or women. Their analyses stay focused primarily on the roles and egos of political and military leaders whose masculinity is very evident. Another very different but relevant resource is Michael Walzer's *Just and Unjust Wars*.

**Works Cited:** *Dr. Strangelove: Or How I Learned to Stop Worrying and Love the Bomb.* Directed by Stanley Kubrick. Performances by Peter Sellers, Sterling Hayden, George C. Scott, and Slim Pickens. Columbia, 1964; Walzer, Michael. *Just and Unjust Wars: A Moral Argument with Historical Illustrations.* 2nd ed. New York: Basic Books, 1992.

## *Gangs of New York* (2002)

Director: Martin Scorsese

Cast: Daniel Day Lewis (Bill "The Butcher" Cutting), Leonardo DiCaprio (Amsterdam Vallon), Cameron Diaz (Jenny Everdeane), Jim Broadbent (Boss Tweed), John C. Reilly (Happy Jack), Henry Thomas (Johnny Sirocco)

Length: 167 min.

Rating: R

Historical Drama: Intense ethnic and gang rivalry result in escalating violence

This film opens in the middle of the nineteenth century with a battle between rival New York gangs. It is a battle between the nativists, those who were born in this country, and newly arrived Irish Catholic immigrants seeking to find their place in the United States. The leader of the immigrants, or "Dead Rabbits," is Priest; "Bill the Butcher" leads the nativists. When Butcher kills Priest, the Dead Rabbits are banished and Priest's son, Amsterdam, is orphaned. Sixteen years later he is released from reform school.

During the second year of the Civil War, divisions among the American people are striking. The abolitionists and the separatists are literally at each other's throats. When a Civil War draft is imposed, clashes erupt between the upper classes who can buy their way out of military service and the lower classes who cannot. The tremendous influx of Irish immigrants only adds to this highly combustible climate. The point of contention Scorsese focuses on in *Gangs of New York* is territory, specifically the area known as Five Points, the center of both commerce and politics in one part of New York City.

The inhabitants of Five Points engage in an endless variety of enterprises, both legal and illegal. Politicians, like Boss Tweed of Tammany Hall, are corrupt, but they also serve the interests of the people by providing them with services they cannot provide for themselves. The complicity between the street gangs and the politicians works for both groups to ensure their control of the legal and illegal commerce in the area.

Amsterdam is bent on revenging his father's death; he is able to develop a relationship with Bill the Butcher because Bill does not know he is Priest's son and because he saves Bill's life. After telling Amsterdam how he killed Priest, Bill says, "He is the only man I killed worth remembering." When Bill learns Amsterdam is Priest's son, however, he punishes him in public, scarring his face for life but not killing him. This signals the return of the Dead Rabbits and the eventual showdown between the Butcher and Amsterdam, a showdown that goes far beyond personal hatred and revenge. The backdrop for their final confrontation involves the election and subsequent murder of an Irish sheriff as well as anger about the draft that is so intense it explodes in four days of mob action against African Americans, politicians, and other authorities, and results in the deaths of hundreds of New Yorkers.

Though extremely violent, *Gangs of New* York is filled with issues related to race/ethnicity. Because it is loosely based on historical events, interesting discussions can be developed on the accuracy of the events and perspectives presented in the film. For example, the role and influence of the Chinese could be researched. They are shown in a variety of scenes throughout the film as shopkeepers, opium peddlers, entertainers, and courtesans and are said to hate the new immigrants as much, if not more, than the nativists. The role of race/ethnicity in the collusion between the politicians of Tammany Hall and the gangs and in the riots that briefly tear New York apart might also be studied. On another level, students could follow up on Bill's observation, while watching an African American dance, that the performance reflects a mixture of cultural styles—in this case African and Irish dance.

Besides written resources like Ronald Takaki's *A Different Mirror* and Roger Daniels's *Guarding the Golden Door*, Ken Burns's *The Civil War* and Thomas Lennon and Mark Zwontizer's *The Irish in America: The Long Journey Home* are excellent resources with which to compare this film.

**Works Cited:** *The Civil War*. Directed by Ken Burns. PBS Video, 1990; Daniels, Roger. *Guarding the Golden Door: American Immigrants and Immigration Policy Since 1882*. New

York: Hill and Wang, 2004. *The Irish in America: The Long Journey Home*. Directed by Thomas Lennon and Mark Zwontizer. A&E Entertainment, 1997; Takaki, Ronald. *A Different Mirror: A History of Multicultural America*, Boston: Little, Brown, 1993.

## *Gentleman's Agreement* (1947)

Director: Elia Kazan

Cast: Gregory Peck (Philip Schuyler Green/Greenberg), Dorothy McGuire (Kathy Lacey), John Garfield (Dave Goldman), Celeste Holm (Ann Dettrey), Ann Revere (Mrs. Green), Dean Stockwell (Tommy Green)

Length: 119 min.

Rating: Not Rated

Drama: An exploration of anti-Semitism within the United States

Philip Green is asked to write a series on anti-Semitism, and even though he does not want the assignment, he reluctantly accepts it. To fulfill the assignment, he assumes the identity of a Jew and immediately encounters all kinds of prejudice. Philip's own engagement party falls through when he refuses to drop his Jewish character for the sake of his fiancée's friends and family. When Philip tries to check into a hotel and asks if they allow Jews to stay there, the manager politely tap dances around the issue while trying to find out if Philip is Jewish. He quietly rings for the bellman to take his bag outside when Philip insists on an answer. Later the same day, his son comes home distraught, because the kids at school called him a "dirty Jew" and a "kike" and refused to play with him. When he asks his father why people hate Jews, Philip has a difficult time finding an answer and ends up saying there are just a lot of mixed-up people in the world.

Philip and Kathy, his fiancée, can't resolve their differences, because even though she understands what Philip is trying to do, she can't make a connection to her own life. In a conversation with Philip's Jewish friend Dave, Kathy comes to realize that she is part of the problem. As she tells Dave about a dinner where one guest expressed anti-Semitic feelings and nobody condemned what was said, she realizes that by not speaking, not acting, she had condoned the speaker. Scenes like this can be effective in helping people understand that it is not only outright bigots, but also law-abiding citizens who fail to act, who keep prejudice and injustice alive.

*Gentleman's Agreement* may not startle today's audiences as it did viewers over sixty years ago, but it remains a powerful vehicle for exploring the prejudice that still exists within mainstream U.S. society. The film goes beyond an examination of prejudice from outsiders against Jews to consider prejudice within the Jewish community. A more in-depth study of this phenomenon occurs in Henry Bean's 2002 film *The Believer*, which is reviewed in this book.

Another issue *Gentleman's Agreement* raises is hate speech. Philip's son talks about being called derogatory names at school. Dave experiences a similar affront when a drunk discovers that Dave's last name is Jewish while he and Philip are in a restaurant. The drunk calls Dave a "Yid" and Dave almost assaults the man. The scene could be an effective catalyst for a discussion on hate speech and on why certain derogatory words should not be tolerated in civic spaces. The Southern Poverty Law Center's website can provide excellent resources and strategies for a thorough study of the issue.

Finally, the two main characters, Philip and Kathy, are excellent role models. Philip is the man of conviction who clearly sees that prejudice in any form is wrong and must be challenged in order to be defeated. Kathy's role is quite different. She first must discover her own hidden prejudice before she is able to articulate it and do something about it. Both roles are important reflections of where people of all ages and cultural backgrounds find themselves even today.

**Works Cited:** *The Believer*. Directed by Henry Bean. Performances by Ryan Gosling, Summer Phoenix, Theresa Russell, and Billy Zane. Fireworks Pictures, 2002; "Teaching Tolerance." Southern Poverty Law Center. http://www.splcenter.org.

## *Gone with the Wind* (1939)

Director: Victor Fleming

Cast: Clark Gable (Rhett Butler), Vivien Leigh (Scarlett O'Hara), Leslie Howard (Ashley Wilkes), Olivia de Havilland (Melanie Wilkes), Hattie McDaniel (Mammy), Butterfly McQueen (Prissy)

Length: 222 min.

Rating: Not Rated

Epic Melodrama: Despiction of the Civil War from the perspective of white Southern aristocrats

*Gone with the Wind* takes viewers from the pre-Civil War South, through the war, and well into the era of Reconstruction. It follows the fortunes of Scarlett O'Hara as she pursues her neighbor, Ashley Wilkes. Though her pursuit seems doomed from the start, it continues through Ashley's marriage to Melanie and Scarlett's own three marriages, including her last to Rhett Butler. The devastation—hunger, illness, madness, and death—experienced by those living through a war and its aftermath intensifies Scarlett's passion and single-mindedness and seem, sadly, to provide an appropriate setting for the melodrama and spectacle the film offers.

Lawrence Reddick, writing in 1944, asserted that "*Gone With the Wind* said in the most effective manner possible that the antebellum South, that wondrous land of beauty and happy slaves, had been destroyed by Union soldiers and carpetbaggers" (14). Herman Vera and Andrew Gordon put it this way in 2001: "Behind the story is a yearning for an impossible reunification of the fantasy Old South and the New, for a blend of the supposed grace and charm of the vanished plantation society with the spirit and enterprise of the rising industrial South" (272). In both of these analyses, the writers focus on the underlying meaning of the film and on the characters as symbols.

Herman and Gordon acknowledge that the characters and the melodrama draw viewers into the story but their primary interest is what the film says about race/ethnicity (272–273). Herman and Gordon see the blacks as "background figures" who "appear primarily as slaves: loyal servants like Mammy . . . , stupid and cowardly servants like Prissy . . . , or clownish servants." If autonomous they "are represented . . . as dangerous and lawless" (273). In contrast, Donald Bogle argues that Hattie McDaniel and Butterfly McQueen transcend their roles, with McDaniel particularly effective and assertive, unafraid to speak up to Scarlett or to any of the O'Haras and "free of the greatest burden that slavery—on screen and off—inflicted on blacks: a sense of innate inferiority" (125).

The making of *Gone with the Wind* was accompanied by a great deal of publicity and when completed became a huge box-office success despite some strong criticism. While it was in production, criticism by the NAACP and other groups was forceful enough to have particularly offensive scenes omitted or softened. Attempted boycotts after the film's release, however, were unsuccessful and probably contributed to its box-office success (Reddick 15–17). For many viewers, objections to the film's depiction of African Americans seem to have been swept aside as they watched Scarlett scheme, suffer, succeed, and fail. Today, when viewing the film, it should be more difficult to lose oneself in Scarlett's melodramatic journey or to ignore her or any of the characters' symbolic meaning. Given those meanings, the film maintains some value as one take on a traumatic period in the history of the United States. Viewers might want to pair it with Ken Burns's documentary *The Civil War.* Given the scope of each, even though—or because—they differ significantly, their contrasting perspectives and approaches can be instructive.

**Works Cited:** Bogle, Donald. *Toms, Coons, Mulattoes, Mammies, and Bucks.* New York: Bantam, 1973; *The Civil War.* Directed by Ken Burns. PBS Video, 1990. Reddick, Lawrence. "Of Motion Pictures." In *Black Films and Filmmakers*, edited by Lindsay Patterson. 3–24. New York: Dodd, Mead, 1975; Vera, Herman, and Andrew Gordon. "Sincere Fictions of the White Self in American Cinema: The Divided White Self in Civil War Films." In *Classic Hollywood,Classic Whiteness*, edited by Daniel Bernardi. 263–280. Minneapolis: University of Minnesota Press, 2001.

## *Green Card* (1990)

Director: Peter Weir

Cast: Gérard Depardieu (George Faure), Andie MacDowell (Bronte Mitchell Faure), Bebe Neuwirth (Lauren Adler), Ethan Phillips (Gorsky, INS Agent), Mary Louise Wilson (Mrs. Sheehan, INS agent)

Length: 107 min.

Rating: PG-13

Romantic Comedy: A marriage of convenience results in mutual love

*Green Card* is a film about two strangers, one a United States citizen who wants an apartment with a greenhouse she cannot get unless she is married, and the other an immigrant seeking to become a U.S. citizen. They arrange a marriage to accommodate both of their desires. Once the deed is done they plan never to see each other again. Things go well until immigration officials begin an investigation to validate the authenticity of their marriage. During the course of his interview with the officials, it becomes quite clear that George does not reside in the apartment he and Bronte allegedly share. The immigration officials request a second interview, forcing this odd pair to live together as though they are really a couple—at least until the next interview.

At a dinner party, George displays his creativity and genius, much to the surprise of Bronte, who to this point has found most of what he does irritating. Slowly he begins to win her heart and they commit to learning and sharing their lives in order to pass the immigration interview. Because Bronte has insisted they tell no one about this arranged marriage, however, their living arrangement leads to one stressful, often comic complication after another. Each, surprisingly, brings them closer together—but not close enough to convince the immigration officials of the validity of their relationship. When George is denied a green card, they realize they are in love with each other. And despite his pending deportation, audiences realize the two will find a way to be together.

A sweet romantic comedy full of humor and anticipation, *Green Card* tells one version of the many immigration stories experienced by people who have come to the United States over several centuries. The film can be a useful tool for introducing students to immigration laws and the Immigration and Naturalization Service (INS), to immigration patterns, to the strategies immigrants use in gaining entry and then remaining in this country, and to their reasons for choosing the United States of America. Samuel J. Ungar's *Fresh Blood: The New Immigrants* is a useful resource for exploring current immigration issues.

As a comedy, *Green Card* approaches serious issues with a light touch; as a Hollywood romance, it ends happily. Steven Okazaki's independent film *Living on Tokyo Time* takes the same situation, an arranged marriage between a citizen of the U.S.A. and an immigrant, and looks at it far more soberly, more pessimistically. A comparison of the two films can help balance some of the negative and positive aspects of the immigrant experience.

**Works Cited:** *Living on Tokoyo Time*. Directed by Steven Okazaki. Performances by Minako Ohashi and Ken Nakagawa. Skouras Pictures, 1987; Ungar, Samuel J. *Fresh Blood: The New American Immigrants*. Urbana: University of Illinois Press, 1998.

## *The Insider* (1999)

Director: Michael Mann

Cast: Russell Crowe (Jeffrey Wigand), Al Pacino (Lowell Bergman), Christopher Plummer (Mike Wallace)

Length: 157 min.

Rating: R

Investigative Story/Drama: A story about a whistle-blower's efforts to expose the dangers of smoking

Based on actual historical events, *The Insider* is a powerful indictment of the tobacco industry's cover-up of their manipulation of cigarettes as a delivery system of nicotine and as a carcinogen. Jeffrey Wigand is the whistle-blower, a high-level chemical research executive at a large tobacco firm who discovers evidence of company practices that threaten the health of smokers. When he makes the CEO of the company aware of the problem, he is fired and required to sign an agreement stating he will not discuss any company policies with the public. The agreement secures the continuation of his family's health benefits and certain salary payouts. Knowing the health risks of cigarette smoking and understanding the implications of the company's deception, combined with wanting to fulfill his roles as husband and father, compromise Wigand's integrity. The discomfort that results makes him particularly vulnerable when Lowell Bergman, a producer with CBS's *60 Minutes* news program, approaches him about what he knows. The company threatens Wigand and attempts to force him to accept a more stringent contract to insure his silence. Wigand refuses and the company escalates its threats toward both Wigand and his family. Wigand retaliates by agreeing to tape an interview with Mike Wallace for *60 Minutes*, setting in motion the immense power of a large corporation to protect and defend itself by silencing the opposition. The result is a confrontation that creates a crisis of ethics for all the players, especially when the CBS corporation is threatened by a claim of "tortuous interference," which leads to a decision not to air the Wigand/Wallace interview. Michael Orey gives further information about this in *Assuming the Risk.*

*The Insider* captures the drama and internal conflict of Wigand, his family, the *60 Minutes* production crew, CBS legal, and CBS corporate. Doing the right thing by not bending to corporate power demands enormous strength, especially on Wigand's part as he sees his family destroyed. He and Bergman prove to be the true heroes of our society, individuals who are willing to sacrifice everything to affect justice.

Bergman's role, as the CBS producer who pushes and prods Wigand to reveal what he knows, however, raises questions about ends and means. Bergman tries his best to protect Wigand while getting the information he has out to the public. An experienced and committed journalist, he is persistent, clever, and sincere in his efforts to support Wigand, but he is not above using some subterfuge in the process of exposing the cigarette corporation. The situation brings up the question of whether the ends justify the means when the means involve a compromise of integrity.

*The Insider* raises issues that are meaningful to people whatever their race/ethnicity. Because it focuses on European Americans and brings up issues of integrity, the public good, justice, and whether a good end justifies questionable means, a comparison of *The Insider* with *Malcolm X* could be interesting. During one period of his life, Malcolm X adopted the motto "by any means necessary." What was behind the cry? What was at stake for African Americans? For the United States? For Malcolm X? What was at stake for Wigand and for Bergman in their efforts to expose the corporations? How are the situations similar? How do they differ? Do race/ethnicity enter into how viewers respond to the characters?

**Works Cited:** *Malcolm X.* Directed by Spike Lee. Performances by Denzel Washington, Angela Bassett, Al Freeman, and Albert Hall. Warner Bros., 1992. Orey, Michael. *Assuming the Risk: The Mavericks, the Lawyers, and the Whistle-Blowers Who Beat Big Tobacco.* New York: Little, Brown, 1999.

## *My Big Fat Greek Wedding* (2002)

Director: Joel Zwick

Cast: Nia Vardalos (Toula Portokalos), John Corbett (Ian Miller), Lainie Kazan (Maria Portokalos), Michael Constantine (Gus Portokalos), Gia Carides (Cousin Nikki), Louis Mandylor (Nick Portokalos)

Length: 95 min.

Rating: PG

Romantic Comedy: Greek American culture explored via a love story

*My Big Fat Greek Wedding* opens with Toula working as a hostess at Dancing Zorba, her father's restaurant. She is thirty years old, single, and rather plain in appearance. According to Gus, her father, she has been getting old since she was fifteen. In her family's estimation she is not likely to ever get married. Toula has two siblings, a sister who married early and already has three children, and a brother who lives at home like Toula. Their home is a virtual museum of contemporary and traditional Greek culture. Gus believes he can trace the origin of any word to the Greek language and is always ready to demonstrate this skill.

Toula is growing tired of her restaurant job and wants to go to college to learn computer skills so she can work in her aunt's travel agency, but her father rejects the idea. Since this is ostensibly a patriarchal family, the women—mother, aunt, and daughter—use deception to get Gus to support Toula's entry into college and her change in jobs. Once away from the Dancing Zorba, Toula gives herself a cosmetic and wardrobe makeover that transforms her from average in appearance to very attractive. Her new appearance and confidence attract Ian, and it is not long before they begin dating. Because Ian is not Greek, Toula attempts to keep their friendship secret. She succeeds only briefly. Discovery creates a major crisis within the family, especially for Gus who is adamant about Toula marrying "a nice Greek boy." Toula and Ian's love eventually triumphs over the objections of both their families; they announce their engagement and, with much fuss and many culturally based social blunders on the part of both families, they marry.

Scenes of these two very different families interacting show viewers some of the complexities that exist within the multicultural milieu we call the United States of America, but the film's humor and panache keep the tone light. The family dinner, marriage ceremony, and reception are full of surprises as each family tries to cope with the different customs each culture brings to the occasion. Because *My Big Fat Greek Wedding* is slanted toward Greek culture, we find out more about Toula's family and traditions than we do about Ian's. The film goes beyond food, holidays, and music to provide insights into gender roles, the meaning of marriage, and childrearing practices.

Dan Georgakas, a film scholar and critic, who is Greek American, has indicated that despite the favorable responses by the general public as well as by many Greek American organizations and newspapers to *My Big Fat Greek Wedding*, many prominent historians of Greek Americans were critical, suggesting that the view of Greek American culture the film offers is "at best fifty years out of date" (37). Georgakas himself finds many aspects of the film out-of-date and offensive. The divergent views point to an issue that frequently surfaces when movies focus on seldom-portrayed cultural groups: how to do justice to the groups' myriad cultural variations, to the complex, ever-evolving individuals within the groups, to the historical as well as contemporary contexts that help define a culture.

Rather than dismiss movies like *My Big Fat Greek Wedding* (or *Waiting to Exhale*, which met similar applause and criticism), viewers might want to savor the filmmakers' accomplishments while also using the films to launch themselves into further cultural explorations, making an enjoyable viewing experience an educational experience as well. Educators can lead the way. *My Big Fat Greek Wedding* is a fun-filled film from beginning to end. Though a small independent film, it stormed into the hearts of viewers across a wide spectrum of cultural backgrounds and became "the most economically successful ethnic film in American cinematic history" (Georgakas 36).

Several factors can account for this film's popularity. For example, its classic fairytale structure gives audiences one more variation of the familiar ugly-duckling-into-beautiful-swan (or Cinderella) scenario but updates it by allowing Toula a more active role in her transformation. Another factor working in the film's favor is its unabashed portrayal of a Greek American family that loves its traditions and heritage and makes these central to its identity and lifestyle. In addition, the unpredictability and awkwardness of the intercultural encounters, though identified with specific cultures in the film, are conveyed with enough humor and basic humanity that audiences can easily recognize and relate to them.

**Work Cited:** Georgakas, Dan. "My Big Fat Greek Gripes." *Cineaste*. 28, no. 4 (2003): 36–37.

## *O Brother, Where Art Thou?* (2000)

Director: Joel Coen

Cast: George Clooney (Ulysses Everett McGill), John Turturro (Pete), Tim Blake Nelson (Delmar), Holly Hunter (Penny)

Length: 103 min.

Rating: PG-13

Comedy Drama: Homer's *Odyssey* set to music in the South in the 1930s

Pete and Delmar are conned into escaping the Depression-era Mississippi chain gang they are part of by Everett's promise he'll share a $1.2-million treasure with them. Almost immediately after they escape, they are told by a blind railroad worker, who sees far more than they do, that they have a long, difficult journey ahead of them, but ultimately they will attain their fortune. He is right: During the four days they have to retrieve the money, they are helped and betrayed several times and must escape sheriffs' posses, an attempted lynching, an assault by a fast-talking swindler, and a flood. They wheedle their way in and out of a recording session, accompany notorious gangster Babyface Nelson as he robs a bank, and successfully disrupt a Ku Klux Klan rally to save a friend. When Everett reveals his real destination and purpose to be reunited with his wife and daughters, they face more challenges but also discover they have become stars as the blues group the Soggy Bottom Boys.

Joel and Ethan Coen blend movie clichés, self-reflexive film homages, and stereotypes of Southern culture into an episodic road movie without losing their light comic touch. Loosely following the narrative structure of Homer's *Odyssey*, the Coens appear unconcerned about the looseness of their plot, the scope of their caricatures, or the overall improbability of most of the events they depict. The filmmakers and the film characters seem to be having fun and to be "looking on the sunny side of life," no matter what their circumstances.

The settings and costumes recall previous movie portraits of the South, but the exaggerations, casual sequencing of events, and surreal images, such as a white-robed religious congregation moving slowly through a woods and sirens mesmerizing the three heroes with their sensual come-ons, make clear the Coens are playing with these portraits. They eschew realism and embrace a comic fantasy that actually provides an effective backdrop for a superb tribute to specific musical traditions. Their choice of narrative context reflects their tendency to play with the conventions of popular culture, but their choice of music and musicians like Emmylou Harris, Alison Krause, Ralph Stanley, and Gillian Welch suggests they have a serious interest in and respect for blues, bluegrass, and country music.

One of the songs frequently singled out as particularly striking is "Oh, Death," ostensibly sung by the *Grand Dragon* of the Klan during the rally that is meant to culminate in a lynching. The song is hauntingly beautiful and fits uneasily within a sequence that is simultaneously chilling—given the song's lyrics and the Klan's intent—and silly because of how the Klan's drill-team type ritual is shown and how Everett, Delmar, and Pete thwart their planned lynching. Does the juxtaposition of aesthetically pleasing music, historical racist activity, and comic form work in the sequence? The question raises the issue of the relationship between form and content in art, an issue that resurfaces again and again in popular as well as fine art. *O Brother, Where Art Thou?* does not settle the issue but is worth exploring because of its self-reflexive portrayal of stereotypes, its use of humor, and its recognition of the rich cultural legacy of regional music.

## *Seabiscuit* (2003)

Director: Gary Ross

Cast: Jeff Bridges (Charles Howard), Tobey Maguire (Red Pollard), Chris Cooper (Tom Smith), William H. Macy (Tick Tock McGlaughlin), Elizabeth Banks (Marcela Howard)

Length: 141 min.

Rating: PG-13

Sport Drama: Depression-era saga of popular racehorse

*Seabiscuit* begins by introducing its central characters separately, but in quick succession. Budding entrepreneur Charles Howard opens a bicycle shop but meets with no success until he switches his focus from bicycles to automobiles. Once he does, he becomes wealthy. His world crashes temporarily when his son dies and his wife leaves him, but his unfailing good will and irrepressible optimism help him move forward despite his grief.

Red Pollard begins life in a close-knit and loving family where he learns to ride horses and study literary classics. Then the Depression hits, his father loses virtually everything, and the Pollards become vagabonds. When Red wins two dollars in a horse race and his parents find he can make a living that way, they make a deal with a horse owner to employ and provide for their son. Keeping in touch is impossible and Red develops a me-against-the-world attitude until he runs into Charles, Tom Smith, and a cantankerous racehorse named Seabiscuit. Tom loves horses and has an uncanny ability to judge both their physical abilities and their spirit. He is hired to purchase a racehorse for the Howards and takes a risk in recommending the relatively small, undisciplined, and surly Seabiscuit.

Small, undisciplined, and surly—the words describe Red as well as Seabiscuit. Horse and rider are clearly compared in a sequence in which shots of Seabiscuit fighting three handlers are intercut with Red fighting five adversaries. Once Tom begins handling Seabiscuit and Charles makes Red part of his family, they all succeed, setting records and making history as Seabiscuit and Red win race after race.

Black and white photographs and film clips are strategically inserted throughout *Seabiscuit* to keep audiences aware of the historical context of Seabiscuit's triumph and to help suggest the horse's metaphorical connection to the common people. Small, initially abused, and underestimated, Seabiscuit thrives under Charles, Tom, and Red's care; similarly in the film, working men and women rebound once Roosevelt's New Deal is in place.

Charles's exuberance, his ability to connect to Tom and Red, his inclusion of ordinary people in Seabiscuit's career, and his support of his workers during economically tough times almost overshadows his identity as an incredibly wealthy CEO. He personifies capitalism at its most appealing while Samuel Riddle, War Admiral's boastful owner, can be linked to an elitist and arrogant class as sure of its superiority as Riddle is of his horse's.

Seabiscuit's ultimate victory over War Admiral, the quintessential racehorse with the genetic linage of champions, also has metaphorical significance in a time when eugenics was a concern of nativists in the United States and, more devastatingly, of Germany's Nazi government. In exploring Seabiscuit's historical backdrop, viewers might want to go further than the Great Depression, New Deal initiatives, and Seabiscuit's extraordinary record to investigate the impact of Hitler's absorption of the principles of eugenics in the same era, and the possible effects of such principles in the United States of America, given its racial/ethnic diversity. To push this toward a further analogy, Seabiscuit's victories in conjunction with those of Jesse Owens, an African American who won four gold medals during the 1938 Olympics in Berlin, seems apropos.

*Seabiscuit* exemplifies traditional Hollywood filmmaking. Its losers-become-winners narrative, excellent cinematography, effective editing, and themes of friendship, family, and trust come together in an engaging feel-good movie. Viewers can enjoy it on this level, but they may want to note that in capturing the 1930s its focus is almost exclusively on white men. Marcela, Charles's second wife, initiates their relationship and then settles into the role of supportive companion with no interests other than her husband's. Similarly, Seabiscuit's African American groom contributes to the horse's success, but he does so silently. While both characters perform essential roles, they seem to exist only to serve the white male protagonists.

*Seabiscuit* can definitely entertain, but it can take viewers beyond entertainment, given its historical and metaphorical links. Because it is so well done, offers many possibilities for introducing important issues to students, and is rated PG-13, educators should find it a useful classroom tool. Comparing the story of *Seabiscuit* as it is told in the film to that told by Laura Hillenbrand in *Seabiscuit: An American Legend* would broaden the discussion possibilities.

**Work Cited:** Hillenbrand, Laura. *Seabiscuit: An American Legend.* New York: Random House, 2001.

## *Sergeant York* (1941)

Director: Howard Hawks

Cast: Gary Cooper (Alvin C. York), Walter Brennan (Pastor Rosier Pile), Joan Leslie (Gracie Williams), Margaret Wycherly (Mother York), Ward Bond (Ike Botkin), Stanley Ridges (Maj. Buxton)

Length: 134 min.

Rating: Not Rated

War Drama: Reconciling religious belief and patriotism

*Sergeant York* is loosely based on the heroic real life experiences of Alvin York, a person who, in the vernacular of his time, might have been classified as a *hillbilly*, a derogatory term referring to European Americans from low socioeconomic backgrounds who live in the hill country of the Appalachian Mountains.

The film opens as a young Alvin York struggles with a wild streak that is enhanced by heavy drinking. At heart a good man who loves his family, York falls in love with Gracie, a local girl being courted by several suitors, but when he can't buy the choice farmland he wants for their home, his wild streak surfaces and he sets out to destroy the man who has thwarted his plan. Literally struck by lightning on his way, he experiences a transformation, embraces Christianity, and puts his life in order. When World War II breaks out and York is drafted, his pastor helps him file for conscientious objector (CO) status on the basis of his religious beliefs. Turned down by the local draft board, he leaves home for basic training, and traveling for the first time outside Appalachia, he encounters men from all over the United States of America, whose language and cultures are as strange to him as his is to them.

Because York's CO petition is on record, his commanding officer, Major Buxton, is baffled by what he perceives to be a contradiction: York's beliefs and his expertise as a marksman and skill as a leader. When he confronts York, Buxton finds him to be a man of deep conviction struggling with whether God would condone his taking another man's life. Buxton grants him a weekend leave, and while back home, York reconciles his beliefs with his military duties. He returns to his unit and is shipped out to the front.

As a soldier, York's skills and bravery are proven again and again, most notably when he almost single-handedly saves his company while killing or capturing a large number of enemy troops. When he returns to the United States, he receives the Congressional Medal of Honor and is heralded as a national hero. He shuns the opportunities for endorsements, however, preferring instead the hills of his homeland, his jubilant family, and his friends.

Many aspects of *Sergeant York* are worth exploring. First, the representation of the Appalachian people as down-to-earth, family-oriented, and morally responsible is refreshing. They may not be wealthy, educated, or worldly, but they value love, respect, and honor as much as anyone else. Second, York represents an everyman, an ordinary guy with whom most viewers can identify. He observes and questions; he wants recognition, but when he acts in a way that brings it to him, he no longer needs it. Third, Sergeant York's story opens the door to an examination of moral development since York confronts several moral dilemmas and tries hard to maintain his integrity while reconciling opposing stands. That he finds a way to salve his conscience and function effectively as a soldier is not surprising, but viewers who cannot condone killing under any circumstance will find his reversal disturbing. The movie seems to equate a willingness to kill with patriotism, and within the context of a war, not defending one's country becomes difficult to justify.

Fourth, *Sergeant York* functions as a metaphor for an expanded manifest destiny that encompasses global spheres of influence and shows democracy and Christianity overcoming fascism and ungodliness. Finally, like so many Hollywood films, this one is devoid of people of color, and women are confined to stereotypical roles. It would be interesting to discuss how these issues intersect and how all of them are connected to the World War II context in which the film was made as well as to current social realities. Thomas Doherty's analysis in *Projections of War: Hollywood, American Culture, and World War II* offers some ideas about the former (100–103). Michael Walzer's *Just and Unjust Wars* should also be of interest.

**Works Cited:** Doherty, Thomas. *Projections of War: Hollywood, American Culture, and World War II*. New York: Columbia University Press, 2001; Walzer, Michael. *Just and Unjust Wars: A Moral Argument with Historical Illustrations*. 2nd ed. New York: Basic Books, 1992.

## *Songcatcher* (2000)

Director: Maggie Greenwald

Cast: Janet McTeer (Professor Lily Penleric), Aidan Quinn (Tom Bledsoe), Jane Adams (Eleanor "Elna" Penleric), Emmy Rossum (Deladis Slocumb), E. Katherine Kerr (Harriet Tolliver), Pat Carroll (Viney Butler)

Length: 109 min.

Rating: PG-13

Drama: A study of Appalachian music through a multifaceted story

Professor Lily Penleric, after having been turned down once again for a promotion to full professor by her male colleagues despite her qualifications, leaves her university to spend time with her younger sister Elna, who teaches in a small rural school in Appalachia. As a music scholar interested in the evolution of folk music, she is immediately drawn to the music of the region and becomes obsessed with scientifically documenting both lyrics and melodies. Among the Appalachians Deladis and Viney are particularly helpful in this process because of their strong voices and wealth of songs, but Alice is also absolutely critical because she recognizes the value of Lily's work and secures Viney's cooperation. Without someone within the community vouching for Lily's integrity and the validity of her work, she could not succeed.

Because Lily is so obsessed with her work and her career, she at times runs roughshod over others, judging them harshly, pushing them to do her will, and ignoring their feelings and needs. She only gradually comes to a deep appreciation of the people she's working with as she recognizes the significance of the music in their lives. Initially she ascribes to "the common view" that the mountain people have no culture and "are dirty, ignorant, and savage," not to mention "illiterate and inbred," but her view changes as she interacts more openly with them. She learns to accept Elna's lesbian relationship with Harriet, to help Alice earn the recognition and money she deserves for her paintings, to appreciate the resilience of people who suffer extreme hardships, to shift her values so people and relationships become more important than her career and recognition from her academic peers. She also falls in love with Tom, Viney's grandson and one of the few people in the area to have spent time away from his mountain home.

Lily's understanding and change in direction come at some cost. When Elna and Harriet's relationship is discovered, two local men punish them by torching their school and home, destroying the buildings as well as all of Lily's transcriptions and recordings. The loss is especially severe for Elna because Harriet, to make it possible for Elna to carry on the work of the school, disappears. For Lily, the loss turns her in a new direction, one that allows her to combine loving relationships with her love for the music she's discovered. She, Tom, and Deladis leave with the intention of preserving the music of Appalachia by recording it, thus combining modern technology with tradition as well as a genuine mission with a way to make a living.

*Songcatcher* is Lily's story, a story of growth and possibility, but in the process of developing her story, filmmakers paint a picture of Appalachian culture that helps counter a pervasive negative view based on stereotypes. The rich tradition of music that pervades the lives of these people is posited alongside the challenges of poor farm land, pressure from coal mining companies, losses suffered because of poverty, poor nutrition, and poor health, and relationships that range from warm and supportive to deadly. The finished picture has greater depth than many and makes *Songcatcher* an appropriate choice when introducing students to another of the many regional cultures that exist within the United States. Its PG-13 rating increases the number of people who can comfortably view the film. Those who do will be treated to some remarkable music and to a culture that has contributed substantially to the amalgam of cultures defining the United States.

Another aspect of *Songcatcher* that educators may find valuable is its critique of a male-dominated academic structure that devalues Lily's work and skill while overvaluing that of her male peers. Lily has much to learn about life, but one thing she is very sure about is her own knowledge and ability in her academic field. Her commitment to her Appalachian project and her genuine excitement about the music she hears help her rise above physical discomfort and interpersonal disagreements while engaged in her research with the people of Appalachia. Her passion for the music ultimately works in her favor, but it doesn't wipe out her recognition of her colleagues' prejudices. To follow up on the music featured in this film, viewers may want to look up *Songcatchers: In Search of the World's Music*.

**Work Cited:** Hart, Mickey, and K. M. Kostval, eds. *Songcatchers: In Search of the World's Music*. Washington, DC: National Geographic Society, 2003.

## *Thelma & Louise* (1991)

Director: Ridley Scott

Cast: Susan Sarandon (Louise), Geena Davis (Thelma), Michael Marsden (Jimmy), Brad Pitt (J. D.), Harvey Keitel (Det. Hal Slocombe)

Length: 128 min.

Rating: R

Road Drama: A cross-country, coming-to-awareness adventure

Louise, a very competent waitress, and her friend Thelma, a housewife, leave for a weekend vacation. Louise has not told her boyfriend, Jimmy, an itinerant musician, of their plans, nor has Thelma told her husband, Darryl. Not long into the trip they stop at the Silver Bullet, a nightclub where Thelma's spontaneity, naiveté, and desire to have fun, coupled with her meeting Harlan, an avid womanizer, lead to her near rape. Louise intervenes using the gun Thelma had given her earlier. When Harlan stops his physical but not his verbal assault, Louise kills him. Though never clearly explained, Louise's violent response is apparently triggered by her own experience of rape. That experience leads her to flee rather than to go to the police. Initially resistant, as Louise heads for Mexico Thelma becomes increasingly convinced Louise made the right decision. Their journey, enmeshing them more deeply in illegal activity while they become stronger, more independent women and better friends, leads to their ultimate decision to drive over the rim of the Grand Canyon rather than surrender to the law.

*Thelma & Louise* is one of countless Hollywood movies that revolve around the lives of European Americans with minimal, if any, self-consciousness about race/ethnicity, but with the implicit assumption that the main characters are American—not European American or Irish or German American but American. The characters in *Thelma & Louise*, with two or three exceptions, are Caucasian. Their racial/ethnic position is less important in defining them culturally than their gender and class because racially/ethnically they are part of the mainstream, the norm, and because gender is highlighted within the narrative.

Though not all feminists agree, many see *Thelma & Louise* as a distinctly feminist film, one in which the protagonists take on a patriarchal society and refuse to submit, even when their refusal leads to their deaths. When they begin their journey, neither woman thinks of herself as feminist. Louise is an independent, single working-class woman while Thelma is an unsophisticated, alternately childish and childlike wife and housekeeper. Their encounter with Harlan precipitates a journey that takes them away from the status quo and into a consideration of their place within a society that is overwhelmingly male-driven. They choose to opt out of that world when they see no viable place for themselves in it.

Paradoxically, from one perspective their position becomes less tenable after they begin breaking the law or taking the law into their own hands, while at the same time their taking the law into their own hands leads to personal empowerment, solidarity, and a clear understanding of the imbalance and injustices created under patriarchal rule. Significantly, the one person who seems to concur with their take on the law is a Rastafarian bicyclist. His brief appearance underscores the prevalence of Caucasian men who are identified with the law and with positions of authority in the movie.

The controversy *Thelma & Louise* stirred up in the popular press and the analysis it prompted among academics suggest the film struck a chord among moviegoers. That chord—or dischord—seems to be the shifting roles of women vis-à-vis men in the contemporary world. The film resonates with some of the changes feminism advanced, particularly in the 1970s and 1980s, and with insights into the impact or implications of those changes within mainstream culture. Given its abrupt and deadly resolution, viewers might try to imagine more satisfactory solutions to the issues the film raises. See "Let's Keep Goin'! On the Road with Louise and Thelma" (Welsch 248–265) for further discussion of the issues.

**Work Cited:** Welsch, Janice R. "Let's Keep Goin! On the Road with Louise and Thelma." In *Ladies and Gentlemen, Boys and Girls: Gender in Film at the End of the Twentieth Century*, edited by Murray Pomerance. Albany: State University of New York, 2001.

## *Witness* (1985)

Director: Peter Weir

Cast: Harrison Ford (John Book), Kelly McGillis (Rachel Lapp), Josef Sommer (Paul Schaeffer), Lukas Haas (Samuel Lapp), Alexander Godunov (Daniel), Danny Glover (McFee), Jan Rubes (Eli Lapp)

Length: 112 min.

Rating: R

Crime Drama: Examination of cross-cultural romance and conflicting world views

Rachel Lapp, the widow of an Amish farmer, is traveling to Baltimore with her son Samuel to visit her sister when Samuel witnesses the murder of an undercover cop in the men's room of Philadelphia's train station. When Samuel identifies another police officer, McFee, as the murderer, he, Rachel, and John Book, the detective investigating the case, become the targets of a ring of corrupt officers that includes Book's superior, Deputy Commissioner Paul Schaeffer. After being seriously wounded by McFee and recognizing the danger to Rachel, Samuel, and himself, Book drives the Lapps back to their farm in Lancaster County. Too weak to drive because of his wound, the Amish care for him and he begins to recover. As he does, he is initiated into Amish life, particularly through his interaction with Rachel, Samuel, and Eli, Rachel's father-in-law. This idyll is cut short, however, by the arrival of Schaeffer and his men. Their violent confrontation ends with Book killing Schaeffer's men, Schaeffer surrendering, and Book leaving the Amish community.

Though John Book and Rachel Lapp fall in love during John's stay on the Lapp farm, the clash between their cultures and between the values those cultures represent is enough to make them realize a lasting relationship would not be possible without one of them giving up their culture. Neither chooses to do so. Peter Weir, the film's director, seems to invite cultural comparisons and to emphasize the differences between the preindustrial world of the Amish and Book's technological world, between rural and city life, between a community-centered society and one centered on individuals, but the contrast is particularly vivid in Book's acceptance of violence and the Amish community's pacifism not only as a philosophy but as their modus operandi in the face of harassment and threats.

The R rating *Witness* has received for violence, profanity, and nudity makes it inappropriate for younger audiences, but the film can work well with college and adult viewers when they evaluate these elements in relation to various cultures in the United States. Violence is rarely critiqued and alternatives rarely suggested in mainstream movies. *Witness* does question its use and value and, by doing so, opens up a space for discussion. Because the film presents easily recognized cultural differences, it also provides a starting point for discussions of culture: how cultures evolve, what culture encompasses, and how culture impacts individuals and communities, for example.

# Latino/a American Films

## OVERVIEW

When beginning this study of Latino/a films, tragic stories of gangs and gang members appeared to dominate. Films like *American Me*, *Blood In Blood Out*, (released as *Bound by Honor*), and *Zoot Suit* quickly surfaced. Even films that focused on family (*Mi familia*), careers (*La Bamba*), or schools (*Stand and Deliver*) incorporated the issue of gang membership and violence. Further exploration, however, revealed another prominent theme: the immigrant experience of Latinos/as. Whether born in the United States of America (*Born in East L.A.*), Mexico (*Mi Familia*), Guatemala (*El Notre*), Puerto Rico (*Almost a Woman*), the Dominican Republic (*My American Girls: A Dominican Story*), or Cuba (*Rum and Coke*), Latino/a immigrants frequently find their citizenship status questioned, their work and educational opportunities limited, and their cultural values challenged.

Some films feature Latino/a families with firmly established roots in the United States (*The Ballad of Gregorio Cortez, Salt of the Earth, The Milagro Beanfield War*) but whose Mexican American identity makes them the objects of prejudice and discrimination. Very few explore family and romantic relationships or career choices in a world that appears to be free of racism, though the comedy *Tortilla Soup* qualifies as such a film and *Spy Kids* and its sequel come close. These latter are action–adventure films featuring a brother and sister who, like their top-of-the-line secret-agent parents, energetically track down and thwart various power-hungry villains.

Apparent from a study of Latino/a films is a pattern of films and filmmaking practices that in many ways reflects civil rights initiatives of the past several decades (Fregoso xiv–xv; Noriega 1992, xix–xxi) and parallels in some ways the trajectories apparent in the film histories of other traditionally underrepresented groups. Very few Hollywood features made before the 1970s went beyond common stereotypes when including Latino/a characters within their stories. When civil rights activists called attention to this phenomenon, a few directors—both Latino and others interested in Latino/a culture—were given the chance to make films that explored themes identified by Hollywood commercial interests with Latino/a culture, such as gang violence, immigration problems, and poverty. Even with their social-problem emphasis, however, positive cultural values emerged in these films, most prominently the centrality of family. In this, Latino/a films are somewhat similar to many films that portray Italian Americans, with their ruthless Mafia destructiveness existing alongside fierce family loyalties and joyous family celebrations.

Family continues to be an immensely important theme even when opportunities to expand the subject matter and genre options of Latino/a films are available, as is apparent in Patricia Cardoso's 2002 *Real Women Have Curves*. Just as filmmakers, many of them Latino/a themselves, have made films about the lives and aspirations of Latinos/as, film scholars, cultural critics, and historians, many also Latino/a, have drawn attention to these films through their analyses. In his introductions to *Chicanos and Film* and *Shot in America*, Chon Noriega discusses some of the challenges and dilemmas these Latino/a and, by extension, other ethnic scholars face as they navigate the spaces between films identified as mainstream and those identified with specific traditionally underrepresented groups.

The analyses certainly deepen readers' and viewers' understanding of the films' overt contents and forms, as well as the more subtle implications of particular representations and narrative patterns. At the same time, they continue the practice of isolating the films and the people they depict, in effect helping to maintain the distinction between our mainstream and marginalized worlds (Noriega 2000, xxvii). The trick—or magic—filmmakers could ideally help effect is to allow individuals who want to sustain their ethnic and cultural distinctiveness to do so while erasing the stigma associated with traditionally underrepresented groups and showing them as legitimate, full-fledged members of our multicultural society. Given the racism that still plagues the United States, such a change will not be accomplished easily, but the increased presence, both qualitative and quantitative, of Latinos/as and other identifiable ethnic groups in films and the accompanying dialogue among scholars, critics, and filmmakers at least pose the possibility of progress.

**Works Cited:** Fregoso, Rosa Linda. *The Bronze Screen: Chicana and Chicano Film Culture*. Minneapolis: University of Minnesota Press, 1993; Noriega, Chon A., ed. *Chicanos and Film: Representational Resistance*. Minneapolis: University of Minnesota Press, 1992; Noriega, Chon A. *Shot in American: Television, the State, and the Rise of Chicano Cinema*. Minneapolis: University of Minnesota Press, 2000.

## THE FILMS

### *Almost a Woman* (2002)

Director: Betty Kaplan

Cast: Ana Maria Lagasa (Negi/Esmeralda), Wanda de Jesus (Mami), Miriam Colon (Tata), Angelo Pagan (Papi)

Length: 80 min.

Rating: Not Rated

Coming-of-age Immigrant Story: Determination, dedication, and family support lead to success

Esmeralda Santiago wrote the screenplay for *Almost a Woman*, a PBS American Collection's film, based on Santiago's 1999 memoir of the same name. The film chronicles Esmeralda's ("Negi" to her family) move from Macún, a small rural town in Puerto Rico, to Brooklyn where she, her mother Mami, and two siblings are welcomed by Mami's parents. Left behind are Papi and four brothers and sisters. These children later join Mami and the rest of the family while Papi stays in Puerto Rico. The move to New York seems to be prompted initially by Mami's determination to get satisfactory medical care for her youngest child, but Negi quickly learns an underlying and more significant reason is the end of her parents' marriage.

While Mami, who speaks very little English, works in a series of low-paying factory jobs, Negi goes to school, insisting that she be admitted to the eighth grade rather than repeat the seventh because of her limited English. Because she proves to be an exceptionally bright and capable student, her junior high principal Mr. Burnett suggests she apply to the prestigious Performing Arts High School in Manhattan, and with her teacher Ms. Brown, he helps her prepare for a successful audition.

Given the demands of performance coupled with her academic classes, however, Negi does not find high school easy. When her drama teacher suggests she enroll in her local public school for her sophomore year, Negi is momentarily dispirited, but taking her teacher's suggestion as only that, a suggestion, she returns to Performing Arts, her determination and initiative convincing the principal she belongs there. *Almost a Woman* concludes with Negi's graduation, an event she and her entire family savor.

Just as important as Negi's academic progress is her relationship to her mother and the rest of her family and her struggles to reconcile her Puerto Rican identity with her life as a teenager in the United States. Negi moves from childhood through adolescence weaving a path through conflicting cultural desires and expectations. She does so successfully with the love and support of Mami and Papi, her grandparents, her stepfather Francisco, and empathic teachers.

*Almost a Woman* sets out its themes clearly. Identity development, family love and support, the immigrant experience, and the value of determination and consistent hard work are interwoven and explored. The film covers five years, multiple relationships, and various aspects of Negi's life, but at times the film introduces elements simply to make a point without integrating them effectively within the story. This happens when, for example, three Latina antagonists appear briefly to harass Negi and when a social worker visits Negi's family, apparently to underscore the difference between an outside view of the family and an insider's view. Even with these slips, *Almost a Woman* offers viewers an engaging coming-of-age story against the background of conflicting cultural values. A companion guide for teachers is available on line at the PBS web site. It provides before- and after-viewing questions, contextual information, an interview with Esmeralda Santiago, and an impressive list of additional resources to help teachers integrate *Almost a Woman* into humanities or social sciences curricula.

**Work Cited:** González, Flora. "*Almost a Woman* Teacher's Guide." 2002. WGBH Educational Foundation. http://www.pbs.org/wgbh/masterpiece/americancollection/woman/tguide.html.

## *The Ballad of Gregorio Cortez* (1982)

Director: Robert M. Young

Cast: Edward James Olmos (Gregorio Cortez), James Gammon (Frank Fly), Tom Bower (Boone Choate), Bruce McGill (Bill Blakely), Brion James (Captain Rogers)

Length: 106 min.

Rating: PG

Historical Drama: Legend and history intersect in the story of a Mexican American folk hero

The setting is Gonzales, Texas, 1901. When Sheriff Morris rides out to Gregorio Cortez's home outside Gonzales to ask Cortez about a horse he traded, Morris depends on Deputy Boone Choate, with his elementary skills in Spanish, to translate for him. Convinced that Cortez lies when he answers, Morris draws his gun and prepares to arrest him. As he does so, Cortez draws a gun, but as they both fire, Cortez's brother Romaldo tries to intervene and is fatally wounded. Cortez responds by killing the sheriff, and after helping his brother, he seeks refuge with a friend. A posse soon descends on the place, and during the gunfight that erupts, two more men—one a sheriff—are killed. Cortez flees. He is pursued by several posses, most comprised of Texas Rangers, but Cortez eludes them for days. When he is finally captured, it is after he has turned in his guns via a third person. During trial preparations, his court-appointed attorney uncovers the fact that a failure to understand a subtle vocabulary distinction led to the Morris–Cortez debacle, but Cortez is found guilty of murder without malice and sentenced to fifty years in prison. Special Deputy Frank Fly successfully deflects a mob bent on lynching Cortez and escorts him safely to the train that will carry him to state prison.

*The Ballad of Gregorio Cortez* is based on a historical event, an event mythologized in the *corrido*, or ballad, alluded to in the film's title and played through the movie. On-screen intertitles intermittently offer historical information about the event, including the fact that Cortez was tried seven times and was pardoned by the governor of Texas after he served twelve years in prison. Young uses history and myth, documentary realism, and subjective points of view to tell Cortez's story. Boone Choate, an Anglo, is the first to recount what happened between Morris and Cortez, but by the time he does so, his prejudice has already been exposed and his reliability undermined. Cortez's account, shown in flashback like Boone's, is given far more credibility. He speaks to his defense attorney through a translator who is visibly moved by the account. She is the person who recognizes that Morris's question, as translated by Boone, rather than Cortez's answer, created the problem leading to their confrontation.

Cortez is introduced as a silhouetted figure galloping across the Texas landscape. The image, with *The Ballad of Gregorio Cortez* on the soundtrack, establishes his mythic status. Later he is shown to be smart, creative, resourceful, and bold while eluding the hundreds of men pursuing him, but right after he learns his brother is dead and the rest of his family is in jail, he in effect turns himself in. From that point he appears very vulnerable and very human. After his trial and the attempted lynching, children line the street with their parents to see Gregorio Cortez—the beginning of the legend. His oldest son sobs, however, as the train taking his father to prison pulls away—a reminder of the reality of the situation.

A journalist's questions prompt most of the flashbacks showing the events surrounding the Cortez–Morris incident, but Bill Blakely from the San Antonio Press does not function as a responsible reporter. He interviews only Anglos and favors exaggeration and distortion, adding one more layer of prejudice to that so evident in Choate and the mob. Other Anglos are committed to fairness, including Cortez's defense attorney and Frank Fly, who reaches heroic status by stopping a hanging and by standing up to the mob that comes after Cortez. Viewers can identify with him as well as with Cortez.

Though the film exposes racial/ethnic prejudice and offers a sympathetic portrait of Gregorio Cortez and his family, like many films that feature traditionally underrepresented groups, it gives viewers almost no information about Cortez's family or other Mexicans living in Texas and glosses over the number harassed and killed during the search for Cortez. Despite this, *The Ballad of Gregorio Cortez* brings to life a legendary Mexican American folk hero. For more on the legend, *corridos*, and the film, see Américo Paredes's *With His Pistol in His Hand: A Border Ballad and Its Hero*, Rosa Linda Fregoso's *The Bronze Screen: Chicana and Chicano Film Culture* (70–85), and Frank Javier Garcia Berumen's *The Chicano/Hispanic Image in American Film* (199–202).

**Works Cited:** Berumen, Frank Javier Garcia. *The Chicano/Hispanic Image in American Film.* New York: Vantage, 1995; Fregoso, Rosa Linda. *The Bronze Screen: Chicana and Chicano Film Culture*. Minneapolis: University of Minnesota Press, 1993; Paredes, Américo. *With His Pistol in His Hand: A Border Ballad and Its Hero*. Austin: University of Texas Press, 1958.

## *Blood in Blood Out/Bound by Honor* (1993)

Director: Taylor Hackford

Cast: Damian Chapa (Miklo), Jesse Borrego (Cruz), Benjamin Bratt (Paco), Enrique Castillo (Montana), Victor Rivers (Magic Mike), Delroy Lindo (Bonafide), Tom Towles (Red Ryder)

Length: 180 min.

Rating: R

Violent Drama: Young Latinos choose divergent paths in this coming-of-age story

*Bound by Honor* is more than just a film about Mexican American culture. A look into the bowels of U.S. society, the film depicts some of the people who did not make it in the United States using the social prescription we know as the Protestant work ethic. This film examines the asocial hierarchy of the graduates of street life in East Los Angeles and the finishing school called prison. This film is remarkably similar to *American Me* (1992), a film directed by and starring Edward James Olmos. Although *Bound by Honor* is not a remake, the plot construction follows the same line of development.

*Bound by Honor* opens with Miklo escaping the abuse of his white father by returning to the barrio where his Mexican American mother lives. In the barrio as well as in prison, he constantly feels the need to compensate for his European American heritage. Cruz, Miklo's cousin and a promising artist, becomes seriously injured as the result of a gang attack. When Miklo and Cruz's half-brother Paco and Miklo join forces to retaliate against the gang that injured Cruz, Spider, a rival gang member, is killed by Miklo and Miklo is shot, eventually losing his leg. After being arrested by the police, Paco, given the choice to join the Marine Corps or go to jail, chooses the military. The service changes his life, and after his discharge he becomes an undercover police officer. Miklo is convicted of murder and sent back to jail, but this time it is to the "big house," a maximum security facility. While in prison he rises in power and eventually takes over the entire Latino gang structure. Eventually Paco's and Miklo's worlds, clearly identified as good and evil, collide.

Director Taylor Hackford shows us a world inside prison that is much different than the almost Disney-like existence that many middle-class people in this country enjoy everyday. Prison life, an ideological world dominated by a whole different set of rules, is about the survival of the fittest. In this film, the competition between the European American, African American, and Latino American gangs as they struggle for control over the prison economy of drugs, sex, and privilege is clear. The most important currency in this world is membership in one of the gangs, without which one has no allies. Strength is in numbers and allegiance the name of the game. While this scenario is harsh, it is real. Not so real is the film's preoccupation with the violence and criminality of the gangs at the expense of every other aspect of Mexican and Latino cultures. Hackford gives only brief glimpses of this rich heritage that encompasses family, music, art, work, education, religion, and spirit. Instead we are bombarded by double crosses, assassinations, and bloodshed.

Is this the vision of the future: the Latino retaking control of the Southwest through the asocial world of gangs and criminals? Or are Cruz and Paco the future? Can the normal middle-class Latino/a American family win? Is it possible for this ethnic group to overcome the problems of discrimination and poverty in order to fulfill their dreams of "making it legally" in society? These are some of the questions raised by *Bound by Honor*. Among the resources available to help with answers are Tomas Benitez's essay "East L.A.: Past and Present" and Linda A. Jackson's research report "Stereotypes, Emotions, Behavior, and Overall Attitudes Toward Hispanics by Anglos."

**Works Cited:** *American Me*. Directed by Edward James Olmos. Performances by Edward James Olmos, William Forsythe, Pepe Serna. Universal, 1992. Benitez, Tomas. "East L.A.: Past and Present." *American Family: Journey of Dreams*. PBS. http://www.pbs.org/americanfamily/eastla.html; Jackson, Linda A. "Stereotypes, Emotions, Behavior, and Overall Attitudes Toward Hispanics by Anglos." Julian Samora Research Institute. http://www.jsri.msu.edu/RandS/research/irr/rr10.html (accessed June 23, 2004).

## *Born in East L.A.* (1987)

Director: Cheech Marin

Cast: Cheech Marin (Rudy), Paul Rodriguez (Javier), Daniel Stern (Jimmy), Kamila Lopez-Dawson (Delores), Jan-Michael Vincent (McCalister)

Running Time: 85 min.

Rating: R

Comedy: A Mexican American's efforts to return home after deportation to Mexico

Cheech Marin wrote, directed, and starred in the film *Born in East L.A.*, a film full of ethnic stereotypes that makes fun of the struggle of the thousands of immigrants caught up in the dilemmas of border crossings, Immigration and Naturalization Service (INS)

raids, and cultural identity. Although Marin occasionally delivers some humorous situations, many of the legitimate social issues raised by the film are never explored deeply enough to qualify as satire. Instead, the film comes off as a kind of farce.

The story revolves around Rudy, a third-generation Mexican American who, on the way to pick up his Mexican cousin Javier at a local sweatshop, is arrested by INS agents and deported to Mexico. He is unable to prove his citizenship because he left his wallet at home and has no identification papers. This triggers a variety of comedic events as Rudy tries to get back to the United States of America. In the course of these mini-skits, we see some of the many struggles immigrants are faced with as they attempt to get to the "land of opportunity" by almost any means. There are several interesting characters Rudy encounters along the way, especially Jimmy, a European American entrepreneur constantly looking for ways to make money and exploit situations like the one Rudy finds himself in. Rudy and Jimmy and their ploys are contrasted with Delores, a Salvadoran refugee portraying the positive immigrant trying to make her way to the United States legally. One of the funnier scenes has Rudy trying to teach some Asian and Latino immigrants how to act cool so they won't be detected as being illegal immigrants once they get to the United States.

Unfortunately, this film is a wasted opportunity because Marin forfeits a chance to enlighten viewers about the struggle of immigrants and instead settles for a few laughs. The film's R rating limits its audience to mature viewers. Even with these drawbacks, the film can still be a useful vehicle for discussion with a knowledgeable facilitator who can pick up where Marin has fumbled. A useful resource to help provide a fuller context for the film's action is Tomas Benitez's "East L.A.: Past and Present."

**Work Cited:** Benitez, Tomas. "East L.A.: Past and Present." *American Family: Journey of Dreams*. PBS. http://wwwpbs.org/americanfamily/eastla.html.

## *Bread and Roses* (2001)

Director: Ken Loach

Cast: Pilar Padilla (Maya Montenegro), Adrien Brody (Sam Shapiro), Elpidia Carrillo (Rosa), George Lopez (Perez), Jack McGee (Bert), Alonso Chavez (Ruben), Monica Rivas (Simona), Frank Davila (Luis)

Length: 110 min.

Rating: R

Immigrant Drama: A fictionalized account of a 1990 L.A. janitor's strike

Maya Montenegro, a spirited, smart, and spontaneous young woman successfully but illegally enters the United States of America from Mexico and finds work as a janitor in an upscale Los Angeles office building. She does so with the help of her sister Rosa, a janitor who has been in the United States for some time. Rosa not only helps Maya but also supports her own family, including two children and a husband suffering from a debilitating illness. The janitors receive minimum wages, no health or other benefits, and have no job security. At the same time that Maya observes coworkers being summarily fired at the whim of their supervisor, she comes in contact with Sam Shapiro, a union organizer who is focusing specifically on the janitors in her building because of the tenants' high profile and prestige and the size of the cleaning service involved.

Using strategies geared to shame the building's tenants and owners and to attract as much media publicity as possible, Sam forges ahead with a "Justice for Janitors" campaign even when his organization tells him to pull back. He recruits Maya and many of her coworkers and energetically leads them in rallies and demonstrations to demand both higher wages and benefits. Their activism leads to more firings, but they persist and eventually win the day. Maya, however, is deported.

Ken Loach, the British director of *Bread and Roses*, is respected internationally for films that explore working class people. In *Bread and Roses*, he explores his characters' family, social, and work relationships since they are interdependent. The film's most dramatic scene illustrates this. It is an intense, painful, accusatory confrontation between Maya and Rosa after Maya learns Rosa has "sold out" her coworkers in exchange for a supervisory position and the higher wages and benefits that go with it. The sisters lash out at each other until Rosa finally reveals that she has met years of family demands and expectations not simply by cleaning offices but through prostitution. Through prostitution she had gotten money to send to their mother in Mexico, to bring Maya to the United States, to secure a job for Maya, and to hold her family together financially despite her husband's illness.

*Bread and Roses* exposes the vulnerability of disenfranchised workers, particularly Latino and Latina immigrants, whether legal or illegal, as they struggle to make ends meet, fulfill family obligations, and create a life in a new country. Access to a living wage often determines whether they succeed or fail. But bread is not enough. To live fully, roses are also needed. Through its title and specific references that Sam makes to the 1912 Lawrence, Massachusetts, textile workers who adopted "Bread and Roses" as their strike slogan, Loach links the janitors of his film to a century of labor movement. For further information specifically focused on the Justice for Janitors campaign, see Roger Waldinger's essay in *Organizing to Win*.

**Work Cited:** Waldinger, Roger, Chris Erickson, Ruth Milkman, Daniel Mitchell, Abel Valenzuela, Kent Wong, Maurice Zeitlan. "Helots No More: A Case Study of the Justice for Janitors Campaign in Los Angeles." In *Organizing to Win: New Research on Union Strategies*, edited by Kate Bronfenbrenner, Sheldon Friedman, Richard W. Hurd, Rudolph A. Oswald, Ronald L. Seeber. Ithaca, NY: Cornell University Press, 2000.

## *The City/La Ciudad* (1999)

Director: David Riker

Distributor: Zeitgeist

Cast: Ricardo Cuevas (Luis), Anthony Rivera (José), Cipriano Garcia (Francisco Lucero), Leticia Herrera (Maria), José Rabelo (Luis), Stephanie Viruet (Dulce), Silvia Goiz (Ana)

Length: 88 min.

Rating: Not Rated

Drama: A series of vignettes depicting the struggles of immigrants in New York

In four poignant vignettes, David Riker sketches a series of Latino/a immigrant experiences in New York City. The city serves as a critical aspect of each narrative and helps emphasize the immigrants' disorientation, their frustration, and their distance from their homes and cultures. In "Bricks," the first vignette, day laborers vie for work and then see Luis, injured when a wall collapses, die while they wait helplessly for assistance. "Home" follows Francisco on his first day in New York as he is drawn to a sweet fifteen party and an encounter with Maria while searching for his Uncle Raphael. "The Puppeteer" takes viewers to a vacant lot where puppeteer Luis lives with his young daughter Dulce and barely ekes out enough money for food much less adequate shelter. A lack of money is also central in "Seamstress." Ana, a sweatshop seamstress who has not been paid for weeks, learns that her six-year-old daughter, Carmelita, whom she left with her mother in Mexico, has been hospitalized. Ana needs $400 immediately to pay for Carmelita's care.

The immigrants' loneliness and longing to be reunited with their families are clearly conveyed in each story through Luis's well-worn, oft-read letter from home, Maria's straightforward admission that she misses the family she hasn't seen for four years, the story/book Dulce and her father share, and Ana's distress over the daughter she had to leave behind. In each situation, the move to New York has been prompted by financial necessity and has torn families apart. Riker's black and white cinematography and the poverty reflected in the settings underscore the sadness and poignancy of the characters' lives. Like the Italian neorealist filmmakers of the post-World War II decade, he shot on location, used actual immigrant workers rather than professional actors, and focused on social issues identified with poverty: uncertain employment opportunities, low wages, poor working conditions, substandard housing, and the lack of health care and education.

The film is beautifully shot, and though only eighty-eight minutes long and covering four separate stories, its pace is very deliberate. Shots are often held longer than average viewers in the United States are likely to expect, adding weight to the situations depicted and giving viewers a chance to think about the situations and the people involved in them. The close shots focused on the faces of secondary as well as main characters give viewers time to see the diversity among them while also revealing the human traits they share with viewers. Beginning each segment with a photographer taking pictures of some of the characters in that story and ending the film with a series of photographs reiterates both aspects of identity.

Because the film's four stories are short, self-contained, and sharply drawn, they can easily be integrated into classroom discussions of the issues they raise, but alerting students that some of the dialogue is in Spanish and translated in subtitles would be wise. Spanish-speaking viewers and students preparing to teach English as a Second Language (ESL) may actually find this aspect of the film a real bonus.

## *El Norte* (1983)

Director: Gregory Nava

Cast: Zaide Silvia Gutierrez (Rosa), David Villalpando (Enrique), Ernesto Gomez Cruz (Arturo), Abel Franco (Raimundo), Lupe Ontiveros (Nacha), Trinidad Silva (Monty)

Length: 139 min.

Rating: R

Family Drama: Immigrants journey from Guatemala to Los Angeles

*El Norte* begins in Guatemala with military action against peasant workers who are trying to organize and reclaim their land. When soldiers extend their murderous campaign to the workers' families, several villagers help the teenage children of one of the organizers to strike out for the United States of America. In Mexico, the siblings, Enrique and Rosa, must find "el coyote," a person willing to help them cross the U.S.–Mexican border. Once across, they move on to Los Angeles, where they depend on other immigrants to help them secure living quarters and jobs. In each of the three countries, the two find people willing to help them and others eager to exploit them. Help comes from Rosa's godmother, a family friend, the Mexican coyote this friend knows, and from acquaintances in L.A. who share Enrique and Rosa's undocumented status.

Family, friendship, and shared origins or status seem to be the ties that elicit concern and assistance, even when they are mixed with a degree of exploitation, as in the case of el coyote. Underlying both their need for help and their exploitation is poverty, the economic, social, and political reality that Enrique and Rosa share with almost everyone with whom they interact. Their father, Arturo, saw his struggle as one in which peasants try "to make the rich understand that [peasants] have hearts and souls" and deserve to be treated equitably. Enrique and Rosa see their journey to *el norte* (the north) as a way to escape death, to maintain family ties, and to improve their lives materially by acquiring the things they think will make their lives more comfortable. As they struggle to do so, other issues surface, including cultural identities, loyalties and enmities, language usage, immigration policies and practices, and stratifications between and within social classes.

*El Norte* is epic in scope, mythic in structure, and to some degree depicts the languages and cultures of Guatemala, Mexico, and the United States. Its narrative gaps and intertwining of realism, dreams, and symbolism can be somewhat confusing for viewers not familiar with a film style known as magical realism, which allows filmmakers to reveal different levels of consciousness by meshing realistic images with dream images that carry symbolic meaning. Enrique and Rosa's dreams, both idyllic and terrifying, occur throughout the film. Particularly disconcerting is the juxtaposition of dream images and reality in the film's final scene. It undercuts the promise of Enrique and Rosa's early experiences in L.A. and confirms Arturo's assertion that to the rich, peasants are "just a pair of arms." Their reality is far from their dreams.

See Rosa Linda Fregoso's analysis of *El Norte* in *The Bronze Screen: Chicana and Chicano Film Culture* for greater insight into the film's style and multiple levels of meaning.

**Work Cited:** Fregoso, Rosa Linda. *The Bronze Screen: Chicana and Chicano Film Culture*. Minneapolis: University of Minnesota Press, 1993.

## *Fires Within* (1991)

Director: Gillian Armstrong

Cast: Jimmy Smits (Nestor Valora), Greta Scacchi (Isabel Valora), Vincent D'Onofrio (Sam), Maribu (Bri Hathaway)

Length: 86 min.

Rating: R

Romantic Drama: Political and personal commitments of Cuban immigrants clash

On the surface, *Fires Within* follows the classic love triangle formula, but just beneath the surface a much more interesting story evolves, a story about how the choices we make change our lives and the lives of everyone around us. Director Gillian Armstrong uses a variety of flashbacks to tell the story of the Valora family. Originally living in Cuba, Nestor is a writer and political activist; Isabel, a wife and mother; and Maribu, their daughter. Together they struggle with the risks Nestor takes as he fights against the Castro regime in the early days of the revolution. The story is somewhat jagged as we leapfrog from the past to present. The film opens with Isabel embracing Sam, her lover, but quickly jumps to where family and friends are gathered as they await Nestor's arrival in Miami after eight years of imprisonment for his political activities. He receives a hero's welcome from the Cuban American community.

Through flashbacks we learn how Isabel opposes Nestor's activism and how his arrest and imprisonment create a chain of events that leads Isabel and Maribu to escape from Cuba, nearly die in the ocean, and be rescued by Sam, who eventually becomes Isabel's lover. After Nestor arrives, Isabel, Sam, and Maribu must reexamine their roles in each other's lives. This creates conflict and dissonance that resonate through a series of events including celebrations and everyday activities, all of which take place in Little Havana, the densely populated, culturally thriving Cuban community in Miami.

Nestor's political past threatens his family unity again when he is courted by community activists who want him to use his hero status to unite the Miami Cuban community in armed struggle against Castro-controlled Cuba. This coupled with his discovery of Isabel's lover creates a serious moral dilemma for Nestor. The main characters have difficult decisions to make, and how they make them impacts not just themselves but everyone around them. This film characterizes the difficulties that exist within a love triangle that involves individuals struggling to make the right personal and political decisions whatever their culture.

Due to some sexually explicit love scenes this film is not for minors, but has great potential for rich discussion among mature audiences. Background information for such a discussion can be found in Maria Christina Garcia's *Havana USA: Cuban Exiles and Cuban Americans in South Florida 1959–1994.*

**Work Cited:** Garcia, Maria Christina. *Havana USA: Cuban Exiles and Cuban Americans in South Florida 1959–1994.* Berkeley: University of California Press, 1997.

## *Girlfight* (2001)

Director: Karyn Kusama

Cast: Michelle Rodriguez (Diana), Jaime Tirelli (Hector), Roy Santiago (Tiny), Paul Calderon (Sandro), Santiago Douglas (Adrian), Elisa Bacanegra (Marisol)

Length: 113 min.

Rating: R

Coming-of-age Drama: The "sweet science" of boxing in an adolescent's life

Diana, a high school senior who embodies hostility, defiance, and a readiness to settle any issue via a fight, whether at school or at home, becomes interested in boxing when she visits a gym on an errand for her father. Her father wants her brother, appropriately nicknamed Tiny, to learn to box as a means of self-protection. Diana wants to box because she is intrigued by the sport. Whatever draws Diana to the sport initially—as an opportunity to strike out at people physically, to vent her frustrations, to challenge a gender taboo, or to find a place where she is comfortable—she finds that boxing suits her. In the process, with help from Hector, her trainer, she learns discipline and quickly shows her mettle in a series of fights, mostly with young men. She also takes on her father, holding him responsible for her mother's suicide years earlier, which is certainly the event behind much of her belligerence and rage.

Diana's prowess in the ring has other effects: under Hector's tutelage she actually becomes less truculent, falls in love, develops more understanding relationships with Tiny and her girlfriend Marisol, and learns to respect Hector as her trainer and as a person. Her attitude changes and her repertoire of responses broadens significantly as she develops discipline, new skills, and self-respect. She is even able to put her own integrity and self-respect above a desire to please her boyfriend when a series of fights puts her in the ring with him and she wins the contest. Ultimately, as played by Michelle Rodriguez, Diana's initial ferocity and anger are mitigated, while she never loses her edge or her intensity as she becomes stronger physically and emotionally.

*Girlfight* is rated R because of some of the language used, unfortunate given its potential to spark discussion among teenagers. The film gives viewers a psychologically compelling portrait of a tough Latina American street kid who finds a way out of the self-destructive attitude and behavior she's adopted to cope with a harsh, often disinterested and violent world. While doing so, *Girlfight* skirts the usual stereotypes and narrow depictions of Latina reality and suggests ghetto life is only one aspect of that reality and rage only one response.

## *La Bamba* (1987)

Director: Luis Valdez

Cast: Lou Diamond Phillips (Richie Valens), Esai Morales (Bob Morales), Rosana De Soto (Connie Valenzuela), Elizabeth Peña (Rosie Morales), Danielle von Zerneck (Donna Ludwig)

Length: 108 min.

Rating: PG-13

Family Drama: The story of rock musician Richie Valens and his family

Richie Valenzuela, his mother, and two younger sisters are migrants working in northern California when Bob, the oldest sibling, rides in on a motorcycle with the money that allows the family to move to southern California. Bob has spent time in prison, but that has not deterred him from dealing drugs, drinking heavily, getting into fights, or seducing women, including Richie's girlfriend. Though his swagger suggests otherwise, Bob is as unfocused and unsure of himself as Richie is focused and purposeful.

Richie's dual purpose is to help his mother and to create and play music, specifically rock 'n' roll. He is virtually never without his guitar. He becomes a member of the Silhouettes when introduced to the group by a friend, but the association is short-lived because he is not given a chance to sing or to play his own music. A hugely successful concert organized by his mother proves to be a major step forward, leading to a contract with Delphi Records, tours throughout the country, and appearances on national television. At age seventeen, as Richie Valens, he is a star and able to buy the house he had promised his mother, but his relationship with Bob waxes and wanes, disrupted not because the two do not love each other but because of Bob's insecurities, lack of success, and envy. The two have reconciled once again and are planning to meet in Chicago when Richie is killed in a plane crash.

Focusing so much on Bob may seem strange, given that *La Bamba* tells the story of Richie Valens, but the film shows that family is as important to Richie as his music is. His relationships with his mother and with Bob are especially significant. His mother gives him constant encouragement and love; Bob alternately gives him support and grief and is responsible for most of the conflict depicted in the film, but ultimately their closeness is underscored in the film's final images before a reprise of "La Bamba": Bob alone on a bridge screaming "Richie" followed by a shot from early in the film of the two of them running up a hill, happy to be together.

In *Selena*, another biographical film about a young Mexican American performer that emphasizes family, sibling rivalry does not exist. In that film, Selena's overprotective father creates much of the drama; in *La Bamba*, Bob does. Both films, even with these tensions, draw attention to the centrality of family within Mexican American culture. Though neither Selena nor Richie are adept at Spanish, both turn to Mexican music for major hits, both identify strongly with their cultures, and both reach large multicultural audiences because of their talent and their comfort in being who they are. To explore Richie Valens's place in rock 'n' roll, an excellent place to begin is the *Rolling Stone*'s history of rock 'n' roll.

**Works Cited:** Decurtis, Anthony, James Henke, Holly George-Warren, and Jim Miller. *The* Rolling Stone *Illustrated History of Rock & Roll: The Definitive History of the Most Important Artists and Their Music*. 3rd ed. New York, Random House: 1992; *Selena*. Directed by Gregory Nava. Performances by Jennifer Lopez, Edward James Olmos, Constance Marie. Warner Bros, 1997.

## *The Mask of Zorro* (1998)

Director: Martin Campbell

Cast: Antonio Banderas (Alejandro/Zorro), Anthony Hopkins (Don Diego/Zorro), Catherine Zeta-Jones (Elena Montero), Stuart Wilson (Don Rafael Montero) Matt Letscher (Captain Harrison Love)

Running Time: 136 min.

Rating: PG-13

Action Adventure: Swashbuckling heroics in the name of justice

*The Mask of Zorro* is a wonderful updated version of the Zorro story and character. This action-packed film has all the right stuff: exciting fight scenes, humor, romance, and themes that include good versus evil, revenge, and betrayal. The actors play their roles convincingly with Hopkins and Banderas capturing the spirit of the hero Zorro, while Wilson and Letscher are credible villains and the beautiful Zeta-Jones provides the energy that fuels the love between Elena and Zorro.

The story is made up of a variety of standard plot elements. Zorro (Don Diego) the aristocratic hero loved by the people, must endure the murder of his wife, the abduction of his infant daughter, and twenty years of imprisonment before he can revenge his loss. The incumbent Zorro (Alejandro) suffers as well, both as a peasant and a thief who loses his brother and then his partner, Jack, at the hands of the mercenary villain Captain Love.

Though unlikely partners, Don Diego and Alejandro join forces to overcome the treachery of Don Rafael as he schemes to take over California.

Director Martin Campbell's film locations in the Southwest, including the large *haciendas*, bring authenticity to the story. The musical soundtrack is also excellent and includes traditional Spanish guitar work along with the compositions that reinforce the period of this early nineteenth-century tale. This is one of few Hollywood films that shows what life was like under Spanish rule in the American Southwest.

Though a great adventure in the tradition of classic Hollywood films that many viewers can enjoy, caution should be applied, however, for very young audiences due to a few scenes that include heightened violent sequences and gore. Parents and teachers should also consider discussing with their children or students the role of revenge as a form of justice as these are portrayed in the film. If using the film to initiate discussion, educators and students may find Tomas Benitez's essay "East L.A.: Past and Present" a valuable resource.

**Work Cited:** Benitez, Tomas. "East L.A.: Past and Present." *American Family: Journey of Dreams*. PBS. http://www.pbs.org/americanfamily/eastla.html.

## *The Milagro Beanfield War* (1988)

Director: Robert Redford

Cast: Ruben Blades (Sheriff Bernabe Montoya), Richard Bradford (Ladd Devine), Sonia Braga (Ruby Archuleta), Chick Vennera (Joe Mondragon), John Heard (Charlie Bloom), Carlos Riquilme (Amarante), Roberto Carricart (Coyote Angel)

Length: 117 min.

Rating: R

Comedy Drama: David versus Goliath/Worker versus Land Developer

When he fails to get work at the Miracle Valley construction site, Joe Mondragon heads home, but on his way he stops to survey the farmland that had sustained his family for decades. As he walks over the dry earth, he angrily kicks at the small gate holding back the water that used to irrigate his fields but is now controlled by Ladd Devine, the Miracle Valley developer. He is surprised and fascinated a few minutes later when the water spreads over one of his fields. In short order, word of the incident spreads through town and Joe's inadvertent act of rebellion becomes Milagro's cause célèbre, Joe's raison d'être, a rallying point for Ruby Achulata's opposition to the Miracle Valley project, and a source of extreme aggravation for Devine.

Lines are drawn: Devine enlists help from the governor, Milagro's mayor, park rangers, a state trooper, and construction site employees; Ruby secures support from a retired 1960s liberal lawyer who edits Milagro's weekly newspaper. Sheriff Bernabe "Bernie" Montoya, moving between the two groups, advises calm and reason and manages to keep the peace despite a series of incidents that threaten to erupt into violence. Through it all Joe tends to his beans and Devine continues bulldozing the surrounding area so he can begin construction. Appropriately, the final confrontation occurs when Joe, having accidentally wounded a neighbor, is threatened with arrest just as he and the townspeople begin harvesting. Bernie's intervention and an unexplained call from the governor's office stop the arrest and turn a potential riot into a lively town festival.

*The Milagro Beanfield War* unfolds within a familiar David versus Goliath format, though it almost bounces along, opting for a light, upbeat mood rather than the seriousness often associated with confrontations between the powerful and the powerless, corporations and laborers. The lightness of tone is established immediately as the spirit of Joe's father, recognized as an angel and the story's virtual emcee, dances across the landscape playing a cheerful melody that recurs as a musical motif throughout the film. Reappearing regularly, but only visible to his old friend Amaranti, Coyote Angel plays the role of amiable trickster, provoking Amaranti to action and, with Amaranti, adding humor and an element of magic to the Milagro–Miracle Valley confrontation.

The magic helps bridge some of the plot's unexplained phenomena, and the humor eases the tension inherent in conflict. For some viewers, they also undermine the seriousness of the issues the film raises even though those issues are articulated by Joe, Ruby, and Charlie and visualized in images like those of bulldozers gouging the earth and ripping up trees. Combining the film with a discussion of the costs and benefits of development that the film raises—among them the displacement of families and traditions, the opportunities for new jobs and growth, the ir/responsible use of the environment—as well as of the processes employed to initiate development could, however, prove an effective way to approach these issues since humor can capture attention when gravity might not.

## *Mi Vida Loca/My Crazy Life* (1994)

Director: Allison Anders

Cast: Angel Aviles (Mona/Sad Girl), Seidy Lopez (Maribel/Mousie), Jacob Vargas (Ernesto), Jesse Borrego (El Duran), Marlo Marron (Giggles), Magali Alvarado (Alicia/Blue Eyes)

Length: 92 min.

Rating: R

Gang Drama: An exploration of female adolescents and gangs

*Mi Vida Loca* consists of three interrelated stories, all set in Los Angeles's Echo Park, featuring some of the same characters in each and flowing chronologically from one to the next. All focus on Latina gang members and their relationships with each other and with various Latinos. In the first, lifelong friends Sad Girl and Mousie turn on each other after they both have affairs with Ernesto; in the second, Giggles returns to the barrio after four years in prison, determined to get a job and become independent; and in the final story, the relationship between Sad Eyes's sister, Blue Eyes, and El Duran is played out.

*Mi Vida Loca* begins and ends with funerals, and though Sad Eyes, in her introductory voice-over, indicates there is no reason to leave Echo Park because residents can get anything they need there, she also indicates, over images of a burial, that they know "what goes around comes around." The stories illustrate most clearly this latter point rather than the former. At the end of the first episode, Ernesto is killed by a client during a drug deal. Subsequently, Duran is killed when Ernesto's "homies" think—wrongly—that Duran stole Ernesto's prize truck. Friends of Duran then set out to kill his murderer but aim badly and kill a little girl instead.

Sad Eyes and Mousie fare better in their confrontation because, even though they both are extremely angry and both are carrying guns, their years of friendship keep them from shooting each other. After Ernesto's death, they actually resume their friendship. Giggles also fares better, though her determination to remain independent and to get a job seems to be replaced by renewed involvement with the gang and at the very end, a resumed relationship with her first love. Blue Eyes, the only one of the young women who is a college student, not a gang member, is described as becoming stronger as a result of her love for Duran.

The connections among all the women in the gang are as important as their individual relationships, especially after Giggles helps them organize in order to take more control over their own lives. Experience has taught them that many of the men they know and love and who have fathered their children "will be disabled, in prison, or dead" by age twenty-one. To make sure they can take care of themselves and their children, they take on their own operations and learn "to pack weapons" because those operations "have become more complicated."

Their reliance on selling drugs—the only financial operation shown—is as disturbing as their solidarity is admirable, but in her last voice-over, Blue Eyes explains this without irony: "It makes me nervous to have so many guns around the kids, but we *are* safe and practical." This and her final point—"Women don't use weapons to prove a point; women use weapons for love"—are immediately undercut when a gang member, intent on avenging Duran's death, kills a child. The film ends with the child's burial and the following images: the child's father, his son, Giggles, and her daughter walking hand in hand, the male gang members together, and finally the female gang with their children, all leaving the cemetery.

Despite the harshness of life in Echo Park, Blue Eyes, Giggles, and their friends demonstrate strong, though at times conflicting, loyalty, love, and generosity toward each other. Within their particular milieu options are limited and mutual dependence, a necessity. *Mi Vida Loca* is one of the few movies that explore the young women who inhabit this world. Viewers may want to pair *Mi Vida Loca* with *Clueless*, a film set in a vastly different part of greater Los Angeles, to see very vividly how the lives of female adolescents can differ and to explore the reasons behind such sharp contrasts. Another possibility is to pair *Mi Vida Loca* with *Blood in Blood Out*, a film that focuses on Latino adolescents, and contrast the lives of the young men with those of the young women.

**Works Cited:** *Blood in Blood Out/Bound by Honor*. Directed by Taylor Hackford. Performances by Damian Chapa, Jesse Borrego, Benjamin Bratt. Buena Vista, 1993; *Clueless*. Directed by Amy Heckerling. Performances by Alicia Silverstone, Paul Rudd, Stacey Dash. Paramount, 1995.

## *My American Girls: A Dominican Story* (2000)

Director: Aaron Matthews

Distributor: Filmakers Library

Length: 63 min.

Rating: Not Rated

Documentary: Intergenerational story of Dominican immigrants

Sandra Ortiz, the oldest of fifteen children, moved from the Dominican Republic to New York assuming she would find a job, work hard, help her family financially, and eventually return to her native land, her home. After marrying Bautista, also a native of the Dominican Republic, the two shared this dream and began building a modest but comfortable home there while continuing to live and work in New York. They did not take into account the complications their three U.S.-born daughters would pose in relation to this dream. Having coped with the pain of leaving her family in the Dominican Republic twenty-five years ago, Sandra now faces the prospect of at least one, perhaps all three, of her daughters choosing to remain in the United States when she and Bautista return home. Monica, a recent Columbia University graduate, has distanced herself from Dominican culture and is balancing a full-time computer job with attempts to become an actor. Aida, age sixteen, is focusing on her last two years of high school and talking about going to college in the United States of America. Fourteen-year-old Mayra spends much of her time hanging out with friends rather than studying, thus causing her mother great concern because she is convinced education will determine Mayra's job opportunities. She would like her daughters to have good-paying, satisfying work rather than have to take on multiple service jobs as she and Bautista have had to do.

Clearly, Sandra is the heart of this documentary even though Bautista, Monica, Aida, and Mayra all voice opinions and perspectives on their lives. Despite her two jobs outside their home, Sandra manages her own household, follows her daughters' progress in school, sponsors other relatives who want to relocate to the United States, and hosts family celebrations, including casual weekend parties, a surprise graduation party for Monica, and a family reunion in the Dominican Republic. Sandra's and Bautista's lives revolve around work and family; they are shown to be remarkably generous people, giving support not only to relatives who emigrate to New York but also to family, friends, and neighbors in their homeland. They both work hard, give generously, and party energetically as they look forward to returning to that land.

As suggested by the title, *My American Girls: A Dominican Story*, much of Sandra's story revolves around her daughters. Though they have lived in the United States their entire lives, they identify with Dominican culture in varying degrees; all three speak Spanish, but only Aida and Mayra still look forward to visits to their parents' home and find themselves relaxed and comfortable there. Despite Sandra's efforts to give her daughters what they need, her long hours at work and her unfamiliarity with formal education mean Mayra and Aida have little supervision after school or guidance with school work, leading to clashes and frustration for everyone. Aaron Matthews documents these as well as the many positive aspects of his subjects' lives.

Though Dominicans are the fastest growing segment of New York's Latino/a population, few films focus on them. Having access to *My American Girls* is, therefore, a boon, especially because it encompasses so many facets of the Dominican immigrant experience. One facet that is not often explored in works about U.S. immigrants is the desire of many Dominicans to return to their native land once they have become more secure financially. The beauty of the island and Sandra's and Bautista's contentment while there make this desire easy to understand.

*My American Girls* premiered on PBS's Point of View (POV) series in 2001. For further information about the film, the filmmakers, and organizational and library resources as well as an update on the Ortiz family, visit the PBS Web site.

**Work Cited:** Point of View. PBS. http://www.pbs.org/pov/pov2001/myamericangirls/.

## *My Family/Mi Familia* (1994)

Director: Gregory Nava

Cast: Jimmy Smits (Jimmy), Edward James Olmos (Paco), Essai Morales (Chucho), Eduardo Lopez Roja/Jacob Vargas (José Sanchez), Elpidia Carrillo (Isabel), Jenny Gago/Jennifer Lopez (Maria), Paul Robert Landon (Carlitos)

Length: 126 min.

Rating: R

Family Epic: Multigenerational saga of Mexican Americans in East L.A.

Paco, the oldest of six children and an aspiring writer, narrates the story of his family in three acts. Act 1 begins in the 1920s in Mexico and concentrates on Paco's father, José Sanchez, his journey to California, his marriage to Maria, Maria's disappearance, and her eventual return. Act 2 skips ahead to the 1950s and turns our attention to Paco's brother Chucho and Chucho's rebellion against his father, while Act 3 covers the 1980s and revolves around José and Maria's youngest son, Jimmy, who as a child witnessed Chucho's death and as an adult has adopted a stance defined by rebellion and alienation.

*My Family* takes viewers through a series of family triumphs and tragedies with joyful, harmonious events—José and Maria's marriage, their daughter Irene's wedding, and Jimmy and Isabel dancing—intermingling with hardships and losses—Maria's deportation to Mexico, Maria's and Chucho's near drownings, José and Chucho's fight, Chucho's death, Jimmy's imprisonment, Isabel's death, and Carlitos's rejection of Jimmy, his father. Guided by Paco, viewers are invited to identify with the characters, to share their delight, their worries, their pain, and even their rage.

*My Family* underscores relationships and emotion, rather than social, economic, or cultural contexts, though these do edge into the story periodically. For example, a bridge separating Los Angeles and its Anglo population from East Los Angeles's Chicano neighborhoods is introduced as the film begins and remains an unobtrusive but eloquent presence throughout the film. A second example revolves around Memo, the Sanchez's third son: Memo's success as a lawyer, his subsequent name choice of William/Bill over Guillermo/Memo, and his embarrassed reactions to his family when he introduces them to his fiancée and her wealthy parents point to personal and social issues that are left unexamined.

Political and social realities, such as the United States' forcible annexation of California, the deportation of Mexican American citizens during the Great Depression of the 1930s, job discrimination, police profiling and brutality directed toward Chicanos, and U.S. policy in El Salvador, surface but, in each case, are explored through their impact on individual lives and personal relationships, not as cause for community action.

*My Family*'s strength lies in its depiction of the multiple relationships within a Chicano family, a human family with which viewers of many backgrounds can relate. It allows audiences to see another milieu and other cultural traditions while recognizing both the similarities and the differences that characterize family interaction. Viewers who choose to move beyond the familial relationships can investigate the social and political contexts suggested by the film's historical references. A useful resource for this exploration is Tomas Benitez's essay "East L.A.: Past and Present."

**Work Cited:** Benitez, Tomas. "East L.A.: Past and Present." *American Family: Journey of Dreams*. PBS. http://www.pbs.org/americanfamily/eastla.html.

## *The Perez Family* (1995)

Director: Mira Nair

Cast: Marisa Tomei (Dorita Perez), Alfred Molina (Juan Raul Perez), Anjelica Huston (Carmela Perez), Chazz Palminteri (Agent Pirelli), Trini Alvarado (Teresa Perez), Celia Cruz (Luz Pat), Diego Wallraff (Angel Diaz)

Length: 112 min.

Rating: R

Political and Family Drama: Cuban immigrants and refugees sort out changing goals

The 1980 Mariel boatlift is the starting point for most of the action in *The Perez Family*. The film follows two of the refugees—former plantation owner and political prisoner Juan Raul Perez and an irrepressible young former field worker, Dorita Perez—as they try to take root in Miami. Juan seems to have the advantage since his wife and daughter, Carmela and Teresa, are well established in Coral Gables, having fled Cuba before Juan's imprisonment twenty years earlier. Dorita, however, has the advantage of youth and an incredibly strong desire to find her way in this land of opportunity. She is quick-witted, flexible, and creative, a survivor and an energetic optimist. No one is deliberately trying to thwart her, while Juan's brother-in-law, Angel, has made it his mission to block Juan and Carmela's reunion. Juan and Dorita's progress is complicated by a government bureaucracy that leads them to connect with two other people with the surname Perez, to form an ersatz family, and thus avoid indefinite detention in a U.S. military camp.

*The Perez Family* lacks a strong cohesive, carefully plotted narrative. The film at times feels as haphazard and improvised as Dorita's spontaneous, patchwork attempts to make it in Miami. Each member of the "family" she puts together contrasts with the others. Juan's seriousness and caution contrast with Dorita's spontaneity and exuberance; Papi's age, loyalty, and mental instability contrast with Phillip's youth, self-centeredness, and nonstop hustling. Similarly, Carmela, beautiful, calm, dignified, and reflective, contrasts with her younger brother whose fiery temper, oversized ego, and obsessive behavior are so broadly drawn, they become farcical. Even Carmela, once she stops waiting for Juan and is attracted to an FBI investigator, takes on contrasting qualities as she combines cunning and charm to keep the investigator checking in to help her.

*The Perez Family*'s plot inconsistencies and improbabilities can be distracting and can put off some viewers. Dorita's knowledge of the United States of America and her expectations are way off the mark, for example, and her wardrobe a puzzle given that she left Cuba only with the clothes she was wearing. Still, the film can generate discussion of a variety of issues, including immigration and refugee policies, Cuban–U.S. relations, and the role of class within Cuban and Cuban American culture and among Cuban exiles. Another question the film raises, given its Indian American director and a cast dominated by actors whose ethnicity is neither Cuban nor Cuban American, is the importance of the ethnicity of the filmmakers and performers when making a movie about a specific ethnic group, especially when that group has been traditionally underrepresented on screen. Viewers who want to learn more about the historical context of Cuban exiles in Miami will find Maria Christina Garcia's *Havana USA: Cuban Exiles in South Florida, 1959–1994* a good place to begin.

**Work Cited:** Garcia, Maria Christina. *Havana USA: Cuban Exiles in South Florida, 1959–1994.* Berkeley: University of California Press, 1997.

## *Raising Victor Vargas* (2002)

Director: Peter Sollett

Cast: Victor Rasuk (Victor), Jude Marte (Judy), Melonie Diaz (Melonie), Altagracia Guzman (Grandma), Silvestre Rasuk (Nino), Krystal Rodriguez (Vicki)

Length: 88 min.

Rating: R

Coming-of-age Story: Intergenerational problems arise between adolescents and their grandmother

Grandma Guzman is raising Victor Vargas, along with his two younger siblings, Vicki and Nino, in New York's East Village. The family is poor, their surroundings reminiscent of the milieu in which gangs thrive and growing to adulthood is precarious, but Peter Sollett focuses not on the crimes so frequently explored in movies set in urban inner-city neighborhoods, but on the family and the personal struggles of adolescence (Dargis 2; Ebert 1).

Victor, enamored with himself and with his dreams of sexual conquest, is attracted to Judy, the object of desire of many of the neighborhood's young men. When his direct approach fails, Victor engages Carlos, Judy's younger brother, to effect a proper introduction. The relationship develops slowly and verges on disaster a number of times, most emphatically when Victor invites Judy to dinner with his family and Grandma matches the lipstick print Judy leaves on a glass with a similar print she'd found earlier. Immediately suspecting the worst of Judy and Victor, she castigates them both. Judy leaves, Victor follows, and, in working through their anger, humiliation, and frustration, they reveal their mutual naiveté and vulnerability. The result is reconciliation.

Paralleling Victor and Judy's attempt at a relationship are those of their best friends, Harold and Melonie, and their siblings, Vicki and Carlos, as well as the younger Nino's budding curiosity about his sexuality. Grandma, witnessing her grandchildren's interests and buying into the image of sexual sophisticate that Victor has worked to project, is quick to blame Victor for every problem that arises because of the gulf between the children's growing fascination with sex and relationships and her very strict traditional views. She is so upset at one point she marches the children to a social service agency with the express intent of having Victor taken from the family. When Victor apologizes and Vicki and Nino support him, Grandma responds with her usual reminder that she is all they have and that they are family, a reminder accompanied by the promise of a new beginning and a nice dinner.

After Victor's reconciliation with Judy, his response to Grandma's "All you have is me," is "No, all you have is us," suggesting his willingness to take on more responsibility as well as Grandma's need to realize the children are growing up and she has to let go, to give them the room to grow. Earlier in the film, she had tried to control them by putting a lock on the phone. By film's end she is ready to let Victor remove the lock, thus acknowledging her willingness to relinquish at least some control.

*Raising Victor Vargas* offers a low-key coming-of-age story that revolves around family and relationships. Yes, the family is poor, but their poverty is accepted; it is not the issue, just as the milieu is not the primary issue. The family's Dominican roots have merged with the cultural influences they have absorbed living in New York, and while their roots still impact their values, the family is firmly situated in the United States. Victor's coming-of-age reflects both his Dominican heritage and his life in New York. His is a story that high school and college students as well as adults can appreciate, though secondary school teachers may want to check the strong language the teenagers use as they flex their coming-of-age muscles.

**Works Cited:** Dargis, Manohla. "In East Village's Grit, Young Love Takes Root." Review of *Raising Victor Vargas. Los Angeles Times*, April 18, 2003. http:www.calendarlive.com/movies/reviews/cl-et-dargis/18apr/8,0,7794266 (accessed June 26, 2004); Ebert, Roger. Review of *Raising Victor Vargas. Chicago Sun Times*, April 18, 2003. http://www.suntimes.com/ebert/ebert_reviews/2003/04/041803.html (accessed June 20, 2003).

## *Real Women Have Curves* (2002)

Director: Patricia Cardoso

Cast: America Ferrera (Ana Garcia), Lupe Ontiveros (Carmen Garcia), Ingrid Oliu (Estela Garcia), George Lopez (Mr. Guzman), Brian Sites (Jimmy), Jorge Cervera, Jr. (Raul Garcia), Felipe de Alba (Grandfather)

Length: 90 min.

Rating: PG-13

Comedy/Drama: A coming-of-age story pitting mother against daughter, traditional against contemporary values

Ana Garcia, having just graduated from high school, wants to go to college and is encouraged to do so by her advisor, Mr. Guzman, but she knows that her family opposes the idea. Ana's mother, Carmen, is especially adamant in her resistance and indicates that she expects Ana to work with her and her sister Estela sewing fashionable gowns in what is essentially a sweatshop. Carmen has worked hard all of her life and adheres to traditional notions about a woman's role within the family, but she is also an accomplished manipulator who is ready to use any available ploy to keep Ana under her control. Ana, however, knows her mother well and is not above countering with her own ploys and deceptions. When she receives a scholarship to Columbia University, her father, grandfather, and sister's support are enough to outweigh her mother's staunch opposition.

Despite her defiance when faced with Carmen's strategies to gain sympathy and assert her will, Ana obviously loves her mother, just as Carmen, in spite of her constant carping, loves Ana and wants the best for her. Their clashes revolve around their definitions of what is best for Ana and their refusal to accept the very different worlds that provide those definitions. Carmen has come to the United States with her traditional beliefs intact and has no interest in adjusting to the realities of her daughter's world. Ana has little interest in her mother's world and in traditions Ana sees as demeaning her as a person. For example, she wants to be loved and respected for her intelligence and personality, not simply found attractive for her appearance, but she is overweight by conventional standards. Carmen continuously berates her because of this, afraid that her weight will diminish her chances to marry. Because marriage, from Carmen's perspective, should be Ana's primary goal, weight becomes a serious issue.

*Real Women Have Curves* explores the difficulty of maintaining family ties across generational differences, changing social values, and evolving educational needs and opportunities. All are serious issues, but the film is as much a comedy as a drama as a result of the director's light touch and America Ferrera's take on her role as Ana. For evidence, viewers can go to the scene in which Ana's coworkers, egged on by Ana's example as much as by her cajoling and the sweltering heat, strip to panties and bras and compare cellulite. To Carmen's horror, these full-bodied women find the exercise freeing and fun—as will most viewers.

*Real Women Have Curves* offers viewers insight into many of the values associated with traditional Latino/a culture while also showing how they can evolve to accommodate a new generation. It does so with engaging humor and with greater realism than do most commercial mainstream movies and is definitely worth viewers' attention.

## *Rum and Coke* (1999)

Director: Maria Escobedo

Cast: Diana Marquis (Linda De Leon), Christopher Marazzo (Steve Banner), Juan Carlos Hernández (Jose Hernández), Kevin A. King (Calvin Whitherspoon), Jacqueline Torres (Norma Gonzales), Angelino Chabrier (Tony De Leon), James Brill (Brian Thomas)

Length: 93 min.

Rating: PG-13

Romantic Comedy: Focuses on assimilation versus acculturation controversy

*Rum and Coke* is a romantic comedy with a Latin American twist. This story explores the internal conflict of Linda De Leon, a TV producer of a syndicated cable talk show. She is beautiful, successful, and seemingly in charge of her life. She lives with a conservative European American photographer named Steve, but their relationship revolves more around their jobs than their romance. In a chance encounter, Linda meets Jose, a firefighter, who comes to her aid as a result of a smoke incident at the TV studio. This encounter reveals her disdain for Latin American men and certain aspects of Cuban culture.

Although Linda's family and close friends are still deeply connected to their Cuban roots, she has chosen the path of assimilation into the predominantly white middle-class culture of the United States. Later in the film, we discover this is the result of her hatred for her father who abandoned her family when she was a child. She converts this experience into a rationale for distancing herself from Cuban culture as well as from the macho advances of Jose. However, Jose's persistence eventually begins to wear her down, and she learns to enjoy some of her Cuban heritage and eventually falls in love with him.

*Rum and Coke* effectively explores the conflict between assimilation and acculturation as alternate strategies for survival in the United States. Although the film is primarily focused on Latino/a culture, its underlying message reaches out to all immigrants and culturally distinctive groups that find themselves on the margins of society. To explore the specific experience of Cuban immigrants to the United States of America, viewers will find Maria Christina Garcia's *Havana USA: Cuban Exiles and Cuban Americans in South Florida, 1959–1994* relevant.

**Work Cited:** Garcia, Maria Christina. *Havana USA: Cuban Exiles and Cuban Americans in South Florida, 1959–1994*. Berkeley: University of California Press, 1997.

## *Salt of the Earth* (1953)

Director: Herbert Biberman

Cast: Rosaura Revueltas (Esperanza Quintero), Juan Chacón (Ramon Quintero), Henrietta Williams (Teresa Vidal), Ernest Velásquez (Charley Vidal), Angela Sanchez (Consuelo Ruiz), Joe T. Morales (Sal Ruiz), Clorinda Alderette (Luz Morales), Will Geer (Sheriff)

Length: 94 min.

Rating: Not Rated

Family Drama: David versus Goliath/Labor versus Management Conflict

*Salt of the Earth* tells the story of a successful strike by Mexican American miners in New Mexico in the early 1950s. An accident within the mine where the men work sends a man to the hospital and sets off a walkout, but the miners have further long-standing grievances against Delaware Zinc, Inc. Compared with the Anglo miners working for the company, the Mexican Americans are subjected to harsher work rules, more dangerous working conditions, and lower wages. Once on strike, the miners refuse to add sanitation to their list of grievances even though their wives urge them to because their company housing, in contrast to that of the white miners, has no indoor plumbing. Anglo and Mexican Americans, bosses and workers, and men and women are divided. The situation grows worse when, after a court order prohibits the miners from picketing, the women replace them on the picket lines, and the men must take on child care and housekeeping.

Based on an early 1950s strike by Mexican Americans against Empire Zinc, *Salt of the Earth* incorporates some of the events and many of the issues of that strike. Its strength lies in the central place it gives Mexican Americans and their struggle to deal with inequality at work and at home. Raised in a culture that defines them as superior to women, the men in *Salt of the Earth* find both their position as worker and as head of the family threatened, while the women, used to obeying their husbands but recognizing their critical function in the strike, discover new abilities and are empowered.

Ramon, a strike leader, finds his wife Esperanza's involvement particularly galling as he stands on the sidelines during the picketing, hangs laundry, or washes dishes. When he angrily confronts her about their changing roles, Esperanza responds: "Why are you afraid to have me at your side? . . . Why must you say to me, 'Stay in your place'? Do you feel better having someone lower than you? . . . I don't want anything lower than I am. . . . I want to rise. And push everything up as I go." Ramon comes to understand this and later is able to publicly acknowledge Esperanza's role. The film ends with this acknowledgement and the mine owners' recognition that they cannot break the union.

*Salt of the Earth* was made under unusual circumstances. Biberman, its director, screenwriter Michael Wilson, and producer Paul Jarrico were all victims of the blacklisting effected by the House Un-American Activities Committee chaired by Joseph McCarthy. Ironically, it is a proworker, pro-union film, made by union members who succeeded in making the film despite the active opposition and interference of a major Hollywood union, the International Alliance of Theatrical and Stage Employees.

Viewers will probably appreciate the film more if they do not expect a glossy Hollywood production. Professional actors play some of the roles; miners play others. Shooting was done on location with black and white film and was limited for a variety of reasons. Yet the resulting documentary quality of the film is appropriate and the story being told is an important one. Background information about the film's production and distribution, Wilson's screenplay, a film critique, and references to other material about *Salt of the Earth* and the strike that prompted it are included in *Salt of the Earth: Screenplay* by Michael Wilson and *Commentary* by Deborah Silverton Rosenfelt. Similar background material is also presented through interviews and newsreel footage in *A Crime to Fit the Punishment* (1982), a documentary by Barbara Moss and Stephen Mack about the making of *Salt of the Earth*.

**Works Cited:** *A Crime to Fit the Punishment*. Directed by Barbara Moss and Stephen Mack. First Run/Icarus Films, 1982; Wilson, Michael, and Deborah Silverton Rosenfelt. *Salt of the Earth: Screenplay and Commentary*. New York: Feminist Press, 1978.

## *Selena* (1997)

Director: Gregory Nava

Cast: Jennifer Lopez (Selena), Edward James Olmos (A. B. Quintanilla), Constance Marie (Marcela Quintanilla), Jackie Guerra (Suzette), Jacob Vargas (Abie Quintanilla), John Seda (Chris Perez), Lupe Ontiveros (Yolanda)

Length: 128 min.

Rating: PG

Family Drama: The story of Selena, her rise to stardom, and her death

The story of Selena was produced by the singer's father, Abraham Quintanilla, and unfolds like a fairytale as it chronicles Selena's career from her childhood to her death. The film sparkles with Selena's charisma and her performances. Her steady rise to fame in both the United States and Mexico is shown to be the result of talent, personality, her father's hard work, and family support. The family members are close. Selena's brother and sister perform in her back-up band, her mother helps in countless ways and serves as Selena's always supportive confidante, and her father provides the vision and determination that open up one opportunity after another for her.

For Abraham, Selena is the fulfillment of his own desire to succeed as a singer, and though he needs a little coaching now and then to keep current, his career decisions for her are sound, and the two share a strong bond of love and respect. When they clash, as they do when Selena falls in love, his initial fury is presented as a result of his love and concern for her. Family is central to the film and to Selena's success. The clash that results in Selena's death comes from outside the family and is sketched in a few brief scenes late in the narrative.

Central to Selena's family identity is its Mexican American ethnicity and culture, a theme introduced when, in the film's opening scenes, the Dinos, a trio composed of

Abraham and two friends, are rejected by European American establishments because they are Mexican Americans and by Mexican American audiences because their music is too European American. When Abraham wants Selena to broaden her repertoire to include songs in Spanish, he tells her that she must be who she is, American and Mexican. Later, in an impassioned exhortation to Selena and her brother, one they have heard often, judging from their playful behavior behind their father's back, Abraham talks about the challenges of being Mexican American, complains they are not accepted in Mexico or the United States, and must work twice as hard.

Selena's initial audiences are Mexican American, but she easily wins over her Mexican audience as well. She is killed as she embarks on a crossover tour that is to take her into predominantly European American settings, which she sees as a little scary because it is a "whole different world." Her identity and her place within the music world are inextricably tied to her ethnicity, but her ethnicity is actually a hybrid, a mix of ethnicities just as her Tejano music is composed of different traditions. *Selena* mirrors significant aspects of Mexican American culture for contemporary audiences, while it demonstrates that people can appreciate other cultures and incorporate elements of those cultures into their own.

To learn more about Selena, her culture, and her music, viewers may want to check Clent Richmond and Shawn Fields's *Selena: The Phenomenal Life and Tragic Death of the Tejano Music Queen.*

**Work Cited:** Richmond, Clent, and Shawn Fields. *Selena: The Phenomenal Life and Tragic Death of the Tejano Music Queen.* New York: Pocket Books, 1995.

## *Spy Kids* (2001)

Director: Robert Rodriguez

Cast: Antonio Banderas (Gregorio Cortez), Carla Gugino (Ingrid Cortez), Alan Cumming (Fegan Floop), Alexa Vega (Carmen Cortez), Daryl Sabara (Juni Cortez), Danny Trejo (Uncle Isadore "Machete/Izzy" Cortez), Cheech Marin ("Uncle" Felix Gumm), Tony Shalhoub (Mr. Alexander Minion)

Running Time: 88 min.

Rating: PG

Action Adventure Comedy: Parents and children save the world and each other

Director Robert Rodriguez has done an about-face with this first installment of his new series of *Spy Kids* movies. Rodriguez is best known for his highly violent adult films like *Desperado*, *The Faculty*, and *From Dusk Till Dawn. Spy Kids* is a genuine family film with a clever Latino flavor that is present but hardly noticeable throughout the film. The subtlety of the use of Spanish language and culture keeps the film available to a wide cultural audience, but at the same time provides very positive ethnic role models for the fast-growing Latino/a population in this country.

The film's plot is fairly basic: On the surface the Cortez family is an upper middle-class family; Gregorio and Ingrid Cortez send their children Carmen and Juni to a private school while they work. Viewers soon find out, however, that Gregorio and Ingrid are really spies. They are kidnapped by the mysterious Fegan Floop and his henchman, Alexander Minion so they cannot thwart Floop's plan to build an army of robot children to take over the world. When Carmen and Juni learn that their parents are spies, they accept the challenge of trying to save their parents—and the world—by learning to use all kinds of fantastic gadgets, many of which have been invented by their uncle, Isadore "Machete" Cortez.

A very strong theme of family runs through *Spy Kids*, illustrated by the constant concern of the parents for their children and the commitment of the children to save their parents. The final piece is the role Uncle Izzy plays in helping to save the day and in reuniting with his estranged brother, Gregorio.

Rodriguez's creative sets, special effects, and nonstop action will keep most viewers on the edge of their seats. His commitment to his Latino culture is evident in a soundtrack with Latino guitar stylings and other subtle reminders of Latino culture, including signs in English and Spanish as well as a variety of minor characters speaking Spanish in park and department store scenes. Rodriguez has crafted a film that represents the ongoing presence of Latinos/as in U.S. culture, a presence that can be traced back centuries.

## *Stand and Deliver* (1988)

Director: Ramon Menendez

Cast: Edward James Olmos (Jaime A. Escalante), Lou Diamond Phillips (Angel), Rosana De Soto (Fabiola Escalante), Andy Garcia (Ramirez), Virginia Paria (Raquel Ortega), Carmen Argenziano (Principal Molina)

Running Time: 105 min.

Rating: PG-13

Drama: Latino/a students learn about discrimination when they learn calculus

*Stand and Deliver* is an outstanding film about adolescents and their efforts to get an education. Given the academic struggles of poor and minority students in this country, this film is a testimony to what a skilled, positively intrusive teacher can do. It is based on the career of math teacher Jaime Escalante, a naturalized citizen who emigrated from Bolivia and begins his teaching career at a predominantly low-income, gang-infested, Latino/a high school in East Los Angeles. He encounters not only apathetic students, but also teachers and administrators who simply do not believe that the students they are teaching have the desire or the ability to take academically demanding classes like advanced placement (AP) calculus.

Escalante sets out to prove them wrong by using a variety of creative techniques to challenge and encourage his students to participate in his new AP calculus class. One of his toughest challenges is Angel, whose initial image is that of a gangbanger for whom school has little if any importance. However, Escalante's persistence gradually breaks through Angel's macho façade. One of the strategies that helps Angel is a simple one: Escalante gives him two calculus books, one to have at home and one to keep at school, so his gang brothers will not see him carrying his books between home and school.

Once Escalante has won the confidence of his students they eagerly meet the challenge of the hard work necessary to prepare for the AP test. When every student passes, student self-esteem is at an all-time high as both school and community members congratulate them. Their sense of achievement is abruptly undercut when Educational Testing Service (ETS) officials, finding it difficult to believe all eighteen students from a low-income Latino/a high school could pass the test, suggest the students cheated. The accusation is supported by the fact that the students all made the same mistakes on the questions they missed. The students are devastated while many of their early critics gloat.

The students once again have to muster the courage to meet a new challenge: retaking the exam under the tight security of suspicious ETS officials. The students and their gallant teacher are victorious and vindicated. The film closes by chronicling the success of Escalante's subsequent classes, each class boasting an increase in the number of successful students.

*Stand and Deliver* is an important film. A straightforward, uncomplicated narrative, the film is unabashedly motivational and, like Escalante and his vindicated students, will leave most viewers smiling happily at its conclusion. Both teachers and students can benefit from this portrait of students' resilience and responsiveness when motivated by a teacher who is convinced of their ability and conveys that conviction to them. The film has relevance for many audiences but has proven particularly valuable in teacher education courses. At least two books about Escalante are available: Ann Byers's *Jaime Escalante: Sensational Teacher* and Jay Matthews's *Escalante: The Best Teacher in America.*

**Works Cited:** Byers, Ann. *Jaime Escalante: Sensational Teacher*. Berkeley Heights, NJ: Enslow, 1996; Matthews, Jay. *Escalante: The Best Teacher in America*. New York: Holt, 1989.

## *Tortilla Soup* (2001)

Director: Maria Ripoll

Cast: Hector Elizondo (Martin), Jacqueline Obradors (Carmen), Elizabeth Peña (Letitia), Tamara Mello (Maribel), Constance Marie (Yolando), Nikolai Kinski (Andy), Julio Oscar Mechoso (Gomez), Paul Rodriguez (Orlando), Raquel Welch (Hortensia)

Length: 102 min.

Rating: PG-13

Romantic Comedy: A father and his daughters learn to get on with their lives

Semiretired chef and widower Martin prepares the meals and keeps house for his three daughters. The oldest, Letitia, is a chemistry teacher and a long-term refugee from a failed relationship; Carmen, in response to her father's prompting, has become a successful businesswoman with an MBA; and the youngest, Maribel, is a high school senior headed for college—maybe. Every Sunday Martin prepares an especially elaborate family dinner, and his daughters are expected to be home for it. It has become the occasion when family announcements are made and when tensions surface because of the family members' ambivalence about their lives.

Martin does and does not want his daughters to leave home and get on with their lives so he can get on with his; Letitia does and does not want to acknowledge her sexual desires; Carmen wants to please her father by succeeding in business, but she wants to please herself by becoming a chef; and Maribel is looking for certainty about who she is and what she wants. Complications and resolutions come in the form of marriages for Martin and Letitia, a career change for Carmen, and a relationship and college for Maribel. All require various levels of acceptance and change.

A disproportionate number of the industry-made feature films that portray Lationos/as are set in urban ghettos and revolve around activities of gangs or the struggles of the working poor. *Tortilla Soup* is an enjoyable exception. Its characters are hard working and comfortable middle or upper-middle class. Martin has been a remarkably accomplished chef, able to turn apples and bread into haute cuisine in minutes. He owns his home, one graced with a large garden and, as one would expect, a big, well-equipped kitchen. Carmen is able to buy a condominium using her savings for the down payment. Because their material needs are so fully met, Martin, his daughters, and their friends focus not on getting by, but on living well, fulfilling their desires, developing satisfying relationships, and choosing work they love.

This focus is not unusual in romantic and family comedies featuring European Americans, but it is unusual in movies that revolve around Latino/a (or African, Arab, Asian, and Native) Americans. *Tortilla Soup* can, on that account, be celebrated, but it can also be enjoyed as a competently made comic venture into the lives of some very charming characters whose family values and culture help define their particular perspectives while allowing them to be distinct individuals.

## *West Side Story* (1961)

Director: Robert Wise

Cast: Natalie Wood (Maria), Richard Beymer (Tony), George Chakiris (Bernardo), Rita Moreno (Anita), Russ Tamblyn (Riff)

Length: 151 min.

Rating: Not Rated

Musical: Gang rivalries and intercultural romance

*West Side Story* retells *Romeo and Juliet* through song and dance, replacing the lovers' feuding families with rival gangs, the Jets and the Sharks, and making ethnicity, race, and turf the points of contention. Maria's brother Bernardo leads the Sharks; Tony cofounded the Jets, and though he has quit gang life, the gang still claims him. When the two gangs agree to settle their turf battle once and for all through a fair fight, Tony's intervention leads to the deaths of both gang leaders and to his own death. He is shot just as he and Maria embrace.

Musicals, almost by definition, depend on stripped down, stylized images and action, so *West Side Story*'s dependence on a short-hand of lyrics and dance movements to convey gang culture is not surprising. Nor is its bold but simple sketch of the enmity between the Puerto Rican Americans and the European Americans. Characterized as having little else, the European Americans want to hang on to what they see as theirs, the streets. Determined to have a part of what they see as the promise of the United States, the Puerto Rican Americans, insist on establishing a place for themselves wherever that seems possible. Both groups, despite their enmity, however, are willing to form a united front when confronted by authority, whether in the guise of the law or elders. They find solidarity in their youth. Maria and Tony find it in their love.

Colorful sets, dynamic musical numbers, and an engaging story made *West Side Story* a popular success when it was released, and it still appeals to many viewers today even though some contemporary film viewers may find its 1960s style and pacing unfamiliar and distancing. The film can be a starting point for discussing culture and questions of turf, for exploring issues of immigration, and for defining "immigrant" within a U.S. context. The functions of friendship and communal ties, the power of love, and the role of violence in the United States are additional themes the film encompasses.

Since practically everyone associated with the production of *West Side Story* was European American, viewers might also discuss how involving Puerto Ricans in key decision-making positions might have changed the storyline, characters, or other aspects of the film. A challenging and valuable starting point for such a discussion is Alberto Sandoval Sanchez's "*West Side Story*: A Puerto Rican Reading of 'America' " (164–179). Sandoval Sanchez describes his incisive analysis as "a differential, alternative, provocative, marginal, and radical reading" (177). In it he uncovers the covert as well as overt racism in the film's story, in its depictions of Puerto Ricans, and in its denigration of Puerto Rican culture. He points to specific scenes, lyrics, and dialogue in the film and to aspects of the original theatrical text to support his position.

**Work Cited:** Sandoval Sanchez, Alberto: "*West Side Story:* A Puerto Rican Reading of 'America.' " In *Latin Looks: Images of Latinas and Latinos in the U.S. Media*, edited by Clara E. Rodriguez. 164–179. Boulder, CO: Westview Press, 1998.

## *Zoot Suit* (1981)

Director: Luis Valdez

Cast: Daniel Valdez (Henry Reyna), Edward James Olmos (El Pachuco), Charles Anderson (George), Tyne Daly (Alice), Abel Franco (Enrique)

Length: 103 min.

Rating: R

Gang Drama: Stylized musical account of the Sleepy Lagoon story

Henry Reyna and three of his friends are identified as members of a Chicano gang and accused of murder. In a trial clearly characterized as discriminatory, they are found guilty and sentenced to prison. While in San Quentin, their families, George, their lawyer, and Alice, a CIO organizer, work tirelessly on an appeal, which they ultimately win. When the four young men leave prison, they are greeted by ecstatic family members and friends.

This brief description, though accurate, reveals very little about *Zoot Suit*. The Sleepy Lagoon murder and subsequent trial on which the movie is based shared headlines with World War II coverage in Los Angeles during the early 1940s and have become part of Chicano legends about *pachucos*, street youth who distinguished themselves visually by wearing flashy zoot suits. Because the events depicted have become mythic, and zoot suits were so clearly stylized themselves, the highly stylized techniques used in *Zoot Suit* seem particularly appropriate. The movie is actually a filmed theatrical performance starring the sinuous, seductive El Pachuco, who serves as narrator and Henry's personified alter ego; there is a three-woman musical chorus that accompanies El Pachuco in song and dance; scene changes are effected instantaneously when El Pachuco snaps his fingers; a reporter—"Press"—provides commentary that supplements and clashes with El Pachuco's; an in-house audience witnesses the stage performance; and alternate endings to Henry's story are offered.

El Pachuco, dressed dramatically in black zoot suit with bright red accents, appears to raise Henry's consciousness about society's stereotyping of pachucos while suggesting he cannot escape those stereotypes and the discrimination they engender. Henry's trial and imprisonment indicate El Pachuco is right, but these experiences, due to El Pachuco's relentless prodding, also lead Henry to escape his own self-loathing and sense of victimization. They lead him, if we are to believe his friends, family, and supporters rather than Press, to a strong identity, encompassing his roots in Aztecan, Mexican, and U.S. cultures.

Because many contemporary film viewers are used to more realistic modes of acting and of storytelling, they may find *Zoot Suit* difficult. As played by Edward James Olmos, El Pachuco's posturing and relentless goading may put them off initially, but the precision of his movements, his strong presence, and his honesty command attention. Viewers willing to suspend disbelief, to accept the theatricality of the performances, and to appreciate the self-reflexive filmmaking techniques will be rewarded with a thoughtful exploration of an important aspect of 1940s Chicano culture.

For an analysis of the Chicano myths and realities in *Zoot Suit*, see Christine List's *Chicano Images: Refiguring Ethnicity in Mainstream Film.*

**Work Cited:** List, Christine. *Chicano Images: Refiguring Ethnicity in Mainstream Film.* New York: Garland, 1996.

# Native American Films

## OVERVIEW

Native Americans have been depicted in countless films beginning early in the twentieth century as the film industry was just getting underway. Angela Aleiss suggests many of the depictions during the silent movie era reflected more effectively the humanity and cultural values of Native Americans than the cowboy versus Indian westerns that took hold during the 1930s and subsequently dominated the industry's representations (2; Hilger 17). Unfortunately, even among early films, Native American cultures were frequently misrepresented, with individual Native Americans stereotypically falling into one of two categories, the first identified with savagery and opposition to European incursions into their homelands, the second identified with a noble but almost extinct species that welcomed and assisted Caucasian settlers (Hilger 17, 25–41). Among the latter is *The Vanishing American*, a critique of racism and of government management of reservations that, like so many Hollywood films dealing with traditionally underrepresented peoples, reveals shortcomings (i.e., casting a European American in the Native American lead and assuming Christianity is superior to native spirituality) as well as strengths (i.e., presenting Native American perspectives and positing the possibility of interracial understanding and cooperation).

Although not denying Native American stereotyping in silent films, Aleiss underscores the integral presence of "Native American actors and directors, authentic artifacts, and sympathetic images" in many early films. She does not answer her own question about why this pattern did not continue (5). Ward Churchill, however, in directing attention to European Americans and identifying them with "as virulent a strain of colonialism as has ever been perfected" (xi), suggests an answer. In the interest of usurping the rich resources on lands occupied by indigenous peoples, "the colonization of Native North America has been simultaneously denied, rationalized, and implicitly, at least, legitimated" (xvi). Film, along with other arts and institutions helped effect this and in the process offered European Americans a license to ignore the complexity, the values and perspectives, and the humanity of indigenous peoples, while simultaneously underscoring their own perceived superiority and sense of entitlement.

The racism directed toward indigenous people is blatant in numerous films, such as John Ford's *Stagecoach* (1939) and John Huston's *The Unforgiven* (1960), more subtle in others like Arthur Penn's *Little Big Man* (1970) and Kevin Costner's *Dances with Wolves* (1990). Whether the stereotyping is negative or positive, given film industry priorities, Native Americans are consistently defined in terms of a European American world and are rarely presented as three-dimensional characters. As Michael Hilger puts it: "These images force the Native American characters into a circle where they are ultimately too bad or too good to be believable fictional characters—a circle in which they also are vehicles for contrast to white heroes of the Westerns and the values of white culture" (1). Distinctions among the more than 400 different Indian peoples (Churchill x) are largely ignored; their separate ways of life, including ceremonies, dwellings, work, and easily identified clothing styles, are collapsed in favor of plot and aesthetic considerations even though in many instances authenticity has been a Hollywood production watchword. Often authenticity has also been overlooked in the casting of European or Latino/a American actors as Native Americans.

Given this history, Native Americans have more recently made concerted efforts to control their screen images, choosing to become film and video producers, directors, actors, and technicians. While including several Hollywood films that portray indigenous people, we have tried to focus on work made, controlled, or significantly influenced by Native Americans. As a result, this section features both documentaries and independent productions.

We include three films that revolve around the American Indian Movement (AIM) members and their 1970s activities on the Pine Ridge Reservation in South Dakota: *Lakota Woman*, *In the Spirit of Crazy Horse*, and *Incident at Oglala*. We also explore documentaries that call attention to other current concerns of American Indians, such as incursions into their sacred lands (*In the Light of Reverence*), the continued appropriation of important cultural rituals (*In Whose Honor? American Indian Mascots in Sports*), and efforts to undercut treaty rights (*Lighting the Seventh Fire*). Several nonfiction and fictional films depict contemporary life; among these are *Skins*, *Grand Avenue*, *Naturally Native*, *Rocks with Wings*, *The Doe Boy*, and *Smoke Signals*. Though they tell very different stories, they are grounded in Native American culture and values, as is Sherman Alexie's experimental *The Business of Fancy Dancing*.

*Dreamkeeper*, *The Fast Runner/Atanarjuat*, and *Skinwalkers* portray American Indian legends and beliefs very directly, even though the latter does so under the guise of a modern murder mystery. Important but often overlooked aspects of U.S. history are documented in *A Warrior in Two Worlds: The Life of Ely Parker* and *True Whispers: The Story of the Navajo Code Talkers*, while bits of history are incorporated into three children's films: *The Education of Little Tree*, *The Indian in the Cupboard*, and the very controversial *Pocahontas*. Addressing the controversy, of course, is important and can lead to considerable insight, not only in the case of Disney's *Pocahontas*, but with any film that tries to chronicle or fictionalize history. The same can be said about films that address sensitive issues. Until recently, however, critical voices and perspectives, those of Native Americans themselves, have been missing from films purporting to portray them. More often, films betrayed Native Americans by grossly distorting their images, values, and history. That Native Americans are creating opportunities to express their perspectives on issues and events that intimately involve them is an important step forward.

**Works Cited:** Aleiss, Angela. "Native Americans: The Surprising Silents." *Cineaste* 21, No. 3 (1995): 34–35; Churchill, Ward. *Fantasies of the Master Race: Literature, Cinema and the*

*Colonization of American Indians*. San Francisco: City Lights, 1998; Hilger, Michael. *From Savage to Nobleman: Images of Native Americans in Film.* Lanham, MD: Scarecrow Press, 1995.

## THE FILMS

### *The Business of Fancy Dancing* (2002)

Director: Sherman Alexie

Cast: Evan Adams (Seymour Polatkin), Michelle St. John (Agnes Roth), Gene Tagaban (Aristotle Joseph), Swil Kanim (Mouse), Kevin Phillip (Steven), Rebecca Carroll (Interviewer)

Length: 103 min.

Rating: Not Rated

Lyrical Drama: Traditional versus contemporary values and lifestyles; intercultural identity

Seymour Polatkin grew up on the Spokane Indian Reservation among family and friends. Among his closest friends were Mouse, a gifted violinist, and Aristotle (Ari), a bright young man with whom Seymour shared high school valedictorian honors. Though Ari and Seymour entered college together, Ari dropped out in his fourth semester, convinced he and Seymour did not belong. Seymour disagreed and went on to complete college and to become an internationally acclaimed poet. Ari returned to the "rez" and let his anger and resentment smolder, at times erupting in violence. When Mouse commits suicide, Agnes, a close mutual friend, calls Seymour, hoping he will return for the funeral. He does, but his return leads not to reconciliation or solidarity with Ari in their shared heritage, former friendship, and loss, but to a reiteration of their differences.

Laid out linearly, the story told in *The Business of Fancy Dancing* can be taken as a straightforward narrative about childhood friends who lose their connection because of different experiences, lifestyles, and values, but describing the film in this way will do little to prepare viewers for the actual experience of the film. Sherman Alexie, a poet, storyteller, and filmmaker, tells his story in discreet segments and weaves into and around them poetry, music, dance, and the persistent questions of an interviewer intent on breaking through Seymour's witty and amiable public persona. The chronology of events becomes evident as the characters interact, but the events come to us in what appears to be random or stream-of-consciousness "order." In an interview, Alexie indicated that he "was interested in making a movie about a writer and a poet specifically, . . . a movie that really featured the poems as well as the poet." He "wanted to have words, images and stanzas be very much a part of the movie" (Glazner). He achieves this by treating scenes like stanzas and incorporating poetry readings as well as printed poems, voice-overs, music, landscapes, and expressive images of dancing into the film.

Alexie's experimental approach conveys the jumble of influences that help identify Seymour and suggests the ambivalence Seymour experiences. He rejects life on the reservation and prospers in a white literary world by appropriating stories from his own life and the lives of his family and friends on the reservation. He becomes an openly gay American Indian poet enjoying success as success is defined in a white academic world. He appears far more comfortable in that world than on the reservation with Ari or

Mouse, and he returns to that white world after Mouse's memorial, but not without a sense of loss. For Seymour the rez reverberates with funny stories about his—or Ari's—grandmother but also with the memory of his six-year-old sister being shot, his parents being drunk, and his mother giving him a gift of a dictionary and urging him to "get out of this place."

Alexie is likely to challenge viewers with his choice of a montage structure for *The Business of Fancy Dancing*, but the effort needed to understand the film's components as well as the whole is worth expending. Alexie's own experience and that of Evan Adams, the actor who plays Seymour, apparently provided the impetus for the work (Curiel 2) and helped shape the director's insights into the costs and rewards of moving from one's relatively small isolated cultural world into the larger universe of diverse people and ideas. Alexie sees the complexity of the move as well as the complexity of refusing to make such a move and avoids romanticizing either. Students will have plenty to research, digest, and discuss as they decipher Seymour's, Aristotle's, Mouse's, and Agnes's choices.

**Works Cited:** Curiel, Jonathan. " 'Fancydancing' Doesn't Sidestep Indian Issues: Loyalty Conflicts with Success." *S F Gate*. August 30, 2002. http://www.sfgate.com (accessed July 25, 2003); Glazner, Gary. "*The Business of Fancy Dancing*: A Review of Sherman Alexie's New Film." In *What You Need to Know About Poetry*, edited by Bob Holman and Margery Synder. November 20, 2002. http://www.poetry.about.com/library/weekly/ca112002a.htm (accessed July 25, 2003).

## *The Doe Boy* (2001)

Director: Randy Redroad

Cast: James Duval (Hunter Kirk), Kevin Anderson (Hank Kirk), Jeri Arredondo (Maggie Kirk), Andrew J. Ferchland (Young Hunter), Judy Ann Herrera (Geri), Gordon Tootoosis (Marvin Fishinghawk)

Length: 87 min.

Rating: Not Rated

Coming-of-age Drama: Intercultural and intergenerational conflicts and resolutions

Hemophilia, coupled with his mother Maggie's concern, keeps Hunter from participating in many of the activities that define masculinity for his father, Hank, including contact sports, hunting, working with tools, and the military. Both Hunter and his father chafe under the restrictions, but Hank finally persuades Maggie to let them hunt together. Unfortunately, Hank falls asleep during their vigil and does not awaken until Hunter shoots a deer. Their pride and satisfaction are dampened considerably when they discover Hunter has violated a code by killing a doe, rather than a buck. Nicknamed the Doe Boy, Hunter lives with his mistake through high school but not without a sizable chip on his shoulder and a complex relationship with his father. When the opportunity to move to his own apartment presents itself, he does not hesitate to take it, but the move does not magically resolve his search for his place in the world.

Hunter's mother, a member of the Cherokee nation, is a nurse; his European American father abandoned his dreams of going to flight school when Hunter was diagnosed with hemophilia. Hank received an honorable discharge from the military, became an auto mechanic, and assumed his responsibilities as a parent while retaining his fascination with planes and his desire to maintain and fly them. Regret colors his relationship with Hunter and, in turn, with Maggie, though the three also love and support each other. This becomes especially clear when they learn Hunter is in danger of contracting AIDS through the blood transfusions he must have. Hunter's relationship with his Cherokee grandfather is easier than that with his father, making him more willing to absorb his grandfather's ideas and values, including the proper—that is, honorable—way to hunt.

Blood metaphors intertwine throughout *The Doe Boy*. They connect Hunter's mixed-blood heritage with his hemophilia and with hunting as well as with his search for an identity and his coming-of-age struggles. His behavior is at times brash and self-destructive, but at other times, as his mother notes, "he wears his heart on his sleeve." Throughout, he is ready with a witty or barbed retort and can readily move from sullenness or seriousness to a smile—or vice versa. Both he and his father manifest a range of emotions that revolve around their particular dreams, fears, and circumstances. Hunter's mother and Marvin, his grandfather, are steadier, less troubled. They provide the anchor Hunter needs.

Marvin also guides viewers through the film via voice-over commentary. For instance, even before we meet the characters, he introduces two of the film's major themes when he says: "Nobody cares about how much blood runs through a deer, but everyone wants to know how much blood runs through an Indian. It's kind of hard to tell unless you cut one of us open and watch all the stories pour out." At the film's end, Marvin suggests that by sorting through the stories comprising his life, Hunter is able to become his own story: "There was a boy who was part deer and part bird, part science and part four-leaf clover. There was a boy who dreamed of becoming a good story . . . and made it happen." Marvin's somewhat enigmatic remarks may baffle, distract, or even annoy some viewers, but they underscore that much of what Hunter experiences is baffling and elusive. Only by confronting it does he come to terms with it.

In the process of coming of age, Hunter deals with his relationship with his father and with his multilayered heritage; he also begins a romantic relationship with Geri, his neighbor. This aspect of *The Doe Boy* prompted filmmaker Chris Eyre (Kadar) to declare that the film "is unique" in presenting "two Indians as principal characters [who] fall in love on the screen." Although not the only film in which this happens, the statement is worth studying given the central role romance has played throughout the history of film. Are characters of color less likely than whites to be portrayed in romantic relationships? If so, why?

Randy Redroad poses multiple questions through *The Doe Boy* that should interest adolescents and adults. Because he has elicited convincing performances from his cast, crafted a well-structured and intriguing story, and used the film medium effectively, viewers should have no problem responding favorably. For an informative interview with the director, check the Smithsonian Institute's National Museum of the American Indian Web site. Reviews by Jon Bastian and Diana Lind offer further insight.

**Works Cited:** Bastian, Jon. Review of *The Doe Boy*. *Film Monthly*, May 30, 2002. http://www.filmmonthly.com/Video/Articles/DoeBoy/Doeboy.html (accessed July 22, 2003); Lind, Diana. "Hunting for an Identity." *Cornell Daily Sun*, October 18, 2001. http://www.cornelldailysun.com/articles/3471/ (accessed July 22, 2003); Kadar Films. Review of *The Doe Boy*. http://www.kader.delpages/freestyle/projects/doeboy_production.html (accessed July 22, 2003); Smithsonian National Museum of the American Indian. Randy Redroad Interview. Native Network. http://www.nmai.si.edu.

## *Dreamkeeper* (2003)

Director: Steve Barron

Distributor: Hallmark Entertainment

Cast: August Schellenberg (Old Pete Chasing Horse), Eddie Spears (Shane Chasing Horse), Sheila Tousey (Janine Chasing Horse), Sage (Mae Little Wounded), Gil Birmingham (Sam Chasing Horse)

Length: 180 min.

Rating: Not Rated

Coming-of-age Drama: A grandfather's stories help his adolescent grandson appreciate their heritage

Old Pete Chasing Horse wants to attend the All Nations Powwow in New Mexico one more time. At age 100 he still fulfills his role as storyteller on the Pine Ridge Reservation in South Dakota, but he is anxious to pass on his stories to another generation so that the tradition of storytelling is kept alive among his people. When his grandson Shane gets himself into trouble with his gang by stealing and then selling a boom box, he quickly agrees to drive his grandfather to the Powwow. His mother suggests the trip, not because she knows of his double-cross, but because she sees the value in having Shane spend time with his grandfather.

Old Pete, often to Shane's chagrin, spins one tale after another as the two journey from South Dakota to New Mexico. Whatever the situation, Grandpa can pull from his memory the legend that will give it meaning beyond the immediately apparent. Despite his resistance, Shane begins to absorb the truths embodied in the tales, and by the time the two spend a night with Sam, Old Pete's son and Shane's father, Shane is ready to put aside his resentment and Sam is ready to return home. Having accomplished this reconciliation and passed on his stories, Old Pete gives up his spirit. Shane completes the journey to the Powwow and assumes his grandfather's role as storyteller.

*Dreamkeeper*, a Hallmark presentation that was broadcast on ABC as a two-part miniseries, rises above most made-for-TV movies in the way it seamlessly weaves legend after legend into the larger story of Old Pete and Shane's journey and in the imaginative way it renders the legends Old Pete tells. Using special effects to transcend the everyday world, *Dreamkeeper* takes viewers into a world of sacred narratives that help identify the beliefs and worldviews of Native Americans.

Viewers may be surprised that although Old Pete and Shane are identified as Lakota, the legends they share come from different Indian nations including the Lakota, Akwasasne Mohawk, Kiowa, Pawnee, Cheyenne, Chinook, and Blackfoot. Subtitles are used to connect the nations with the appropriate legends as they unfold on screen, cueing educators to the possibility of using *Dreamkeeper* as an introduction to Native American cultures in the United States of America. For educators who choose to do so, "The *Dreamkeeper* Guide for Educators" offers some resources that could prove helpful. They include background information, vocabulary, discussion questions, activities, and a short bibliography that includes several books of myths and legends. Though geared primarily to middle and junior high students, teachers can adapt the material to other grade levels or use it as a point of departure for alternate approaches to the film.

*Dreamkeeper* was given top honors at the 28th Annual American Indian Film Festival in 2003.

**Work Cited:** Onish, Liane B. "The *Dreamkeeper* Guide for Educators." Edited by Peg Kolm. KIDSNET, 2003. http://www.kidsnet.org/studyguides/.

## *The Education of Little Tree* (1997)

Director: Richard Friedenberg

Cast: James Cromwell (Granpa), Tantoo Cardinal (Granma), Joseph Ashton (Little Tree), Graham Greene (Willow John), Mika Boorem (little girl), Leni Parker (Martha)

Length: 112 min.

Rating: PG

Family Drama: Home and countryside become a young boy's primary sources of education

When eight-year-old Little Tree is orphaned in 1935, his European American Granpa and Cherokee American Granma take him to their Eastern Tennessee mountain home to live. They do so despite the clearly racist objections of his Aunt Martha. Through the love and care of his grandparents and the friendship of Willow John, Little Tree thrives. He learns to love the earth, to read and appreciate nature, to understand the consequences of his choices, and to help his Granpa make moonshine liquor, the source of the small amount of cash the family needs. When Martha learns of the boy's involvement in this enterprise and of the fact he is not attending school, she initiates action that results in his being sent to Notched Gap Indian School.

Before leaving, Granma tells Little Tree about the Dog Star, the brightest star at dusk, and assures him if he needs her or Granpa he can let them know through the star. Though he tries to fit in, he soon finds himself being punished for an unexplained offense and after several days of isolation turns to the star. Almost immediately, Granpa makes his way to Notched Gap to rescue him. Once back home Little Tree continues to grow under the tutelage of Granma, Granpa, and Willow John, while successfully evading authorities whenever they come looking for him.

*The Education of Little Tree* is a delight and a welcome change from fast-paced, action-filled movies that have dazzling special effects but little substance. James Cromwell, Tantoo Cardinal, Joseph Ashton, and Graham Greene inhabit their roles with apparent ease and with grace. Granma and Granpa give Little Tree love and security but do not coddle him. With Willow John's help, they initiate him into Cherokee history and culture effortlessly, telling him about efforts to force the Cherokee off their lands and conveying their appreciation of the earth, of nature, to him. For example, Granma makes Little Tree a pair of moccasins to replace his hard-soled shoes so he can feel and get to know the earth.

The trio teaches him reading, writing, and arithmetic, but they are primarily interested in nurturing his spirit. They succeed because of their own generous spirits. Little Tree's education involves challenges, including the loss of both parents and later of Granma and Granpa, but the film presents these realities gently, and as one door closes for Little Tree, another opens. Because this is so, the film could be an excellent introduction to discussions with students, particularly elementary and middle school students, about different cultures, worldviews, and perspectives. Before screening the film, however, educators may want to read the introductory material to the Smithsonian Institution's Bibliography on North American Indians for K–12. The information and insight found there is invaluable and the bibliography itself an immensely useful resource.

**Work Cited:** Anthropology Outreach Office. "Critical Bibliography on North American Indians, for K–12." Smithsonian Institution, 1996. http://www.nmai.si.edu/.

## *The Fast Runner/Atanarjuat* (2001)

Director: Zacharias Kunuk

Cast: Natar Ungalaaq (Atanarjuat), Sylvia Ivalu (Atuat), Peter-Henry Armatsiaq (Oki), Lucy Tulugarjuk (Puja), Pakhak Innukshuk (Amaqjuag)

Length: 172 min.

Rating: R

Drama: Inuit Legend, conveys clan values, conflicts, and family structure

Though Atuat has been promised by Sauri, the clan leader, to his son Oki, she falls in love with Atanarjuat. When challenged by Oki to a fight to decide who will marry her, Atanarjuat wins. He and Atuat happily begin a family while Oki nurses a growing hatred and a desire for revenge. Succumbing to the wiles of Puja, Oki's sister, Atanarjuat takes her as his second wife. When Puja and Atanarjuat's brother Amaqjuag are caught committing adultery, their spouses are actually able to accept their expressions of sorrow and forgive them. Not so Oki. With the help of two friends, he attacks Atanarjuat and Amaqjuat while they are sleeping and kills Amaqjuat. Atanarjuat escapes, running naked across miles of ice and snow until his pursuers finally give up.

Convinced he hasn't survived, Oki later searches unsuccessfully for Atanarjuat's body. He then tries to convince his father to let him claim Atuat, but when Sauri refuses, Oki kills him and rapes Atuat. Paralleling these events are Atanarjuat's rescue by an isolated clan family, his healing, and, to Atuat's relief and delight, his return home. In a clan ceremony, Atanarjuat calls for an end to revenge killings. An elder firmly banishes Oki, his cohorts, and Puja from the clan, and harmony is restored.

Stripped of the particulars that distinguish *The Fast Runner* as an Inuit legend, the film's events are similar to the legends and stories familiar to many cultures, including those told in Greek and Shakespearean literature and today in melodramas and soap operas (Ebert; Hoberman). What distinguishes *The Fast Runner* are the particulars. The first feature made by the Inuit, *The Fast Runner* integrates several versions of an eleventh-century Inuit legend that still holds meaning for today's Inuit people. The film chronicles in closely observed detail their customs and values. Because those customs are so new to most viewers and their setting so unfamiliar, the film opens up a new world while simultaneously demonstrating just how universal human traits and relationships are.

*The Fast Runner* integrates several levels of reality by incorporating mythic and spiritual elements with the more realistic portrayal of the characters' interaction and work. It makes visible the magical power of ritual and the presence of evil in human form while also showing viewers how animal skins are cleaned, birds' eggs cooked, and cooking oil stored. The film's epic, multilayered dimensions make the film ideal for a comparative study of cultures, though its three-hour length and deliberate pacing may prove challenging to some viewers. Educators can find ways around both by creative scheduling and by helping viewers appreciate the film's distinct Inuit rhythm. The film's uniqueness and ability to mesh this with universal themes, the beauty of its landscape, the skill and freshness of its actors, and its focus on cultural values and customs suggest the effort to make it accessible to students would be well worth the time and energy needed to do so.

**Works Cited:** Ebert, Roger. Review of *The Fast Runner. Chicago Sun-Times*, June 28, 2002. http://www.suntimes.com/ebert/ebert_reviews/2002/06/062806.html (accessed August 13, 2003); Hoberman, J. "Let There Be Light." Review of *The Fast Runner. The Village Voice*, June 5–11, 2002. http://www.villagevoice.com/print/issues/0223/hoberman.php (accessed August 12, 2003).

## *Grand Avenue* (1996)

Director: Daniel Sackheim

Cast: Sheila Tousey (Mollie), Deeny Dakota (Justine), Dianne Debarsige (Alice), Cody Lightning (Sheldon), Jenny Gago (Anna), Simi Mehta (Jeanne), A. Martinez (Steven), Irene Bedard (Reyna), Alexis Cruz (Raymond), Tantoo Cardinal (Nellie)

Length: 167 min.

Rating: Not Rated

Family Drama: A story of complex interwoven family and community relationships

When Mollie's husband, Jack, dies on the Lokaya Reservation, Mollie and her three children, Justine, Alice, and Sheldon, are forced to leave because, though they are Native Americans, they are Pomo and not Lokaya. They drive to Santa Rosa, where they are warmly welcomed by Mollie's cousin Anna, who finds a house for them on Grand Avenue, a predominantly low-income neighborhood populated by African, Latino/a, and Native Americans. Shortly after their arrival, Mollie discovers that Steven, her high school sweetheart and Justine's father, lives a few houses away with his second wife Reyna and his teenage son, Raymond, from his first marriage. Both Steven and Mollie have been silent about the identity of Justine's father, and Mollie still deeply resents Steven for choosing college rather than marriage when she became pregnant. When Raymond and Justine become interested in each other, Steven sets off a whole series of angry emotional confrontations by breaking the silence.

The confrontations take place as other relationships and issues within the neighborhood unfold: Justine invites trouble by being too friendly with a gang member; Mollie repeatedly seeks refuge in alcohol; Anna's adolescent daughter Jeanne faces a second round of chemotherapy; and other tribal members oppose Nellie and Steven when they try to prevent the sale of the Pomo burial ground. Interactions are not all negative, however: Alice learns traditional basket-weaving and healing from Nellie; Jeanne and Justine give each other support; Mollie finally acknowledges her anger and seeks help. The plot twists and turns are often melodramatic, but the performances are strong enough to keep audiences concerned about the characters and curious about their interaction.

None of the characters are heroes in a Hollywood sense, yet they all struggle and each acts valiantly at times. They relate in different degrees to their traditional indigenous culture, with Anna's father, Nellie, Steven, and Alice most in tune with it and best able to respond effectively to crises. Alice becomes Nellie's protégée and apprentice, affirming through her actions that the life of the spirit can take root in an urban area as well as on a reservation.

Ward Churchill has noted that *Grand Avenue* "received the highest viewer ratings of any HBO program for the [1996] season, and was described in the *New York Times* as 'a giant step toward offering a gritty and unsparing depiction of urban Indian life' " (205). Though "gritty and unsparing," the portrayal is also extremely moving. The characters are frequently at odds, but intertwined with the clashes are gestures of love and support that together indicate difficulties American Indians—and other people—cope with, while also introducing cultural resources that can help pull them through.

Conflict is part of the structure of almost all narrative films so its conspicuous role in *Grand Avenue* is expected. Viewers might want to question, however, how often, especially in stories in which adolescents figure prominently, gangs are used as the narrative convention to spark conflict between parents and their children and between adolescent peers. How pervasive is gang activity in low-income urban settings? In middle—or upper—income settings? What determines the existence of a gang and its level of activity in a given setting? How are gang members depicted? With what racial/ethnic groups are they most frequently associated? Do these associations have negative repercussions that go beyond gang members? What other situations cause conflict among teenagers and their parents and peers? Could they be used as effectively as identification with a gang to create conflict or to further a story? These questions are relevant in discussions of *Grand Avenue* because of Justine's interest in a gang member, but they can be asked when discussing other films as well.

The raw language, though realistic, will probably put *Grand Avenue* out of bounds for high school students but should not dissuade college-aged and adult viewers from seeing this powerful, well-acted film.

**Work Cited:** Churchill, Ward. *Fantasies of the Master Race: Literature, Cinema and the Colonization of American Indians*. San Francisco: City Lights Books, 1998.

## *In the Light of Reverence* (2000)

Producers and directors: Christopher McLeod and Malinda Maynor

Distributor: Bullfrog Films

Length: 73 min.

Rating: Not Rated

Documentary: An analysis of conflicting spiritual values and worldviews

*In the Light of Reverence* presents three groups of Native Americans—the Lakota, the Hopi, and the Wintu—within the context of their struggles to maintain their sacred sites: *Mato Tipila*, also known as Devils Tower and the Lodge of the Bear, in the Black Hills of Wyoming; the Colorado Plateau, including *Tsimontukwi* or Woodruff Butte, *Nuvatukaovi* or the San Francisco Peaks, and *Tuuwanasavee* or Black Mesa; and Mount Shasta, or *Bulyum Puyuik*, the "Great Mountain." The struggles all to some extent revolve around the very different concepts of sacred places that European and Native Americans have. Generally speaking, European Americans build churches, houses of worship, "where it's convenient for people," while Native Americans see the earth itself as sacred and "believe that sacred places define themselves and that it's up to humans to find them and care for them, not create or own them" (Rogow 31).

These differing philosophies have led to conflicts over land use. Lakota and other Indian nations revere *Mato Tipila* and perform sun dances and vision quests nearby; to them the activities of rock climbers are acts of desecration and violations of the sacredness of the tower. In the Southwest, pumice, gravel, and coal mining interests as well as private property rights have been given precedence by the U.S. government over Hopi shrines and the Hopi spiritual covenant to care for their desert homeland. The result has been the bulldozing of sacred sites and the loss of vital Hopi village springs. In the Mount Shasta area, the Winnemem Wintu successfully worked against a proposed ski resort that threatened a sacred spring but subsequently have faced growing numbers of spiritual seekers whose New Age practices appear to the Wintu to mock their traditional ceremonies and offend the mountain (Rogow 6–7).

In their representation of each of these situations, McLeod and Maynor are primarily concerned about the irreparable losses that result from incursions into sacred lands, but this does not mean they ignore the perspectives of the rock climbers, the mine owners, or the New Age spiritual practitioners. Members of each of these groups are interviewed and given opportunities to articulate their positions. *In the Light of Reverence* thus becomes a remarkable illustration of the profound differences in the worldviews and values of various cultural groups and clearly shows how difficult, and at times impossible, reconciliation of these differences can be.

Because *In the Light of Reverence* explores the crisis experienced by the Lakota, the Hopi, and the Wintu separately, the individual segments lend themselves to classroom use. In addition, two comprehensive teachers' guides open up a variety of avenues for further study. Between the two, issues related to social studies, environmental studies, language, and religion are covered. The guides also point the way to more resources, offer extensive bibliographical information, and suggest a variety of activities that can be adapted to different age groups and situations.

**Works Cited:** Mok, Bettina, and Patricia St. Onge. "*In the Light of Reverence*: Discussion Guide." Television Race Initiative, 2001. http://www.sacredland.org/teach. Rogow, Faith. Teacher's Guide: *In the Light of Reverence*. With Christopher McLeod. La Honda, CA: The Sacred Land Film Project, 2002.

## *In the Spirit of Crazy Horse* (1991)

Director: James Locker

Distributor: PBS Video

Length: 60 min.

Rating: Not Rated

Historical Documentary: History from a Native American perspective

*In the Spirit of Crazy Horse* is a documentary that chronicles the struggles of the Lakota Sioux from the time of the legendary Sioux Chief Crazy Horse to the contemporary challenges facing his descendants. The story is told through the experiences of Milo Yellow Hair, a descendant of the warriors who fought with Crazy Horse in the defeat of General Armstrong Custer at the Battle of the Little Big Horn. This is a significantly different perspective from the majority of films on Native Americans since most are European American narratives. In this film, viewers hear the authentic Native

American voices of participants in the twentieth-century siege at Wounded Knee, South Dakota, like American Indian Movement (AIM) leader Leonard Peltier and goon squad member Duane Brewer, as well as Native American historians like Vine Deloria, Jr., Dennis Banks, and Charlotte Black Elk.

Film director James Locker supplies additional authenticity to this account by incorporating archival film footage depicting the history of the Lakota Sioux, but he also provides essential facts about the current socioeconomic conditions on the Pine Ridge Reservation. This is effectively contrasted with the tourist-rich Badlands anchored by Mount Rushmore. Perhaps the most poignant scene in the film is a family of European American tourists taking their pictures with an elderly Native American in a full headdress and the father encouraging his son to ask, "How's the Injun?" This scene is symbolic of how most mainstream Americans think and feel about Native Americans, sealing them into historically inaccurate scenarios, relegating them to tourist-attraction status, and ignoring their contemporary situation.

*In the Spirit of Crazy Horse* can be an effective tool for middle and secondary school and college students. It provides a quality chronology for one of many little known Native American stories. The story of the Lakota Sioux's struggle to reclaim their ancestral holy lands in the Black Hills is ongoing and offers an opportunity for this generation to apply, in a meaningful way, the social justice identified with this nation.

Several other films deal with events at Wounded Knee and life on the Pine Ridge Reservation. Among them are a feature-fiction film, *Thunderheart*, and a documentary, *Incident at Oglala*, both directed by Michael Apted; Chris Eyre's recent feature, *Skins*, about two brothers living on the "rez"; Frank Pierson's *Lakota Woman*, a fictionalized biographical film based on Mary Crow Dog's life, which centers on her participation in the 1973 siege at Wounded Knee; and *Homeland*, a documentary about four contemporary Lakota families.

*Thunderheart* has been harshly criticized for its continuation of an unspoken policy of having Native Americans' lives and issues interpreted through European American (and in this case, British) eyes. *Incident at Oglala*, while giving the FBI and other government spokesmen opportunities to present their side of the events surrounding the murder of two FBI agents on the Pine Ridge Reservation in 1975, provides testimony that clearly undercuts the government's position while suggesting Leonard Peltier was wrongly convicted of the murders.

*Lakota Woman* tells the story of Wounded Knee from a woman's perspective. Like *Thunderheart*, it incorporates a portrait of life on the Pine Ridge Reservation. Chris Eyre makes this the center of *Skins*, underscoring the poverty and hopelessness of a people whose unemployment rate is significantly over 50 percent. In contrast, *Homeland*, though it too chronicles contemporary life at Pine Ridge, features parents and a grandparent who have not given up hope. Each is creating a better life through work and strong commitments to their families and their cultures. Viewers who want to read more about the activities of AIM and the events leading up to Leonard Peltier's conviction should find Peltier's *Prison Writings* an excellent place to start.

**Works Cited:** *Homeland*. Directed by Jilann Spitzmiller and Hank Rogerson. UC Extension Center for Media and Independent Learning, 2000; *Incident at Oglala*. Directed by Michael Apted. Miramax, 1992; *Lakota Woman*. Directed by Frank Pierson. Performances by Irene Bedard, Casey Camp-Horinek, Tantoo Cardinal, and Pato Hoffman. Warner Home Video, 1994; Peltier, Leonard. *Prison Writings: My Life Is My Sun Dance*. New York: St. Martin's Press, 2000; *Skins*. Directed by Chris Eyre. Performances by Eric Schweig, Graham Greene, Gary Farmer, and

Lois Red Elk. First Look Pictures, 2002; *Thunderheart*. Directed by Michael Apted. Performances by Val Kilmer, Sam Shepard, and Graham Greene. Columbia Tristar, 1992.

## *In Whose Honor? American Indian Mascots in Sports* (1997)

Director: Jay Rosenstein

Distributor: New Day Films

Length: 46 min.

Rating: Not Rated

Documentary: The University of Illinois Chief Illiniwek controversy

*In Whose Honor? American Indian Mascots in Sports* opens with this 1940 quote by James Gray: "It has ever been the way of the white man in his relation to the Indian, first, to sentimentalize him as a monster until he has been killed off . . . and second, to sentimentalize him in retrospect as the noble savage." These words suggest Jay Rosenstein's perspective on the issue of Indian mascots and team names. He quickly confirms his empathy for the position of Native Americans by introducing Charlene Teters, a Spokane Indian invited to enter—and help diversify—the graduate program in art at the University of Illinois (UI). Teters publicly protested the university's use of Chief Illiniwek because of its trivialization of symbols and dances sacred to American Indians. Rosenstein weaves an extended interview with Teters with footage showing her protesting alone and with others, sometimes silently and sometimes loudly. Interspersed with this footage are interviews with UI trustees, alumni, and students who support the continued use of Indian names, dress, and caricatures to identify their teams.

The controversy surrounding the performance of the fictitious Chief Illiniwek at UI games receives most of the attention in *In Whose Honor?*, perhaps because the UI community has been most determined to retain their seventy-year Illiniwek tradition, even taking the issue to the Illinois legislature for official confirmation. They persist in holding on to a tradition, including a dance choreographed by successive European American individuals playing Chief Illiniwek, despite attempts by American Indian activists to explain how painful, damaging, and offensive the presentation is to them. Viewers familiar with authentic indigenous dances and ceremonies will immediately recognize the gulf between these and the athletic leaps, twists, and midair splits that have become part of the UI performance. The gulf between the people on the opposing sides of the controversy appear just as great. They seem incapable of listening to each other. Failing this, they are unable to understand each other's positions.

While the Chief Illiniwek impasse continues, other universities, school districts, and sports teams have understood the perspective of Native Americans and responded by changing their names. *In Whose Honor?* provides this information without exploring in any depth how these changes came about. Educators could use *In Whose Honor?* as an impetus to investigate how the changes were effected and to compare them to the situation at UI. Another direction viewers could take, using *In Whose Honor?* as their starting point, is a study of possible compromises that American Indians and their opponents might work out. They might also want to study some authentic American Indian symbols and dances and learn their significance and use.

If the mainstream, and even other people of color, truly wants to honor Native Americans, their history, and their culture, Native Americans surely must play a central role in determining how this can be done. Elements of indigenous cultures cannot simply be appropriated, twisted into a different shape and placed in a new context while the people themselves are dismissed, if the object is to honor them. Understanding and respect precede honor.

A very comprehensive report, "The Chief Illiniwek Dialogue Report," is available on the University of Illinois at Urbana-Champaign Web site. It incorporates extensive testimony and arguments from people on both sides of the Illiniwek issue as well as historical and contextual information. Another important source of information in discussions of Native Americans and their cultures is the Smithsonian Institution's National Museum of the American Indian Web site.

**Works Cited:** "The Chief Illiniwek Dialogue Report." University of Illinois at Urbana-Champaign, 2001. http://www.uiuc.edu/dialogue/report/ (accessed June 27, 2004); National Museum of the American Indian. Smithsonian Institution. http://www.nmai.si.edu.

## *Incident at Oglala* (1992)

Director: Michael Apted

Distributor: Miramax

Length: 90 min.

Rating: PG

Documentary: Events surrounding the 1975 killing of two FBI agents on the Pine Ridge Reservation

On the 26th of June, 1975, two FBI agents, Jack Coler and Ronald Williams, and an American Indian Movement (AIM) member, Joe Stuntz, were killed on the Pine Ridge Reservation in South Dakota at the Jumping Bulls compound, triggering an intensive search for the individuals who shot the agents. The investigation led to the arrest and trial of Robert Robideau and Darrelle "Dino" Butler, while a third suspect, Leonard Peltier, fled to Canada. All were AIM members. Robideau and Butler were tried together and found not guilty. Peltier was subsequently extradited, tried, found guilty, and given two consecutive life sentences. *Incident at Oglala* is an account of the original confrontation and the investigations and trials that followed, but the film also contextualizes the incident by depicting the tension-filled atmosphere that prevailed on the reservation in the 1970s.

Much of the tension arose because of the deeply felt differences in outlook and values expressed by the Native Americans who favored a traditional way of life and looked to AIM for help, and by those led by Tribal Council President Richard Wilson who supported U.S. government policies with their shift away from tribal tradition. The differences resulted in incredible violence and fear, much of it generated by heavily armed Wilson vigilantes who intimidated reservation residents on a regular basis through attacks that left even elders, women, and children dead or wounded.

Because appeals on behalf of Peltier were ongoing, interviews with FBI investigators are not part of *Incident at Oglala*, but interviews with U.S. attorneys convinced of the accused men's guilt are included. Much stronger, more compelling prodefendant arguments, however, are made by the accused themselves, their attorneys, other AIM members, the jury foreman for the Butler–Robideau trial, and other interviewees. Given the information and perspectives shared, most viewers are likely to side with the defendants even though exactly what happened at the Jumping Bull compound is not completely clear. The government's strategies appear to be directed more at avenging the deaths of Coler and Williams than ensuring justice, more at perpetuating failed policies than at supporting the efforts of the indigenous people to become autonomous.

The filmmakers make it absolutely clear they believe Butler, Robideau, and Peltier were prosecuted unjustly by beginning *Incident at Oglala* with this note: "At the conclusion of this film, information will be provided on how you can support Leonard Peltier." Following the end credits they urge viewers to express support by writing to the chairs of the Senate Select Committee on Indian Affairs, the House Civil and Constitutional Rights Subcommittee, and the president of the United States. They also invite viewers to contact the Leonard Peltier Defense Committee for further information about the case. Their openness about their perspective is helpful and underscores the fact that documentaries are always interpretations rather than completely objective accounts. Because they incorporate dissenting voices and so carefully scrutinize evidence, the declaration of their position makes their presentation more rather than less trustworthy.

*Incident at Oglala* takes a particularly dramatic event, identifies circumstances that help explain why it could happen when it did, and then investigates the consequences for those most deeply involved. The film can not only make viewers aware of the specific historical and contemporary events it chronicles, but also introduce them to the serious problems Native Americans continue to face within a country that has frequently treated them unjustly. Viewers who are prompted to investigate further on their own may want to begin with Leonard Peltier's own *Prison Writings: My Life Is My Sun Dance* or the *Trial of Leonard Peltier* by criminologist Jim Messerschmidt.

**Works Cited:** Messerschmidt, Jim. *Trial of Leonard Peltier*. Boston: South End Press, 1983; Peltier, Leonard. *Prison Writings: My Life Is My Sun Dance*. New York: St. Martin's Press, 2000.

## *The Indian in the Cupboard* (1995)

Director: Frank Oz

Cast: Hal Scardino (Omri), Litefoot (Little Bear), Lindsay Crouse (Jane), Richard Jenkins (Victor), Rishi Bhat (Patrick)

Length: 97 min.

Rating: PG

Children's Fantasy: An introduction to Native American culture through play

*The Indian in the Cupboard* is a fascinating family film. At face value, it is about magic and children's ways of dealing with themselves, their peers, and the world. Underneath, this film is complex and requires a well-developed adult intellect to understand the feasibility of the phenomenon as well as the moral and ethical issues it presents.

The film revolves around an old wooden cupboard Omri receives for his birthday. His mother finds a key that unlocks the magic properties of the cupboard. Place an inanimate object like the plastic Indian his friend Patrick gives him in the cupboard, turn the key, and the plastic figure comes alive. This puts into motion an incredible assortment of adventures Omri and Patrick experience with Little Bear, Boone, and a variety of other toys that are brought to life.

Omri and Patrick are faced with huge moral and ethical dilemmas: What are the consequences of playing God in the lives of these animated beings that are literally snatched from the conscious worlds they inhabit to the bedroom reality of Omri? There is enough here to write a doctoral dissertation.

The selection of *The Indian in the Cupboard* for this category was based on the authenticity of Litefoot as a historical character. His recollection of his identity is solid and will be instructive to the children who see what he does and listen to what he says. For example, in the scene where Omri gives Litefoot a toy tepee to live in, Litefoot reacts with an astonished "What is this?" He then requests the materials to construct a longhouse which, he informs Omri, is the shelter characteristic of his people. Through scenes like this, the cultural value of the film shines through.

*The Indian in the Cupboard* can be used to teach about a variety of issues, such as morality, ethics, ethnicity, and culture. It can be approached from a child or an adult perspective without losing relevance or the interest of the audience. Viewers can turn to Pauline Turner Strong's essay "Playing Indian in the 1990s" for an analysis that focuses specifically on *The Indian in the Cupboard* and children's films. An appropriate and accessible accompaniment to the film for viewers who want to learn more about the indigenous peoples of North American is *The Complete Idiot's Guide to Native American History* written by Walter C. Fleming (Kickapoo), an associate professor and director of Native American Studies at Montana State University. Another source definitely worth pursuing is the Smithsonian Institution's "Critical Bibliography on North American Indians, for K–12," beginning with the Foreword and Preface.

**Works Cited:** Anthropology Outreach Office. "Critical Bibliography on North American Indians, for K–12." Smithsonian Institution, 1996. http://www.nmai.si.edu/anthro/outreach/Indbibl/bibliogr.html; Fleming, Walter C. *The Complete Idiot's Guide to Native American History*. New York: Alpha Books, 2003; Strong, Pauline Turner. "Playing Indian in the 1990s: *Pocahontas* and *The Indian in the Cupboard*." In *Hollywood's Indian: The Portrayal of the Native American in Film*. 187–205. Lexington: University Press of Kentucky, 1998.

## *Lakota Woman* (1994)

Director: Frank Pierson

Cast: Irene Bedard (Mary Crow Dog), Casey Camp-Horinek (Elsie Flood), Tantoo Cardinal (Emily Moore), Pato Hoffman (Spencer), Lawrence Bayne (Russell Means), Michael Horse (Dennis Banks)

Length: 113 min.

Rating: Not Rated

Political Drama: Coming-of-age narrative linked to the 1973 siege of Wounded Knee

As a precredit title indicates, *Lakota Woman* "is the story of Mary Brave Woman who survived the siege at Wounded Knee, Pine Ridge, South Dakota, 1973." It is based on the biography *Lakota Woman* by Mary Crow Dog (later named Mary Brave Woman) and Richard Erdoes and begins with Mary's voice-over account of the stories her grandfather told about the Ghost Dance and the U.S. army's massacre of the Lakota Sioux at

Wounded Knee in the nineteenth century. Mary loses her secure place in her family and her Indian nation when she and her sister are sent to St. Tristan's, a Christian boarding school that replaces their native culture, including their language and history, with a more mainstream U.S. culture.

After her sister runs away, Mary manages to get herself expelled, but when she returns home, she clashes with her mother and begins a self-destructive mode of behavior that she describes as "one big wild party." She stops drifting when she meets Spencer, an Apache working with the American Indian Movement (AIM), and becomes deeply committed to the movement. Though pregnant at the time, she takes an active part in the seventy-three-day siege of Wounded Knee and finds renewed strength and purpose in her solidarity with other Native Americans who dedicate themselves to the preservation of their culture, their lands, and their rights.

*Lakota Woman* is one of several film accounts of the siege at Wounded Knee and the events surrounding that political action by AIM and its supporters. This chronicle is from a woman's point of view and is introduced explicitly as such in an opening statement: "This is the way [Mary Crow Dog] saw it." Throughout the film, Mary focuses on her life and the events that led her from content child to rebellious adolescent to mature woman. When she returns from St. Tristan's, her mother Emily, a nurse, describes her as a "person permanently on the warpath," and at another point, Mary describes herself as a drifter, but her association with AIM leads her back to her roots, to her grandfather, to her Aunt Elsie Flood, a medicine woman, and to political awareness. For her, despite the precariousness of the situation much of the time, Wounded Knee, the place where her first child is born, becomes the place where Mary finds her center, her voice, where she experiences great happiness, where she, with the rest of the Wounded Knee community, "reached out and touched [their] history." She sees the event, despite its violence and the arrests and broken promises that followed, as full of promise.

*Lakota Woman* is a coming-of-age film that focuses on an individual's journey to a strong self-identity, but it is more, since Mary Brave Woman's journey is intricately intertwined with a political awakening that takes her back to Lakota history and culture while simultaneously propelling her forward through meaningful political action. Her personal growth depends on her integration into a community with clear and meaningful purpose. The two are inseparable, making *Lakota Woman* an excellent starting point for discussions of the relative importance of individuality and community within various cultures, the role of cultural history in personal identity development, and the significance of active engagement in personal empowerment.

**Work Cited:** Dog, Mary Crow, and Richard Erdoes. *Lakota Woman.* New York: HarperPerennial, 1991.

## *Lighting the Seventh Fire* (1999)

Director: Sandra Osawa

Distributor: Upstream Productions

Length: 48 min.

Rating: Not Rated

Documentary: A clash of cultures centered on fishing rights in Wisconsin

At the beginning of *Lighting the Seventh Fire*, the following information appears on screen: "There is a Chippewa Indian prophecy that speaks of 7 fires, representing 7 periods of time. Today many Chippewas see the return to traditional ways as a sign that the 7th fire is beginning. The reemergence of traditional fishing rights reflect both the start of a new fire and the end of the previous fire, marked by a loss of traditions and intense conflicts." The video moves on to show the 1492 Chippewa Land Base and briefly examine the treaties through which the Chippewa lost or ceded 19 million acres of that land to the U.S. government but reserved their fishing and hunting rights on the ceded land. The difficulty of asserting those rights then becomes the video's central focus.

Though federal courts have upheld the treaty rights when challenged, opposition to the Chippewa's (Ojibwé's) exercise of those rights was galvanized in northern Wisconsin in 1985 when the Native Americans, as part of their return to tradition, left their reservation to spearfish. They became the focal point of an inordinate amount of hostility and racist activity that ranged from particularly ugly insults to death threats. The controversy led to the appointment of the Ad Hoc Committee on Racism in Wisconsin and a mandate to teach Native American history in the state's public schools. The controversy also strengthened the resolve of American Indians like Tom Maulson, President of Lac du Flambeau, to become more intensely involved with his people and his native traditions.

The spearfishing controversy, the racism it revealed, the studies it sparked, and the official responses it evoked are chronicled in *Lighting the Seventh Fire*, primarily through interviews and footage documenting a number of the protests. That the filmmakers as well as the Chippewa envision a positive end to the conflict is suggested through the return to the prophecy with which the film began: "The first 5 fires foretold of the Chippewa journey to the Great Lakes area, the coming of the fair-skinned race to America, and a time period of intense struggle. The 6th fire predicted a time of great loss, to be followed by the 7th fire, a time when lost traditions would be renewed."

Unfortunately the struggle is ongoing. *Lighting the Seventh Fire* can serve to introduce and document one aspect of the struggle, prompting viewers to investigate further the history of indigenous Americans and the treaty rights they continue to pursue. Larry Nesper's *The Walleye War: The Struggle for Ojibwé Spearfishing and Treaty Rights* could provide a next step in that study.

**Work Cited:** Nesper, Larry. *The Walleye War: The Struggle for Ojibwé Spearfishing and Treaty Rights*. Lincoln: University of Nebraska Press, 2002.

## *Naturally Native* (1999)

Directors: Valerie Red-Horse and Jennifer Wynne Farmer

Cast: Valerie Red-Horse (Vickie Lewis Bighawk), Irene Bedard (Tanya Lewis), Kimberly Norris Guerro (Karen Lewis), Pato Hoffman (Steve Bighawk), Mark Abbott (Mark Bighawk)

Length: 108 min.

Rating: PG-13

Family Drama: Middle-class sisters combine traditional Native American and contemporary values in their lives

In 1972, Native American sisters Vickie, Karen, and Tanya Lewis were adopted by a European American couple after their mother, an alcoholic, died and their impoverished father could not care for them. Twenty-six years later, Vic lives with her husband, Steve, and their two children, Courtney and Derek, in the spacious home left to her and her sisters by their adoptive parents. Karen has just graduated from college with an MBA and is about to accept a job in Chicago, while Tanya is between careers after concluding she would not succeed as an actor. Both are temporarily living with Vic and her family.

Vic was seven when she left the Viejas Reservation, but she returned as an adult to spend some time with her natural father. While there, she learned much from him about herbs and their medicinal and cosmetic value. When Karen tells Vic and Tanya about her dream to develop her own business, Vic immediately responds by showing them her herb garden and suggesting they start a business producing and marketing herbal medicines. The three quickly explore the idea, redirect their focus from medicines to cosmetics, and begin turning a dream they now share into reality. As they perfect their formulas for lotions and shampoos, they develop a business plan and begin looking for the $25,000 necessary to launch their Naturally Native products.

Securing financing proves difficult. Rejection follows rejection, each integrally intertwined with questions of their Native American identity, of how the women see themselves and how others see them. At one point they are asked to provide the government-issued identification cards that indicate their blood quantum by Indian nation to prove they are Native Americans. Interpersonal crises also surface, but the sisters' mutual support, persistence, willingness to reconsider some of their choices, and return to their Viejas roots lead not only to a successful business enterprise but also to a clear sense of their identities as women with ties to family, friends, their tribal nation, and the larger world.

The origins and development of *Naturally Native* parallel the story of Vic, Karen, and Tanya and attests to Valerie Red-Horse's own persistence and to the combination of talent, business acumen, and good fortune that helped her realize her dream of a career as a filmmaker. Her unhappiness about being turned down for a script development grant juxtaposed with a casual comment by her husband—"Maybe that's [the rejection] your real story!"—became the impetus for *Naturally Native*, the first Hollywood feature film written, produced, directed, edited by, and starring American Indian women and funded entirely by an American Indian tribal nation, the Mashantucket Pequot (Red-Horse).

Red-Horse has indicated that Tanya, Karen, and Vickie represent various stages of her life. Tanya, the youngest, is more interested in romance than in her heritage while Karen is looking for her identity through her education and has learned to navigate mainstream culture well. Vic, having steeped herself in American Indian culture, is not only secure in that culture but also very knowledgeable and articulate about issues of concern to indigenous peoples, such as Bureau of Indian Affairs policies, alcoholism and poverty on reservations, the use of Indian names for sports teams, and the usurpation of American Indian sacred rituals by the devotees of New Age religions. References to these issues are integrated into the action somewhat self-consciously at times, but the movie remains an entertaining and engaging story.

By articulating the issues as she does, Red-Horse provides audiences with points of departure for further research. For example, an issue Vickie raises is the blood quantum requirement imposed by the federal government on American Indians who want to be recognized as such. What are the ramifications of this policy? Why was it written? How is it enforced? Blood quantum has been an issue for African Americans as well as Native Americans. When? Where? Why? How does the use of the concept differ in its application to the two groups?

In telling Vickie, Karen, and Tanya Lewis's story, *Naturally Native* tells an acculturation success story, a story of women from a historically underrepresented group who hold on to the traditional values of their native culture while adapting to their contemporary circumstances. The film is unique in its focus on contemporary middle-class Native American women, on their dreams, their personal anxieties, their romantic and family relationships, and their political and cultural concerns. Its fresh perspective can help counter the stereotypical depictions of American Indians that have dominated commercial cinema. It assures us that members of traditionally underrepresented groups in our society have many stories to tell, and given the chance, they can tell them in ways that are meaningful to their own communities as well as to society as a whole.

**Work Cited:** Red-Horse, Valerie. "Naturally Native . . . the Journey." Tarzana, CA: Red-Horse Productions, 2001.

## *On and Off the Res with Charlie Hill* (2000)

Producer and director: Sandra Sunrising Osawa

Distributor: Upstream Productions

Length: 59 min.

Rating: Not Rated

Documentary: Biography of a Native American stand-up comedian

The notion that Native Americans have no sense of humor crops up regularly in *On and Off the Res with Charlie Hill*, and just as regularly it is countered by Charlie Hill himself or by one of the other people interviewed in this video. Charlie Hill's principal means of rebutting the notion is his own humor, which is well documented in this exploration of his work as a stand-up comic and an American Indian. Video clips of Hill's television and comedy club appearances, and interviews with Hill, other comedians and activists, and family members offer further evidence of the rich, satiric humor that justifies this video tribute.

Hill in effect narrates *On and Off the Res* via interviews that allow him to tell his story from childhood through adolescence and three decades as a successful comedian. He takes viewers to his childhood home on the Oneida reservation in Wisconsin, speaks of the strong family relationships that helped shape his comedic sense, and guides us from one performance to another, including appearances on "The Big Show" with Steve Allen, "Latino Laugh Festival," "The Richard Pryor Show," "The Tonight Show" with Johnny Carson, and Canada's "Indian Time." Hill's observations and insights are complemented by those of, among others, scholar, historian, and satirist Vine Deloria, Jr., comedian Dick Gregory, film actors Floyd Westerman and Evan Adams, and activist Dennis Means.

Astute and often stinging, Hill's humor revolves around the history and politics of the United States of America, or, in his words, "Europe, Jr.," as these have affected American Indians, their lands and cultures. Riffs on Thanksgiving, Columbus Day, broken treaties, Indian mascots, sports team names, the Bureau of Indian Affairs, and European Americans' sense of entitlement—all are part of his repertoire. Sharp and uncompromising, his wit can make listeners sit up and take notice, can initiate reflection, and effect a shift in perspective.

Given this, *On and Off the Res with Charlie Hill* should prove an appropriate and effective tool in discussions of Native American cultures, especially since Hill addresses ongoing issues of great significance but coats his comments with engaging humor and human values. His career illustrates how Native Americans use humor to negotiate the injustices they have experienced as a people and as individuals while also making the larger population aware of these injustices. Several Native American filmmakers share Hill's commitment to incorporating humor into their work, including Chris Eyre and Sherman Alexie. Included in their film repertoires are *Smoke Signals*, *Skins*, and *The Business of Fancy Dancing*.

**Works Cited:** *The Business of Fancy Dancing*. Directed by Sherman Alexie. Performances by Evan Adams, Michelle St. John, Gene Tagaban, and Swil Kanim. Outrider Pictures, 2001; *Skins*. Directed by Chris Eyre. Performances by Eric Schweig, Graham Greene, Gary Farmer, and Lois Red Elk. First Look Pictures, 2002; *Smoke Signals*. Directed by Chris Eyre. Performances by Adam Beach, Evan Adams, Tantoo Cardinal, Gary Farmer, and Irene Bedard. Miramax, 1998.

## *Pocahontas* (1995)

Directors: Mike Gabriel and Eric Goldberg

Voices: Irene Bedard and Judy Kuhn (Pocahontas), Mel Gibson (John Smith), Linda Hunt (Grandmother Willow), James Apaumut Fall (Kocoum), David Ogden Stiers (Governor Ratcliffe/Wiggins), Russell Means (Powhatan)

Length: 81 min.

Rating: G

Animated Drama: Intercultural romance and conflict in the seventeenth century

The story of the legendary Pocahontas comes to life through the magic of Disney's animation. Although historical accuracy has been sacrificed to increase the entertainment value for its targeted younger audience, directors Gabriel and Goldberg attempt to show in broad, simple—or simplistic—strokes some of the cultural differences between the Native Americans and the English colonists. Powhatan's tribe is seen as communal and harmonious. Members live in peace with each other and with nature in a virtual paradise. The English, on the other hand, are exemplified by their despicable leader, Governor Ratcliffe, and are depicted as greedy, exploitive, and violent fortune hunters.

The film's heroine, Pocahontas, is drawn with Barbie-like adult features even though, historically, she was actually only eleven or twelve years of age when she met John Smith in 1608. She is intelligent, curious, thoughtful, observant, courageous, and athletic. Smith is given Mel Gibson's voice and portrayed as a strikingly handsome, appropriately Ken-like adventurer, with many of the same qualities as Pocahontas, though he assumes he is culturally more advanced and, therefore, superior. The film is formulaic and uses most of the devices Disney has made famous, including the use of mischievous animals and other natural phenomena with anthropomorphic qualities, such as a talking tree called Grandmother Willow.

The Disney studio has been heavily criticized for the racist and sexist subject matter found in many of its previous thirty-two animated features. In this film, the studio seems to have gone out of its way to develop a story that celebrates interracial relationships, anticolonialism, ecology, and some feminist values, while taking a negative stand on elitism, imperialism, and greed. Sometimes this comes across as preachy, but the film is a small positive step in Disney's efforts to make products that are more culturally sensitive.

When embedded in memorable songs, the messages are palatable. It can be argued that the film's soundtrack actually carries the film while several delightful songs add social commentary about the cultural context of both the Seneca and the British. One song in particular deserves mention: "Savages, Savages" illustrates the differences each culture brings into its social interaction and demonstrates how differences can quickly be used to justify hate and scorn for another group.

The heart of *Pocahontas* is the love affair between Pocahontas and John Smith, which crescendos into her heroic stand to save Smith's life after the death of her Native American suitor Kocoum. Kocoum's death has a domino effect that leads to an impending battle between natives and colonists and sets the stage for Smith's heroism as he takes a bullet intended for Chief Powhatan, Pocahontas's father. Uncharacteristically, the film ends with Pocahontas refusing to return to England with Smith even though her refusal leaves both hero and heroine heartbroken and, arguably, the audience less than satisfied. The ending parallels that of the Hollywood classic *Casablanca* in that the protagonists choose duty over personal desire, community well being over individual gratification.

Even with its historical inaccuracies, this film can be used effectively to teach about Native American culture. Educators will need to research the actual historical circumstances surrounding Pocahontas's interaction with John Smith from both European and Native American perspectives. Potential starting points for that research include David Price's *Love and Hate in Jamestown: John Smith, Pocahontas, and the Heart of a New Nation* and Paula Gunn Allen's *Pocahontas: Medicine Woman, Spy, Entrepreneur, Diplomat*. They may also want to check other responses to the film that are available in print or online, such as Jacquelyn Kilpatrick's *Cineaste* article "Disney's 'Politically Correct' Pocahontas" and the Pocahontas Web site hosted by Lehigh University.

**Works Cited:** Allen, Paula Gunn. *Pocahontas: Medicine Woman, Spy, Entrepreneur, Diplomat*. San Francisco: HarperSanFrancisco, 2003; Kilpatrick, Jacquelyn. "Disney's 'Politically Correct' Pocahontas." *Cineaste* 21, no. 3 (1995): 34–35; "Pocahontas." Lehigh University. http://www.Lehigh.edu/~ejg1/pocahontas/poca-title.html; Price, David. *Love and Hate in Jamestown: John Smith, Pocahontas, and the Heart of a New Nation*. Westminster, MD: Knopf, 2003.

## *The Return of Navajo Boy* (2001)

Producers and directors: Jeff Spitz and Bennie Klain

Distributor: University of California Extension, Center for Media and Independent Learning

Length: 57 min.

Rating: Not Rated

Documentary: Biography, film history, and social critique

*The Return of Navajo Boy* explores three intertwined stories. *Navaho Boy: The Monument Valley Story*, a short fictional film made by Robert J. Kennedy and Rex Fleming in the early 1950s, sparked the first of the three stories. Kennedy's son Bill and documentary filmmaker Jeff Spitz began with a desire to return *Navaho Boy* to the Navajo people, but they were also interested in identifying the individuals who starred, without credit, in the film. Pursuing and reaching their goal took them to Monument Valley and resulted in increasing involvement in the lives of Elsie Mae Cly Begay and her extended family, several of whom appeared in *Navaho Boy*.

During their research and their visits with Elsie Begay, the filmmakers learned much about Navajo culture and the history of Monument Valley. They also learned, from the personal perspectives of Elsie and her family, of the impact government policies have had on their lives. Two policies in particular stand out: the placement of Native American children in European American families or institutions with no regard for the wishes of their natural families; and the withholding of information about the health hazards associated with uranium. The connection between these two policies becomes clear when Elsie, seeing shots from *Navaho Boy* of her mother holding her youngest brother, breaks into tears and links missionaries taking her two-year-old brother John Wayne Cly (he was named after—and by—the actor) to her mother's death apparently due to a respiratory illness related to radiation exposure. Though the missionaries promised to return John to his family at age six, they did not, and the family lost touch completely.

Serendipitously, forty years after being taken from the Navajo reservation, John saw an article that combined coverage of testimony by Bernie Cly at a uranium miner's rally with a Spitz interview about his bringing *Navaho Boy* back to the Clys. The information in the article was enough to prompt John to contact the Clys and led to a deeply emotional reunion with his sister Elsie and the rest of his family. Spitz was on hand to document the reunion, making the return of John Wayne Cly to his family the second story covered in his film. The third chronicles the ongoing repercussions of living and working around uranium as well as efforts by victims of uranium-related illnesses to secure compensation from the U.S. government.

Given its interwoven stories, *The Return of Navajo Boy* can enliven discussions on several aspects of Navajo—and more broadly, Native American—experience. The documentary covers both historical and contemporary issues and shows how government policies affect individuals over generations. Originally meant to refer to Bill Kennedy's intent to give the film *Navaho Boy* to the Navajos, *The Return of Navajo Boy* has been identified primarily with John Wayne Cly's very moving reunion with his family. Though ending happily, his story can help viewers understand the pain caused to both children and their families when a policy of assimilation meant children could be taken from their homes and legally placed with other families or in boarding schools with the specific intent of cutting their ties to their native language and culture.

When granting Spitz formal permission to include them in his documentary, the Clys did so on the condition the film direct some attention to the health hazards associated with uranium mining (Sula). Spitz does so. For example, he chronicles Bernie Cly's testimony at the April 1998 uranium miners' rally in Window Rock, but ultimately he urges viewers to follow this issue via the worldwide web and provides them with a place to begin. The site offers articles about the uranium issues as well as about *The Return of Navajo Boy*, among them a very comprehensive essay, "Mystery in the Desert," written by Mike Sula and originally published in the *Chicago Reader*.

**Work Cited:** Sula, Mike. "Mystery in the Desert." http://www.navajoboy.com/artread.htm.

## *Rocks with Wings* (2001)

Director: Rick Derby

Distributor: Shiprock Productions

Length: 113 min.

Rating: Not Rated

Sports Documentary: African and Native American cultures intertwine to produce a winning high school basketball team

*Hoosiers* and *Hoop Dreams* are two basketball movies that have been recognized as exemplary. *Rocks with Wings* belongs in that same category. Director Rick Derby has crafted a complex but very entertaining documentary about winning not just basketball games, but winning in life. The tale encompasses members of a Navajo community, European American assistant coaches, and an African American head coach. It examines the strengths and weaknesses of the cultural traditions of family and community as well as issues of gender and hierarchy. It is a bittersweet tale full of lessons for our lives and times.

The story begins in Shiprock, a small community in the heart of Navajo country that is as culturally rich as it is economically poor. The Shiprock High School boys' sports teams dominate the community's attention while the girls' basketball program functions as just something for the girls to do. Up the road in Kirtland, the girls' team has won seven consecutive state championships. The Lady Chieftains pose no threat to Kirtland Central's powerhouse until Jerry Richardson arrives to coach the Shiprock team. In less than four years, the Lady Chieftains face Kirtland Central for the state championship, but on the eve of the big game, the team virtually falls apart as tensions that have been fermenting for months spill out from the coaches, the team mother, and the players. These tensions, a complicated mix of race/ethnicity, gender, age, culture, and tradition have become a powder keg ready to explode. It does. Instead of destroying the team, however, the explosion clears the air and draws the team closer together. Even though they lose in overtime by one point, they win the right to rededicate themselves as a team and to compete again for the championship. The following year the Lady Chieftains do win the championship and go on to repeat that feat for four consecutive years.

The element that is most likely to captivate both adolescent and adult viewers of *Rocks with Wings* is footage from the actual championship games and the broadcast dialogue that captures not only the excitement of the games, but the intensity of the fans' reactions. As important are Derby's intersecting interviews with the players, coaches, and community members that show how their different assumptions, expectations, and cultural values led initially to misunderstandings and friction. *Rocks with Wings*, however, goes further, inviting viewers to explore the spiritual journey that each player, and by extension each human being, must take to realize her or his potential.

Throughout the film, Derby uses the art of Navajo weaving as a metaphor that connects individuals and generations. The positioning of the "spirit line" connects each weaving to the next, just as their work together connected the Lady Chieftains and their coach, Jerry Richardson. The spirit line also presents a way out of a woven pattern. A willingness to listen to each other became a way out for the players and their coach when they found themselves boxed in and stymied by misunderstandings.

The film is dedicated to Jerry Richardson. His vision was both the spirit and the heart line that wove the Lady Chieftains into a winning unit. His influence continued in the lives of the players and the entire Shiprock community after he left to coach at the University of Central Florida and even after his untimely tragic death in a car accident. The story of Richardson, the Lady Chieftans, and the Shiprock community is full of potential for teaching about the intersection of diverse cultures in our pluralistic society, and about how understanding and appreciation of diverse cultural perspectives can bring people together in positive ways.

## *Skins* (2002)

Director: Chris Eyre

Cast: Eric Schweig (Rudy Yellow Lodge), Graham Greene (Mogie Yellow Lodge), Gary Farmer (Vernell Weasel Tail), Noah Watts (Herbie Yellow Lodge), Lois Red Elk (Aunt Helen), Michelle Thrash (Stella)

Length: 84 min.

Rating: R

Family Drama: An exploration of love, frustration, alcoholism, family ties, violence, and humor

Rudy Yellow Lodge divides his time among fulfilling his duties as a cop on the Pine Ridge reservation in South Dakota, keeping tabs on his alcoholic older brother Mogie, mentoring his nephew Herbie, carrying out vigilante "justice" in the area, seeking refuge in a relationship with Stella, the wife of a first cousin, and trying to maintain a deep commitment to a spiritual life and to his heritage. Rudy sees this commitment as justifying his vigilante activities (breaking the knees of two teens who killed another, setting fire to a liquor store), but he is increasingly frustrated and tortured by his actions, especially when Mogie is severely burned in the liquor store fire. Mogie's burns send him to the hospital where he is diagnosed with alcohol-related medical problems that are life threatening. Mogie dies shortly after this diagnosis, but not before Rudy confesses his vigilante actions to him and Mogie encourages Rudy to take a different tack, that is to express his anger, frustration, despair, and disappointment symbolically—on the face of Mount Rushmore's George Washington sculpture. Rudy does. The action leaves Washington with a giant red tear running down his face. It leaves Rudy smiling, relaxed, satisfied.

*Skins* underscores the deep love and commitment Rudy and Mogie have for each other and for their Lakota heritage though their interaction at times belies this. Mogie, a Vietnam veteran who earned three purple hearts, is seldom sober and seems to be picked up regularly by the cops, Rudy among them. Director Chris Eyre, however, "wanted to humanize a social untouchable, . . . to put a face to the alcoholics that people see in . . . any reservation border town in this country" (Brockman 16), and he succeeds in making Mogie a person who retains his humanity and his sense of humor under the most painful circumstances. Eyre does this primarily through Mogie's relationship with Rudy, but it is also evident in his interaction with his son Herbie.

When Mogie asks Rudy to help him blow off the nose of the Washington sculpture, he suggests it will give the people a good laugh and adds, "maybe that's all we need." Actor Eric Schweig, after reminding viewers that the pre-Columbian indigenous population in the Americas was around 100 million and now is less than three million, suggests that "sometimes laughing is all you have." Gary Farmer, who plays Mogie's friend Vernell, says "how you survive . . . [is] by maintaining the ability to laugh at the harshest circumstances." Eyre was drawn to *Skins* because of its humor (Eyre). Humor is essential for Mogie, Rudy, and the other people on the reservation who are able to retain their humanity. But not everyone succeeds in doing this, given the poverty, the unemployment, and the loss of hope.

Actor Graham Green quotes Lyle Long Claws, a medicine man, when he says, "Before the healing can take place, the poison must be exposed," and Schweig suggests *Skins* "will force people to look at themselves and look at what they're doin' to their lives" (Eyre). Besides alcoholism and poverty, the movie shows domestic abuse, violence, and murder, the poisons that have infected the people of Pine Ridge. *Skins* also shows healing elements of Lakota culture and spirituality that, coupled with humor, do offer hope. It is on this note that the film ends.

*Skins* will have special meaning for Native American viewers but should not be limited to them since its themes are universal and its portrayal of contemporary American Indian lives and culture can lead to greater understanding among Indians themselves and among people within other cultural groups. One of a small but growing number of feature films made by Native Americans, *Skins* is to be celebrated and studied.

**Work Cited:** Brockman, Joshua. "Telling the Truth From Inside Indian Country." *New York Times*, September 29, 2002: 15–16. *Skins*, DVD. Directed by Chris Eyre. First Look Media, 2003.

## *Skinwalkers* (2002)

Director: Chris Eyre

Cast: Adam Beach (Jim Chee), Wes Studi (Joe Leaphorn), Alex Rice (Janet Pete), Michael Greyeyes (Dr. Stone), Sheila Tousey (Emma Leaphorn), Saginaw Grant (Wilson Sam), Nicholas Bartolo (Tommy Nakai)

Length: 100 min.

Rating: Not Rated

Mystery: Traditional Native American values versus contemporary perspectives

Lt. Joe Leaphorn, an experienced detective, reluctantly teams up with Officer Jim Chee of the Navajo Tribal Police to investigate the death of a medicine man on the Diné (Navajo) reservation. Leaphorn has rejected his traditional Native American culture and absorbed the values of mainstream society, including empirical investigative methods. Chee, however, embraces Navajo tradition and spirituality and is being mentored by Wilson Sam to take on the role of a medicine man. Their investigation expands when two more medicine men, including Wilson, are killed. The evidence suggests to Chee that the deaths are the work of an avenging spirit, a *skinwalker*, but Leaphorn interprets the evidence more pragmatically. Their separate approaches have them looking at different aspects of crime scenes and evidence, but ultimately they lead to the same suspect at the same time—Dr. Stone, an extremely competent practitioner of modern medicine who takes on the trappings of a skinwalker to avenge his father's suicide and his mother's illness.

The skinwalker investigation begins shortly after Leaphorn and his wife Emma, at her insistence, move from Phoenix to the reservation. Emma wants to come home to the reservation after battling cancer, but she is back only a short time before the illness returns. In contrast to her usually grouchy, abrupt husband, Emma is warm, hospitable, and, like Chee, very much in tune with Diné culture. Though Leaphorn does not believe in the supernatural, share Emma's connection to the land of the Navajo, or see a need for social amenities, his deep love for Emma and his readiness to respond to her needs are apparent. His role as supportive spouse balances that of hard-nosed detective.

Chee, who lost his parents as a child and was taken in by Wilson Sam, balances his role as a police officer with that of healer. He can lose control when faced with some situations, most notably child abuse, but he is basically responsible, good-humored, and intelligent. He and Leaphorn learn to respect each other. Both Leaphorn and Stone turn away from their native culture, but with different consequences. For Leaphorn, the rejection is not irrevocable; for Stone, it is, and the hatred behind it leads to murder.

*Skinwalkers* works as an engrossing mystery and as an engaging story that can be used to open discussion about many issues, among them the role of culture in peoples' lives, the importance of balancing the past and the present, government and corporate intrusions on native lands, the cost of revenge, and Diné values and spirituality. There are many resources one can access to help provide further background for such discussions. Among them are the Smithsonian Institution's National Museum of the American Indian and Peter Nabokov and Vine Deloria, Jr.'s *Native American Testimony*.

**Works Cited:** Nabokov, Peter, and Vine Deloria, Jr. *Native American Testimony: A Chronicle of Indian–White Relations from Prophecy to the Present, 1492–2000*. Hopkinton, MA: Penguin Books, 1999; National Museum of the American Indian. Smithsonian Institution. http://www.AmericanIndian.si.edu.

## *Smoke Signals* (1998)

Director: Chris Eyre

Cast: Adam Beach (Victor Joseph), Evan Adams (Thomas Builds-the-Fire), Irene Bedard (Suzy Song), Gary Farmer (Arnold Joseph), Tantoo Cardinal (Arlene Joseph)

Length: 89 min.

Rating: PG-13

Drama: Road movie and coming-of-age narrative focusing on father-son relationships

*Smoke Signals* chronicles the lives of two Coeur d'Alene Indians from infancy into early adulthood. Besides having the same tribal affiliation and living in the same Idaho community, Victor and Thomas are connected through Victor's father, Arnold, who saved Thomas during a July 4, 1976, fire that killed Thomas's parents. They are very different in physical appearance, temperament, and worldview. Thomas is small in stature, wears large, dark-framed glasses, and tells stories incessantly, whether he has a willing listener or not. He is gregarious, outspoken, and open. Victor is tall and physically imposing, but taciturn and apparently unable to forgive his alcoholic father for abandoning him a decade earlier. His outlook is summed up when he says to Thomas: "Don't you know anything? People are awful . . . you can't trust anybody." When Arnold dies in Arizona, it becomes Victor's task to retrieve his father's ashes and his truck. Thomas offers Victor the money for the trip—with a condition: Victor must take Thomas with him. Victor reluctantly agrees, and the two set off on what becomes, with

Thomas's incessant pushing, Victor's journey toward reconciliation with his father and the world.

*Smoke Signals* touches on serious issues affecting American Indians, among them poverty, unemployment, alcoholism, family violence, alienation, and media myths, but through wry humor, low-key playfulness, and affection for its characters, it offers a more multidimensional portrait of Native American culture than is usual in film. Despite his best efforts to maintain a mean warrior look, for example, Victor can't resist enjoying his own riff on John Wayne's teeth: "Are they false or are they real? Are they plastic or are they steel?" Medicine-man-initiate Thomas mixes flights of word fancy with down-to-earth observations as when Victor asks him how he'd heard of his father's death: "I heard it on the wind. I heard it from the birds. I felt it in the sunlight. And your Mom was sittin' here cryin!" And when Victor and Thomas trade a ride to the bus stop for one of Thomas's stories, the young women providing the ride not only point out "We're Indians, remember? We barter," but after hearing the story also remark that it is "A fine example of the oral tradition."

The film's levity and self-aware stance vis-à-vis American Indian myth and reality do not undercut its seriousness. The first U.S. feature made by Native Americans (producers, writer, director, actors, and crew) and based on short stories from Sherman Alexie's *The Lone Ranger and Tonto Fistfight in Heaven*, *Smoke Signals* explores interdependence, healing, friendship, forgiveness, and relationships between past and present and between one generation and the next through the vignettes it embeds within its overarching story and through visual and aural poetry. Its pace is slower than many contemporary films and its interest is in interpersonal interaction rather than in action and special effects. Its glimpse of Native American culture is by turns funny, sad, moving, and life-affirming.

**Work Cited:** Alexie, Sherman. *The Lone Ranger and Tonto Fistfight in Heaven*. New York: HarperPerennial, 1994.

## *True Whispers: The Story of the Navajo Code Talkers* (2002)

Producers and directors: Valerie Red-Horse and Gale Anne Hurd

Distributor: Red-Horse Native Productions, Inc.

Length: 57 min.

Rating: Not Rated

Documentary: A story told through interviews and historical film footage

One image quietly dissolves into another as Valerie Red-Horse tells the story of the World War II Navajo Code Talkers through images and the words of the Code Talkers themselves. The images depict the beauty of the Navajo, or Diné, landscape, the faces of the Navajo Marine veterans as they talk about their experiences as code talkers, and the devastation of some of World War II's bloodiest battles. Through these images, Red-Horse contrasts the peacefulness and beauty of the Navajos' sacred land, and some of the spiritual dimensions of Diné culture, with the horrific loss of human life at Guadalcanal, Iwa Jima, and other Pacific Islands. The story they tell is that of the Navajo Code Talkers, a special contingent of 429 Marines who developed and implemented an unbreakable communications code that proved critical in U.S. victories during World War II.

The Code Talkers' story does not begin with their recruitment and training. Rather, Red-Horse provides the context for their service by taking viewers back to an 1863 government treaty that forced the Navajo into a 300-mile walk to a small area of the 17 million acres they had previously occupied. Not only was the treaty used to justify taking Navajo lands; it was also used to justify taking Navajo children and placing them in boarding schools where they could be assimilated into mainstream culture. This was accomplished in part by absolutely forbidding them to speak Navajo or to engage in any native cultural or spiritual practices. Much of this background is given by Navajo Code Talkers who actually experienced boarding school life and the harsh punishments meted out to children discovered speaking Navajo. That they held onto their language despite these consequences became evident when the military, desperate to find a communications code the Japanese could not break, began recruiting young men fluent in both English and Navajo who could develop a code as effective as the one developed by the Cherokee and Choctaw during World War I. The Navajo Code Talkers did just that. They developed an incredibly complex code and committed it to memory, then used it successfully while serving on the front lines in major battles throughout the Pacific.

Despite their critical contributions to the success of the Pacific campaign, the Code Talkers' work was kept secret not only during the war, but for decades afterward. They did not receive veterans' benefits and were virtually forgotten until records of their work were declassified in 1968. It wasn't until 2001, after many had died, that they were awarded gold and silver medals for outstanding service. Their story, however, does not end with this recognition. As one of them suggests, their contribution was a contribution of the Navajo nation since their language belongs to all of the Navajo people. Unfortunately, the story of the Navajo nation is one of continued neglect on the part of the federal government, as is evident from statistics indicating that the employment rate among them is six times the national average and the average annual salary of Native American families is less than $12,000, two-thirds lower than the average for the rest of the nation. The Navajo Code Talkers, despite these grim statistics and their own shabby treatment as veterans who risked their lives for this country, seem to be grounded in a spirituality that allows them to focus on healing and on positive change even as they and their people struggle for life.

Valerie Red-Horse does a superb job of blending images and interviews to give the Navajo Code Talkers a voice. They tell of their boarding school experience, their recruitment, their service under harrowing battlefield circumstances, of the aftermath of the experience, and of their reintegration into their communities. They weave Navajo culture and values into their stories, making it possible for viewers to come to some understanding of their worldview and motivation. Red-Horse makes clear to viewers the ironies underlying the government's position vis-à-vis these men: its attempt to take away the Navajo language and subsequent reliance on that language at a critical time in our history; its denial of veterans' benefits while recognizing the Navajo contributions to the war effort.

*True Whispers* is not the only film that documents the history and experience of the Navajo Code Talkers, but it is arguably the most accomplished and the most comprehensive. It includes graphic war images and stories and for that reason would not be appropriate for elementary students, but for teenagers and adults, the film offers a compelling account of a chapter in our history that has been largely overlooked. It easily trumps the feature film *Windtalkers* that purports to tell this story but reduces the Code

Talkers to a problem for the film's central character, a European American. The Tribal Ink Web site provides additional information about the content and background of Red-Horse's film.

**Works Cited:** White, Cara. *"True Whispers."* Tribal Ink News, 2002. http://www.tribalink.org/archives/whispers.htm (accessed June 27, 2004); *Windtalkers*. Directed by John Woo. Performances by Nicholas Cage, Adam Beach, and Christian Slater. MGM, 2002.

## *The Vanishing American* (1925)

Director: George B. Seitz

Cast: Richard Dix (Nophaie), Noah Beery (Henry Booker), Lois Wilson (Marian Warner), Malcolm McGregor (Capt. Earl Ramsdell)

Length: 109 min.

Rating: Not Rated

Epic Drama: Relations between indigenous peoples and European Americans

Set in Monument Valley, *The Vanishing American* begins with a brief overview of various peoples who inhabited the valley over several centuries before focusing on the interaction between Native Americans and the U.S. government in the early part of the twentieth century. At that point, the story of Nophaie, a Navajo warrior, unfolds as he tries to mediate between his people and government officials. His efforts are frequently thwarted by the greed and corruption of the officials, but he holds out hope, partly because of his love for Marian Warner, a European American school teacher who encourages him to think of the United States as his country and Christianity as his religion. He and many other Native Americans volunteer for military service during World War I and fight bravely but return home to find more of their land confiscated and more of their rights curtailed. They decide to fight back—all except Nophaie, who tries to save the white settlers and mediate a peaceful settlement. He is killed in the attempt, but his sacrifice helps bring about a promise of peaceful coexistence for his people and European Americans.

*The Vanishing American* begins with a quote from Herbert Spencer: "We have unmistakable proof that throughout all past time there has been a ceaseless devouring of the weak by the strong, . . . a survival of the fittest." The conquests of the "Basket Makers" by the Slab-House People, the Slab-House People by the Cliff Dwellers, the Cliff Dwellers by a "younger, fiercer, harder people, . . . of the race we now call 'Indian,' " and the Indians by Spanish conquistadors and other European Americans illustrate this premise.

The earlier conquests are "justified" by the incompetence, indolence, pride, or naiveté of the vanquished, but the conquest of the Indians is presented more ambivalently, especially through the heroic status accorded Nophaie, through his relationship with Marian, and through the incompetence and greed of several government officials. Viewers are invited to identify with Nophaie. But who is Nophaie? He wants to save his people and is ready to be an American, to fight for his country in the hope that the "country will deal fairly with [his] people." It does not. He is willing to give up "the simple faith of his fathers" and appeal to the "God of the white man" to help his people, but finds this God willing to "let his people perish!"

As he is dying, Nophaie comes to understand a passage from the New Testament that had baffled him earlier: "He that findeth his life shall lose it; and he that loseth his life for my sake, shall find it." At the same time, he has a vision of his people coming home. Is the conquest of the Native Americans by European Americans inevitable, or can Nophaie's heroism and sacrifice prevent it? Immediately after his death, the corrupt official is replaced by someone who understands and respects the Indians, suggesting coexistence is possible and thus contradicting the premise on which the narrative is built.

Despite its contradictions, *The Vanishing American* remains an intriguing film for a number of reasons, one being the romantic interracial relationship between a Native and a European American. Even when a young white military captain comes onto the scene and falls in love with Marian, her relationship with Nophaie takes precedence. Though very respectful and reserved in each other's presence, their love for each other is evident and neither the native peoples nor the European Americans seem to question it. Of course, with Nophaie's death the possibility of their marrying ends; however, according to Angela Aleiss, their interracial relationship, was not unique in silent movies (34–35).

As Nophaie and the other Native American volunteers ride off to begin their military service, the captain looks on in awe and exclaims: "Pitiful—and tremendous! Riding away to fight for the white man!" Unpacking that exclamation could provide the starting point for a discussion of this unusually perceptive on-screen depiction of American Indians. Peter Nabokov and Vine DeLoria, Jr.'s *Native American Testimony* could be a great help.

**Works Cited:** Aleiss, Angela. "Native Americans: The Surprising Silents." *Cineaste* 21, no. 3 (1995): 34–35; Nabokov, Peter, and Vine DeLoria, Jr. *Native American Testimony: A Chronicle of Indian–White Relations from Prophecy to the Present, 1492–2000.* Hopkinton, MA: Penguin Books, 1999.

## *A Warrior in Two Worlds: The Life of Ely Parker* (1999)

Producers and directors: Richard Young and Ann Spurling

Distributor: Chip Taylor Communications

Narrator: Wes Studi

Length: 55 min.

Rating: Not Rated

Documentary: Biography that depicts the costs of assimilation

*A Warrior in Two Worlds* is the amazing story of Ely Parker, a Seneca born in 1828. His mother prophesied at his birth that he would become a great leader in both the Seneca's and the white man's worlds. It would not take long for the prophecy to be realized. Ely took his name from the missionary school he attended. One summer, while working at a stable tending horses, he had an encounter with some British soldiers who mocked him for his use of English. He vowed he would master the language so that no one could ever scorn him again. He later attended Yates Academy. Though the only Native American in the school, his academic determination quickly distinguished him as one of its top students. His academic and social skills were soon utilized by the Seneca nation in negotiations with the state and federal governments over land and treaty rights and, while still a teenager, he interpreted and signed treaties on behalf of the chiefs of the Seneca nation.

By the time Parker turned forty-one, he had been a Seneca chief, a federal engineer, a Civil War secretary, and a significant participant in General Lee's surrender at Appomattox. His skills and his friendship with Ulysses S. Grant elevated him from captain to brigadier general. In 1867, he shocked Washington, D.C., society by announcing his engagement to an 18-year-old white debutante. When Grant became president in 1869, he named Parker the first Native American Commissioner of Indian Affairs. At this point in Parker's career, almost anyone would agree that his life of service to Native Americans as well as to the United States of America had been exemplary. However, this appointment may well have pushed Parker from being a person who had successfully bridged two cultures to one who accepted assimilation as a way of life. The change is apparent in his backing an army officer responsible for killing innocent Native Americans. Additional controversies led Parker to resign his position in 1871 and to retreat into the private sector, where he worked as an obscure clerk for the last nineteen years of his life.

The Ely Parker story is a poignant example of the dangers historically underrepresented ethnic people encounter as they straddle ties to their first culture while embracing the opportunity structure of a second, mainstream culture. Parker's assimilation would be viewed by most mainstream historians as successful, but it jeopardized Parker's connection to his Seneca cultural identity and to the roots that helped sustain his spirit. In hindsight, Parker realized the necessity of holding onto his native culture to maintain balance and to successfully navigate mainstream culture. Because this basic truth is just as meaningful today as it was in Ely Parker's time, members of traditionally underrepresented groups are still questioning the wisdom of assimilation when the cost is so great.

Educators who want to explore this issue further by using Ely Parker's life as a point of departure will find a wealth of resources and additional information about Parker at the PBS Web site.

**Work Cited:** WXXI Rochester Public Broadcasting. "Ely Parker." PBS. 1999. http://www.pbs.org/warrior.

# Intercultural Films

## OVERVIEW

Though many racial and ethnic distinctions exist in the United States of America and those distinctions still lead to discrimination, much progress toward equity and positive interaction has been made since the Civil Rights Act of 1965 was passed. Many people are willing to cross the lines of racial/ethnic diversity and interact with people whose racial/ethnic heritage and culture differ from their own. Movies reflect this change. Films made in the United States, whether they are produced in Hollywood or by independents, are far more likely to have diverse characters and subjects than films made fifty years ago.

Not only are film characters more racially/ethnically diverse, characters from traditionally underrepresented groups are more likely to appear in leading roles or even in secondary and minor roles in which their dignity and integrity remain intact. They are no longer relegated almost solely to service roles or to demeaning bits of comic relief or villainy. They no longer exist only to serve European American characters and are no longer presented exclusively from Eurocentric points of view.

More interracial and interethnic friendships exist on screen along with an increased number of intimate love relationships. Communication and interaction occur between colleagues at work (*Blue Collar*), and peers at school (*Higher Learning*), between native-born citizens and recent immigrants (*In America*), between young children (*Hey Arnold! The Movie*), adolescents (*The Incredibly True Adventures of Two Girls in Love*), and adults (*Norma Rae*), between an adopted child and a parent (*Lovely and Amazing*), and between lovers (*Lone Star*). Multiple examples of each can be found. At times the relationships begin tentatively (*Far from Heaven*) or even antagonistically (*In the Heat of the Night*); at other times they are presented as preexisting (*Unforgiven*), or they simply blossom because the characters have a chance to meet and to take the time to observe each other (*Holes*). In other words, they follow the patterns of relationships among people whose racial/ethnic identity is the same. Which, of course, is as it should be.

Many of the movies in which characters do cross racial/ethnic lines actually focus on that as a central issue. For instance, in *Giant*, the interracial marriage between European and Latina American characters becomes a significant focal point in the final third of the film and motivates a major statement about the many similarities of people whose racial/ethnic backgrounds differ. In *The Human Stain*, the decision of the central character to deny his African American roots hovers over all of his relationships. In *White Man's Burden*, the inequality between European and African Americans that has played out in U.S. history is reversed and determines how the plot unfolds, and *In the Heat of the Night*, African American and European American law enforcement officers clash repeatedly, largely because of the racial/ethnic stereotypes they have absorbed.

Increasingly, race/ethnicity functions as an important aspect of a character's identity but is not the core conflict driving the plot. We see this in *Because of You*, *Finding Forrester, Moscow on the Hudson, Philadelphia*, and *Silverado*, to give but a few examples. This acceptance of people of diverse racial/ethnic backgrounds has been an unrealized ideal in the United States' pluralistic society and remains elusive, but an investigation of representations of African, Arab, Middle Eastern, Asian, European, Latino/a, and Native Americans in film since its beginning reveals progress. The progress suggests society itself is moving forward, given that motion pictures reflect the society that produces them.

The picture being drawn here may seem naive or overly optimistic since the media, including films, still incorporate racial/ethnic stereotypes far too often. And European Americans continue to dominate every aspect of the industry; they still carry the vast number of motion pictures not only in terms of star power, but in terms of the perspectives and values that underlie the plots. In this, too, they reflect the dominant Eurocentric presence in the United States. Their dominance is not guaranteed, however, and African, Arab, Middle Eastern, Asian, Latino/a, and Native Americans are not likely to stop pushing for more equitable representation. Given the number of stories they have to tell and the creative energy they have at their disposal, why should they step back? They are far more likely to use their creativity to open up new opportunities for everyone. Ideally, European Americans will move forward with them.

## THE FILMS

### *Because of You* (Video title, 2000)<br>*Kyoko* (Japan, 1995)

Director: Ryu Murakami

Cast: Saki Takaoka (Kyoko), Carlos Osorio (Jose), Scott Whitehurst (Ralph), Angel Stephen (Angel)

Length: 100 min.

Rating: Not Rated

Drama: Intercultural friendship; road movie

Kyoko meets Jose, a Cuban American, who is in the service and stationed in Japan for six months. Jose teaches the eight-year-old Kyoko the dances most popular in his community: the cha cha, the rumba, the mambo. When his tour of duty is over, the two exchange gifts. Jose gives her a pair of dance shoes and his address; she gives him a wind chime. Twelve years later, Kyoko, now an aspiring dancer as well as a truck driver, comes to New York to visit Jose. Because he no longer lives at the address she has, Kyoko begins a search to locate him with the help of Ralph, a limousine chauffeur.

Their search takes them from Manhattan to Queens, from dance studio to posh hotel to Bowery bar, and finally to the Latino hospice where Jose is an AIDS patient. Though Jose suffers from dementia and does not remember her, Kyoko, undaunted, offers to drive him to Miami when she learns of his desire to see his mother. The series of culturally diverse encounters prompted by Kyoko's search for Jose in New York continues as she and Jose make their way to Florida.

Director Ryu Murakami appears to be well aware of the stereotypes through which people in the United States see members of cultural groups other than their own, whether the stereotypes are related to nationality, ethnicity, gender, sexual orientation, or geography. In her encounters, Kyoka not only cuts through the stereotypes but frequently challenges them as she goes about the business of locating and then helping Jose. Her responses to individuals are straightforward and clear, prompted by their behavior rather than her preconceptions. Initially she may seem naive, but because she is not, she proves to be an admirable guide as we travel with her from north to south.

Though Murakami does not avoid all of the movie clichés associated with the South or with traditionally underrepresented groups, he does succeed in telling a story of cross-cultural friendship and human interaction that is quietly engaging and often moving.

## *Blade Runner* (1982)

Director: Ridley Scott

Cast: Harrison Ford (Rick Dekard), Rutger Hauer (Roy Batty), Sean Young (Rachael), Edward James Olmos (Gaff), M. Emmet Walsh (Captain Bryant), Daryl Hannah (Pris), William Sanderson (J. F. Sebastian)

Length: 115 min.

Rating: R

Futuristic Science Fiction: Replicants pose questions about humans and humanoids

Rick Dekard belongs to the Blade Runners, a special police unit whose job is to "retire" (kill) humanlike genetically engineered androids called *replicants*. After a violent escape during an uprising on one of the out worlds, six replicants led by Roy Batty have returned to earth seeking information on how to extend their limited lives. Billionaire scientist Tyrell contracts the Blade Runners to retire the rebel replicants, and in the process of getting information about them, Dekard meets and falls in love with one of Tyrell's most recent and advanced creations, Rachael.

*Blade Runner* is a futuristic view of U.S. society. Its stylish, dark setting helps create a world where androids or replicants have become barely distinguishable from the human counterparts they were designed to serve. In this future world, Los Angeles has become populated by a fusion of races and ethnicities exemplified by the character Gaff, the police detective who appears to be Latino or Native American, but whose signature origami figures identify him with Japanese culture as well. A strong Asian presence is evident through food vendors, street hawkers, and the stereotypical Asian scientist Hannibal Chew, the eye-maker.

Characters who hold positions of power and influence are typically European American in appearance, like Tyrell, the sinister genius who masterminds the development of the replicants, and J. F. Sebastian, an engineer. Interestingly, the latter is affected with a unique gland condition resulting in hyperacceleration of his aging process, which is essentially the same problem faced by the replicants and adds one more dimension to the comparison of humans and replicants that the film invites. All of the replicants are European American in appearance, none more strikingly so than the Aryan-looking Batty. Their appearance belies their role as slaves.

Essentially, the vision of this futuristic film represents our current status quo in terms of the hierarchical relationships among people of different races/ethnicities. Little has changed in this future: European Americans are still in power and are taking advantage of opportunities on the off-world colonies of distant planets while a vast underclass, mostly people of color, barely eke out an existence on a polluted earth. This situation, though not the film's principal focus, is significant, especially when exploring this underclass in relation to both the powerful elites and the replicants who serve these elites, a role one might assume was filled by the underclass on earth before the off-world colonies were developed and the elites replaced their human servants/slaves with replicants. Were they able to do this because they regarded people of color, the underclass, as less than human? Or did they dare not go that far, and "merely" regard them as insignificant instead? Did the existence of the underclass prick the consciences of the elite and lead them to question their own humanity? Did they abandon them in an effort to avoid the discomfort these questions caused? Was this why they were left behind and replaced with nonhumans, with androids? *Blade Runner* questions notions of humanity in another way. It asks if the characteristics normally used to define humanity are the exclusive province of homo sapiens since humankind as traditionally defined and genetically engineered androids are wrestling with the same issues. Have the replicants become human? What does it mean to be human?

Much has been written about *Blade Runner*, so educators who choose to introduce it to their students will have multiple resources to consult should they want to do so. One place to start is Scott Bukatman's *Blade Runner*, published by the British Film Institute as part of its Modern Classic Series. Bukatman provides the production history of the film, a comparison of the 1982 release with the version distributed in 1992 as the director's cut, and an in-depth, very academic analysis. An alternate place to begin is the remarkably inclusive Web site David Caldwell and Lukas Mariman maintain.

**Works Cited:** Bukatman, Scott. *Blade Runner*. London: British Film Institute, 1997; Caldwell, David, and Lukas Mariman. "*Blade Runner* Movie." http://www.brmovie.com/analysis/index.htm.

## *Blue Collar* (1978)

Director: Paul Schrader

Cast: Richard Pryor (Ezekiel "Zeke" Brown), Harvey Keitel (Jerry Bertowski), Yaphet Kotto (Smokey), Ed Begley, Jr. (Bobbie Joe), Harry Bellaver (Eddie Johnson)

Length: 114 min.

Rating: R

Drama: Management versus workers

Zeke, Jerry, and Smokey share the same bleak working conditions at an auto assembly plant in Detroit. Constantly pushed by hard-to-satisfy supervisors, they, with their coworkers, chafe under the continual harassment, noise, and inadequate wages that go with their jobs. At odds with their union as well as with management, the men find camaraderie at Little Jo's Bar and at parties Smokey hosts. All three are pressed financially.

Zeke's financial struggles become apparent through a visit from an IRS agent, who is after him for declaring exemptions for six rather than three children and not reporting wages from a weekend painting job. Jerry's tight money situation is dramatized when his daughter tries to make her own braces because Jerry can't afford to send her to an orthodontist. Though Smokey does not have the responsibilities of a family, he is $1,000 in debt to an unforgiving loan shark who threatens to take his superbly maintained Cadillac if the debt is not paid. After their attempt to rob their union's safe nets them little money but a journal detailing illegal loans, they turn to blackmail as the way to get out of debt, but Smokey's murder and the union's divisive tactics have Zeke and Jerry running scared. Ultimately, fear and self-interest not only divide them, but turn them violently against each other.

An important emphasis in *Blue Collar* is the power unions and management have to control and direct people's lives and the gulf in resources—financial, intellectual, material, human—that exists between powerful institutions and individuals. Ironically but not surprisingly, the union and management collude to divide Smokey, Zeke, and Jerry. Smokey understands this and articulates it passionately when he says that the company will "do anything to keep you on their line. They pit the lifers against the new boys, the old against the young, the black against the white—everybody to keep us in our places. . . . [I]t's the money that makes the difference."

Almost all of this monologue is reprised in voice-over by Smokey at the very end of the film when Zeke and Jerry are caught in a freeze-frame as they try to attack each other physically. Their friendship breaks down after Zeke is reminded by his union boss that he is black and owes his job to the union. In turn, when they confront each other after Smokey's murder, Zeke reminds Jerry of their differences, of his own limits within a racist society and of opportunities Jerry, as a white man, can expect. They share working-class status and challenges, but their difference in color leads them finally in different directions.

The profanity in *Blue Collar* is likely to offend some viewers, not only because of the language itself, but because of its stereotypical use in portraying male working-class culture. If one can get beyond the language, the film offers a rare look at an important segment of the working poor while also showing how friendships can cross racial/ethnic lines and then erode under pressure. To study the film within the context of the role unions play in the American workplace, viewers can consult *American Worker, American Unions: The Twentieth Century*. To probe more deeply into the economic structure that places Zeke, Jerry, and Smokey at a disadvantage financially, *The American Class Structure* could be helpful.

**Works Cited:** Gilbert, Dennis. *The American Class Structure in an Age of Growing Inequality*. 6th ed. Belmont, CA: Wadsworth, 2003; Ziegler, Robert H., and Gilbert J. Gail. *American Worker, American Unions: The Twentieth Century*. Baltimore: Johns Hopkins University Press, 2002.

## *Bowling for Columbine* (2002)

Director: Michael Moore

Length: 119 min.

Rating: R

Documentary: Gun violence in the United States

Michael Moore's *Bowling for Columbine* won the Oscar in 2002 for the best documentary film. This film, while funny, is also sobering. It challenges its viewers to understand how the United States of America has accepted the gross level of gun violence it experiences every day. Moore expertly—and devastatingly—uses a variety of techniques to make his points; he blends statistical data and interviews with clips from historical feature films, television footage, an animated sequence, and video clips of contemporary acts of gun violence.

Moore's comparison of the annual murder rates of Canada and other industrialized countries with the United States is striking. Although Canada and the United States have relatively the same ratio of guns per capita, for example, the number of gun-related deaths in the United States is astronomical compared to Canada. Such arresting juxtapositions are Moore's stock and trade and are evident in his interviews, whether he is speaking with a bank teller, members of a Michigan paramilitary group, a spokesperson for Lockheed Martin, television producers, Marilyn Manson, or the principal of Buell Elementary School in Flint, Michigan, where one six-year-old shot a classmate.

Perhaps Moore's most poignant interaction is with Mark and Richard, two wounded survivors from the Columbine High School massacre. Moore takes these victims of gun violence to K-Mart's corporate headquarters and the three ask officials why they permit their stores to carry handgun ammunition. Though they receive little satisfaction on their initial visit, when they return with newsmen and cameras, K-Mart officials have a response ready: They will remove handgun ammunition from all of their stores. The film captures the surprise the three ambassadors experience from this rapid and positive, but unexpected, outcome. Their success provides a powerful real-life lesson on how consumers can influence the decisions of corporations.

The interview with Charlton Heston will definitely evoke mixed reviews. On the one hand, viewers are apt to question the timing of the rallies Heston and the organization he represents, the National Rifle Association (NRA), held in Colorado and Michigan immediately following the killing of students in public schools in those states. On the other hand, Moore seems to use his own NRA membership to secure an interview with Heston and then appears to badger Heston after he invites Moore into his home. Heston appears to be trying to answer Moore's questions honestly, but Moore keeps pushing for an apology. Complicating viewer responses further are the Heston comments that hint at racist attitudes as well as the frailty evident when he ends the interview by walking somewhat unsteadily away from Moore. For some viewers, Moore's relentless questioning undercuts his effectiveness, justifying at least to some extent his reputation for going too far. For other viewers, however, his hard-hitting persistence is exactly what makes him effective.

Moore's film, while humorous in many places, is a stern wake-up call about the violent culture that exists in the United States, the pervasive fear that underlies it, and the complacency with which citizens accept this reality. Moore challenges people in the United States to stop, reflect, and rethink this nation's history of killing—killing that takes place at a rate higher than in any other industrial or postindustrial society in the world.

The way the film is edited lends itself to classroom use. This is especially true of the DVD version since that format allows easy access to any one of the thirty-two descriptively titled chapters. In addition, the DVD contains background information on the making of the film as well as lectures and award presentations in which Moore talks about the making of this engrossing film.

Because of the excitement this film created, a number of Web sites, some supportive, some critical, have been established. Some call into question the authenticity of Moore's statistics as well as his "attack" on Heston. Moore uses his own Web site to counter his critics and bolster his own arguments. Regardless of the film's flaws, *Bowling for Columbine* has already proven an effective catalyst for discussion of one of the most serious, intractable, and divisive issues the United States faces. The issue affects people of every race/ethnicity, class, gender, and sexual orientation.

**Work Cited:** Moore, Michael. http://www.michaelmoore.com.

## *The Brother from Another Planet* (1984)

Director: John Sayles

Cast: Joe Morton (the Brother), Daryl Edwards (Fly), Steve James (Odell), Leonard Jackson (Smokey), Maggie Renzi (Noreen), David Strathairn (Man in black), Bill Cobbs (Walter)

Length: 110 min.

Rating: R

Science Fiction: Variation on the immigrant experience

This is the story of a visitor from another planet who just happens to be black. His body can regenerate a limb if it becomes severed, and he has highly developed empathic skills and the ability to relive past experiences by merely touching the surface of physical objects like walls or wooden tables; but he lacks the ability to communicate orally. Ironically, his ship lands at a deserted Ellis Island, port of entry for so many immigrants to the United States.

As he begins to explore New York City, he encounters a variety of people and cultures. Because he does not understand how money is used to pay for goods and services, he runs into trouble with the police, but his flight from the police is serendipitous. It brings him into contact with the African American community. Though members of this community find him a curiosity, they see him as a brother, try to communicate with him, and help him out.

Two white alien bounty hunters, posing as immigration agents, appear on the scene with a contract on the Brother. When they find him, a full-scale battle erupts, but the Brother's new community comes to his assistance and the group is able to drive the bounty hunters away. The film concludes with the bounty hunters closing in and almost capturing the Brother a second time, but he escapes again, this time because, as he is fleeing, from out of the shadows come other alien brothers and sisters, and together they chase and trap the bounty hunters.

Sayles exposes viewers of *The Brother from Another Planet* to some incisive social commentary throughout the film. He does so entertainingly, humorously, as in the hilarious sequence in which two European American men get lost and end up getting drunk at a bar in Harlem. They have an experience bordering on a religious epiphany as the result of their positive interaction with the African Americans in the bar.

This imaginative and provocative film explores many aspects of our race-conscious society and draws a clear parallel between African Americans who endured slavery and the extraterrestrials, people of color who are being hunted by white bounty hunters. For example, the film alludes to the Underground Railroad, to the experiences of runaway slaves, and to the fictive kinship support system that has long helped African Americans survive in a racist society. Though made on a minuscule budget and shot very quickly (Ryan 97–98), an excellent script, cast, and crew worked together effectively to produce an insightful critique of contemporary U.S. society by using science fiction to evoke history.

Several in-depth analyses of *The Brother from Another Planet* exist and are well worth investigating. Among these are Ed Guerrero's critique in *Framing Blackness: The African American Image in Film* (44–50), Jack Ryan's reading in *John Sayles, Filmmaker* (97–114), and Sayle's own comments in *Sayles on Sayles* (104–118).

**Works Cited:** Guerrero, Ed. *Framing Blackness: The African American Image in Film*. Philadelphia: Temple University Press, 1993; Ryan, Jack. *John Sayles, Filmmaker*. Jefferson, NC: McFarland & Company, 1998; Sayles, John. *Sayles on Sayles*. Edited by Gavin Smith. Boston: Faber and Faber, 1998.

## *China Girl* (1987)

Director: Abel Farrare

Cast: James Russo (Alby), David Caruso (Mercury), Joey Chinn (Tsu Chin), Russell Wong (Yung Gan), Sari Chang (Tai), Richard Pannebianco (Tony)

Length: 90 min.

Rating: R

Multiethnic Urban Drama: Romeo and Juliet within a gang setting

*China Girl* opens with a frenetic dance scene of young ethnically diverse—Asian, African, and European American—adolescents. While everybody is on the dance floor grooving, it doesn't take long to notice that the dancers in each group are segregated ethnically, until Tony, an Italian American, begins dancing with Tai, the China girl of the film's title. Once the dancers notice, Tony is chased from the club by a gang of Asians who continue to pursue him into a rival neighborhood where a fight between gangs ensues. Both Tai and Tony are warned about their incursions into cultures other than their own, but they continue to see each other, endangering and enraging their communities as they fall in love.

Underlying Tai and Tony's story is the story of the organized crime rampant in both communities. In each community, young gang members challenge the leadership of the aging crime bosses, violating the mutual respect for turf that has been established by the older generation. Intragroup tensions escalate when an established Chinese restaurant owner moves out of Chinatown into the Italian neighborhood and refuses to pay protection money to the young Chinese mobsters. Violence on all levels grows, though the possibility for peaceful coexistence is suggested briefly during an Italian festival. When Yung attacks and kills Alby, however, further violence erupts and is symbolically underscored when a statue of the Virgin Mary being carried in a procession crashes into the street.

*China Girl*'s focus is not on the cultural traditions of either ethnic group; instead the film shows viewers the gang life that exists in both communities and the difficulty of bridging racial/ethnic differences. On a personal level, Tai and Tony do bridge these differences. They refuse to stay within their own cultures. When they pay for their love with their lives, the parallels between their story and Shakespeare's *Romeo and Juliet* are hard to ignore. Like *West Side Story*, *China Girl* translates Romeo and Juliet's warring families into warring gangs, making race/ethnicity a central focus.

Interracial or interethnic relationships are still problematic for many people, whether they revolve around intimate interpersonal relationships such as Tai and Tony's or around integrated neighborhoods and schools. Tai and Tony's relationship leads to deadly physical violence. Seeing it and understanding its senselessness could help initiate discussion about the kinds of interethnic violence that exists in contemporary society, whether it is blatant physical violence or the more subtle and pervasive violence evident in segregated neighborhoods and schools.

**Work Cited:** *West Side Story*. Directed by Robert Wise. Performances by Natalie Wood, Richard Beymer, Rita Moreno, and George Chakiris. MGM, 1961.

## *Conrack* (1974)

Director: Martin Ritt

Cast: Jon Voight (Pat Conroy), Paul Winfield (Mad Billy), Madge Sinclair (Mrs. Scott), Tina Andrews (Mary), Ruth Attaway (Edna), Hume Cronyn (Superintendent)

Length: 106 min.

Rating: PG

Drama: Traditional versus innovative educational practices; high versus low expectations

Pat Conroy is a "born-again" Southern liberal who has escaped his racist upbringing and is hired to teach in an all-African American school located on the barrier islands off the South Carolina mainland. During the protest years of the Vietnam War, he takes over a one-room schoolhouse, administered by an African American principal, Mrs. Scott, who tells him all of the children are slow but can learn what is beaten into them. The school children quickly demonstrate their lack of academic knowledge. Most cannot read, write, or do basic math; their knowledge of fundamental facts about the world, such as the names of continents, mountains, and oceans, is virtually nonexistent. Because of Conroy's eagerness to teach and protect these children, he soon wins their hearts and minds, but his unorthodox instructional methods offend the principal and the white superintendent. He is fired before the beginning of his second year.

Director Martin Ritt chooses to emphasize the isolation of these island inhabitants from mainland realities. Many of the children and adults have never been to the mainland. By also virtually ignoring the rich Gullah culture of these islanders, however, Ritt leaves the children appearing to be far more culturally deprived than they actually are.

What Conroy decides to teach them is a cross between the content of the Discovery Channel and *National Geographic*. He selects such Eurocentric subjects as Beethoven's Fifth Symphony, Rimsky-Korsakov's "Flight of the Bumblebee," Picasso paintings, Errol Flynn movies, and the origins of the races. On a very pragmatic level, when he discovers that none of the children can swim, he teaches them to swim.

Though Conroy's idealism, energy, and creativity make him a very likable hero, his limited view of what constitutes knowledge and his assumption that the Gullah people have little or no culture pose some problems, especially in retrospect. Viewers might also want to ask what the previous African American teacher was teaching. How could the children have so little book knowledge? Why was this lack of knowledge condoned by the principal and the superintendent? Exploring these questions could lead to some interesting discussions, but researching the African American Southern cultural experience, especially the Gullah culture, would also be valuable. William S. Billitzer's *The Gullah People and Their Heritage*, Julie Dash's *Daughters of the Dust*, and Marquetta L. Goodwine's *The Legacy of Ibo Landing* offer starting points. Viewers might also compare the experience of Conroy and his students with other areas in the United States during the early 1970s.

Some viewers might read *Conrack* as one more liberal tribute to the "genius" of European American culture at the expense of African Americans, another example of the stereotype of the white man saving the poor uneducated black. It certainly can be read that way. Other viewers might see it as an example of how important the teacher–student relationship can be or as the beginning of a conversation about teacher–administrator relationships.

**Works Cited:** Billitzer, William S. *The Gullah People and Their Heritage*. Athens: University of Georgia Press, 1999; *Daughters of the Dust*. Directed by Julie Dash. Performances by Barbara O. Jones, Adisa Anderson, and Cora Lee Day. MGM, 1992; Goodwine, Marquetta L. *The Legacy of Ibo Landing: Gullah Roots of African American Culture*. Atlanta, GA: Clarity Press, 1998.

## *Faith and Doubt at Ground Zero* (2002)

Producer: Helen Whitney

Length: 120 min.

Rating: Not Rated

Documentary: The impact of 9/11 on the faith of survivors

*Faith and Doubt at Ground Zero* is a remarkable documentary. It examines the impact that the tragedy of 9/11 has had upon the faith of those who were personally affected by this event. This includes members of the religious community as well as survivors and the family and friends of victims.

The film is divided into segments; each follows a specific theme through interviews with a variety of people who were connected to the destruction of the World Trade Center in New York. The interviews are punctuated by actual film footage of the terrorist action. In the first segment the events of 9/11 are retold; the second segment examines the reaction of families and friends of the victims; the third explores the impact this event had on the faith of survivors and religious leaders; the next deals with the implications of religious absolutism as it is being practiced in the world today; and the final segment is an epilogue that examines one of the most striking 9/11 images caught on film: the scene in which two strangers reach for and hold each other's hands as they leap from the towers to their deaths. Other footage incorporated into the film captures the despair and disbelief of firefighters, police officers, emergency medical technicians, and spectators.

*Faith and Death at Ground Zero* is an excellent film to open discussions of many issues, from terrorism to religious absolutism. Because it is multilayered and can be approached from so many levels of consciousness and belief or disbelief, it can be a useful catalyst for talking about cultural differences and the lack of knowledge that keeps cultures apart. The film's structure, the music and background settings used to create and steer emotions, and the film's imbalances as well as its apparent breadth in its choice of interviewees are all worth considering. Given the level of culturally based tensions in the United States at the beginning of the twenty-first century, this film is an important contribution to cross-cultural dialogue. It can be used effectively with adolescent and older audiences, but given the graphic nature of some of the footage, caution must be used with younger audiences. Frontline provides a comprehensive Web site with extended interviews and background information that can encourage and facilitate in-depth discussion of the issues *Faith and Doubt* presents.

**Work Cited:** Frontline. *Faith and Doubt at Ground Zero*. PBS. http://www.pbs.org/wgbh/pages/frontline/shows/faith.

## *Far from Heaven* (2002)

Director: Todd Haynes

Cast: Julianne Moore (Cathy Whitaker), Dennis Quaid (Frank Whitaker), Dennis Haysbert (Raymond Deagan), Patricia Clarkson (Eleanor Fine), Viola Davis (Sybil)

Length: 107 min.

Rating: PG-13

Melodrama: Critique of racism and homophobia

Looking from the outside of their perfectly appointed upper-middle class home, Cathy and Frank Whitaker appear to have achieved an ideal life. Dubbed Mr. and Mrs. Magnatech, Frank garners the respect and admiration of his colleagues for his success with the company while Cathy willingly and ably fulfills her role as mother of their two children and as a prominent Hartford socialite. Helping them keep their lives and home in order are two African Americans: their maid, Sybil, and their gardener, Raymond. This "idyllic" 1950s world begins to crumble when Frank can no longer deny or control his homosexual desires.

Under the guise of working late, Frank begins a series of assignations with gay partners but is caught when Cathy, hoping to support him by bringing dinner to his office, innocently walks in on one such encounter. Though Frank readily opts for counseling to deal with the issue, and both he and Cathy make an effort to return to "normal," Frank's growing tenseness and dependence on alcohol undercut their resolve. When Frank announces he has fallen in love, the situation can no longer be contained, and the two prepare for a divorce.

Paralleling Frank's crisis is Cathy's growing friendship with Raymond. Seen together just enough to fuel gossip and anger among both African and European American communities, Cathy and Raymond find themselves at the center of critical attention and disapproval so intense that their situation actually overshadows Frank's. Raymond's daughter is even seriously injured in a rock-throwing incident as a result of their interaction.

Though set in the 1950s and exploring issues that can certainly be identified with that or any other era, *Far from Heaven* could not have been made in Hollywood then because the myths and ignorance surrounding homosexuality, race, and interracial relationships were so strong. *Far from Heaven* begins to get at the psychological damage and pain such misinformation and ignorance generate as well as the social and psychological limitations and losses they impose. As a melodrama, the film emphasizes the social and psychological dimensions of interpersonal relationships and resolves the crisis it explores through the clandestine fulfillment of Frank and his new partner's desires and the denial of Cathy and Raymond's.

The Whitakers' world, as presented in the beginning of *Far from Heaven*, is a world of perfect artifice, with everything and everybody—except perhaps Cathy and Frank's son, David, who speaks out of turn and obeys only reluctantly at times—performing according to their easily recognized scripts. Perfectly coordinated décor, beautiful fall foliage, bandbox-fresh attire, polite conversation, and courteous interaction appear to be hallmarks of this world. When it shatters, it does so with tears, violations of propriety, and even violence on Frank's part. Cathy, however, responds with restraint and concern, because neither she nor Raymond allows personal attraction or desire to outweigh their social roles or the responsibilities the roles impose. Cathy's restraint is in large part due to Raymond's clear signals that a relationship is impossible. Because of her naiveté and desire, Cathy attempts to hold onto it, but Raymond has seen the consequences of doing so in the assault on his daughter. He is more in touch with the reality of their situation.

By highlighting Cathy's role, *Far from Heaven* suggests Cathy and Raymond's responses are more acceptable than Frank's, but the film still invites viewers to ponder the merits of sacrificing or circumscribing personal happiness because of social and familial roles, especially when those roles are at least partially defined by prejudice and injustice.

*Far from Heaven* clearly echoes two earlier melodramas: Douglas Sirk's 1955 *All That Heaven Allows* starring Jane Wyman and Rock Hudson, and Rainer Werner Fassbinder's 1974 German tribute to Sirk, *Ali: Fear Eats the Soul*. In *All That Heaven Allows*, friends and family object to a relationship between a middle-aged wealthy widow and her younger gardener because of age and class differences. In *Ali: Fear Eats the Soul*, age, race/ethnicity, and nationality evoke objections to the relationship of an older German widow and a Moroccan immigrant thirty years her junior. For Todd Haynes, age is not an issue, and class concerns are somewhat muted since Raymond is college-educated and his gardening is just one aspect of the business he owns. Race/ethnicity and sexual orientation are the film's central issues, reflecting, as the earlier films do, the society that produced it. Viewing it alone or with the other two films can prompt multifaceted discussions of race and ethnicity as well as the intersections of race and ethnicity with class, gender, and sexual orientation.

Among the materials on *Far from Heaven* that can help viewers probe the issues it raises are the article, interview, and review printed in the March 2003 issue of *Sight and Sound*.

**Works Cited:** *Ali: Fear Eats the Soul*. Directed by Rainer Werner Fassbinder. Performances by Brigitte Mira and El Hedi Ben Salem. New Yorker Films, 1974. *All That Heaven Allows*. Directed by Douglas Sirk. Performances by Jane Wyman and Rock Hudson. Kino International,1955; Falcon, Richard, and Nick James. "Magnificent Obsession." *Sight and Sound* 13, no. 3 (2003): 12–15, 40–41.

## *Finding Forrester* (2000)

Director: Gus Van Sant

Cast: Sean Connery (William Forrester), Rob Brown (Jamal Wallace), F. Murray Abraham (Professor Robert Crawford), Anna Paquin (Claire Spence), Busta Rhymes (Terrell Wallace)

Length: 136 min.

Rating: PG-13

Drama: Rites of passage for an adolescent and his adult mentor

*Finding Forrester* opens with a panoramic view of the ghetto that is quickly contrasted with a close-up of a bookshelf holding impressive intellectually weighty volumes. Jamal wakes, gets instructions from his mother, shoots hoops with his friends, and accepts a challenge to break into the apartment of Forrester, the neighborhood's mysterious and near-legendary "man in the window." Accepting the challenge unexpectedly leads Jamal and Forrester into a relationship that benefits both. Jamal, a potentially brilliant student and an avid writer, has hidden his intellectual abilities from his sports-minded peers, but he finds Forrester fascinating and accepts his mentoring.

The relationship between Jamal and Forrester begins uneasily and is repeatedly threatened by one or the other. For Jamal, much of the pressure comes from outside: transfer to a new school, the demands of academics and sports, peer competition and jealousy, and the low expectations of teachers. For Forrester, a loss of faith in his own abilities and accomplishments, fear of social interaction, and years of seclusion have virtually encased him in his apartment and in his past.

As a result of their friendship and mutual support, Jamal improves his writing skills and comes to understand that a successful writer writes from the heart before revising with the head. Forrester begins to regain his confidence, initially venturing outside his apartment with Jamal and later visiting Scotland and resuming his own writing. Jamal is considering college scholarship offers when a lawyer informs him of Forrester's death. In a letter Forrester thanks him for his friendship. He has completed a new manuscript and asks that Jamal write the foreword.

This is a film about the rites of passage for an aging European American writer and an adolescent African American novice writer. The two individuals need each other as they transition into old age and young adulthood, respectively. They see each other, listen to each other, challenge each other, and support and love each other. Race/ethnicity mean very little in their relationship, but in Jamal's world it means a lot and affects how he sees himself, how he interacts with his friends, and how he is viewed and evaluated by his teachers. For Forrester, race/ethnicity is almost a nonissue. However, age has significance for him, as it has for Jamal—and for all cultures, races, and ethnic groups.

## *Follow Me Home* (1996)

Director: Peter Bratt

Distributor: Speak Out Speakers and Artists Agency

Cast: Alfre Woodard (Evey), Benjamin Bratt (Able), Jesse Borrego (Tudee), Steve Reevis (Freddy), Calvin Levels (Kaz)

Length: 101 min.

Rating: R

Drama: Road movie and pointed social critique of racism

*Follow Me Home* is a road film that depicts the cross-country journey of four artists. Like most road movies, the action takes place on both the physical and psychological levels and revolves around the protagonists' interactions with each other and with the people they meet along the way. This independent film is distinctive not only because the sojourners are two Chicanos (Tudee and Able), an African American (Kaz), and a Native American (Freddy), but also because they are driving to Washington, D.C., to paint the White House with their own rainbow colors. Among the people they meet along the way are Evey, the executive director of the NAACP's Washington chapter, who is mourning the death of her daughter, and a small group of European Americans in cavalry uniforms who are historical reenactment enthusiasts.

*Follow Me Home* is a difficult film, though one worth seeing and discussing. Viewers can follow the progress of the protagonists' trip with relative ease on the level of the physical action, but that action is repeatedly interrupted by enigmatic dreams and reveries that transcend the realism with which many audiences are comfortable. Through the dreams, viewers enter a surreal world of symbols that is not so easily understood. For example, in several of Tudee's reveries, he is seen serving an authoritative older white man who seems, in successive scenes, to be identified with government, economics, and art, and who is described by the film's distributor as "a Machiavellian wordsmith and manipulator who [Tudee] has subconsciously internalized." The dreams also help convey, along with the audio background of prayer and drumming, a spiritual dimension not often found in Hollywood feature films but an integral aspect of indigenous cultures.

The stereotypical portrayals of the European Americans in the film and Able's initial behavior, the angry, self-destructive kind associated with guns, drugs, and gangs, also make the film difficult. Director Peter Bratt explains his use of stereotypical white characters as "a playful cinematic turn of the tables," given film's history of stereotyping people of color, and ultimately Able's rage is revealed as a cover for deeply felt but unrecognized pain. Understanding this may make the film easier to watch for some viewers, though perhaps not for all.

That Bratt does want audiences to understand *Follow Me Home* despite its difficult subject matter and experimental film techniques is apparent in the film's distribution arrangement which calls for a postscreening discussion led by Bratt or his sister Lakota whenever the film is shown. Through the discussion, viewers can explore the film's multiple layers of meaning and, as Alfre Woodard suggests, contribute to a much-needed "national dialogue on race."

## *Giant* (1956)

Director: George Stevens

Cast: Elizabeth Taylor (Leslie Lynnton Benedict), Rock Hudson (Jordan "Bick" Benedict), James Dean (Jett Rink), Carroll Baker (Luz Benedict II), Dennis Hopper (Jordan Benedict III), Fran Bennett (Judy Benedict), Elsa Cárdenas (Juana Benedict)

Length: 201 min.

Rating: Not Rated

Family Drama: Intergenerational and intercultural relationships

Leslie Lynnton and Bick Benedict marry shortly after they meet at her home in Maryland and then make their home at the 595,000-acre Benedict Reata Ranch in Texas. Leslie—strong-willed, independent, intelligent, and compassionate—quickly shows her mettle as she takes on the responsibilities of a rancher, a wife, and a neighbor. Periodically she and Bick clash over her refusal to maintain a "proper" distance from the concerns of their Mexican employees or to stay within the male-prescribed boundaries for women, but their love and respect for each other help move them past these challenges. Together they raise three children—the twins, Jordy (Jordan III) and Judy, and Luz, who is named after Bick's sister—and weather the changes made necessary when oil interests supersede their interests as ranchers. Bick very slowly and reluctantly relinquishes his desire that his son—or his daughters—take his place at the head of the Reata Ranch. Just as slowly he comes to accept Mexicans and Mexican Americans as full-fledged Texans.

Leslie's biggest challenges come from Luz, Bick's only sister, who refuses to accept Leslie as her brother's wife, from the harshness of the Texas sun, and from the rigors of cattle ranching. She meets these challenges more easily than Bick meets his, just as she learns to accept and embrace the children's choices, including their choices of marriage partners, more readily. She proves to be the catalyst for the major shifts in Bick's attitude in relation to his son's career and family and to Mexicans and Mexican Americans. Leslie's relationship to the Latinos/as who work at Reata becomes clear as soon as she arrives: They may be working for the Benedicts, but they are worthy of respect and decent living conditions.

Because Leslie's involvement in the lives of the Latinos/as centers primarily on ensuring they receive satisfactory medical care, Jordy's decision to become a doctor and to focus his practice on Mexican Americans is not surprising. Neither is his marriage to Juana, a Mexican American. Bick has reservations about the marriage because he fears the family will be hurt by it and also because of his own prejudice—a prejudice Jordy and Leslie consistently challenge. That this is a major theme of *Giant* is underscored in the film's final scene when Leslie and Bick discuss the issue while babysitting their two grandchildren. As Bick suggests that the prejudice of his generation will lessen in future generations, the camera cuts to the little boys standing together. The sons of Judy and Juana, their similarities are as evident as their distinct ethnic features. *Giant* ends with close-ups of their faces dissolving from one to the other. The close-ups, Leslie's social consciousness, and Bick's rejection of racism make *Giant* "a fascinating anomaly" that "treated Chicanos humanely and contributed meaningfully to the discourse on American prejudice" (Berg 126) before the multiple civil rights movements of the 1960s and 1970s.

Though *Giant* is often recognized for its stars and epic sweep rather than its emphasis on social justice, the latter makes it particularly worth seeing and discussing within the context of race and ethnicity.

**Work Cited:** Berg, Charles Ramirez. *Latino Images in Film: Stereotypes, Subversion, Resistence.* Austin: University of Texas Press, 2002.

## *Hey Arnold! The Movie* (2002)

Director: Tuck Tucker

Cast: Spencer Klein (Arnold), Francesca Smith (Helga/Deep Voice), Jamil Walker Smith (Gerald), Dan Castellaneta (Grandpa)

Length: 80 min.

Rating: PG

Animated Comedy, Drama: Community action counters vengeful land developer

Arnold, Gerald, and Helga live in a neighborhood that has been targeted for urban renewal by corporate mogul Schrek. Armed with the approval of the mayor, the latest technology, and a slogan that insists "change is good," Schrek is all set to destroy both homes and businesses and to replace them with a shimmering new mall despite the protests of the people living in the neighborhood. The ever-optimistic Arnold, his more pragmatic friend Gerald, and their neighbors try various tactics to stop Schrek, but he successfully blocks each of their attempts. With time running out, Grandpa inadvertently gives Arnold information that could prompt the mayor to reverse her decision: The neighborhood was the site of the nineteenth-century Tomato Incident, an event with enough significance to make the area an official historical landmark. All Arnold and Gerald have to do is find out if it is a historical site and produce the document verifying its status—within the 46 hours and 19 minutes left before Schrek begins the demolition. Their task is not made easier when they learn Schrek has the document they need. They get help, however, from the mysterious sleuth Deep Voice and gadget inventor extraordinaire Bridget.

This animated movie is the work of Nickelodeon Movies and originated in the television program featuring Arnold, Gerald, Helga, and their friends. *Hey Arnold! The Movie* overtly lauds the values of community, tradition, hard work, an optimistic outlook, and determination. Arnold's world is culturally diverse. Its people appreciate their heritage but defy stereotypes; Arnold (European American) and Gerald (African American) are best friends. Mayor Dixie is a woman; so is the character who comes up with one James-Bond-type gadget after another; so is Deep Voice, the super sleuth who is usually several steps ahead of Arnold and furnishes him and Gerald with critical information and direction. The neighborhood butcher can cry when the situation calls for it and experience no shame. Grandma Gertie can go to jail for protesting, manage an escape, and get back to the neighborhood in time to use Schrek's own heavy machinery against him.

That *Hey Arnold!* reverses stereotypes and lauds community and individual responsibility is not difficult to see. A more subtle message comes from Schrek. While he's declaring "change is good," he is harboring resentment for his family's loss in the Tomato Incident when the tyranny of an ancestor, General Von Schrek, was defeated by community action and solidarity. He is motivated by revenge and has become obsessed with a desire to reverse this earlier defeat, illustrating in the process, the danger of clinging to old enmities and refusing to change an attitude. In contrast the neighborhood community is able to make changes without giving up those aspects of the past that are worth preserving. The challenge is to sort out what aspects of tradition are good and which call for change.

All this from a cartoon for children, that is peopled with colorful characters of great variety and multiple talents, and that offers action, suspense, humor and a happy ending? Perhaps that is why adults as well as children can enjoy it.

## *Higher Learning* (1995)

Director: John Singleton

Cast: Omar Epps (Malik Williams), Ice Cube (Fudge), Lawrence Fishburn (Professor Maurice Phipps), Michael Rapaport (Remy), Jennifer Connelly (Taryn), Tyra Banks (Deja), Kristy Swanson (Kristen Connor)

Length: 127 min.

Rating: R

College Drama: First-year experiences of culturally diverse students

John Singleton's *Higher Learning* brilliantly depicts college life at a major university. It portrays the complexity of group and individual interaction as young men and women from various geographic areas, ethnic/racial groups, sexual orientations, socioeconomic levels, and political beliefs try to live and study together. For some of the students, the arrangement works; others can't get beyond their own narrowly defined cultural boxes.

Beneath the veneer of collegiality, Columbus University is a web of segregated groups competing and sometimes warring against each other. Singleton does an excellent job of allowing viewers to sample some of the inner workings of Greek life, African American cliques, white racist groups, feminist organizations, and sports teams. He gives viewers a glimpse of how these groups sometimes connect, interact, and disconnect, and he examines the difficulty of making friends in a new social setting when past experiences shape and often distort one's perceptions of the world. Particularly volatile intercultural exchanges occur when Fudge, an African American intellectual and activist, or Malik, a first-year student athlete with a sense of entitlement, and Remy, a loner with a survivalist background and ideology, cross paths; when a fraternity member insults a black woman; and when campus police treat African American students much more harshly than white students. Some of the cultural differences that are exposed appear to be too vast to bridge.

A brief elevator scene early in the film neatly but disturbingly points to the distrust that exists between African and European American students. When Kristen, a European American student, registers the fact that she is alone in an elevator with an African American male, her nonverbal communication is so pointed that it can't be ignored. As she clutches her purse more tightly and draws it more closely to her, Malik shrugs his recognition of what is going on. This single interaction can spark a discussion that covers issues of race/ethnicity, class, and gender, but *Higher Learning* offers much more as it follows Malik and Kristen through the first few months of their college careers.

Remy, another first-year student, fails to connect with any other students until he is recruited into a white supremacist group and is then goaded into killing an African American during a campus rally. His lack of social skills, his outsider status, and his desire to fit into a group of his peers are palpable. His eruption into violent action may have seemed unrealistic in 1995, but the Columbine massacre and similar events give credence to Singleton's painful vision.

*Higher Learning* effectively examines late adolescence and early adulthood in a world dominated by popular culture and the stereotypes and anxieties it can generate. The competition for social space and self-definition on the Columbus University campus exemplifies what is taking place in many cultural milieus within the United States.

## *Holes* (2003)

Director: Andrew Davis

Cast: Shia LaBeouf (Stanley Yelnats IV), Khleo Thomas (Hector "Zero" Zeroni), Sigourney Weaver (The Warden), Jon Voight (Mr. Sir), Tim Blake Nelson (Dr. Pendanski), Patricia Arquette (Kissin' Kate Barlow), Dulé Hill (Sam), Eartha Kitt (Madame Zeroni)

Length: 117 min.

Rating: PG

Preadolescent Adventure: Intercultural friendship and cooperation

Stanley Yelnats IV seems to be the latest Yelnats to exemplify the power of a curse placed on the Yelnats men three generations earlier. Though innocent, he is found guilty of stealing a pair of shoes and is sentenced to Camp Green Lake for eighteen months. Despite its name, the camp occupies a huge dry lake-bed in Texas and serves as a cover for Warden Walker's search for a huge amount of money she thinks is buried there. Helped by two self-important but easily cowered henchmen, Mr. Sir and Dr. Pendanski, the Warden carries out a methodical search by having the boys assigned to the camp dig five-by-five-foot holes each day.

When he arrives at camp, Stanley goes through the usual initiation process, shows his mettle, and is accepted, even by Zero, a tough loner who bears the brunt of Dr. Pendanski's badgering. Eventually, Zero is pushed beyond his limit and runs away. Stanley goes after him, finds him, and, aided by his grandfather's stories, not only breaks the curse but, with Zero's help, finds a treasure that belongs to the Yelnats family. Honoring his friendship with Zero, Stanley shares the treasure with him, making it possible for Zero to find his mother.

*Holes*, adapted for screen by Louis Sachar from his very popular, prize-winning children's novel, intercuts its main storyline with two background stories. The three tales intersect neatly, serendipitously justifying the friendship of the movie's main characters, Stanley and Zero. Stanley's grandfather supplies the background stories. The first is set in Latvia in the nineteenth century and tells how Stanley's great-great-grandfather came to the United States under the curse of Madame Zeroni, a fortune-teller. She had told him how to win his love, Myra, but, angered by Myra's game-playing and without fulfilling his promise to Madame Zeroni, he abruptly takes off for the United States and sets in motion her curse. Though his son wins a fortune in stocks, he loses it in a stagecoach robbery. The family has been poor ever since.

The robbery, seen as the result of Madame Zeroni's curse, links the Yelnats to Zero, her descendant, and to Warden Walker, whose grandfather figures prominently in the second background story. The elder Walker, used to getting his way, is rebuffed by Catherine Barlow, a schoolteacher in love with the young African American Sam. After Walker incites the townspeople to lynch Sam and destroy her schoolhouse, Catherine begins a campaign of revenge and becomes known as Kissin' Kate Barlow, a notorious robber and murderer. Among her victims is Stanley's great grandfather. The money and other valuables she has stolen comprise part of the treasure Warden Walker is after.

*Holes* lives up to its reputation as a children's movie that appeals to its primary audience but also captures and holds the attention of adults. At once funny and serious, it takes up several themes, among them friendship, family, and greed. Beyond these it examines racial/ethnic relationships. Explicitly explored in the Walker story through Catherine and Sam's love, it surfaces more quietly in the first Yelnats' interaction with the darker-skinned Madame Zeroni and in Stanley Zelnats IV's friendship with Hector "Zero" Zeroni. The prejudice of the elder Walker and the townspeople escalates to hatred and violence, but the Yelnats cross racial/ethnic lines with ease, whether in Latvia or in Texas.

At Camp Green Lake racial/ethnic prejudice seems not to exist for Stanley or his peers. They test each other and at times fight, but neither friends nor enemies are determined by race/ethnicity. The possibility and desirability of alliances and friendships across ethnicity and race clearly surfaces. An exception may be seen in Dr. Pendanski's completely inappropriate and demeaning attitude and behavior toward Zero. Though his stance is hard to fathom, perhaps Zero's light skin implies a blend of European and African ancestry and brings to mind—or to the subconscious—interracial marriage, a possibility evident in the Walker story and Catherine's relationship with Sam.

Even with its multiple flashbacks and interwoven stories, *Holes* is accessible to children. Laced with elements of legend and fairytale it carries its messages lightly—and effectively.

## *The Human Stain* (2003)

Director: Robert Benton

Cast: Anthony Hopkins (Coleman Silk), Nicole Kidman (Faunia Farley), Gary Sinise (Nathan Zuckerman), Ed Harris (Lester Farley), Wentworth Miller (Young Coleman Silk)

Length: 106 min.

Rating: R

Psychological Drama: Identity, denial, and redemption

*The Human Stain* begins with the deaths of its protagonists, Coleman Silk and Faunia Farley, in an automobile crash deliberately caused by Lester, Faunia's ex-husband. Coleman's friend Nathan Zuckerman narrates their story, beginning with Coleman's angry resignation as dean of Athens College after being accused of racism. His wife collapses and dies when he tells her what has happened. Not long after, Coleman seeks out Nathan to suggest he write the story of the events. The subsequent interaction between Coleman and Nathan moves forward in the film's present, as does a relationship between Coleman and Faunia, a janitor at both Athens College and the local post office.

Through flashbacks we learn that Coleman, though identified as Jewish, is African American and, following his father's death, chose to go to the University of Pennsylvania rather than to Howard University, the historically black university his father had chosen for him. Flashbacks also show that Coleman chose, after being rejected by his Danish American fiancée because of his race, to pass as white, a decision that effectively cuts him off from his mother, brother, and sister as well as his race/ethnicity and his culture, but that advances his career. He subsequently excels as an academic.

Coleman meets Faunia after his resignation from Athens. By that time he had been comfortably entrenched in the life of a well-educated, successful professional for several decades. In contrast, she is juggling two janitorial jobs as well as feeding and milking cows in exchange for a room. Their relationship begins when her car breaks down, Coleman offers her a lift, and she offers him sex. Coleman becomes increasingly drawn to her, but she maintains a distance that he finds difficult to understand. When Lester intrudes and accuses her of killing their children, she reveals the horror and anguish she has experienced since the death of the children in a fire.

In fits and starts the two confide in each other; eventually Faunia expresses a willingness to try to break through the protective distance she has built around herself, and Coleman, for the first time since he decided to pass as white, reveals his African American identity. The crash in which both are killed occurs immediately after they have revealed and committed themselves to each other.

His awareness that his father has had to work as a train porter despite his keen intellect and knowledge points Coleman in the direction of passing; the loss of his fiancée when he introduces her to his mother cements that decision, though his desire to be recognized as an individual, as a classics professor, rather than as a representative of his race/ethnicity, a Negro classics professor, strongly influences his choice. He sees identification with white mainstream society as a value so great that he chooses that identity over his birth family, but after attaining the success he desires, we can see via the flashbacks that the denial haunts him. The accusation of racism intensifies memories of his family, and the meaning and impact of his deception prompts his move toward honesty, making possible greater intimacy and acceptance.

*The Human Stain* is primarily Coleman's story told from his perspective and narrated by his friend; viewers are not given comparable access to Faunia's past or to the trauma that shaped her present. Her ex-husband's erratic appearances and psychotic outbursts, supplemented by brief sessions with his psychotherapist, provide access to that information. His presence is the catalyst forcing Faunia to deal with her self-imposed emotional shutdown just as the racism charges are the catalyst for Coleman.

Viewers might want to begin a discussion of *The Human Stain* by asking if Coleman's rejection of his family and his racial/ethnic identity can be justified. What personal, social, and historical circumstances led to his denial? What were the implications or consequences of his decision for himself, his birth family, his fiancée, his wife, and the society in which he lived? What made Faunia's acceptance of Coleman possible? What is the human stain of the title? Why did Coleman identify as Jewish?

Another question raised by *The Human Stain*, given Anthony Hopkins's role as Coleman, is the casting. The Hollywood film industry has a history of casting European Americans in roles calling for light-skinned African Americans—Ava Gardner in *Show Boat* and Jeanne Crain in *Pinky*, for example—but given the Civil Rights Movement and the current availability of accomplished African American actors, why was Hopkins cast to play Coleman? Was it a matter of star status, audience appeal, and actor availability? Was it based on a conviction the casting should be determined by the actor's ability to transcend his and the character's racial/ethnic differences? Is the casting of Wentworth Miller as the young Coleman significant? And what is one to make of the fact, as Roger Ebert points out in his *Chicago Sun-Times* review, that the "racist white man who berates the porter is played by Allison Davis, a Chicago attorney who is black" (2)? Does the industry have any obligation, a moral or ethical one, to provide opportunities for traditionally underrepresented groups when casting films like *The Human Stain*? This same question arises in relation to Renee Zellweger's role in *Cold Mountain*, where she plays a character who, in the novel on which the film is based, is a mulatto.

*The Human Stain* is definitely worth discussing as a story of relationships, identity, and redemption and as a product of what appears to be a very canny commercial enterprise given the status of the actors chosen as the film's leads.

**Works Cited:** *Cold Mountain*. Directed by Anthony Minghella. Performances by Nicole Kidman, Jude Law, and Renee Zellweger. Miramax, 2003; Ebert, Roger. "The Human Stain." *Chicago Sun-Times*, October 31, 2003. http://www.suntimes.com/ebert/ebert_reviews/2003/10/103104 (accessed December 28, 2003); Frazier, Charles. *Cold Mountain*. New York: Vintage Books, 1997. *Pinky*. Directed by Elia Kazan. Performances by Jeanne Crain, Ethel Barrymore, and Ethel Waters. Twentieth Century-Fox, 1949; *Show Boat*. Directed by George Sidney. Performances by Kathryn Grayson, Howard Keel, and Ava Gardner. Warner Bros., 1951.

## *Imitation of Life* (1959)

Director: Douglas Sirk

Cast: Lana Turner (Lora Meredith), Juanita Moore (Annie Johnson), Sandra Dee (Susie), Susan Kohner (Sara Jane), John Gavin (Steve Archer)

Length: 124 min.

Rating: Not Rated

Melodrama: Intercultural friendships, racism, mother-daughter relationships

*Imitation of Life* skillfully intertwines two distinct stories into one. The first is a familiar rags-to-riches tale of a young aspiring actress from a small town who comes to New York City in search of stardom and eventually has to choose between her career and a traditional marriage. The second centers on a daughter's attempts to establish her own identity, apart from that of her mother. Each of these stories has atypical twists. Lora Meredith is a blonde European American widow and a mother as well as an actress. Annie Johnson is a dark-skinned African American whose daughter, Sara Jane, is light enough to pass as white.

Lora and Annie meet by chance, but their mutual needs quickly evolve into a barely articulated agreement that Lora will pursue her career and provide Annie and Sara Jane with a place to stay while Annie manages the household and cares for Lora's daughter Susie as well as for Sara Jane. Given the film's 1950s pre-Civil Rights Movement setting, the friendship between Annie and Lora merits the attention of viewers interested in multicultural issues, but Annie and Sara Jane's relationship is of even greater significance. Seeing clearly the dichotomy between the opportunities available to her and her mother as African Americans and those Lora and Susie can access as whites, Sara Jane chooses to pass as white.

*Imitation of Life* makes it easy for viewers to identify with Annie, a long-suffering, devoted mother who loves her daughter and wants above all to protect her from the pain of societal rejection. Sara Jane, even as a child, comes across as ungrateful, always wanting more, always wanting what she can't have, and pointedly protesting what she is given: a black doll, a bedroom off the kitchen, Annie's—not Lora's—love. As a young adult, she pursues a white boyfriend and a career as a white performer, refusing the possibility of a relationship with the son of a black chauffeur or the type of service work her mother accepts without question.

Annie's kindness, her consideration and concern for others, and her constant selflessness contrast vividly with Sara Jane's rebelliousness, her continual contrariness. Yet, as Marina Heung suggests in her exceptionally insightful analysis, " 'What's the Matter with Sara Jane?': Daughters and Mothers," Annie essentially accepts a racist society as a given, she accepts her place in it and, in an effort to protect her daughter, tries to persuade Sara Jane to do the same. Annie does not challenge the status quo. Sara Jane does and her refusal to conform is irritating, especially since her rebellion affects Annie most directly; it breaks her heart.

Sara Jane sees an unjust society and recognizes in her light skin a way to escape the worst of it. Hers is a personal solution to a social, political, and economic problem. She does not challenge the system of injustice itself, as the Civil Rights Movement was just beginning to do. That Sirk broaches the issue in the late 1950s, however, makes *Imitation of Life* an unusually rich film, one worth exploring for its representation of women vis-a-vis men and biracial female friendships as well as its representation of the difficulties of challenging social hierarchies and its exploration of the issues of "passing" and marginalization within the United States.

The Sirk script for *Imitation of Life* as well as background essays, reviews, and commentaries including Heung's article, are included in *Imitation of Life* edited by Lucy Fischer.

**Works Cited:** Fischer, Lucy, ed. *Imitation of Life*. New Brunswick, NJ: Rutgers University Press, 1991; Heung, Marina. " 'What's the Matter with Sara Jane?': Daughters and Mothers." *Cinema Journal* 26, no. 3 (1987): 21–43.

## *In America* (2002)

Director: Jim Sheridan

Cast: Jim Sheridan (Johnny), Samantha Morton (Sarah), Sarah Bolger (Christy), Emma Bolger (Ariel), Djimon Hounsou (Mateo)

Length: 103 min.

Rating: PG-13

Family Drama: Irish and Haitian immigrants cross racial/ethnic lines to become friends

*In America*, though a British–Irish production, fits well into a guide to the multiculturalism that defines the United States because it so effectively epitomizes the optimism of many immigrants to this country and shows in a simple, straightforward way the possibility of friendship across race/ethnicity.

Johnny and Sarah come to New York with their daughters, Christy and Ariel. Filled with hope and an incredibly strong belief in the American Dream, they are able to turn an upper-floor apartment in a dark, dirty, and rundown drug house in lower Manhattan into a colorful, even magical, space. Transformed by optimism and love, the apartment becomes a setting for creativity, games, and much family happiness. Johnny, an aspiring actor, may fail audition after audition, but he does not give up even when tempted to do so; at those rare moments when he is down, Sarah is there with her effervescent spirit and a plea, "for the children." Sarah gets a job as a waitress and Johnny keeps trying while Christy and Ariel begin classes at a Catholic school.

Poorer than their classmates, Christy and Ariel stand out when they show up for a Halloween party in homemade costumes, but their spirits are raised when their parents allow them to go trick-or-treating in their building. Convinced they can demand treats from their neighbors, they pound on door after door with no luck until Ariel dares Christy to knock on Mateo's door, a door made more formidable by its emphatic message to stay away. Annoyed by their persistent knocking, Mateo finally opens the door and instead of the bogeyman they expect, they find a friend—thanks to Ariel's ready acceptance of this massive black man who, they learn later, is dying of AIDS and has withdrawn from a comfortable life to live alone and to rage at his situation.

Gradually it becomes clear the family's move from Ireland to the United States was prompted at least in part by deep sorrow over the accidental death of their two-year-old son/brother, Frankie. Each of the family members still grieves over the loss and struggles because they have been unable to accept it. When Sarah becomes pregnant, complications jeopardize the lives of both mother and baby and make early hospitalization necessary but unaffordable. When born, the baby's life depends on a blood transfusion, a procedure made possible when eleven-year-old Christy, identified as a compatible donor, steps forward. By cross-cutting between Mateo as he lies dying in another hospital room, it becomes clear that Christy's gift of blood is being supplemented by Mateo's giving up his life so the baby lives.

Christy's clear vision and wisdom, Ariel's guilelessness, Sarah's radiance and generosity, Johnny's indefatigable spirit, and Mateo's strength and openness make the film exceptionally positive and appealing. Beneath the surface and almost always held in check for the sake of the others is the family's deep sadness, a sadness relieved by Mateo's friendship, by the birth of the baby—named Mateo in honor of that friendship—and by the family's kindness, concern, and care for each other.

*In America* was written by Jim Sheridan and his two daughters, Naomi and Kirsten, as a semiautobiographical account of their family's move to New York. Interestingly, the story is told from Christy's perspective and reflects the rich, magical world of a child who sees and experiences the sadness enveloping her parents and works hard to make things right. As the film opens, Christy tells us in voice-over that she has received the gift of three wishes from Frankie and she is determined to use them to good effect. The first she uses to secure the family's entry into the United States. The second is invoked at a particularly low point, when her father is in danger of losing hope, the family's rent money, and Ariel's belief in his power to make things happen. The third wish saves the new baby and opens the way for the family to exorcise their grief over Frankie's death.

Given its focus on the children's roles in the family and their ready acceptance of people regardless of skin color, *In America* effectively illustrates the beauty and value of cross-cultural interaction and connection while also showing not only how children learn from their parents' example, but also how parents learn from their children's. Ariel's love for Mateo is particularly eloquent.

## *In the Heat of the Night* (1967)

Director: Norman Jewison

Cast: Sydney Poitier (Detective Virgil Tibbs), Rod Steiger (Chief Bill Gillespie), Warren Oates (Officer Sam Wood), Lee Grant (Mrs. Leslie Colbert), Larry Gates (Eric Endicott) Quentin Dean (Delores Purdy), James Patterson (Purdy)

Length: 110 min.

Rating: Approved (suggested for mature audiences)

Interracial Murder Mystery: Northern African American detective and Southern police chief learn to work together

*In the Heat of the Night* opens with a passenger train arriving in Sparta, Mississippi. A well-dressed man exits the train, but we never see his face. Wood, a local police officer, finishes his coffee at the local restaurant and, continuing his late night patrol, discovers a homicide victim in an alley in town. Chief of Police Gillespie is summoned and he and Wood begin their investigation. The stranger from the train is arrested at the train station, brought into the police station, and questioned by the chief, who assumes he is the murderer. The stranger introduces himself as Virgil Tibbs and Gillespie quickly learns that Tibbs is a Philadelphia police officer. When his commanding officer suggests that Tibbs assist in the investigation, neither Tibbs nor Gillespie like the idea, but they go along with it.

As the investigation moves forward, the war of wills between the African American, big city, well-educated, Northern detective and the European American, street-smart, small town, Southern chief of police becomes more and more apparent. Director Norman Jewison uses several dramatic devices to portray the differences between the two, but he emphasizes the racial divide in particular. Tibbs, for example, is consistently referred to as "boy," and any time he tries to question a European American, the character responds with a mix of disbelief, defiance, and disgust. Tibbs does not, however, follow Southern protocol and overlook the insults. When Tibbs confronts Endicott, a plantation owner and local economic power broker, Endicott is so insulted by Tibb's questioning that he slaps Tibbs in the face and is totally unprepared when, without hesitating, Tibbs slaps him back. Endicott expects Chief Gillespie to avenge the affront, but he does not.

In 1967, this scene, at the height of the civil rights struggle, symbolized the social changes taking place in this country and created a stir that rippled through the whole nation. Through the film, audiences can still glimpse the social stratification that existed during this time; it is evident in Endicott, his mansion and servants, in the African Americans and their shanties in the colored section of town, and in Gillespie's position between the two. Another significant element of the film's depiction of the era is the fictive kinship that exists among African Americans. Apparent when Tibbs is quickly accepted and provided housing within the community, this extended familial connectedness was and is an essential part of African American survival.

Both Tibbs and Gillespie struggle with their own prejudice and contempt, Tibbs assuming the police officers and inhabitants of a small racist Southern town to be slow-witted and unsophisticated, and Gillespie resenting an "uppity" African American Northerner, a big-city detective who makes more money and has more book knowledge than he has. However, for all their differences, they are similar in that they are both loners who have sacrificed personal relationships for their love of the law. Their commitment to the law makes their bonding possible because it makes them realize they need each other's unique skills to solve a murder case.

*In the Heat of the Night* effectively captures the attitudes and nuances of Jim Crow Mississippi in the 1960s through its highly stylized characters and their interactions, the accuracy of its settings, and its brilliant Quincy Jones soundtrack. Couched in a complicated and absorbing murder mystery, the film entertains as it teaches. It can further viewers' understanding of the history and feelings of an era. C. Vann Woodward's *The Strange Career of Jim Crow* can help shed light on an important aspect of the era.

**Work Cited:** Woodward, C. Vann. *The Strange Career of Jim Crow*. New York: Oxford University Press, 2001.

## *The Incredibly True Adventure of Two Girls in Love* (1995)

Director: Maria Maggenti

Cast: Laurel Holloman (Randall "Randy" Dean), Nicole Parker (Evelyn "Evie" Roy), Dale Dickey (Regina), Stephanie Berry (Evie's mother, Evelyn Roy), Maggie Moore (Wendy), Kate Stafford (Rebecca), Sabrina Artel (Vicky), Nelson Rodriguez (Frank)

Length: 94 min.

Rating: R

Adolescent Romantic Comedy: Interracial lesbian romance

High school senior Randy Dean lives with her Aunt Rebecca and Rebecca's partner Vicky because her mother, having carried her antiabortion protests too far, is in prison. Randy works with Regina at a gas station, dreams of playing guitar in a rock band, and shows minimal interest in school. Correctly identified as a lesbian by her classmates and at least superficially reveling in her rebel status, she has few friends. When Evie, an African American senior at the same school Randy attends, comes by the gas station in her Range Rover to have a tire checked, Randy is immediately smitten. The two meet again when they independently seek refuge in the girls' room at school—Randy to let off steam after a reprimand and Evie to try to sort out her conflicting feelings after breaking up with her boyfriend. When they are discovered smoking, they share detention after school. Their friendship develops from there, with the wealthy, accomplished, and proper Evie intrigued by Randy and her lifestyle. The two girls become increasingly close.

When Evie's overprotective mother, a very successful agricultural economist and consultant, leaves Evie alone for a weekend while she attends a conference, Evie invites Randy to spend the weekend with her and help her celebrate her eighteenth birthday. Using her friend Frank as a cover, Randy accepts. The two girls, under the influence of marijuana and wine, prepare an elaborate dinner, talk, and eventually go to bed together. Evie's mother, ever anxious about her daughter, returns home early, and finds the house an absolute mess and the girls sleeping together. She becomes hysterical and the girls flee to a motel. Eventually Frank, Evie's mother, Rebecca, Vicky, and an assortment of friends gather outside the motel and, in a comically chaotic scene, clamor for the girls to come out. When they do emerge, they have promised to stay together; they seal their agreement with a kiss and an embrace while their "audience" watches in silence.

The "incredibly" of the film's title is apt given Maria Maggenti's over-the-top treatment of Randy and Evie's night together, the incredible mess they leave in their wake, and the circuslike atmosphere that accompanies their escape to the motel. Race/ethnicity does not become an issue in Randy and Evie's relationship or in those of the adults they answer to. It surfaces only once when, after having dinner with Randy's family, Evie asks if Rebecca hates her because she is black. Randy assures her Rebecca does not hate her and the subject is dropped. A brief assessment of the film in *Halliwell's 2002 Film and Video Guide*, suggests that "[a]part from the fact that its protagonists are of the same sex, this is otherwise a predictable movie of teenage angst and rebellion" (413).

The comfort level shown in Randy and Evie's interracial relationship—and its non-issue status—suggests race/ethnicity does not present the same problems for adolescents in the 1990s that it did for earlier generations. A comparison of *The Incredibly True Adventure* with other films featuring culturally diverse teenagers could be interesting. Is Maggenti's film, a low-budget independent movie, an anomaly or an indication young people are accepting cultural pluralism not simply as a political or social reality, but as an integral part of their own personal reality? If this is the case, is it significant that Evie, the African American, is wealthy and enjoys the lifestyle and advantages of that class while Randy, the European American, is lower-middle class? Do their class differences make their relationship more or less viable than their racial/ethnic differences? Would their relationship be possible or likely if their racial/ethnic identities remained the same but Randy were wealthy and Evie lower-middle class?

Though *The Incredibly True Adventure* comes across as a light and—in its second half—even madcap comedy, it raises some interesting and engaging questions for adolescents and adults.

**Work Cited:** Halliwell, Leslie. *Halliwell's 2002 Film and Video Guide*. New York: HarperResource, 2001.

## Ken Burns's Documentaries

### *The Civil War* (1990), *Baseball* (1994), *Jazz* (2001)

Director: Ken Burns

Distributor: PBS Video

Length: *The Civil War*, 690 min.; *Baseball*, 1,140 min.; *Jazz*, 1,140 min.

Rating: Not Rated

Historical Documentaries: Explorations of major aspects of U.S. history and culture

Ken Burns is one of the best historical documentary filmmakers of our times. His diligence in pursuing evocative details, his superb research skills, and his interview abilities give his work an authenticity that has earned the respect of his peers. Burns's selection of subject matter chronicles some of the most central elements of our society. *The Civil War*, for example, is a monumental work in nine segments and covers this event from its causes through Reconstruction. Likewise, *Jazz*, an epic effort, distills from a vast history many major artists, styles, and eras of the music that best celebrates the shared culture of the people of the United States. Finally, *Baseball* is an examination of the quintessential American pastime and represents the best and worst in our culture, from its racism and scandals to its opportunities and riches.

In each of these films, Burns features primary source documents such as letters, newspaper articles, photographs, and motion pictures, and then supplements these using interviews with distinguished historians and other experts who are connected to the events in some way. A narrator, often a well-known public person, brings these many disparate elements together to give a coherent well-crafted and multidimensional account of Burns's subjects. This process gives viewers a broad perspective on the topics being covered and assures a well-crafted, unified presentation.

Burns's films lend themselves to classroom use because of their subject matter, but also because they break down into short segments very easily. In addition to *The Civil War*, *Baseball*, and *Jazz*, titles that could be considered in a study of culture are *The West*, *Lewis and Clark*, and *The Shakers*, all available through PBS Video. Most of his major films are complemented by textbooks and Web sites that enhance their utility. Educators are also likely to find Gary R. Edgerton's *Ken Burns's America* of interest since he analyzes the evolution of Burns's documentary approach as well as several of his major projects.

*The Civil War* effectively documents some of the many reasons behind the Civil War. The differences between the North and South and the role of slavery in the events leading up to secession are examined. Once the war begins, its impact on families, communities, and friends is effectively illustrated, and major battles are covered in detail, with perspectives from both Union and Confederate combatants and civilians. The lives of key figures like Ulysses S. Grant and Robert E. Lee are chronicled in sufficiently vivid detail and with enough input from historians to allow viewers to connect with these men, but the letters from "ordinary" men and women help viewers identify with them as well. A soundtrack that includes sound effects to help bring the film's images to life and period music to help convey the climate of the era contributes to the import of this impressive documentary. The comprehensive PBS Web site will help educators and their students follow up on the many facets of the Civil War the film introduces.

Although *Jazz* has been praised for the artists such as Billie Holiday, Louis Armstrong, Duke Ellington, Winton Marsalis, and many others that Burns included, it has been equally criticized for the contemporary artists left out. Obviously a single work, even a work of this magnitude will never satisfy all the critics, but this is a comprehensive work that not only looks good but sounds good as well.

The film is divided into ten segments beginning with a synopsis of African American music from Africa through slavery. Subsequent chapters deal with jazz from New Orleans to Kansas, Chicago, New York, and the Pacific coast, and with the development of various styles and stages of jazz. According to the PBS catalog description, *Jazz* "blends 75 interviews, more than 500 pieces of music, 2,400 still photographs, and over 2,000 rare and archival film clips." Much of the music had not been released to the public previously but is now available in a wonderfully mastered set of five CDs. The Web site is a valuable resource and accompaniment to *Jazz*. It contains the actual interview transcripts and audio clips of many of the contributing artists as well as a timeline, other background information, and links to other sites. A children's section offers lots of age-appropriate materials including timelines and suggestions for interactive activities.

Jazz is one cultural phenomenon that could lead a person to an understanding of the history of the United States. Baseball is another. As America's favorite pastime, baseball's role has been as indelible as it has been inclusive. Ken Burns and his associate Lynn Novich believe "[t]he story of baseball is also the story of race in America, of immigration and assimilation, of the struggle between labor and management, of popular culture and advertising, of myth and the nature of heroes, villains, and buffoons; of the role of women and class and wealth in our society" (WETA).

*Baseball* effectively chronicles the role of the Negro Leagues and the significance of baseball's integration by Jackie Robinson of the National League and Larry Doby of the American League. Once again the Burns style of intermixing interviews, archival photos, and film brings this subject alive, and the PBS Web site provides excellent supplementary material.

**Works Cited:** Edgerton, Gary R. *Ken Burns's America.* New York: Palgrave, 2001; WETA. "Ken Burns on PBS." http://www.pbs.org/kenburns/.

## *Lone Star* (1996)

Director: John Sayles

Cast: Chris Cooper (Sam Deeds), Elizabeth Peña (Pilar), Kris Kristofferson (Charlie Wade), Matthew McConaughey (Buddy Wade)

Length: 134 min.

Rating: R

Drama: Personal and public investigations help establish identities and define relations

After his divorce, Sam Deeds returns to Frontera, his hometown along the Texas–Mexico border, and becomes sheriff, a position his deceased but still idolized father, Buddy, held for over thirty years. Two years into his term, the bones of Charlie Wade, his father's feared and despised predecessor, are found on an abandoned army firing range. Along with the bones is evidence Charlie was murdered. Sam is convinced his father killed Charlie and is intent on discovering exactly what happened—preferably before a monument to honor Buddy is dedicated.

While Sam carries on his investigation, he renews his relationship with Pilar, his first—and perhaps only—love, now a widow with two adolescent children. Pilar's relationship with her mother, Mercedes, is as problematic as Sam's is with his father. A third difficult parent–child relationship being played out is between tough-as-nails Colonel Paine and his father, Otis, who had abandoned his family when his son was eight. Otis, known as the "Mayor of Dark Town" because of his interventions on behalf of the African Americans in town, owns a bar whose patrons are almost all black. His son commands a nearby army base.

The town's official mayor is Hollis, once one of Charlie's deputies. He, Otis, Mercedes, and Buddy all figure prominently in the history Sam uncovers. He learns that Hollis actually killed Charlie as Charlie was about to kill Otis in cold blood, and that Buddy, entering the scene just as the shooting occurred, helped bury the body and create an explanation for Charlie's disappearance.

Sam also learns that Buddy is Pilar's father as well as his, having had an extramarital affair for fifteen years with Mercedes after her fiancé was killed by Charlie. Sam decides to drop the Charlie Wade investigation even though dropping it means Buddy will be assumed to have been responsible (Sam: "Buddy's a . . . legend; he can handle it!"). He then meets Pilar and tells her about Buddy's ties to her and her mother. Together they decide to forget their histories and "start from scratch" in their relationship.

The past. History. How important are they? To whom are they important? How are they important? Pilar teaches history and clashes with the parents of her Anglo students when she tries to discuss Texas history from both Mexican and Anglo perspectives. The parents' opposition does not stop her from doing so. Otis's passion is his small but impressive museum where the history of black Seminoles is traced through photos and artifacts. He obviously wants to reconnect with his son, but he realizes too that "blood only means what you let it."

Much of Sam's investigation revolves around Frontera's past. His and Pilar's adolescent past resonates strongly in the present and is Sam's motivation for returning to Frontera. His strained relationship with Buddy also reverberates in the present and affects how he sees and does things. Mercedes prefers to forget her past, but a memory of an incident from her youth determines what she does in a critical situation involving one of her employees. Sayles seems to suggest that only in acknowledging and understanding history—personal and public—can we choose how best to respond to it.

The past Sayles explores in *Lone Star* is that of culturally diverse people and involves Mexicans, Mexican Americans, African Americans, Anglos, and, to some extent, Native Americans. He reveals prejudice, especially among some Anglos as they lose majority status in their border town, but he also shows, through multiple examples, that cooperation, interaction, and even intimate personal relationships among people from different racial/ethnic groups are possible though each comes with its own set of challenges. Sayles presents an unusually broad spectrum of such relationships. In doing so he questions the nature and function of borders—the borders we construct to organize and define our lives, to establish control, to assert identity, to determine legality, to distinguish between good and evil. He suggests that the lines drawn by individuals, communities, and governments are often elusive and prove inadequate given the complexity of our lives and our relationships. Sayles invites viewers to explore this complexity and the multiplicity of cultures in play within the United States through a popular genre that goes beyond the usual conventions and stereotypes. Because of the depth of Sayles's exploration in *Lone Star*, much has been written about it; two of the most accessible resources are *Sayles on Sayles* and *John Sayles, Filmmaker.*

**Works Cited:** Ryan, Jack. *John Sayles, Filmmaker.* Jefferson, NC: McFarland, 1998; Sayles, John. *Sayles on Sayles*, edited by Gavin Smith. Boston: Faber and Faber, 1998.

## *Lovely and Amazing* (2001)

Director: Nicole Holofcener

Cast: Catherine Keener (Michelle Marks), Brenda Blethyn (Jane Marks), Emily Mortimer (Elizabeth Marks), Raven Goodwin (Annie Marks), Aunjanue Ellis (Lorraine), Jake Gyllenhaal (Jordan), Dermot Mulroney (Kevin McCabe)

Length: 91 min.

Rating: R

Family Drama: Individual insecurities and their impact on relationships

Jane Marks has decided to have liposuction surgery and asks her daughter Michelle, an aspiring artist, wife, and mother, to look after Annie, her adopted eight-year-old African American daughter, while she recovers. Michelle reluctantly agrees, but when medical complications require Jane to remain in the hospital several days, Jane's other daughter, Elizabeth, offers to stay at Jane's house with Annie. Between hospital visits the three daughters wrestle with various problems, all apparently rooted in low self-esteem and insecurity.

Michelle makes a couple of attempts to sell her artwork but immediately responds with hostility and self-pity when the work is rejected. Her husband, Bill, is carrying on an affair with her friend Donna, and Michelle is aware of this. When she gets a job at a one-hour photo shop, she responds ambiguously to the advances of Jordan, her 17-year-old boss. Jordan's infatuation and ardor and her response, though limited, result in Michelle being arrested and charged with statutory rape.

Elizabeth works as a model and actor but limits her own possibilities because of her inability to project "sexy." Her insecurities bore her boyfriend Paul and lead to their break-up, but a chance meeting with television star Kevin McCabe, with whom she has had a failed audition, leads to an evening together and the possibility of another. She directs much of her energy and a desire to be needed to the care of injured and stray dogs; they usually respond well to her attention though one attempt results in her being bitten on the lip.

Annie—feisty, overweight, and also insecure—identifies with and loves Jane as her mother though she is clear about who her natural mother is. At one point she tells Jane she wants skin like hers. Despite Jane's assurances that her skin is beautiful, Annie is not convinced. She picks up on Michelle's hostility toward her and responds in kind. When Lorraine, a young African American woman becomes her Big Sister, Annie cons her into straightening her hair, upsetting Elizabeth and Jane, but the result actually prompts a rapprochement between Annie and Michelle.

Though Jane is a loving mother and sees her daughters as "lovely and amazing," her own insecurity comes across in the humor she uses to deflect an examination of her own needs, and in her decision to have surgery, an act that undermines her attempts, for example, to assure Annie she is beautiful. Jane seems to understand her daughters and their lack of self-confidence, but she doesn't make the connection between her own mixed signals and their sense of self. She worries about Annie, convinced she will have a more difficult time than her older daughters. By enrolling her in the Big Sister program, Jane facilitates Annie's interaction with Lorraine, but after Annie lies and then scares her by floating face down in the swimming pool, Lorraine opts out. In becoming a Big Sister, she did not envision a relationship with a middle-class African American living in mainstream society. She wants to help someone from the black community who doesn't have the advantages Annie has.

Annie's behavior seems to shout "Pay attention to me; love me; give me some assurance I belong." She lives in a white world, interacting primarily with a loving but insecure mother and with sisters who are three or four times her age, are hard pressed to deal with the expectations of their own culture, and have little understanding of African American culture. Rather than become part of an African American or culturally diverse community, they hand Annie over to Lorraine, apparently expecting her to take responsibility for Annie's initiation into black culture.

Intriguing and relevant, *Lovely and Amazing*, despite its inward focus, invites analysis. It differs from many films about cultural diversity in its focus on an alternative family, the members' interactions and their personal strengths and weaknesses, and the insecurity cultural demands can impose on individuals. The film poses questions, too, about the challenges and rewards of interracial adoptions and about the complex personal and social web they create. For viewers who want to explore these questions further, Maria P. P. Root and Matt Kelley's *Multiracial Child Resource Book* could prove an excellent source of information and insight.

**Work Cited:** Root, Maria P. P., and Matt Kelley. *Multiracial Child Resource Book: Living Complex Identities*. Seattle: Mavin Foundation, 2003.

## *Matewan* (1987)

Director: John Sayles

Cast: Chris Cooper (Joe Kenehan), Mary McDowell (Elma Radnor), Will Oldham (Danny Radnor), David Strathairn (Sid Hatfield), James Earl Jones ("Few Clothes" Johnson)

Length: 132 min.

Rating: PG-13

Political Drama: Union organizer attempts to unite African, Appalachian, and Italian miners

In the 1920s, when miners in the small town of Matewan, West Virginia, decide to strike for better wages and working conditions, the mine owners bring in African Americans and newly arrived Italian immigrants to replace the strikers. The union sends in Joe Kenehan to organize the workers—strikers and strikebreakers alike—to press their demands more effectively. Committed to nonviolence on principle and as a strategy that will thwart the mine owners' attempts to bring hostile government forces in against the strikers, Kenehan finds his efforts undermined by a member of the union who is actually a spy for the mine owners.

Violence breaks out several times, but the workers unite despite their racial/ethnic differences when the African and Italian Americans refuse to enter the mines, thus becoming strikers and union men themselves. When a young striker is brutally killed and the Stone Mountain Coal Company brings in a posse of armed men to evacuate the workers from their camp, all of Joe's efforts to avoid violence prove fruitless as miners and company men fight each other in a bloody massacre. Kenehan is among those killed in what becomes known as the Matewan Massacre and the beginning of the Great Coal Field War.

Because their experiences differ so radically, the miners find it difficult to trust each other. The African and Italian Americans, for example, are initially hired as scabs when the white miners strike. Racism and anti-immigrant sentiment are rampant. African Americans have reason to distrust whites given their experiences with race-related violence in the United States, and the Italians, new to the country and unfamiliar with the language and the culture, are wary of alliances with people they do not know. Understandably, the men initially identify more as West Virginians, African Americans, or Italian Americans than as workers with common challenges and goals. One of Kenehan's primary tasks is to convince them they not only share goals, but they can reach them only by uniting and working together.

Living together in a camp set up after the three groups join forces against the mine owners gives them the chance to see around their cultural differences to their shared humanity and values. Playing baseball and music together as well as sharing food prove simple but effective ways of crossing the lines that initially separate them. Their views on violence, however, continue to divide them, with the African and Italian Americans choosing not to join the West Virginians in the violence of the Matewan Massacre. Given their vulnerability and more tenuous status within the country, their decision makes sense though it does not go as far as Kenehan would like them and all people to go: to a complete rejection of violence even at the cost of personal suffering. Ironically, Joe's cry, an attempt to avoid the confrontation that ends in the massacre and his own death, sparks the first shots and suggests how difficult it is to refrain from violence when confronted with power and money, in this case the mine owners' and the state's.

*Matewan* invites discussion of the role of violence within the United States and within the diverse cultural groups that comprise this country. The film also invites discussion of how, why, and with what effect these diverse groups have been brought together at times. When discussing the film in relation to these issues, John Sayles's comments in the chapter titled "Why Matewan?" in his book *Thinking in Pictures: The Making of the Movie* Matewan and in his interview covering the movie in *Sayles on Sayles* can be helpful and informative.

**Works Cited:** Sayles, John. *Sayles on Sayles*, edited by Gavin Smith. Boston: Faber and Faber, 1998; Sayles, John. *Thinking in Pictures*: *The Making of the Movie* Matewan. Boston: Houghton Mifflin, 1987.

## The *Matrix* Trilogy: *The Matrix* (1999), *The Matrix Reloaded* (2003), *The Matrix Revolutions* (2003)

Directors: Andy and Larry Wachowski

Cast: Keanu Reeves (Neo), Laurence Fishburne (Morpheus), Carrie-Anne Moss (Trinity), Hugo Weaving (Agent Smith), Gloria Foster/Mary Alice (Oracle), Jada Pinkett Smith (Niobe), Helmut Bakaitis (Architect)

Length: *The Matrix*, 136 min.; *The Matrix Reloaded*, 138 min.; *The Matrix Revolutions*, 129 min.

Rating: R

Futuristic Science Fiction Drama: The struggle between human beings and technology

The *Matrix* trilogy, a futuristic epic, is about the struggle between man and machine. In this story the machines have overtaken the world. Humans, in a desperate effort to stop the machines, cover the earth with a shroud of clouds to blot out the sunlight and deprive the machines of this essential energy source. This strategy backfires. It fails because the machines learn to harvest energy from humans themselves. They create massive farms containing billions of humans to produce the energy they need to control the world. In order to pacify their human chattel, the machines create an illusory computer-generated world called the Matrix. The captive humans live their entire conscious lives in this world without ever knowing the reality of their existence.

Morpheus, a leader among the free humans who live outside the control of the machines and the Matrix, is fighting to free the enslaved humans but believes he and his fellow humans need the intervention of the "One" in order to succeed. He is convinced, after meeting with the Oracle, that Neo is the One, capable of leading humans to freedom from their bondage. To assume this role, however, Neo must evolve, must mature intellectually and spiritually. Only then will he be able to meet the threats posed by the Matrix and by Agent Smith, the chief antagonist of the humans and their desire for freedom.

In this future the humans of Zion are definitely a multicultural nation. Characters of color are influential throughout the film, in sharp contrast to the many futuristic Hollywood films that are dominated by European Americans. In the *Matrix* trilogy, African Americans in particular have very significant roles: the Oracle is the second most powerful computer entity, Morpheus, the revered prophet of the Zions, and Niobe, the captain of a war ship. On the ruling council of Zion, males and females of different races/ethnicities wield power, and females, such as the Oracle, Niobe, and Trinity, play powerful and decisive roles throughout the trilogy. On the other hand, the Architect, the most powerful computer entity, Zion's council leader, and Agent Smith whose growing power threatens everything and everyone, are all European American males.

This trilogy can be studied on many levels, as is evident from the numerous Web sites, articles, books, and reviews it has spawned. Whether viewers' interests are in cultural diversity, philosophy, religious studies, history, aesthetics, or technology, they will have little difficulty locating material to assist them in their pursuit of information and insight. Matt Lawrence's *Like a Splinter in Your Mind: The Philosophy Behind the Matrix Trilogy* is one place to begin, but Frank M. Robinson, Robert E. Weinberg, and Randy Broecker's *Art of Imagination* provides another point of entry.

**Works Cited:** Lawrence, Matt. *Like a Splinter in Your Mind: The Philosophy Behind the* Matrix *Trilogy*. Malden, MA: Blackwell Publishing, 2004; Robinson Frank M., Robert E. Weinberg, and Randy Broecker. *Art of Imagination: 20th Century Visions of Science Fiction, Horror, and Fantasy*. Portland, OR: Collectors Press, 2002.

## *Midnight in the Garden of Good and Evil* (1997)

Director: Clint Eastwood

Cast: John Cusack (John), Kevin Spacey (Jim Williams), Jack Thompson (Frank/Lady Chablis), Irma P. Hall (Minerva), Jude Law (Billy Hanson)

Length: 155 min.

Rating: R

Southern Gothic Melodrama: Mystery, murder, and complex sexual and racial relationships

*Midnight in the Garden of Good and Evil* is a multilayered examination of the modern South. John, a New York-based journalist from *Town and Country* magazine, comes to Savannah, Georgia, to write a 500-word article on a Christmas party at an eccentric millionaire's restored mansion. Jim Williams's party list includes politicians, the rich, and the famous. Following the Christmas party, Jim kills Billy Hanson. The ensuing investigation draws John into the mystery of the murder. He is subpoenaed as a material witness because he overheard Hanson threaten Williams before the party, but he also wants to turn the whole incident into a book and highlight the strange culture he has observed in this small southern town.

As John begins to investigate Hanson's life, he encounters a whole spectrum of characters: Chablis, a drag queen who knew Hanson prior to his death; Minerva, a voodoo queen and medium who operates between the realms of good and evil and seeks to break the spell Hanson placed on Jim; the upper echelon of black society in the region; the ladies of the Bridge Club; people from the gay community; and Jim's resourceful and cunning lawyer who successfully argues his case. Shortly after Jim is released from custody, Minerva summons him and John to the garden, where she beckons Billy Hanson's spirit to pass on, but it refuses to rest. When later that night Jim dies mysteriously at his mansion, audiences are left to decide if he died of natural causes or was killed by Hanson's restless spirit.

This macabre tale shows viewers some of the rich variety that makes up Southern culture. Defined primarily by class, sexual orientation, and race/ethnicity, the interplay among these cultural variations still reflects traditional hierarchies and prejudices. African Americans are largely portrayed in service roles as cooks, servants, dog walkers, and entertainers. Although we get a glimpse of the African American elite, there is no evidence that they participate equally in the professional life of the society. Interracial interactions are still at the margins of this society, especially when they involve voodoo, certainly a part of African culture but one that is largely hidden even among African Americans.

European American culture is shown to be stratified by social classes that range from the Southern gentry and noveau riche to the middle class and the poor. This stratification is complicated further by the alternative lifestyles of Jim, Billy, and Lady Chablis. Like the voodooism practiced by Minerva, the homosexuality of these characters exists below the surface of socially acceptable behavior. In both, what is hidden or taboo proves mysterious and fascinating, but also easy to condemn. Because it exposes so many levels of an intricate social order, *Midnight in the Garden of Good and Evil* can be used to initiate discussion of the complex hierarchies and social interaction imposed by variations in culture.

## *Mississippi Masala* (1991)

Director: Mira Nair

Cast: Denzel Washington (Demetrius), Sarita Choudhury (Mina), Roshan Seth (Jay), Sharmila Tagore (Kinnu), Charles Dutton (Tyrone), Kongo Mbandu (Okelo)

Length: 118 min.

Rating: R

Drama: An interracial romance develops despite family and community opposition

*Mississippi Masala* begins in 1972 with Indian Ugandan attorney Jay, his wife Kinnu, and daughter Mina being forced to leave Uganda under the dictatorship of Idi Amin. They leave property but also friends, among them Okelo, a particularly close black family friend who had earlier risked his life to get Jay out of prison. Despite their personal relationship, Jay and Okelo take different political stances, Jay arguing he has every right to stay in Uganda since he sees it as his country, the country with which he identifies and to which he gives his allegiance. Okela sees 1972 as a time for Africans to take back their country: "Africa is for Africans—black Africans."

Having been displaced, Jay, Kinnu, and Mina, emigrate to the United States, settling in Greenwood, Mississippi, in an Indian American community. After almost twenty years there, they live in a motel owned by friends, own a small liquor store, and manage to get by with help from Mina, now twenty-four-years old and cleaning rooms at the motel. Jay is still obsessed with Uganda and spends considerable time writing letters to the Ugandan government in an effort to get his property back.

Both Jay and Kinnu are concerned about Mina's future and want her to marry well—and within the Indian American community. Mina and Demetrius Williams meet when she literally runs into his van. They meet again the same day at the Leopard Lounge, where they dance and Demetri ends up taking Mina home. Demetri doesn't hesitate introducing Mina to his family, but she is not so open with her family about their budding relationship. When the two meet in Biloxi and are discovered in a motel room together, the repercussions are immediate and severe: Demetri's rug cleaning business is threatened when his Indian American customers drop him, and in turn, his loan payments are jeopardized. Jay decides to separate the two by taking Mina and Kinnu with him to Uganda when settling his lawsuit against the government. Mina, not ready to leave without saying goodbye, however, finds Demetri. As they talk through what has happened, they decide to stay together despite the obvious hurdles ahead. Jay returns to Uganda alone and finally comes to terms with the changes there and with the reality of his life in the United States.

Jay's story, his loss of status because of political and ideological change, frames Mina and Demetri's story of an interethnic relationship. Jay's acceptance of his Ugandan experience signals his acceptance of Mina and Demetri's relationship though this is not played out in the film. Both situations, despite their enormous differences, involve intercultural relationships that demand that Jay rethink his assumptions, priorities, and point of view. Unfortunately, it takes Okelo's death, which Jay learns of when he returns to Uganda, to effect this rethinking.

Jay's story, in a sense, is privileged since it begins and ends *Mississippi Masala*, but for most viewers, Mina and Demetrius's relationship is probably of primary interest. Both are initially identified with their families and communities, but as they fall in love and are judged to have violated familial and cultural norms, with few exceptions family, friends, and associates withdraw support. They are effectively kept from each other until Mina, about to leave for Africa, defies her parents in order to see Demetri again. In typical Hollywood and Romeo-and-Juliet fashion, they choose each other over family and community and set off for a life together somewhere outside of Mississippi. Not so typically Hollywood are the phone calls each makes to their parents to explain their decision to leave, keeping open the door for reconciliation and reunion.

*Mississippi Masala*'s portrayal of cross-cultural romance has been viewed as a positive step in the history of interethnic relations (Ebert), but bell hooks sees the film as a "cavalier and shallow treatment of serious material" (41). She and her colleague Anuradha Dingwaney, in a critique published in *Z Magazine*, find the film problematic for a number of reasons: stereotypical portrayals of secondary characters, the identification of the major characters with "attitudes and perspectives that represent the white supremacist norm" (43), the undercutting of community in favor of personal freedom (43), and the suggestion "that romantic love . . . enables individuals to move beyond systems of domination," without changes occurring within the larger community (41). Their analysis is compelling and brings up several issues, among them audience expectations and responses to commercial cinema.

The Hollywood film industry, with its interest in entertainment and profit, rarely explores political or social issues in a serious or complex way. Stereotypes, romance, and feel-good answers are what it offers and what the average viewer expects. When it ventures into new territory, even if it does so only marginally, as *Mississippi Masala* does, many viewers, as well as critics, are likely to applaud.

In *Mississippi Masala* we are given a familiar formula, a light romantic drama, with two important twists: an interethnic couple at the film's center and a relationship framed by international political conflict. Is this worth applauding? Yes and no. Yes, because the film acknowledges the multiculturalism integral to U.S. society and the desires we share as humans. No, because with its focus on individual fulfillment, the film reinforces ideas that confirm the status quo and strengthen the notion that individual happiness is more important than community (hooks 43). Yes, because by giving Jay's struggle a significant role, the film acknowledges the need to adapt to new circumstances and to accept change even at great personal loss.

hooks and Dingwaney point out that when Jay returns to Uganda, he finds his former property in ruins, but they overlook the energy and joy evident in the people Jay sees. When, in a letter to Kinnu, he writes "home is where the heart is," however, he glosses over complex political situations and falls into Hollywood's pat reaffirmation that the personal, not the political, is its priority.

Critiques like hooks and Dingwaney's go below the surface of commercial films and point to their shortcomings and contradictory stances. Such in-depth explorations invite viewers to examine assumptions they rarely question. For example, taking a cue from hooks and Dingwaney but following it in another direction, we might note that in the United States Jay identifies as a Ugandan when pursuing his property claim, but he identifies as Indian in choosing a community in which to live and work. He never identifies as African American, nor is he or his family identified as such by Indian or African Americans. Can one be Ugandan without being African? Ugandan American without being African American? The questions complicate the distinctions made on the basis of race/ethnicity, but they could simplify the issue if they lead to a recognition of how artificial such tags are.

Looking deeply and asking questions help make us more astute viewers. We should, therefore, acknowledge the insights of critics such as hooks and Dingwaney while we, at the same time, appreciate and enjoy the recognizable steps forward media have taken in their depiction of our culturally diverse society. *Mississippi Masala* provides one starting point.

**Works Cited:** Ebert, Roger. Review of *Mississippi Masala*, directed by Mira Nair. *Chicago Sun-Times*, February 14, 1992. http://www.suntimes.com/ebert/ebert_reviews/1992/02/741134.html (accessed September 2, 2003); hooks, bell, and Anuradha Dingwaney. Review of *Mississippi Masala*, directed by Mira Nair. *Z Magazine* (July/August 1992): 41–43.

## *Moscow on the Hudson* (1984)

Director: Paul Mazursky

Cast: Robin Williams (Vladimir Ivanoff), Cleavant Derricks (Lionel Witherspoon), Maria Conchita Alonso (Lucia Lombardo), Alejandro Rey (Orlando Ramirez)

Length: 107 min.

Rating: R

Comedy Drama: A Russian defector adapts to a new country and culture

*Moscow on the Hudson* opens as a troupe of circus performers in the Soviet Union is being prepared by the KGB for a visit to New York City. Before they leave, a glimpse of life in Russia shows harsh living conditions that include long lines for food, for clothing, for every kind of commodity, except, it seems, vodka. The simple act of bringing home toilet paper is cause for a minor celebration. The KGB is practically omnipresent, but when not present, citizens are expected to keep an eye on each other, even friends. This constant scrutiny undercuts their enjoyment of the conveniences they do have, such as color television, a modern transportation system, and access to the arts. When the circus troupe arrives in New York, the KGB is so concerned about Vladimir's good friend Tolya defecting that they actually allow Vladimir to do so. His escape involves a hilarious chase with the KGB that includes the KGB leader begging Vladimir not to defect because of reprisals to his own career.

Vladimir is invited by Lionel, the African American security guard who helps in his defection, to live with his family temporarily, and they become friends. Vladimir also develops a relationship with Lucia, an Italian American immigrant, and with Orlando, a Cuban American who becomes his lawyer. As his circle of friends grows, he finds each of them is an immigrant and has a unique story to tell about becoming "American."

Vladimir works at a variety of jobs as he waits for his immigration hearing, though he fails to get work as a musician. His relationship with Lucia dissolves and Lionel moves back to Alabama. During this dark period he also learns his grandfather has passed away. When he is robbed and assaulted on his way home one evening, he begins to question the whole idea of freedom and the United States. Later, talking with Orlando and other immigrants, the sound of fourth-of-July fireworks pulls him back to the country's promise.

*Moscow on the Hudson* is a very entertaining film that can help viewers remember why this country is great, even with all its flaws. Robin Williams is brilliant as a new immigrant trying to make it in New York City, the Big Apple. The multiethnic/racial mix of the characters lends authenticity to this bittersweet story of the trials and tribulations of the new immigrant experience. The film's balance of positive and negative experiences makes it more realistic and more useful in classroom situations. The many comic scenes, such as one in which Vladimir suffers a mental meltdown when grocery shopping because of the overwhelming array of product choices, will help assure attention. Though the film is rated R because of some profanity and violence as well as brief nudity and suggested sex, educators may want to consider its appropriateness for adolescents as well as adults. Viewers can find further insights and information about contemporary immigrants to the United States in Samuel J. Ungar's *Fresh Blood: The New American Immigrants*.

**Work Cited:** Ungar, Samuel J. *Fresh Blood: The New American Immigrants*. Urbana: University of Illinois Press, 1998.

## *The New Americans* (2004)

Directors: Steve James, Gordon Quinn, Indu Krishnan, Susana Aikin, Carlos Aparicio, Renee Tajima-Peña, Jerry Blumenthal.

Distributor: PBS Video

Length: 360 min. (miniseries, 3 episodes)

Rating: Not Rated

Documentary: A chronicle of contemporary immigrants and their experiences over several years

*The New Americans*, begun in 1997 and first aired in 2004, tells the stories of several recent immigrants to the United States. It chronicles the lives of two Nigerian families, two aspiring Dominican baseball players, a Palestinian woman and her Palestinian American husband, a Mexican family of eight, and an Indian computer programmer. They begin their stories in their homelands as they explain why they are leaving countries and, to a great extent, cultures they know and love.

For Israel and Ngozi Nwidor and Barine Wiwa-Lawani, Nigerian Ogonis who face discrimination because of their opposition to a military government and to Shell Oil Company's exploitation of their land, immigration is necessitated by oppression. Naima chooses to leave the West Bank because, given the precarious position of Palestinians, she cannot expect to find what she wants in life if she stays. Ricardo Rodriguez and José Garcia see playing major league baseball in the United States as a means to escape the poverty and lack of job opportunities in the Dominican Republic. Economic necessity and a desire to be together as a family motivate Pedro Flores, his wife, and six children to leave Mexico for the United States. Though not compelled by financial need to leave India, Anjan Bacchu, a young computer programmer, is anxious to participate in the Silicon Valley dot.com boom and to see more of the world before settling down in his home country.

Much of the value of this six-hour miniseries springs from its comprehensiveness. By beginning in their homelands, viewers get a much better understanding of the circumstances of these people's lives, and of the deep family and community relationships they must sacrifice when choosing to emigrate. By following them as they try to adjust to a new life in a land with different cultural values and expectations, viewers can see how much struggle is involved. Although their situations differ markedly, they all struggle because of the demands of living within a foreign culture. For most, establishing a firm economic base is critical, but for all, finding meaningful work and retaining their dignity are also major concerns and challenges.

The producers of *The New Americans* are to be applauded for following their subjects for an extended period of time because by doing so they are able to give a balanced picture of the lives they are documenting. They are able to include triumphs and failures, moments of joy and sadness. What becomes apparent is the strength of the immigrants, their persistence even when their dreams of America clash with their day-to-day experiences. Also evident is the continued importance of their cultural roots. This comes across in their comments about the food available in the United States, but more significantly, in the enjoyment of celebrations with people from their homelands, whether they are members of their extended family, friends, or new acquaintances.

*The New Americans* is supplemented by extensive educational material, including a series guide and activity book. In the introduction to this book, the filmmakers indicate they chose immigrants who differ in homeland, race/ethnicity, education, and socioeconomic status, but they also acknowledge that "[n]o single story or group of stories can ever hope to encompass the entire immigrant or refugee experience." They want *The New Americans* to become a catalyst for further study (Independent Lens 2). The background material, suggestions for discussion, and activity options offered in the supplement will facilitate such study and can be accessed on the Independent Lens Web site. Further information is available at the PBS Web site. Educators, whether they are working with elementary, secondary, college, or adult students, should find the video as well as the printed material of immense value. Their breadth and depth make them extraordinarily powerful.

**Works Cited:** Independent Lens. "*The New Americans*: Learn More." http://www.ITVS.org/outreach/newamericans/guide; ITVS. "*The New Americans*: Series and Activity Book." PBS Online. http://www.pbs.org/independentlens/newamericans/learnmore.html.

## *Norma Rae* (1979)

Director: Martin Ritt

Cast: Sally Field (Norma Rae Wichards Webster), Ron Leibman (Reuben Warshawsky), Beau Bridges (Sonny Webster), Pat Hingle (Vernon Wichards)

Length: 113 min.

Rating: PG

Drama: Efforts to establish a union in a textile factory

Spunky and smart, Norma Rae, along with her two children, Millie and Craig, lives with her parents. All three adults, with the majority of the adults in the area, work in the town's textile factory, the O. P. Henley Mill, under very poor conditions; these include low pay, few benefits, and a toxic environment. Because earlier efforts to unionize have failed, the workers greet Reuben, an organizer for the Textile Workers Union of America, with indifference or hostility. Management is clearly hostile, and after a few workers join the union, it blocks Reuben in every way possible, including cutting the work week to three days.

Shortly after the cutback, Vernon, Norma Rae's father, dies suddenly at work and Norma increases her commitment to the union. When she boldly copies a letter posted on a bulletin board to cause friction between black and white workers, management tries to fire her. Rather than leave quietly, she climbs onto a table, prints the word UNION on a piece of cardboard, and lifts it above her head so everyone can see it. Slowly, her coworkers shut down their machines and stand with her. Her arrest galvanizes more of the workers, and the union, by a vote of 425 to 372, wins the right to organize the factory.

Shortly after Norma Rae meets Reuben, she asks him if he is a Jew. His response is "Born and bred." Norma Rae goes on to say she'd never met a Jew before and had heard they had horns, then allows that he doesn't seem different from other people. She goes on to become his strongest ally. Later, when her minister refuses to let her schedule a union meeting at the church because blacks will be participating, she holds the meeting in her home. When management posts the incendiary letter calculated to split black and white workers, she acts immediately to undercut its effect.

As the moral center of the film, Norma Rae's ability to cross racial/ethnic lines is critical in her effectiveness as a leader. She is backed by Reuben who, in his first meeting with the mill workers, insists the union is open to everyone, joining "black and white, Irish and Polish, Catholic and Jew" in one voice. *Norma Rae* shows this to be true despite the segregated church and the mill management's attempt to block the union by turning whites against blacks.

Norma Rae and her coworkers are empowered through their commitment to the union and to each other. They learn the value of taking risks, of cooperating, and of working long, exhausting hours to improve their situation. They get on each other's nerves at times as they push and are pushed to do and give more, but when they succeed they savor the victory, the pure joy of doing something extremely difficult and doing it effectively.

*Norma Rae* was not an easy sell to studio executives, but once distributed, it was widely seen and applauded as testimony to the human spirit. To a significant extent it is based on the lives of Crystal Lee Jordan, a worker at the J. P. Stevens textile mill in Roanoke Rapids, North Carolina, and union organizer Eli Zivkovich, as these are chronicled in *Crystal Lee: A Woman of Inheritance* by Henry P. Leifermann (Wolf 24). This link deepens the film's potential to spark discussions about interracial/interethnic cooperation, the challenges and complexities of organizing unions, and the culture and values of working class people. As Jackie Wolf has suggested, "Though *Norma Rae* obviously focuses on the development and growth of the character played by Sally Field, it also emphasizes the group effort of an organizing drive" (8). Henry A. Giroux explores the film from the perspective of the class culture it dramatizes in "*Norma Rae*: Character, Culture, and Class" (1, 7). More general references to unions and to class differences in the United States include Dennis Gilbert's *The American Class Structure* and Robert H. Ziegler and Gilbert J. Gail's *American Worker, American Unions: The Twentieth Century*.

**Works Cited:** Gilbert, Dennis. *The American Class Structure In an Age of Growing Inequality*. 6th ed. Belmont, CA: Wadsworth, 2003; Giroux, Henry A. "*Norma Rae*: Character, Culture, and Class," *Jump Cut* 22 (May 1980): 1, 7; Leifermann, Henry P. *Crystal Lee: A Woman of Inheritance*. New York: Macmillan, 1975; Wolf, Jackie. "Filmmakers Take on J. P. Stevens." *Jump Cut* 22 (May 1980): 8, 24, 37; Zeigler, Robert H., and Gilbert J. Gail. *American Worker, American Unions: The Twentieth Century*. Baltimore: Johns Hopkins University Press, 2002.

## *Philadelphia* (1993)

Director: Jonathan Demme

Cast: Tom Hanks (Andy Beckett), Denzel Washington (Joe Miller), Jason Robards (Charles Wheeler), Mary Steenburgen (Belinda Conine), Antonio Banderas (Miguel Alvarez)

Length: 119 min.

Rating: PG-13

Courtroom Drama: An African American lawyer defends a gay European American attorney in an AIDS discrimination suit

After an exceptionally promising beginning, Andy Beckett is suddenly fired from his position as a senior associate at Philadelphia's most prestigious law firm. He is convinced he was terminated not for incompetence as alleged, but because he is gay and has AIDS, a condition he had had difficulty concealing just prior to his dismissal. After an exhaustive search, Andy hires Joe Miller, an ambulance-chasing lawyer, to represent him in a suit against his former employers. During the trial Andy must come to terms with his declining health and imminent death while Joe must match wits with Wheeler's team of top-notch lawyers and work through his own homophobia and fear of AIDS.

Race/ethnicity becomes part of the context for this exploration of homophobia, but it is not the major issue. That Joe Miller, as an African American, has firsthand experience as the victim of prejudice and discrimination can be assumed in the way he is watched by—and in turn watches—one of the clerks as he does research in a public library. He chooses to intervene when, immediately afterwards, he observes the discomfort and polite suggestions made to Andy, doing research a few tables away, that he work in a private room. Joe approaches Andy's table and via his gaze challenges the clerk who quietly backs off. The two then begin a conversation that ends with them reviewing the court case that will provide the precedent for Andy's. The case clearly links Andy's and Joe's experiences when Joe reads this critical part of the court decision: "This is the essence of discrimination, formulating opinions about others not based on their individual merits but rather on their membership in a group with the same characteristics."

Joe's experience of discrimination does not mean he is free from prejudice. Nor does the connection he makes between homophobia and racism in the library scene mean he has overcome his homophobia. His wife is far more accepting than he is, and her comfort with gay and lesbian relatives and friends contributes to his eventual change of heart, but it is his professional and personal interaction with Andy that influences Joe most strongly and gradually permits him to recognize and value Andy as a human being, a person who has needs, desires, fears, and aspirations similar to his own. *Philadelphia* suggests that getting to know a person is key to acceptance and a most effective means of countering the stereotypes so often used to define unfamiliar groups, and the individuals within those groups.

*Philadelphia* is noteworthy because it unabashedly and directly addresses difficult subjects: homosexuality, AIDS, and prejudice. It does this while normalizing the multiethnic society that the United States is by casting actors of different races/ethnicities, most visibly African and Latino Americans, in major and minor roles, an indication we have made some progress in telling this country's stories. The casting of Tom Hanks and Denzel Washington and their exceptional performances enrich this particular story by adding another dimension to the study of prejudice and by broadening the film's audience across lines of race/ethnicity and of sexual orientation.

Viewers who want to pursue the film's focus on sexual orientation may want to read Robert Mazur's *The New Intimacy*.

**Work Cited:** Mazur, Robert. *The New Intimacy: Open-Ended Marriage and Alternative Lifestyles*. Lincoln, NE: Iuniverse, 2000.

## *Romeo Must Die* (2000)

Director: Andrzej Bartkowiak

Cast: Jet Li (Han Sing), Aaliyah (Trish O'Day), Isaiah Washington (Mac), Russell Wong (Kai), DMX (Silk), Delroy Lindo (Isaak O'Day), Edoardo Ballerini (Vincent Roth), Henry O (Ch'u Sing)

Length: 115 min.

Rating: R

Urban Drama: A martial arts action film with culturally diverse players

*Romeo Must Die* tells of two families, at once different and very similar. The heads of each family, Chinese American Ch'u Sing and African American Isaak O'Day, are involved with the multimillionaire businessman Vincent Roth in the quasi-legal acquisition of properties that will lead to the development of a new professional football franchise and stadium. Because Sing and O'Day also share the recent tragic experience of having a son mysteriously killed, they are suspicious of each other. Each has a surviving child who wants to uncover the person responsible for the death of their sibling. Finally, each family has a trusted ally who is a traitor, a key to the untimely deaths of their children and to their future.

Central to the action in *Romeo Must Die* are Sing's son Han and O'Day's daughter Trish, who unite to unravel the mystery of their brothers' deaths and who fall in love. Their interracial relationship reflects the growing ease with which individuals can move beyond traditional social taboos. With the exception of African American soldiers and Southeast Asian women during the Vietnam War years, this kind of "race mixing" rarely occurred and is virtually absent from mainstream movies.

*Romeo Must Die* is one of the new genre of martial arts adventure films like *Rush Hour*, *Rush Hour II*, and *Replacement Killers* featuring well-known Chinese actors like Jackie Chan, Yun Fat Chow, and Jet Li. They are the new Asian superheroes and they are garnering fans in the United States. Unfortunately, most of the martial arts films do little to educate us about Chinese culture other than the aspects connected to organized crime. Fans have limitless exposure to the drug trade, prostitution, illegal immigration, and the excesses of the rich and powerful. And they can see how important the family is to the patriarchs who control the crime, not unlike the family in Italian Mafia films. The strength of the patrilineal connections between father and son as well as brother and brother is emphasized while women usually exist only as sexual objects.

*Romeo Must Die*, despite its focus on action and adventure, suggests through Roth that the game they are playing in the business world, like golf, is a game of finesse and skill rather than power. This theme plays out several times, especially in the fight scenes in which African American characters are repeatedly beaten by Han and Kai. Despite the violence and crime, a refreshing aspect of the film is the number of legitimate black businesses and businessmen that are incorporated into the narrative and counter the usual stereotypes.

Though not a great film, *Romeo Must Die* is an example of the changes that are taking place in society. At times, filmmakers can move beyond stereotypes to depict relationships that cross racial/ethnic lines and portray characters who escape narrow traditional roles.

## *Silverado* (1985)

Director: Lawrence Kasdan

Cast: Kevin Kline (Paden), Scott Glenn (Emmett), Kevin Costner (Jake), Danny Glover (Mal), Linda Hunt (Stella)

Length: 127 min.

Rating: PG-13

Western Drama: A self-reflexive western with four heroes, multiple villains, and much action

*Silverado* is a self-reflexive film posing as an old-school western full of action and plenty of heroes and villains. The heroes are four very different cowboys: two brothers, Emmett and Jake, who plan to go to California; Paden, a drifter who readily joins Emmett when Emmett rescues him; and Mal, who wants to rejoin his family after working in Chicago slaughterhouses for a time. The story begins with Emmett fighting for his life as he is being ambushed. After surviving this incident he happens upon Paden, who has been left for dead by bushwhackers after stealing everything from him except the red long johns he wears.

As Emmett and Paden move on together, they cross paths with Mal when they observe him being discriminated against in a bar while trying to buy a drink of whiskey. A fight ensues and Mal is asked to leave town by Sheriff Langston, who then informs Emmett and Paden that Jake, Emmett's brother, is being held in prison—arbitrarily—and is scheduled to be hung the next day. Before that can happen, Paden is also jailed. Emmett springs both Jake and Paden, and as they make their escape, Mal protects them from the pursuing posse with some excellent long-range shooting. As a result they unite against the evil of the expanding West as this is personified chiefly in four villains.

The villains are characterized by a desire for wealth and power, unlike the heroes who are committed to fairness and equality. Though Sheriff Cobb, Deputy Tyree, and ranch owner Ethan McKendrick identify with roles associated with law, order, and respectability, they along with the gambler Slick, represent the dark side of the new frontier; each finds his nemesis in one of the "good guys." While the film is ripe with gun violence, the clear distinction between good and evil seemingly justifies the killing and mayhem. Kasdan certainly avoids a realistic portrayal of gun violence and colors his film with a great deal of humor, making it palatable for viewers who see the film as a very self-reflexive comic take on earlier westerns. Comparing *Silverado* with Clint Eastwood's *Unforgiven* (1992), a film in which violence is far more realistically depicted, could be an extremely worthwhile exercise.

A strong theme of family runs through *Silverado* motivating much of the violence and helping to justify it, but also linking its heroes with people who are nonviolent. Through Mal, his sister Rae, and his father Ezra, we get a rare glimpse of an African American family dealing with the challenges of frontier life. True to the times, they experience prejudice and discrimination, but ultimately Mal and Rae are united and are able to settle into the role of homesteaders. Emmett and Jake are also involved in family. They are close to each other and to their sister and her husband and son. Family loyalties and relationships play a central role in the film's plot.

Lawrence Kasdan has created a rich landscape upon which the clashes between good and bad are played out in a variety of vignettes. We are witness to the different sides of those European and African Americans who were part of this nation's "manifest destiny," though we see no Native Americans or the impact of this philosophy on them.

## *Solaris* (2002)

Director: Steven Soderbergh

Cast: George Clooney (Chris Kelvin), Natascha McElhone (Rheya), Jeremy Davies (Snow), Viola Davis (Gordon), Ulrich Tukur (Gibarian)

Length: 99 min.

Rating: PG-13

Futuristic Science Fiction Drama: Definitions of reality are questioned

When Chris Kelvin, a psychiatrist, journeys to a space station orbiting Solaris, one of the moons of Jupiter, a member of the space team there asks him to help figure out the bizarre phenomena taking place among the crew. Kelvin observes their very strange behaviors, but it isn't until he falls asleep that he experiences the phenomena they have been facing. He wakes to an encounter with Rheya, his dead wife, now apparently alive and conversing with him. Overwhelmed, he, like other crew members, attempts to find the logic in what is occurring.

Gordon, the mission scientist, is particularly obsessed with the need to explain and defeat the phenomena by using the scientific method. She has no patience with mystical explanations, so when no logical explanation emerges, she focuses on returning home. Kelvin receives a warning that if he doesn't leave Solaris, he will die. Leaving the station becomes even more imperative when they learn that Solaris is expanding and pulling the space station into its gravitational field. Gordon begins prepping the Athena spaceship for the return voyage to earth, but Kelvin, still deeply in love with his wife, is persuaded by her to stay; after the Athena departs he awakens with Rheya's manifestation in a new reality.

*Solaris* can work as a metaphor for examining many of the philosophical underpinnings of Judaeo–Christian–Islamic traditions that stress dichotomies of good and evil, heaven and hell, angels and demons. Some of the questions the film poses are the following: Is there life after death? Do heaven and hell exist? Do angels? Are humans given second chances in another world? What is the nature of the manifestations the crew experiences? Is eliminating them murder?

*Solaris* presents viewers with a picture of a future highly advanced, postindustrial fourth-wave society in which people of color and women play vital roles in the exploration of space and race/ethnicity and gender are no longer issues. However, even with the technological and intercultural advances, human fragility, both mental and physical, still plague the species. Mental illness, depression, fear, and violence are among the major hurdles still facing humankind and jeopardizing an individual's happiness. This being so, Susan Sontag's 1965 essay "The Imagination of Disaster" is still pertinent, but viewers may also want to look into Frank M. Robinson, Robert E. Weinberg, and Randy Broecker's *Art of Imagination: 20th Century Visions of Science Fiction, Horror, and Fantasy*.

**Works Cited:** Robinson, Frank M., Robert E. Weinberg, and Randy Broecker. *Art of Imagination: 20th Century Visions of Science Fiction, Horror, and Fantasy*. Portland, OR: Collectors Press, 2002; Sontag, Susan. "The Imagination of Disaster." In *Against Interpretation and Other Essays*. 209–225. New York: Octagon Books, 1978.

## *Soylent Green* (1973)

Director: Richard Fleischer

Cast: Charlton Heston (Det. Robert Thorn), Leigh-Taylor Young (Shirl), Chuck Connors (Tab), Joseph Cotton (Simonson), Edward G. Robinson (Sol Roth), Brock Peters (Lt. Hatcher), Paula Kelly (Martha)

Length: 97 min.

Rating: PG

Futuristic Science Fiction Drama: Posits the extremes to which those in power will go to retain power

The year is 2022 and Earth is suffering from global warming. The United States is overpopulated: New York alone has 40 million people, and food and water are scarce. Food production is in the hands of a giant company called the Soylent Corporation.

When Simonson, one of the key members of its board of directors, is murdered, Police Detective Thorn is assigned to the case. He is assisted by his roommate, Sol Roth, his "book," who does his investigative research. Thorn and Roth discover that Simonson has actually been assassinated.

As the investigation of the assassination widens, threats are made on Thorn's life, and Hatcher, his commanding officer, orders him to drop the investigation. Meanwhile, Roth is so disturbed by what he learns about Soylent Corporation that he volunteers for the state-sanctioned ethical suicide program. As part of the legal arrangement for this procedure, he is given twenty minutes of privacy and a ceremony that includes seeing films of the earth as it once was—beautiful, pristine, and full of life.

After Roth's death, Thorn follows his body to a Soylent Corporation processing plant and discovers that the body, like other deceased bodies, is turned into a food supplement called Soylent Green. The supplement is currently feeding most of the population of New York. As soon as the corporation finds out that Thorn is on to them, they put a bounty on him. Thorn kills his would-be assassin but is fatally wounded in the process. Before he dies he tries to alert others to Soylent's operations, but his effort is futile.

In the world of *Soylent Green*, the middle class barely exists while the extremes of the haves and have-nots are highly apparent. The very rich still have access to hot water, fresh fruit, vegetables, and occasionally even meat. Wealthy men live in comfort and dominate society. Women come with apartments like they were furniture, to be kept or exchanged at the whim of the owners. Everyone, including the police, seems to be corrupt. African Americans have survived and are viable though very little racial/ethnic diversity is shown despite New York's population of over 40 million people.

Like most science fiction, *Soylent Green* is based on a fear of the unknown, a fear of the future. Its what-if scenario serves as a warning about what could happen if megacorporations acquired unrestrained power and population growth continued unchecked. It dramatizes the danger that could follow if individual rights and freedoms are not protected and if access to information is limited to those in the highest echelons of corporations and law enforcement agencies. In visualizing the worst, *Soylent Green* remains fundamentally linked to the here and now, and to what is familiar, suggesting that action to preserve human rights for everyone is needed now to secure those rights for the future. Given these broad themes, *Soylent Green* gives viewers much to discuss. Its PG rating and engaging story make it accessible to a wide audience.

## *To Kill a Mockingbird* (1962)

Director: Robert Mulligan

Cast: Gregory Peck (Atticus Finch), Mary Badham (Scout), Philip Alford (Jem), Brock Peters (Tom Robinson), Robert Duvall (Boo Radley), Collin Wilcox (Mayella Ewell)

Length: 129 min.

Rating: Not Rated

Courtroom Drama: Integrity in the face of racial injustice

Though based on a Pulitzer Prize-winning novel by Harper Lee, *To Kill a Mockingbird* did not generate much excitement in Hollywood initially, probably because the story, though told from a child's perspective, dealt with difficult social issues and lacked romance as well as physical action. The story unfolds in the small Southern town of Macon in 1932 and 1933, when six-year-old Scout Finch and her nine-year-old brother, Jem, observe their father Atticus as he defends Tom Robinson, a "colored" man wrongly accused of raping Mayella Ewell, a white woman. They become part of the violence when Mayella's father, not satisfied even after Tom is killed, attacks them to get back at Atticus. They are rescued by Boo Radley, a developmentally disabled neighbor whom they have never actually seen but imagine to be an ogre because of the mystery surrounding him.

Scout, as an adult, looks back to that eventful time in the early 1930s and in voice-over narrates the story, but Jem's perceptions and experiences are given as much weight as hers. Their mother had died three years earlier, and Atticus gets help with the children from Cal, the family's black housekeeper, while he carries on his law practice. Jem thinks of him as "too old for anything" because he won't play football, but as he witnesses Atticus's handling of a rabid dog and, more importantly, his defense of Tom Robinson in the face of the racism many townspeople personify, Jem's attitude changes to admiration and respect. As a six-year-old, Scout is less analytical than Jem, but she has absorbed Atticus's commitment to honesty and his sense of justice; she is straightforward and guileless in her observations and interactions with adults as well as children, virtues through which she actually disarms a mob of angry white men intent on lynching Mr. Robinson.

Tom Robinson's trial is the emotional and thematic center of *To Kill a Mockingbird*, with Atticus's candid statement about the racist codes in play in 1930s Macon a clear indictment of the racism still in play in the United States of 1962—and today. Interwoven with this powerful exploration of this critical issue is the story of Boo Radley (played by Robert Duvall in his film debut), a man hidden from the world because of his disability, whose attempts to communicate are usually thwarted, but who manages to establish a bond with Jem, and later with Scout, and who saves their lives when they are threatened.

*To Kill a Mockingbird* goes far beyond teaching tolerance of people who are different. The film embodies lessons of respect, which Atticus sums up when he tries to help Scout get along with her schoolmates. He says, "You never really understand a person until you consider things from his point of view . . . until you climb inside his skin and walk around in it." Jem and Scout learn the lesson well thanks to Atticus's example. It is incorporated vividly within a well-made, forceful, and entertaining movie that effectively recreates the culture of a given time and place. Viewing the special thirty-fifth anniversary commemorative edition is particularly rewarding because it includes interviews with the filmmakers and many of the performers, among them Gregory Peck and Mary Badham.

## *Twelve Angry Men* (1957/1997)

Directors: Sidney Lumet (1957), William Friedkin (1997)

Cast (1957): Henry Fonda (Juror 8), Martin Balsam (Jury Foreman), Lee J. Cobb (Juror 3)

Cast (1997): Jack Lemmon (Juror 8), Courtney B. Vance (Jury Foreman), George C. Scott (Juror 3), Ossie Davis (Juror 2), Edward James Olmos (Juror 11)

Length: 95 min.

Rating: PG-13

Courtroom Drama: Personal integrity, responsibility and peer pressure are explored

A jury of twelve men is given the task of determining the guilt or innocence of an eighteen-year-old boy accused of murdering his father. An initial poll of the jurors indicates that all except Juror 8 are ready to declare him guilty. This sets in motion a debate that forces each juror to consider more closely the evidence presented during the trial, as well as perceptions and prejudices influencing his response to the evidence. From an eleven-to-one vote of guilty, the men move, step-by-step, to a unanimous vote of not guilty. Their deliberations are often heated, made more so because "it is the hottest day of the year," they are locked in a relatively small room, and they have very different agendas.

The 1957 film differs significantly from the 1997 version of *Twelve Angry Men* even though the story, the setting, and much of the dialogue, remain the same. The differences reflect cultural changes that occurred over the twenty years between the two productions. The judge and the jury in the 1957 movie are, with one possible exception, European American. The 1997 cast includes a female European American judge and greater racial/ethnic diversity among the all-male jurors, with the African American jurors ranging from mild-mannered and open-minded (Juror 2) to extremely bigoted (Juror 10). The ethnicity of the defendant in the 1957 film is somewhat unclear whereas he is clearly identified as Latino and given slightly more screen time in the remake.

The Civil Rights Movement and the persistent call by people of color for greater representation in movies and on television no doubt influenced the decision to diversify the 1997 cast, a possibility that probably was not considered two decades earlier. Both casts are unusually strong and the acting in both is powerful enough to hold viewers' attention even though dialogue is far more important than physical activity. The psychological explorations outweigh the need for lots of movement. These explorations show how personal experience and subconsciously held attitudes can determine what one sees and how one judges other people's behavior and character. Only through a willingness to listen to other perspectives and to examine one's own assumptions and prejudices are we likely to reach well-reasoned and fair judgments and be able to work effectively in a culturally diverse world. Studying either film can be rewarding; studying both within the social contexts in which they were made can extend their relevance in interesting ways.

## *Unbowed* (2000)

Director: Nanci Rossov

Distributor: Filmanthropic

Cast: Tembi Locke (Cleola Banks), Jay Tavare (Waka Mani), Chuma Hunter-Gault (Richard Singletary III), Catero Alain Colbert (Junius Parker), Fran Bennett (Miss Cooper), Vincent McLean (Simon Crow), Mark Abbott (Jumping Elk), Michelle Thomas (Anna), Ron Glass (President Duesquene), Hattie Winston (Mother), Edward Albert (General Grollen)

Length: 122 min.

Rating: Not Rated

Historical Drama: African and Native American conflict and cooperation

*Unbowed* is set in the late nineteenth century at a Negro college. Six students, Cleola, Richard, Anna, Junius, Lewis, and Isaac, having been chosen for the honor, are staying at Beckwourth College over the summer to take classes and help with preparations for the school's twenty-fifth anniversary celebration, a celebration that President William Duesquene hopes will bring in much-needed financial support.

The carefully managed order of the residents is disrupted when General Grollen, one of the college's patrons, brings three Lakota (Sioux) prisoners, Waka Mani, Simon Crow, and Jumping Elk, to Beckworth with an impossible-to-refuse request that they be accepted as students. Reluctantly, President Duesquene agrees, opening up the possibility for rivalries and/or alliances between the black and Indian students.

Rivalries do develop when Cleola, Richard's fianceé, falls in love with Waka Mani, but Junius, not Richard, proves to be most disturbed and hostile toward his new classmates, particularly Waka Mani. While Junius nurses his hatred of all Native Americans, Lewis moves in the opposite direction, recognizing the parallels between African and Native Americans and learning to respect the Lakota, their values, and culture. Waka Mani is determined to resist "white man's ways," to regain his freedom, and to return to his own people, but Jumping Elk sees value in what he is learning and is not so anxious to leave Beckwourth.

By characterizing the small number of students as it does, *Unbowed* becomes somewhat schematic, with various characters personifying diverse attitudes through the stances they take in relation to one another and to Beckwourth's mission. Within their closed world and despite their real accomplishments as scholars and leaders, the African American students assume positions of superiority similar to those taken by European Americans vis-à-vis African Americans in schools dominated by whites. Given the history of African Americans as it is often taught in the United States, the intense hatred Junius expresses toward Native Americans may surprise some viewers; he indicates its roots when he tells Isaac and Lewis that Choctaw killed his grandfather just days after the Civil War ended. Comments the other black students initially make about the Indians suggest they are also responding to them as stereotypes, not as individuals. Given their lack of previous contact, they do not have enough information to go beyond the stereotypes.

General Grollen's interest in the Native Americans stems from his clear identification with them and from the loss of his own cultural heritage when his parents, Cheyenne and Iroquois, " 'passed' and cut all ties" to their Indian heritage. His intent is to "show [Native Americans] are not all bloodthirsty savages." That he chooses Beckwourth rather than Harvard, the university his son is attending, suggests the limits of his own influence and prestige within the European American world and his use of white privilege and power within African and Native American spheres. Though the general doesn't appear to recognize the irony of his situation, President Duesquene is clear about his own status. He realizes that at Beckwourth he is a leader who wields authority and commands respect while outside the institution he is simply a "colored." His mission: to help his students get the education and acquire the skills that can help them become leaders within the upper echelons of African American society.

*Unbowed*'s exploration of intercultural relationships that are rarely seen should hold viewers' attention whether they are secondary-school or college-age students or adults, but some viewers may find *Unbowed* a challenge to watch because of its period flavor, its focus on nineteenth-century manners, and its deliberate pace. It was made on a limited budget and does not look or feel like a major Hollywood production. Educators can steer students around these possible stumbling blocks by preparing them for the film experience. Providing questions or suggesting they pay attention to particular issues can give them the focus they need as they explore an often overlooked aspect of the post-Reconstruction era and of racial/ethnic relations in the United States.

Drawing viewers' attention to the film's production history may also stimulate interest because *Unbowed* was produced by Filmanthropic, a Hollywood-based nonprofit corporation founded by Nanci Rossov to help individuals from traditionally underrepresented groups acquire filmmaking skills. Over seventy such individuals—people of color, women, and people over forty—worked on *Unbowed.* Many were economically disadvantaged (Filmanthropic 3). *Unbowed* is the first feature film Rossov has directed and the first of Mildred Inez Lewis's scripts to be produced. It received Best Film and Best Actor (Jay Tavare) awards at the American Indian Film Festival and was an Audience Favorite at the Pan African Film Festival.

**Work Cited:** Filmanthropic. "*Unbowed* Background." Filmanthropic@aol.com.

## *Unforgiven* (1992)

Director: Clint Eastwood

Cast: Clint Eastwood (Will Munny), Morgan Freeman (Ned), Gene Hackman (Little Bill), Jaimz Woolvett (Schofield Kid), Richard Harris (English Bob)

Length: 130 min.

Rating: R

Western Drama: A gritty, realistic exploration of gun violence

The year is 1880; the place, Big Whiskey, Montana. In the middle of the night, a cowboy assaults a hooker in a brothel for laughing at the size of his privates. In anger he uses his knife to permanently disfigure the woman's face. Little Bill Dagget, the town's usually ruthless sheriff, lets the cowboy and his partner off with just a fine. The brothel's madam and other prostitutes are outraged by this injustice and decide to take the law into their own hands. They pool their money and put out a bounty on the lives of the cowboys who wronged them. Their revenge is about the condition of their lives, the hazards of their occupation, and the powerlessness they feel as human beings.

The Schofield Kid, a young would-be gunfighter, visits the ranch of William Munny seeking a partner to collect the bounty. Will, now a responsible widower and the father of two children, is approached because of his past history as a merciless, cold-blooded gunfighter. Munny initially turns down the offer, but later, desperate for money to support his family, he recruits his old partner, Ned Logan, and the two join the Kid in his quest. On the road they recount some of Will's infamous deeds, killings he associates with his earlier excessive drinking. They also discover the Kid is nearsighted and far from the *pistolero* he claims to be.

Little Bill makes an example of English Bob when he comes to Big Whiskey to claim the bounty by nearly beating him to death in front of the whole town. When Will, Ned, and the Kid arrive they, too, quickly run afoul of the law and Little Bill's sadistic control. Will is badly beaten and all three are run out of town. The beating leaves Will weak and ill, but once he regains his strength, he and his partners begin the process of hunting down the cowboys and collecting the bounty.

After killing the first cowboy, Ned, no longer able to justify such killing, tries to return home but is caught, tortured, and dies in Little Bill's custody. His body is displayed in a coffin in front of the saloon while Will and the Kid hunt down and kill the other cowboy. When they collect the bounty, Will learns of Ned's death. Instead of returning to his farm, Will heads into town to avenge his friend's death. He kills the brothel owner and Little Bill and warns the townspeople that he'll be back to kill them if they fail to give Ned a Christian burial.

In some ways *Unforgiven* follows the structure of a typical western, but it is far from typical. Rather, it is a compelling critique of the genre's glorification of violence and of a heroism based on violence. Introducing Will as he ineptly tries to control feverish pigs in a muddy pen, Eastwood quickly and incisively undercuts his traditional majestic image as gunfighter extraordinaire. The Kid has romanticized Will's exploits in a way numerous westerns have romanticized the West. Eastwood sets about undermining the idyllic images and heroic deeds of these films by showing how difficult it can be to take a life, how messy, painful, and even sickening. He shows the weaknesses of heroes, the sadism and arbitrariness of those enforcing the law, the hard work and struggle necessary to provide for a family. Eastwood also, however, shows the value—and cost—of loyalty and friendship and, in a scene familiar to viewers from classic westerns, ultimately resorts to "justifiable" brutality when avenging Ned's death.

This Academy Award-winning film encompasses many themes worth discussing, among them violence, loyalty, revenge, heroism, and youthfulness versus maturity. It prompts numerous questions: How did the treatment of "good women," such as Will's wife, differ from that of prostitutes? If the assault that took place in the brothel had taken place in the home of "respectable" townspeople, how might Little Bill have responded? How much or how little has our society changed? How does our contemporary understanding of revenge and justice differ from that of the nineteenth-century wild west? Can an evil man ever truly redeem himself and become a good man? Is evil in alcohol or in the man? In the deed or in the person? Why was English Bob's life spared and Ned's life taken? Was racism a factor? Was Ned's presence in the West (or in a western) unusual? Was his and Sally Two Trees' interracial marriage unusual?

*Unforgiven* is justifiably rated R because of its violence and profane language, but mature audiences should find its themes and the questions it raises definitely worth discussing. For those wanting further information about African Americans in the West, Monroe Lee Billington and Roger D. Hardaway's *African Americans on the Western Frontier* offers a point of departure.

**Work Cited:** Billington, Monroe Lee, and Roger D. Hardaway. *African Americans on the Western Frontier*. Boulder: University of Colorado Press, 2001.

## *The Way Home* (1998)

Director: Shakti Butler

Distributor: New Day Films

Length: 92 min.

Rating: Not Rated

Documentary: Conversations among women of color

*The Way Home* documents the conversations of eight councils of women who came together over eight months to discuss issues of race/ethnicity, gender, class, and culture. Each group is composed of women identified in terms of race/ethnicity. Their differences as well as their similarities become apparent as they are introduced in turn: indigenous, Latina, African, European, Jewish, multiracial, Asian, and Arab Americans. Themes that surface during the introductory dialogues include their intragroup diversity, skin color and identity, white privilege, and oppression.

Following the introductions, these issues are addressed more specifically by one or more of the councils under headings that include "controlling the land," "the power of silence and privilege," "becoming American," "finding identity," "individual versus cultural reality," "standards of beauty," "oppression institutionalized," and "consciousness and healing." In the course of their discussions, the women share insights, reveal extremely painful personal experiences, and ultimately move toward greater awareness, healing, and self-affirmation.

Shakti Butler, director of *The Way Home*, conceived the work as a "catalyst for transformative learning, conversation, healing, and change." She sees it not as a self-contained entity, but as the prompt for conversations among viewers on the questions raised by the council women. Ideally, their dialogues will be as deep and illuminating as those of the original participants, whose stories and analyses reveal just how complex and powerful race/ethnicity, gender, class, and sexual orientation are in determining how individuals see themselves, how they are perceived by others, and how they are positioned within society. To help facilitate such discussions, a conversation guide has been prepared to accompany the film.

Because the council women are articulate and their experiences diverse and multifaceted, *The Way Home* can easily hold the attention of viewers interested in women's and intercultural issues. Butler makes this even easier by imaginatively intercutting her shots of the council women with family and historical photos, dance sequences, and a variety of other images to make a video that is also visually appealing.

**Work Cited:** Butler, Shakti, Laura Rifkin, and Gretchen Rohr. "*The Way Home* Heart-to-Heart Conversation Guide." Oakland, CA: The World Trust, 1998.

## *White Man's Burden* (1995)

Director: Desmond Nakata

Cast: Harry Belafonte (Thaddeus Thomas), John Travolta (Louis Pinnock), Kelly Lynch (Marsha Pinnock), Margaret Avery (Megan Thomas), Tom Bower (Stanley), Andrew Lawrence (Donnie Pinnock), Bumper Robinson (Martin)

Length: 89 min.

Rating: R

Racial Drama: A reversal of the racial hierarchy

*White Man's Burden* juxtaposes race and social class in the United States. Louis Pinnock, a working-class European American, represents a race/ethnicity that is culturally inferior in a society dominated by African Americans like Thaddeus Thomas, a well-educated, socially prominent entrepreneur and patron of the arts. Their lives are connected only because Louis works in Thaddeus's factory. They are set on a collision course when Louis volunteers to deliver a package to the Thomas mansion, mistakenly enters the wrong part of the estate, and accidentally views Thaddeus's wife as she is dressing.

Because of a miscommunication about this incident, Louis is fired from his job and his life quickly spirals out of control. He is even evicted from his home and separated from his wife and two children. In desperation, he confronts Thaddeus for the money he feels he is owed and, getting no satisfaction, kidnaps him at gunpoint. The action leading up to the kidnapping, and Louis and Thaddeus's conversations following it create a variety of opportunities to show the cultural and social distance between the lives of these two men. The reversal of roles is especially effective in underscoring that distance.

*White Man's Burden* is an excellent teaching tool to use when examining race and social class in the United States. The film can be easily broken down into vignettes to focus discussion on specific issues like color privilege, police brutality, eugenics, generational poverty, prejudice, and discrimination. Because the film is so didactic, however, viewers may have to be prepared for it. Its moral lessons are not presented subtly. The characters and plot seem to exist primarily to convey a message rather than to entertain, but if students can get beyond this, they can find what the film has to say relevant and insightful. Examining Louis's experience in terms of the Jim Crow laws of the twentieth century would be an interesting avenue to pursue. See C. Vann Woodward's *The Strange Case of Jim Crow* for help with this.

**Work Cited:** Woodward, C. Vann. *The Strange Case of Jim Crow*. New York: Oxford University Press, 2001.

## *Woodstock* (1970/1994)

Director: Michael Wadleigh

Length: 184/228 min.

Rating: R

Rock Festival Documentary: Focus on performers and participants

*Woodstock* documents one of the watershed cultural events of the late 1960s; it marks the celebration of a changing age and became a prophetic anthem of the future. Richie Haven's howling protest song "Freedom" and his hopeful "Here Comes the Sun" set in motion "Three Days of Peace and Freedom" for over 400,000 people who gathered on a farm in New York State to celebrate and to protest. Director Michael Wadleigh at times employs split screens to capture this massive event, from preconcert preparation of the stage and the concert facilities through the arrival and interaction of the overwhelming throng of fans and the electrifying performances of some of the best-known musicians of the time, to the breakup of the crowd as the concert ends. Public service announcements and interviews intercut with concert footage help convey the sense of immediacy and spontaneity of the event.

Besides Richie Havens, performers included folksingers Joan Baez, John Sebastian, and Arlo Guthrie; blues singer Joe Cocker; Afro-Latino guitarist Carlos Santana; and rock groups The Who, Country Joe and the Fish, Crosby, Stills and Nash, Ten Years After, Sha Na Na, Sly and the Family Stone, and Jefferson Airplane. Though the performances of Jimi Hendrix and Janis Joplin are phenomenal, the early deaths of these artists attest to the downside of the hippie counterculture, which was evident to some extent at Woodstock along with the musical genius on display. Despite a storm that drenched the field and the participants, despite inadequate food and sanitary facilities, overdoses and promiscuity, individuals from diverse racial/ethnic groups created community and shared a sense of peace and freedom, love and hope. The music unified the crowd.

Wadleigh chronicles the positive and negative aspects of Woodstock, as he strives to provide a full account of the event. Interviews with participants are balanced by interviews with people from the area. Favorable and unfavorable comments from both groups are included just as are images of elation, frenzy, chaos, distress, generosity, warmth, and wonder. *Woodstock* reflects an incredible moment in the history of the hippie generation and dramatically illustrates its strengths and weaknesses. Though the film's R rating restricts educators working with preadolescents and adolescents from using *Woodstock* in its entirety, using appropriate excerpts could be helpful in conveying this extraordinary moment.

Because music is central to *Woodstock*, following up with an exploration of *The Rolling Stone Illustrated History of Rock and Roll* would be appropriate.

**Work Cited:** Decurtis, Anthony, James Henke, Holly George-Warren, and Jim Miller. *The* Rolling Stone *Illustrated History of Rock and Roll: The Definitive History of the Most Important Artists and Their Music*. 3rd ed. New York: Random House, 1992.

## *X-Men* (2000)/*X2* (2003)

Director: Bryan Singer

Cast: Patrick Stewart (Professor Xavier), Ian McKellen (Magneto), Hugh Jackman (Wolverine), Halle Barry (Storm), Famke Janssen (Dr. Jean Grey), Brian Cox (General Stryker), Alan Cumming (Night Crawler), Aaron Stanford (Pyro), Shawn Ashmore (Ice Man)

Rating: PG-13

Length: *X-Men*, 104 min.; *X2*, 134 min.

Futuristic Science Fiction Drama: Explores how differences are valued or feared

The *X-Men* series is another in the long list of Marvel Comic Books that have come to the big screen. Directed by Bryan Singer, *X2* is the second of what is likely to become a long-running series. The premise of the films is that the human race has spawned a new species of mutants that possess superhuman powers. Certain factions within the government fear these mutants and want them registered and monitored. In *X-Men*, Professor Xavier recognizes the value of the mutants and wants to integrate them into human society for the benefit of humans and mutants. Magneto, also a powerful mutant leader, wants to turn normal human beings into mutants because of the hatred humans have for mutants. With the help of Wolverine, Storm, Cyclops, and Jane, all mutant allies of Xavier, Magneto is captured and held in a prison of plastic at the end of *X-Men*. In *X2*, he escapes. Though recaptured, he still leads a band of militant mutants who do not want to live peacefully with humans, and in this differ from Professor Xavier's X-Men and the gifted mutant children in the school he runs.

In *X2*, viewers are introduced to General William Stryker, head of the country's top secret agency charged with studying, observing, and neutralizing any mutant threat. Stryker is obsessed with controlling the mutants and bitterly opposes Professor Xavier, whom he blames for the death of his wife. When Stryker organizes an attack on the school with his special forces, he encounters the mutant Wolverine and a group of mutant children with formidable powers. Though Magneto and Professor Xavier join forces against Stryker, he is able to control them using a chemical extracted from his mutant son's brain. His attempt to kill all the mutants on the planet sets the scene for the X-Men to utilize their unique powers to quell this diabolical threat.

The significance of this futuristic tale is threefold. First, in the future portrayed here, diversity of race/ethnicity is insignificant compared with the concerns generated by mutancy. Second, mutancy seems to appear within all cultures and societies. Third, genetic differences, like the historic differences of skin color, hair texture, and eye shape, have been heightened by a diversity of physical and mental abilities. These factors revive old societal fears, leading to prohibitions and ostracism. Both *X-Men* and *X2* give examples of the internal as well as external dilemmas prejudice creates and can be used effectively as teaching vehicles for some preadolescent and all older students.

Because the futuristic settings and superhuman characters differ from their own experience but are applicable to it, students may more readily see the harm prejudice and fear create and can be encouraged to transfer this understanding to contemporary situations. For example, when Pyro, Wolverine, and Ice Man visit Ice Man's family, his younger brother turns them in to the authorities and his mother asks him why he can't "just be normal." A similar question is frequently asked of members of traditionally underrepresented ethnic groups when they choose a lifestyle that reflects their ethnic culture, or of gay and lesbian family members whose choices mirror their sexual orientation. The films also tackle the ages-old battle between good and evil, loyalty and betrayal, while entertaining viewers with action that offers a virtual rollercoaster ride for the senses.

# Films by Theme

## ACCULTURATION/ASSIMILATION

*Business of Fancy Dancing, The*
*Education of Little Tree, The*
*Grand Avenue*
*Moscow on the Hudson*
*My Big Fat Greek Wedding*
*Naturally Native*
*Rum and Coke*
*Vanishing Americans, The*
*Warrior in Two Worlds, A*

## ADOLESCENCE

*Almost a Woman*
*Almost Famous*
*Bronx Tale, A*
*Clueless*
*Covered Girls*
*Doe Boy, The*
*Girlfight*
*Holes*
*Hoop Dreams*
*Incredibly True Adventure of Two Girls in Love, The*
*La Bamba*
*Mi Vida Loca*
*My American Girls*
*Raising Victor Vargas*
*Rocks with Wings*
*Selena*
*Stand and Deliver*
*Two Lies*
*West Side Story*

## AWAKENING

*Antwone Fisher*
*Blade Runner*
*Bronx Tale, A*
*Clueless*
*Dreamkeeper*
*Fail Safe*
*Far from Heaven*
*Finding Forrester*
*Gentleman's Agreement*
*Giant*
*Girlfight*
*Green Card*
*Human Stain, The*
*Lakota Woman*
*Malcolm X*
*Mississippi Masala*
*Philadelphia*
*Raisin in the Sun, A*

*Rocks with Wings*
*Salt of the Earth*
*Sergeant York*
*Skins*
*Slam*
*Smoke Signals*
*Songcatcher*
*Thelma & Louise*
*To Sleep with Anger*
*Two Lies*
*Unforgiven*
*Warrior in Two Worlds, A*
*Way Home, The*
*Witness*

## BIOGRAPHY

*Almost a Woman*
*Antwone Fisher*
*Ballad of Gregorio Cortez, The*
*Beautiful Mind, A*
*Bird*
*Collecting Stories from Exile*
*Covered Girls*
*Heaven & Earth*
*Hoop Dreams*
*In America*
*In the Spirit of Crazy Horse*
*Insider, The*
*La Bamba*
*Lakota Woman*
*Malcolm X*
*Maya Lin: A Strong Clear Vision*
*My American Girls*
*New Americans, The*
*On and Off the Res with Charlie Hill*
*Return of Navajo Boy, The*
*Seabiscuit*
*Selena*
*Sergeant York*
*Stand and Deliver*
*Warrior in Two Worlds, A*
*When We Were Kings*

## CHILDREN'S (K-5) FILMS

*Education of Little Tree, The*
*Hey Arnold! The Movie*
*Indian in the Cupboard, The*
*Pocahontas*

## CIVIL RIGHTS

*Africans in America*
*Autobiography of Miss Jane Pittman, The*
*Ballad of Gregorio Cortez, The*
*Eyes on the Prize*
*Gentleman's Agreement*
*In the Spirit of Crazy Horse*
*Incident at Oglala*
*Lakota Woman*
*Lighting the Seventh Fire*
*Snow Falling on Cedars*
*To Kill a Mockingbird*
*Who Killed Vincent Chin?*

## CIVIL WAR

*Birth of a Nation, The*
*Gone with the Wind*
Ken Burns's Documentaries: *The Civil War*
*Warrior in Two Worlds, A*

## CLASS STRATIFICATION

*Africans in America*
*Bamboozled*
*Blue Collar*
*Bread and Roses*
*Business of Fancy Dancing, The*
*City, The/La Ciudad*
*Clueless*
*Giant*
*Gone with the Wind*
*Heaven & Earth*
*Hey Arnold! The Movie*
*Hoop Dreams*
*Incredibly True Adventure of Two Girls in Love, The*
*John Q*
*Milagro Beanfield War, The*

*My Family/Mi Familia*

*New Americans, The*

*Norma Rae*

*Real Women Have Curves*

*Salt of the Earth*

*White Man's Burden*

**COMING OF AGE**

*Almost a Woman*

*Almost Famous*

*Antwone Fisher*

*Baby Boy*

*Blood in Blood Out*

*Bronx Tale, A*

*Clueless*

*Doe Boy, The*

*Dreamkeeper*

*Education of Little Tree, The*

*Eve's Bayou*

*Finding Forrester*

*Gangs of New York*

*Girlfight*

*Higher Learning*

*Hoop Dreams*

*Incredibly True Adventure of Two Girls in Love, The*

*La Bamba*

*Lakota Woman*

*Raising Victor Vargas*

*Real Women Have Curves*

*Seabiscuit*

*Slam*

*Smoke Signals*

**COURTROOM DRAMA**

*Amistad*

*Ballad of Gregorio Cortez, The*

*Incident at Oglala*

*Insider, The*

*Midnight in the Garden of Good and Evil*

*Philadelphia*

*Snow Falling on Cedars*

*To Kill a Mockingbird*

*Twelve Angry Men*

*Zoot Suit*

**DANCE**

*Stormy Weather*

*West Side Story*

*Zoot Suit*

**DOCUMENTARY**

*Africans in America*

*Almost a Woman*

*Bowling for Columbine*

*Collecting Stories from Exile*

*Covered Girls*

*Eyes on the Prize*

*Faith and Doubt at Ground Zero*

*Hoop Dreams*

*In My Own Skin*

*In the Light of Reverence*

*In the Spirit of Crazy Horse*

*In Whose Honor? American Indian Mascots in Sports*

*Incident at Oglala*

Ken Burns's Documentaries

*Lighting the Seventh Fire*

*Maya Lin: A Strong Clear Vision*

*Miles of Smiles, Years of Struggle*

*My American Girls*

*New Americans, The*

*On and Off the Res with Charlie Hill*

*Return of Navajo Boy, The*

*Rocks with Wings*

*Sa-I-Gu*

*Tales of Arab Detroit*

*True Whispers*

*Warrior in Two Worlds, A*

*Way Home, The*

*When We Were Kings*

*Who Killed Vincent Chin?*

*With Us or Against Us*

*Woodstock*

## EDUCATION

*Almost a Woman*
*Beautiful Mind, A*
*Conrack*
*Education of Little Tree, The*
*Finding Forrester*
*Higher Learning*
*Hoop Dreams*
*My American Girls*
*Rocks with Wings*
*Songcatcher*
*Stand and Deliver*
*Unbowed*

## FAMILY

*Almost a Woman*
*Antwone Fisher*
*Avalon*
*Baby Boy*
*Blood in Blood Out*
*Bread and Roses*
*Bronx Tale, A*
*Catfish in Black Bean Sauce*
*China Girl*
*Chutney Popcorn*
*City, The/La Ciudad*
*Color Purple, The*
*Daughters of the Dust*
*Doe Boy, The*
*Dreamkeeper*
*Eat a Bowl of Tea*
*Education of Little Tree, The*
*El Norte*
*Eve's Bayou*
*Far from Heaven*
*Fast Runner, The/Atanarjuat*
*Fires Within*
*Giant*
*Girlfight*
*Gone with the Wind*
*Grand Avenue*
*Great Wall, A*
*Heaven & Earth*
*Holes*
*Hoop Dreams*
*House of Sand and Fog*
*Imitation of Life*
*In America*
*John Q*
*Joy Luck Club, The*
*La Bamba*
*Lakota Woman*
*Lone Star*
*Lovely and Amazing*
*Mask of Zorro, The*
*Mississippi Masala*
*My American Girls*
*My Big Fat Greek Wedding*
*My Family/Mi Familia*
*Naturally Native*
*New Americans, The*
*Norma Rae*
*Perez Family, The*
*Philadelphia*
*Raisin in the Sun, A*
*Raising Victor Vargas*
*Real Women Have Curves*
*Return of Navajo Boy, The*
*Roots*
*Salt of the Earth*
*Selena*
*Sergeant York*
*Silverado*
*Skins*
*Smoke Signals*
*Snow Falling on Cedars*
*Soul Food*
*Sounder*
*Spy Kids*
*Tales of Arab Detroit*
*To Kill a Mockingbird*
*To Sleep with Anger*
*Tortilla Soup*
*Two Lies*
*Wedding Banquet, The*

## FOOD

*Catfish in Black Bean Sauce*
*Combination Platter*
*My Big Fat Greek Wedding*
*Soul Food*
*Tortilla Soup*
*Wedding Banquet, The*

## IDENTITY DEVELOPMENT

*Almost a Woman*
*Almost Famous*
*Antwone Fisher*
*Baby Boy*
*Believer, The*
*Blood in Blood Out*
*Bronx Tale, A*
*Business of Fancy Dancing, The*
*Clueless*
*Color Purple, The*
*Conrack*
*Doe Boy, The*
*Dreamkeeper*
*Girlfight*
*Higher Learning*
*Imitation of Life*
*Lakota Woman*
*Lovely and Amazing*
*Malcolm X*
*Mi Vida Loca*
*My Big Fat Greek Wedding*
*Naturally Native*
*Raising Victor Vargas*
*Rocks with Wings*
*Rum and Coke*
*Slam*
*Smoke Signals*
*Tales of Arab Detroit*
*Tortilla Soup*

## IMMIGRANT EXPERIENCE

*Africans in America*
*Almost a Woman*
*Avalon*
*Born in East L.A.*
*Bread and Roses*
*Chan Is Missing*
*City, The/La Ciudad*
*Combination Platter*
*Eat a Bowl of Tea*
*El Norte*
*Fires Within*
*Gangs of New York*
*Green Card*
*Green Dragon, The*
*Heaven & Earth*
*House of Sand and Fog*
*In America*
*In My Own Skin*
*Joy Luck Club, The*
*Living on Tokyo Time*
*Lone Star*
*Matewan*
*Mississippi Masala*
*Moscow on the Hudson*
*My American Girls*
*My Big Fat Greek Wedding*
*My Family/Mi Familia*
*New Americans, The*
*Perez Family, The*
*Picture Bride*
*Sa-I-Gu*
*Tales of Arab Detroit*
*Wedding Banquet, The*
*With Us or Against Us*
*Who Killed Vincent Chin?*

## INTERGENERATIONAL RELATIONSHIPS

*Africans in America*
*Antwone Fisher*
*Autobiography of Miss Jane Pittman, The*
*Avalon*
*Baby Boy*
*Bronx Tale, A*
*China Girl*
*Chutney Popcorn*

*Color Purple, The*
*Daughters of the Dust*
*Doe Boy, The*
*Dreamkeeper*
*Eat a Bowl of Tea*
*Education of Little Tree, The*
*Eve's Bayou*
*Eyes on the Prize*
*Fast Runner, The/Atanarjuat*
*Finding Forrester*
*Gangs of New York*
*Giant*
*Girlfight*
*Grand Avenue*
*Great Wall, A*
*Imitation of Life*
*In America*
*Joy Luck Club, The*
*Lone Star*
*Lovely and Amazing*
*Matewan*
*My American Girls*
*My Big Fat Greek Wedding*
*My Family/Mi Familia*
*New Americans, The*
*Picture Bride*
*Raisin in the Sun, A*
*Raising Victor Vargas*
*Real Women Have Curves*
*Return of Navajo Boy, The*
*Roots*
*Smoke Signals*
*Soul Food*
*Sounder*
*Spirit of Crazy Horse, The*
*Spy Kids*
*Tales of Arab Detroit*
*To Kill a Mockingbird*
*To Sleep with Anger*
*Tortilla Soup*
*Two Lies*
*Witness*

## INTERRACIAL/INTERETHNIC RELATIONSHIPS

*Because of You*
*Bird*
*Blade Runner*
*Blue Collar*
*Bronx Tale, A*
*Catfish in Black Bean Sauce*
*China Girl*
*Chutney Popcorn*
*Conrack*
*Doe Boy, The*
*Education of Little Tree, The*
*Far from Heaven*
*Finding Forrester*
*Follow Me Home*
*Gangs of New York*
*Giant*
*Girlfight*
*Gone with the Wind*
*Green Card*
*Heaven & Earth*
*Hey Arnold! The Movie*
*Higher Learning*
*Holes*
*House of Sand and Fog*
*Human Stain, The*
*Imitation of Life*
*In America*
*In the Heat of the Night*
*Incredibly True Adventure of Two Girls in Love, The*
*Lone Star*
*Lovely and Amazing*
*Midnight in the Garden of Good and Evil*
*Mississippi Masala*
*My Big Fat Greek Wedding*
*Naturally Native*
*Norma Rae*
*Philadelphia*
*Pocahontas*
*Rocks with Wings*

*Romeo Must Die*
*Sa-I-Gu*
*Silverado*
*Snow Falling on Cedars*
*To Kill a Mockingbird*
*Twelve Angry Men (1997)*
*Unbowed*
*Unforgiven*
*Vanishing Americans, The*
*Wedding Banquet, The*
*West Side Story*
*White Man's Burden*
*Who Killed Vincent Chin?*
*Woodstock*

## JIM CROW ERA

*Autobiography of Miss Jane Pittman, The*
*Bird*
*Birth of a Nation*
*Color Purple, The*
*Eyes on the Prize*
*In the Heat of the Night*
*Malcolm X*
*Miles of Smiles, Years of Struggle*
*Raisin in the Sun, A*
*Soldier's Story, A*
*Sounder*
*Sweet Sweetback's Baad Asssss Song*
*To Kill a Mockingbird*

## LABOR UNIONS

*Blue Collar*
*Bread and Roses*
*Matewan*
*Miles of Smiles, Years of Struggle*
*Norma Rae*
*Salt of the Earth*

## MATRIARCHY

*Autobiography of Miss Jane Pittman, The*
*Baby Boy*
*Chutney Popcorn*
*Daughters of the Dust*
*Imitation of Life*
*Joy Luck Club, The*
*Lovely and Amazing*
*My American Girls*
*Raisin in the Sun, A*
*Soul Food*

## MENTORING

*Antwone Fisher*
*Bread and Roses*
*Bronx Tale, A*
*Doe Boy, The*
*Dreamkeeper*
*Education of Little Tree, The*
*Finding Forrester*
*Girlfight*
*Green Dragon, The*
*Higher Learning*
*Matewan*
*Norma Rae*
*Rocks with Wings*
*Seabiscuit*
*Skinwalkers*
*Stand and Deliver*

## MILITARY

*Fail Safe*
*Gone with the Wind*
*Green Dragon, The*
*Heaven & Earth*
Ken Burns's Documentaries: *The Civil War*
*Sergeant York*
*Siege, The*
*Soldier's Story, A*
*True Whispers*
*Warrior in Two Worlds, A*

## MUSIC/MUSICIANS

*Almost Famous*
*Bird*
Ken Burns's Documentaries: *Jazz*
*La Bamba*
*O Brother, Where Art Thou?*

*Selena*
*Songcatcher*
*Stormy Weather*
*West Side Story*
*Woodstock*
*Zoot Suit*

### NATIVISM/NATIONALISM

*Birth of a Nation, The*
*Fail Safe*
*Fires Within*
*Gangs of New York*
*Perez Family, The*
*Snow Falling on Cedars*
*Zoot Suit*

### POST 9/11 EXPERIENCES

*Faith and Doubt at Ground Zero*
*In My Own Skin*
*With Us or Against Us*

### PRISON EXPERIENCES

*Ballad of Gregorio Cortez, The*
*Blood in Blood Out*
*Malcolm X*
*My Family/Mi Familia*
*Sounder*
*Zoot Suit*

### RACISM

*Africans in America*
*Amistad*
*Autobiography of Miss Jane Pittman, The*
*Ballad of Gregorio Cortez, The*
*Bamboozled*
*Birth of a Nation, The*
*Blood in Blood Out*
*Eyes on the Prize*
*Gangs of New York*
*Higher Learning*
*In the Heat of the Night*
*In the Spirit of Crazy Horse*
*Incident at Oglala*
Ken Burns's Documentaries: *Baseball*
Ken Burns's Documentaries: *The Civil War*
Ken Burns's Documentaries: *Jazz*
*Lighting the Seventh Fire*
*Lone Star*
*Malcolm X*
*Mississippi Masala*
*Raisin in the Sun, A*
*Silverado*
*Soldier's Story, A*
*Sounder*
*Snow Falling on Cedars*
*Sweet Sweetback's Baad Asssss Song*
*To Kill a Mockingbird*
*True Whispers*
*White Man's Burden*
*Who Killed Vincent Chin?*

### RECKONING

*Believer, The*
*Fast Runner, The/Atanarjuat*
*Follow Me Home*
*Grand Avenue*
*Holes*
*Insider, The*
*Lone Star*
*Midnight in the Garden of Good and Evil*
*Milagro Beanfield War, The*
*Silverado*
*Skins*
*Skinwalkers*
*Smoke Signals*
*Stand and Deliver*
*Sweet Sweetback's Baad Asssss Song*

### REFUGEES

*Catfish in Black Bean Sauce*
*Collecting Stories from Exile*
*Green Dragon, The*
*Heaven & Earth*
*Perez Family, The*

### RELIGION/SPIRITUALITY

*Believer, The*
*Covered Girls*

*Daughters of the Dust*
*Eve's Bayou*
*Eyes on the Prize*
*Faith and Doubt at Ground Zero*
*Fast Runner, The/Atanarjuat*
*In the Light of Reverence*
*In My Own Skin*
*In the Spirit of Crazy Horse*
*Malcolm X*
*Midnight in the Garden of Good and Evil*
*Naturally Native*
*New Americans, The*
*Sergeant York*
*Skinwalkers*
*Smoke Signals*
*Snow Falling on Cedars*
*To Sleep with Anger*
*True Whispers*
*Witness*
*Woodstock*

**RURAL**

*Africans in America*
*Autobiography of Miss Jane Pittman, The*
*Ballad of Gregorio Cortez, The*
*Color Purple, The*
*Conrack*
*Daughters of the Dust*
*Dreamkeeper*
*Education of Little Tree, The*
*Fast Runner, The/Atanarjuat*
*Giant*
*Holes*
*In the Light of Reverence*
*In the Spirit of Crazy Horse*
*Incident at Oglala*
*Lakota Woman*
*Lighting the Seventh Fire*
*Mask of Zorro, The*
*Milagro Beanfield War, The*
*O Brother, Where Art Thou?*
*Picture Bride*
*Pocahontas*
*Return of Navajo Boy, The*
*Salt of the Earth*
*Sergeant York*
*Skins*
*Skinwalkers*
*Smoke Signals*
*Songcatcher*
*True Whispers*
*Unbowed*
*Unforgiven*
*Vanishing American, The*
*Witness*

**SCIENCE FICTION**

*Blade Runner*
*Brother from Another Planet, The*
*Matrix* Trilogy, The
*Solaris*
*Soylent Green*
*X-Men/X2*

**SELF-HATRED**

*Bamboozled*
*Believer, The*
*Human Stain, The*
*Soldier's Story, A*
*Two Lies*

**SEXUALITY**

*Almost Famous*
*Antwone Fisher*
*Baby Boy*
*Catfish in Black Bean Sauce*
*Chutney Popcorn*
*Color Purple, The*
*Eat a Bowl of Tea*
*Eve's Bayou*
*Far from Heaven*
*Fast Runner, The/Atanarjuat*
*Incredibly True Adventure of Two Girls in Love, The*
*Midnight in the Garden of Good and Evil*
*Raising Victor Vargas*

*Real Women Have Curves*

*Sweet Sweetback's Baad Asssss Song*

*Wedding Banquet, The*

*Woodstock*

## SLAVERY

*Africans in America*

*Amistad*

*Birth of a Nation*

*Gone with the Wind*

Ken Burns's Documentaries: *The Civil War*

*Roots*

## SMALL TOWN

*Africans in America*

*Autobiography of Miss Jane Pittman, The*

*Doe Boy, The*

*Eve's Bayou*

*In the Heat of the Night*

*Lone Star*

*Matewan*

*Milagro Beanfield War, The*

*Norma Rae*

*Rocks with Wings*

*Silverado*

*Snow Falling on Cedars*

*Thelma & Louise*

*To Kill a Mockingbird*

## SOCIAL PROTEST

*Amistad*

*Ballad of Gregorio Cortez, The*

*Bamboozled*

*Bowling for Columbine*

*Bread and Roses*

*Brother from Another Planet, The*

*Collecting Stories from Exile*

*Education of Little Tree, The*

*Fail Safe*

*Follow Me Home*

*Gentleman's Agreement*

*In the Light of Reverence*

*In the Spirit of Crazy Horse*

*In Whose Honor? American Indian Mascots in Sports*

*Incident at Oglala*

*Insider, The*

*John Q*

*Lakota Woman*

*Lighting the Seventh Fire*

*Malcolm X*

*Mask of Zorro, The*

*Matewan*

*Milagro Beanfield War, The*

*Norma Rae*

*On and Off the Res with Charlie Hill*

*Sa-I-Gu*

*Salt of the Earth*

*Skins*

*Snow Falling on Cedars*

*Soylent Green*

*Sweet Sweetback's Baad Asssss Song*

*Thelma & Louise*

*To Kill a Mockingbird*

*Two Lies*

*Way Home, The*

*White Man's Burden*

*Who Killed Vincent Chin?*

*Woodstock*

*Zoot Suit*

## SPORTS

*Girlfight*

*Hoop Dreams*

Ken Burns's Documentaries: *Baseball*

*Rocks with Wings*

*Seabiscuit*

*When We Were Kings*

## TERRORISM

*Birth of a Nation, The*

*Faith and Doubt at Ground Zero*

*Siege, The*

## URBAN LIFE

*Avalon*
*Baby Boy*
*Bamboozled*
*Believer, The*
*Blade Runner*
*Blood in Blood Out*
*Blue Collar*
*Bread and Roses*
*City, The/La Ciudad*
*Clueless*
*El Norte*
*Finding Forrester*
*Gangs of New York*
*Girlfight*
*Grand Avenue*
*Green Card*
*Hoop Dreams*
*In America*
*Mi Vida Loca*
*Moscow on the Hudson*
*My Family/Mi Familia*
*New Americans, The*
*Philadelphia*
*Real Women Have Curves*
*Romeo Must Die*
*Sa-I-Gu*
*Siege, The*
*Slam*
*Stand and Deliver*
*Sweet Sweetback's Baad Asssss Song*
*West Side Story*
*Zoot Suit*

## WAR

*Collecting Stories from Exile*
*Fail Safe*
*Gone with the Wind*
*Heaven & Earth*
Ken Burns's Documentaries: *The Civil War*
*Sergeant York*
*True Whispers*
*Vanishing Americans, The*
*Warrior in Two Worlds, A*

## WORKING CLASS

*Almost a Woman*
*Blue Collar*
*Bronx Tale, A*
*Combination Platter*
*Doe Boy, The*
*Hoop Dreams*
*In America*
*John Q*
*Mississippi Masala*
*My American Girls*
*My Family/Mi Familia*
*New Americans, The*
*Norma Rae*
*Picture Bride*
*Real Women Have Curves*
*Salt of the Earth*
*Thelma & Louise*
*Who Killed Vincent Chin?*

# Film Distributors

A&E Television Networks, http://www.aetv.com.

American Film Foundation, http://www.americanfilmfoundation.com.

American Indian Film Institute, http://www.aifisf.com.

Arab Film Distribution, http://www.arabfilm.com.

Asian American Film News, http://www.AsianAmericanFilm.com.

Chip Taylor Communications, http://www.chiptaylor.com.

Cinema Guild, http://www.cinemaguild.com.

Direct Cinema, http://www.directcinema.com.

Facets Multi-Media, http://www.facets.org.

Filmakers Library, http://www.filmakers.com.

Filmanthropic, http://Filmanthropic.com.

First Americans in the Arts, http://www.firstamericans.org.

First Run/Icarus Films, http://www.frif.com.

Frameline, http://www.frameline.org.

National Asian American Telecommunications Association (NAATA), http://www.naatanet.org.

National Museum of the Amerian Indian, http://www.americanindian.si.edu.

New Day Films, http://www.newday.com.

Public Broadcasting System (PBS), http://www.pbs.org.

Red-Horse Native Productions, http://www.naturallynative.com.

Resolution Inc./California Newsreel, http://www.newsreel.org.

Rich-Heape Films, Inc., http://www.richheape.com.

Third World Newsreel, http://twn.org/index.html.

UC Extension, Center for Media and Independent Learning, http://www.cmil.unex.berkeley.edu.

Women Make Movies, http://www.wmm.com.

Zeitgeist Films, http://www.zeitgeistfilms.com.

# Selected Bibliography


## GENERAL

Allport, Gordon W. *The Native of Prejudice*. Reading, MA: Addison-Wesley, 1954.

Banks, James A. *Teaching Strategies for Ethnic Studies*. 7th ed. Upper Saddle River, NJ: Allyn and Bacon, 2002.

Cavalli-Sforza, L. Luca, Paolo Menozzi, and Alberto Piazza. *The History and Geography of Human Genes* [Abridged]. Princeton, NJ: Princeton University Press, 1996.

Levy, Emanuel. *Cinema of Outsiders: The Rise of American Independent Film*. New York: New York University Press, 1999.

Omi, Michael, and Howard Winant. *Racial Formation in the United States*. 2nd ed. New York: Routledge, 1994.

Rollins, Peter C., ed. *The Columbia Companion to American History on Film: How the Movies Have Portrayed the American Past*. New York: Columbia University Press, 2003.

Rothenberg, Paula S., ed. *White Privilege: Essential Readings on the Other Side of Racism*. New York: Worth, 2002.

Weber, Lynn. *Understanding Race, Class, Gender, and Sexuality: A Conceptual Framework*. New York: McGraw-Hill, 2001.

## AFRICAN AMERICAN

Bogle, Donald. *Toms, Coons, Mulattoes, Mammies, and Bucks: An Interpretive History of Blacks in American Films*. New York: Viking, 1973.

Boyd, Todd. *Am I Black Enough for You? Popular Culture from the 'Hood and Beyond*. Bloomington: Indiana University Press, 1997.

Cripps, Thomas. *Black Film as Genre*. Bloomington: Indiana University Press, 1978.

———. *Slow Fade to Black: The Negro in American Films, 1900–1942*. New York: Oxford University Press, 1977.

Diawara, Manthia, ed. *Black American Cinema*. New York: Routledge, 1993.

Donalson, Melvin. *Black Directors in Hollywood*. Austin: University of Texas Press, 2003.

Dyson, Michael Eric. *Reflecting Black: African-American Cultural Criticism*. Minneapolis: University of Minnesota Press, 1993.

Gray, Herman. *Watching Race: Television and the Struggle for "Blackness."* Minneapolis: University of Minnesota Press, 1995.

Guerrero, Ed. *Framing Blackness: The African American Image in Film*. Philadelphia: Temple University Press, 1993.

Harris, Erich Leon. *African-American Screenwriters Now: Conversations with Hollywood's Black Pack*. Los Angeles: Silman-James Press, 1996.

hooks, bell. *Reel to Real: Race, Sex, and Class at the Movies*. New York: Routledge, 1996.

Klotman, Phyllis R., and Janet K. Cutler, eds. *Struggles for Representation: African American Documentary Film and Video*. Bloomington: Indiana University Press, 1999.

Leab, Daniel. *From Sambo to Superspade: The Black Experience in Motion Picture*. Boston: Houghton Mifflin, 1976.

Martin, Michael T., ed. *Cinemas of the Black Diaspora: Diversity, Dependence, and Oppositionality*. Detroit, MI: Wayne State University Press, 1995.

Massood, Paula. *Black City Cinema: African American Urban Experiences in Film*. Philadelphia: Temple University Press, 2003.

Reid, Mark A. *Redefining Black Film*. Berkeley: University of California Press, 1993.

Rhines, Jesse Algeron. *Black Film/White Money*. New Brunswick, NJ: Rutgers University Press, 1996.

Rocchio, Vincent Q. *Reel Racism: Confronting Hollywood's Construction of Afro-America Culture*. Boulder, CO: Westview, 2000.

Ross, Karen. *Black and White Media: Black Images in Popular Film and Television*. Cambridge, England: Polity Press, 1996.

Smith, Valerie, ed. *Representing Blackness: Issues in Film and Video*. New Brunswick, NJ: Rutgers University Press, 1997.

Snead, James. *White Screens Black Images: Hollywood from the Dark Side*. New York: Routledge, 1994.

Wilson, Julius Wilson. *The Truly Disadvantaged: The Inner City, the Underclass, and Public Policy*. Chicago: University of Chicago Press, 1987.

———. *When Work Disappears: The World of the New Urban Poor*. New York: Vintage Books, 1996.

Yearwood, Gladstone L. *Black Film as a Signifying Practice: Cinema Narration and the African-American Aesthetic Tradition*. Trenton, NJ: African World Press, 2000.

## ARAB AMERICAN/MIDDLE EASTERN

Bernstein, Matthew, and Gaylyn Sludlar, eds. *Visions of the East: Orientalism in Film*. New Brunswick, NJ: Rutgers University Press, 1997.

"Bibliography: Arabs in Film and Television." A Bibliography of Materials in the UC Berkeley Library. http://www.libberkeley.edu/MRC/arabbib.html.

Boosahda, Elizabeth. *Arab American Faces and Voices: The Origins of an Immigrant Community*. Austin: University of Texas Press, 2003.

Eisele, John C. "The Wild East: Deconstructing the Language of Genre in the Hollywood Eastern." *Cinema Journal* 41, no. 4 (2002): 68–94.

Goodstein, Laurie. "Hollywood Now Plays Cowboys and Arabs." November 1, 1998. http://www.library.cornell.edu/collden/mideast/arbholl.htm (accessed June 21, 2004).

Karim, Persis M., and Mohammad Mehdi Khorrani, eds. *A World Between: Poems, Short Stories, and Essays by Iranian-Americans*. New York: George Braziller, 1999.

O'Donnell, Terence. *Seven Shades of Memory: Stories of Old Iran*. Washington, DC: Mage Publishers, 1999.

Shaheen, Jack G. *Reel Bad Arabs: How Hollywood Vilifies a People*. New York: Olive Branch Press, 2001.

Simon, Scott J. "Arabs in Hollywood: An Undeserved Image." http://www.pages.emerson.edu/organization/fas/latent_image/issues/1996~04/arabs.htm.

Steinberg, Shirley. "French Fries, Tezzes, and Minstrels: The Hollywoodization of Islam." *Cultural Studies/Critical Methodologies* 21, no. 2 (2002): 205–210.

## ASIAN AMERICAN


Daniels, Roger. *Prisoners Without Trial: Japanese Americans in World War II*. New York: Hill and Wang, 1993.

Do, Hien Duc. *The Vietnam Americans*. Westport, CT: Greenwood, 1999.

Feng, Peter X., ed. *Screening Asian Americans*. New Brunswick, NJ: Rutgers University Press, 2002.

Garcia, Maria Christina. *Havana USA: Cuban Exiles and Cuban Americans in South Florida, 1959–1994*. Berkeley, CA: University of California Press, 1997.

Gee, Emma, ed. *Counterpoint: Perspectives on Asian America*. Los Angeles: Asian American Studies Center, University of California, 1976.

Hamamoto, Darrell Y., and Sandra Liu. *Countervisions: Asian American Film Criticism*. Philadelphia: Temple University Press, 2000.

Lowe, Lisa. "Heterogeneity, Hybridity, Multiplicity: Marking Asian American Differences." *Diaspora* 1, no. 1 (1991): 24–44.

Marchetti, Gina. *Romance and the "Yellow Peril": Race, Sex, and Discursive Strategies in Hollywood Fiction*. Berkeley: University of California Press, 1993.

Nisbett, Richard E. *The Geography of Thought: How Asians and Westerners Think Differently . . . and Why*. New York: Overlook Press, 1994.

Okihiro, Gary Y. *Whispered Silences: Japanese Americans and World War II*. Seattle: University of Washington Press, 1996.

Palumbo-Liu, David, ed. *The Ethnic Canon: Histories, Institutions, and Interventions*. Minneapolis: University of Minnesota Press, 1995.

Takaki, Ronald. *Strangers from a Different Shore: A History of Asian Americans*. New York: Little, Brown, 1989.

Wong, Eugene Franklin. *On Visual Media Racism: Asians in the American Motion Pictures*. New York: Arno Press, 1978.

Xing, Jun. *Asian America Through the Lens: History, Representations, and Identity*. Walnut Creek, CA: AltaMira Press, 1998.


## EUROPEAN AMERICAN


Benshoff, Harry M., and Sean Griffin. *America on Film: Representing Race, Class, Gender, and Sexuality at the Movies*. Malden, MA: Blackwell Publishing, 2004.

Bernardi, Daniel, ed. *Classic Hollywood, Classic Whiteness*. Minneapolis: University of Minnesota Press, 2001.

Bondanella, Peter. *Hollywood Italians: Dagos, Palookas, Romeos, WiseGuys, and Sopranos*. New York: Continuum, 2004.

Girgus, Sam B. *America on Film: Modernism, Documentary, and a Changing America*. New York: Cambridge University Press, 2002.

Guglielmo, Jennifer, and Salvatore Salerno. *Are Italians White? How Race is Made in America*. New York: Routledge, 2003.

Johnson, Allan G. *Privilege, Power, and Difference*. Mountain View, CA: Mayfield Publishers, 2001.

McIntosh, Peggy. *White Privilege: Unpacking the Invisible Knapsack*. Wellesley, MA: Wellesley College Center for Research on Women, 1998.

Shohat, Ella, and Robert Stam. *Unthinking Eurocentrism: Multiculturalism and the Media*. New York: Routledge, 1994.

Takaki, Ronald. *A Different Mirror: A History of Multicultural America*. Boston: Little, Brown, 1993.


## LATINO/A AMERICAN


Berg, Charles Ramirez. *Latino Images in Film: Stereotypes, Subversion, Resistance*. Austin: University of Texas Press, 2002.

Berumen, Frank Javier Garcia. *The Chicano/Hispanic Image in American Film*. New York: Vantage, 1995.

Fregoso, Rosa Linda. *The Bronze Screen: Chicana and Chicano Film Culture*. Minneapolis: University of Minnesota Press, 1993.

Keller, Garry D., ed. *Chicano Cinema: Research, Reviews, and Resources*. Tempe, AZ: Bilingual Press, 1985.

———. *Hispanic and United States Film: An Overview and Handbook*. Tempe, AZ: Bilingual Press, 1994.

Limón, José E. *American Encounters: Greater Mexico, the United States, and the Erotica of Culture*. Boston: Beacon Press, 1998.

List, Christine. *Chicano Images: Refiguring Ethnicity in Mainstream Film*. New York: Garland, 1996.

Mayer, Vicki. *Producing Dreams, Consuming Youth: Mexican Americans and Mass Media*. Piscataway, NJ: Rutgers University Press, 2004.

Noriega, Chon A., ed. *Chicanos and Film: Representation and Resistance*. Minneapolis: University of Minnesota Press, 1996.

———. *Shot in America: Television, the State, and the Rise of Chicano Cinema*. Minneapolis: University of Minnesota Press, 2000.

Noriega, Chon A., and Ana M. López, eds. *The Ethnic Eye: Latino Media Arts*. Minneapolis: University of Minnesota Press, 1996.

Rodriguez, Clara E., ed. *Latin Looks: Images of Latinas and Latinos in the U.S. Media*. Boulder, CO: Westview Press, 1998.

Valdivia, Angharad. *A Latina in the Land of Hollywood and Other Essays on Media Culture*. Tucson: University of Arizona Press, 2000.

## NATIVE AMERICAN

Bataille, Gretchen M., and Charles L. P. Silet, eds. *The Pretend Indians: Images of Native Americans in the Movies*. Ames: Iowa State University Press, 1980.

Berkhofer, Robert F., Jr. *The White Man's Indian: Images of the American Indian from Columbus to the Present*. New York: Vintage Books, 1978.

Bird, S. Elizabeth, ed. *Dressing in Feathers: The Constitution of the Indian in American Popular Culture*. Boulder, CO: Westview Press, 1996.

Churchill, Ward. *Fantasies of the Master Race: Literature, Cinema and the Colonization of American Indians*. San Francisco: City Lights Press, 1998.

Fleming, Walter C. *The Complete Idiot's Guide to Native American History*. New York: Alpha Books, 2003.

Hilger, Michael. *From Savage to Nobleman: Images of Native Americans in Film*. Lanham, MD: Scarecrow Press, 1995.

Kilpatrick, Jacquelyn. *Celluloid Indians: Native Americans and Film*. Lincoln: University of Nebraska Press, 1999.

Leuthold, Steven. *Indigenous Aesthetics: Native Art, Media, and Identity*. Austin: University of Texas Press, 1998.

Nabokov, Peter, and Vine Deloria, Jr. *Native American Testimony: A Chronicle of Indian–White Relations from Prophecy to the Present, 1492–2000*. Hopkinton, MA: Penguin Books,1999.

O'Connor, John E. *The Hollywood Indian: Stereotypes of Native Americans in Film*. Trenton, NJ: New Jersey State Museum, 1980.

Owens, Louis. *Mixedblood Messages: Literature, Film, Family, Place*. Norman: University of Oklahoma Press, 1998.

Rollins, Peter C., and John E. O'Connor, eds. *Hollywood's Indian: The Portrayal of the Native American in Film*. Lexington: University Press of Kentucky, 1998.

Singer, Beverly R. *Wiping the War Paint Off the Lens: Native American Film and Video*. Minneapolis: University of Minnesota Press, 2001.

## INTERCULTURAL

Carson, Diane, and Lester D. Friedman, eds. *Shared Differences: Multicultural Media & Practical Pedagogy*. Urbana: University of Illinois Press, 1995.

Daniels, Roger. *Guarding the Golden Door: American Immigrants and Immigration Policy Since 1882*. New York: Hill and Wang, 2004.

Denzin, Norman K. *Reading Race: Hollywood and the Cinema of Racial Violence*. Thousand Oaks, CA: Sage, 2002.

Friedman, Lester D., ed. *Unspeakable Images: Ethnicity and the American Cinema*. Chicago: University of Illinois Press, 1991.

Gabbard, Krin. *Black Magic: White Hollywood and African American Culture*. Piscataway, NJ: Rutgers University Press, 2004.

Girgus, Sam B. *America on Film: Modernism, Documentary, and a Changing America*. New York: Cambridge University Press, 2002.

Ungar, Samuel J. *Fresh Blood: The New American Immigrants*. Urbana: University of Illinois Press, 1998.

Willis, Sharon. *High Contrast: Race and Gender in Contemporary Hollywood Film*. Durham, NC: Duke University Press, 1997.

# Index

## About the Authors

JANICE R. WELSCH has taught courses in film criticism and history, women's studies, and multicultural studies since joining the English and journalism faculty of Western Illinois University in 1975. She has served as codirector of the Expanding Cultural Diversity Project for more than ten years and has coedited *Multiple Voices in Feminist Film Criticism*. She recently received the Society for Cinema and Media Studies Service Award for her distinguished contributions to the Society and to the profession.

J. Q. ADAMS teaches in the Department of Education and Interdisciplinary Studies at Western Illinois University. He has worked extensively in the area of multicultural education as a consultant, presenter, and curriculum development specialist in K-12 schools and school systems as well as colleges, universities, and community organizations for more than 25 years. In 2004 he was named outstanding teacher in the College of Education and Human Services. He codirects the Expanding Cultural Diversity Project at WIU.